The River

at the Center of the World

A Journey Up the Yangtze,
and Back in Chinese Time

SIMON
WINCHESTER

Picador
Henry Holt and Company
New York

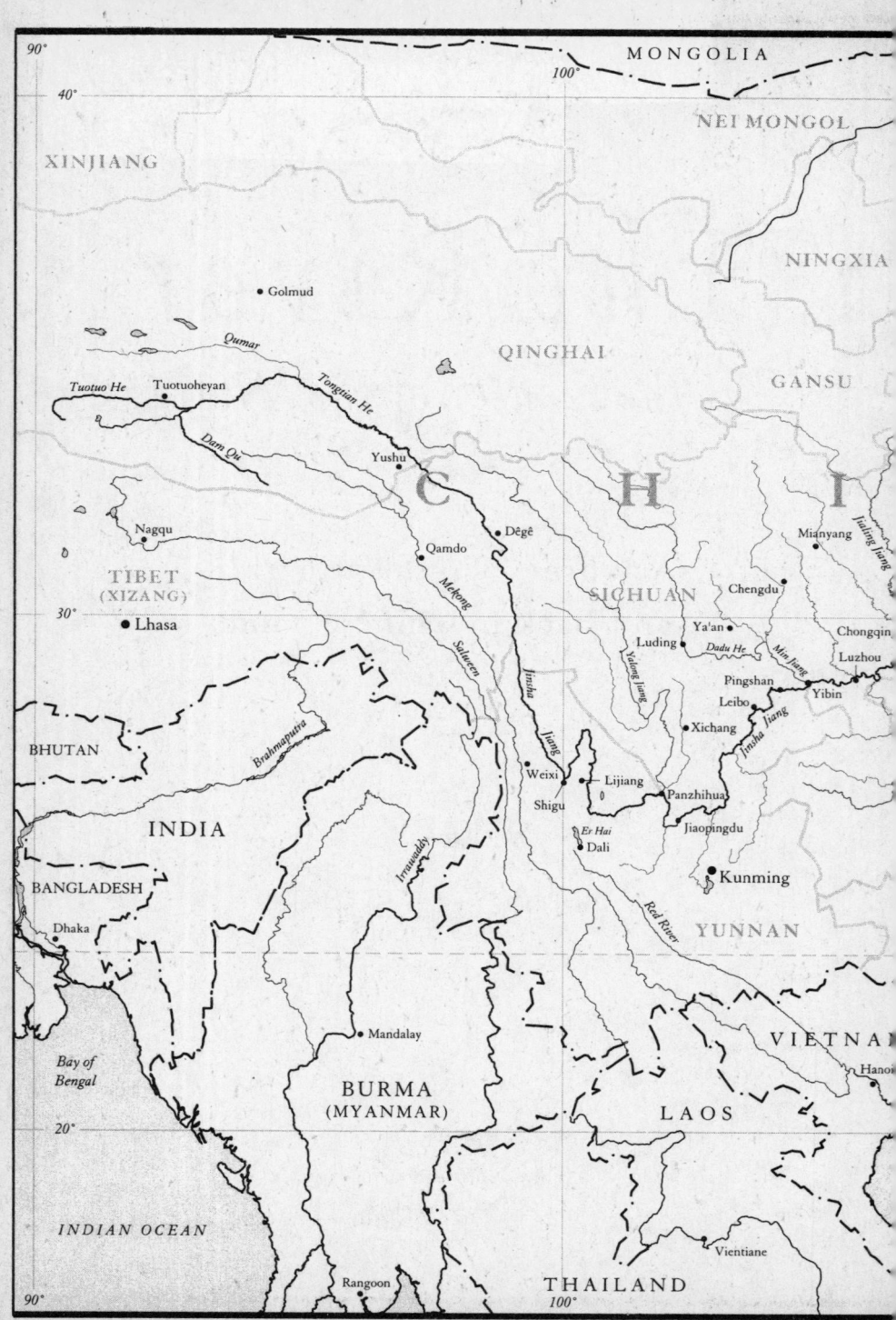

This book is dedicated to
Lucy and David Tang—
a small token of a great delight

www.picadorusa.com

Picador® is a U.S. registered trademark and is used by Henry Holt and Company under license from Pan Books Limited.

For information on Picador Reading Group Guides, as well as ordering, please contact the Trade Marketing department at St. Martin's Press.
Phone: 1-800-221-7945 extension 763
Fax: 212-677-7456
E-mail: trademarketing@stmartins.com

Designed by Paula Russell Szafranski
Cartography by Jeffrey L. Ward

Library of Congress Cataloging-in-Publication Data

Winchester, Simon.
    The river at the center of the world : a journey up the Yangtze, and back in Chinese time / Simon Winchester.
        p. cm.
    Includes index and bibliographical references.
    ISBN 0-312-42337-3
    1. Yangtze River Region (China)—Description and travel.

DS793.Y3W56 1996
915.1'20459—dc20

96-12399
CIP

First published in the United States by Henry Holt and Company

10 9 8 7 6 5 4 3

Contents

In Gratitude

My thanks go first to two people I have never met, Andrea and Harry Crane of Chicago. It was their unanticipated kindness that led me to meet the extraordinary and enthusiastic Wan-go Weng in his house in remotest New Hampshire, and it was he who in turn showed me the Wang Hui picture called the *Ten thousand li Yangtze*—the picture that truly set this journey in train. To all three, connected to each other only by the faint incandescent trails of digital electronics, I owe a very great deal.

A journey of this scale demands the very best maps, and I am glad to count as my good friend Francis Herbert, the curator of the Map Library at the Royal Geographical Society in London: he found for me some of the best old French maps and portolanos of the Upper Yangtze, and then led me to other sources of good modern charts— the firm of Brupacher Landkarten in Switzerland, who supplied me with the frighteningly excellent Soviet General Staff maps of western China, and a young lawyer named Julie Jones of the Defense Mapping Agency in Washington, D.C., an agency which—after a tussle with officials that Ms. Jones gamely fought on my behalf—came up with all the relevant sheets from the normally classified map series known as Joint Operations Graphics.

David Yiu, the ebullient and unforgettably generous figure behind Regal China Cruises, then helped me to make a number of reconnaissance trips along the navigable reaches of the river. His three vessels proved superbly comfortable refuges from which I could plan journeys by more rudimentary transport—and one of them acted as a floating hotel for me during my frequent visits to Shanghai. If there were ever moments when my enthusiasm for continuing the voyage wavered, it was David's eagerness and sense of fun that always managed to restore it.

I cannot hope to express my gratitude to the young woman whom current Chinese circumstance obliges me to disguise with the English name of Lily. This courageous and unflappable Manchurian, who rightly hesitated long before deciding to accompany me, turned out to be absolutely central to the successful completion of the journey. The fact that the trip up the great river was as much an adventure for her as a Chinese citizen, to whom the Yangtze means so much, as it was for me as a curious foreigner perhaps offers some practical measure of my thanks for her participation. As I say elsewhere, sad reality makes it too risky to identify her more fully than I do, but she knows who she is, and I hope that when she reads these words she will understand a little more easily how very real and lasting is my admiration for her.

Among the others to whom I owe thanks in varying measure are these following, along with very many more unnamed people for whom identification in China would be similarly perilous. I was helped enormously by: Richard Bangs of Mountain Travel–Sobek in California; Betty Barr of Fudan University in Shanghai; David Brown of the Royal Navy Historical Branch in London; Jeremy Brown of Jardines; Peter Cann of the University of Pennsylvania, a specialist in Pearl Buck; Daniel Desmond, General Manager of the Holiday Inn, Lhasa; Dave Fairty and Anne McAndrew of Backcountry Outfitters in Kent, Connecticut, who sent me off properly clothed and shod; Simon Featherstone, the current British Consul-General in Shanghai; William Goodman of the Ertan Dam Project on the Yalong River; my old friend Richard Graham, who gave valuable time during his own interesting moments spent running the Barings office, post-trauma, in Shanghai; Charlotte Havilland of Swires; Huang Guo Guang, who plied me with strong drink at the Wuliangye Distillery, Yibin; Michael Ingram of Monenco Agra in Ottawa, who had much useful to say about the new dam, both when we met in Yichang and later in Canada; Penny King at the Asian Music Centre in London, who organized the Nakhi orchestra's successful tour of Britain; Li Shou Kun and Helen Jin of the Yun Ying art gallery in Wuhan; the splendid Julia Liu of the Ramada Hotel in Wuhan; the writer Madeleine Lynn in Hong Kong, who collects arcana from the Yangtze and was happy to share it; Rick Jacobs of Northwest Airlines in Minneapolis; Patrick McCully and Owen Lammers of the International Rivers Network in Berkeley, California; the magnificent Hong Kong medical personality Dr. Jake O'Donovan, who made sure that I was able to keep fit and unblistered in the wildest reaches of Tibet; Pam Logan and her colleagues at the China Exploration and Research Society; Ma Jishen, Professor of Archaeology at Sichuan United University, a hugely knowledgeable source about the losses that are to be sustained in the wake of the Three Gorges flooding; the eternally good-humored Washington writer Rudy Maxa, who accompanied me on an early scouting trip and insisted that I write this book; a number of members of the ill-fated Ken Warren rafting expedition who talked to me anonymously about that extraordinary episode; Professors Suo Lisheng, Yu Kehua and their colleague dam designers at Hohai University in Nanjing; my great friend Iain Orr of the British Foreign Office, who knows much about rivers, islands—and China; Cynthia Shiu of Grid Media in Hong Kong, who first brought the world of interactive electronics to the Yangtze by publishing a CD-ROM about it; Professor Lyman van Slyke of Stanford University, who generously gave me material about Cornell Plant and shared his own long experience of writing about the river; the amusing and flamboyant Tao Chang An in Wuhan; Frank and Irene Walker, who when we met had been transplanted from their home in Lochcarron in Western Ross to the banks of the Yalong River near Panzhihua; Tom Wallace, the editor-in-chief of *Condé Nast Traveler,* and the magazine's senior editor Gully Wells, who both helped support many of my travels to the region; my former agent Lois Wallace, who helped so ably with the initiation of this book, and my present agent Peter Matson and his colleague Jennifer Hengen at Sterling Lord Literistic of New York; Wang Naili of the Shanghai Tourism Administration; Wen Zi Jian of Jiujiang; my son Rupert Winchester of Hong Kong; Wu Wei, of the People's Insurance Company of China in Panzhihua, who loaned me his car and his driving skills to take Lily and me to and around Lijiang; Terry Xu of Malone's Café, Shanghai; Xu Xiaoyang in Chengdu, who was inexpressibly kind in a score of ways, and who loaned us a second car to take us from Chengdu to Lhasa and to the upper reaches of the Tuotuo River; the great musicologist Xuan Ke in Lijiang; the Misses Mirra Ye and Lulu Uy and the rest of the public relations staff at the great Portman Shangri-La Hotel, Shanghai; and finally in this list, the first man whom I was to meet officially in China, at the very start of the journey—Mr. Zhang Zu Long of the Woosung Supervision Station. He is the official whose task is, among other things, to keep a constant watch, as navigators have done for more than a century and a half, over the highly contentious and historically memorable phenomenon known as The State of the Woosung Bar.

All of these people gave more information, told me stories, offered me help and advice. In the end, though, I interpreted what they said and I wrote the book, and if there are errors, misjudgments or infelicities in the pages that follow, responsibility should be laid squarely at my door, and at mine alone.

The idea for this book came first from a discussion with my London agent and friend of many years, Bill Hamilton: my thanks to him for setting me on the trail that led from the high seas to High Tibet are unqualified. My delight in having Marian Wood as editor at Henry Holt is similarly unbounded: she and her colleagues have shown the greatest diligence during all the phases of the book's creation and production, and I am proud to be associated with them and their work.

Finally it goes almost without saying that a serene and comfortable domestic environment provides a wonderful base for writing a book about a place that is as difficult and distant as China. That Catherine, my wife, was despite her own busy life well able to keep our home cozy and welcoming, and that she put up with my occasional frustration and ill temper, is a measure of what a remarkable woman she is. The making of this book was an endurance test through which she came with flying colors.

Wassaic, New York
Summer 1996

Author's Note

Generally speaking I have used the pinyin form of the transliteration of the Chinese place-names and personal names that are used in this book. However, since this account deals with the past as well as the present—the Yangtze journey being deliberately chronological as well as topographical—there are occasions when it seemed to me much more suitable to use the old and officially discarded Wade-Giles form.

So although I visit the city of Nanjing, as it is presently known, I also make references to the Rape of Nanking and the Treaty of Nanking. Similarly, the river takes us to the grimy city that is now called Wanxian; but the infamous Wahnsien Incident took place there seventy years ago, and to refer to those remarkable events by the more modern name would make for greater confusion, I believe, than my small lexical inconsistency. In any case the names used in these and other examples sound to the Western ear usually more or less similar: only when the variant forms are very different—Tibet and Xizang, for instance, or Changan and Xian—do I interrupt the narrative to explain.

The name of the river itself is so complex and historically fascinating as almost to justify an entire chapter to itself. From this, however, I spare the reader—with the single caveat that the proper pinyin rendering of Yangtze is actually Yangzi, and the pronunciation, offered very approximately, is rather less *Yang-tzee* than it is *Young-zer*. But since the Chinese rarely if ever use either version, I have stuck with the most familiar, albeit barbarian, form.

As to how it became saddled with the non-Chinese name Yangtze—there is more mystery than agreement. Some nineteenth-century references speak of the word meaning "Son of the Sea," while others refer to it as deriving from "the Blue River"—and both of these interpretations are fairly reasonable, given that Chinese and its English transliterations enjoy an almost limitless elasticity. However, the most likely explanation probably results from a mishearing. Early western sailors on the river undoubtedly asked local boatmen for the name of their stream, and these boatmen—who may well have come from, or have been well aware of the great local influence of, the city of Yangzhou, which was then the greatest metropolis in the estuary region (and was where Marco Polo worked in the bureaucracy)—mouthed something to the effect that this was *the river of the Yang Kingdom*. Since Jiang is unequivocally the word for river, the combination of mumbling and elision of the words Yang and Jiang could quite possibly, to the untutored ear of a London-born sailor, have come across as Yangtzee-kiang. This name would have been reported back to the ship's captain; it would have eventually found its way into a report; the Admiralty would have issued orders relating to the said-named stream; and thus would geography, cartography and history have been gifted with an enduring new addition.

Common usage has it that a river's left bank or right bank is that which is seen on a downstream journey—the bank that is regarded from the point of view, as it were, of the flowing waters. I have tried to stick to this hydrographers' convention throughout my account. However, since my journeying was intentionally and relentlessly upstream this did produce moments that managed even to confuse me: I would see, from the deck of my upriver ship, a pagoda on the bank that lay on my *right* side, but I would have to note down that it in fact stood on the bank that, by convention, was actually the river's *left*. I have in places tried to lessen the confusion by mentioning north or south, or east or west, if doing so seems to clarify the situation; but I have to confess that this didn't always work.

The most difficult part of writing any book about the sad situation of contemporary China is not being able—thanks to the present government's unquenchable capacity for cruelty and revenge—to give the real names of many of the participants.

Many of the men and women whom I met along the four thousand miles and many months of this journey said things to me that were well worth including in the narrative; many others helped me in undertaking an expedition that was in no way officially sanctioned, nor even officially known about. I realized when I was writing, even if these people did not, that by relating their comments or the tales of their assistance in this book, I would cause retribution of some unpleasantly imaginative kind to befall them at some untold moment in their various futures. So I have, and with great reluctance, altered several names, and I have rendered deliberately vague one or two—but only one or two—locations.

Of the changes I have been forced to make I am sorriest of all to have to refer to Lily, my trusted guide and mentor, by this invented English name, and not by her real one—which, as well as enjoying the singular merit of being hers, is in its Chinese form very much more lovely, too.

Without Lily this book could not have come about, at least not in its present state. And yet to draw too much attention to her by writing of her as fully as I would like would be to invite a cascade of official wrath which she in no way either deserves or would be in a position to deflect. Lily is a remarkable and courageous young woman, the likes of which China should be proud to count among its own. I am sure I am not alone in hoping that young men and women just like her will eventually find some way to inherit the management of their vast country, and thus one day, perhaps, to allow China to offer some kind of decently humanitarian future for its marvelous and almost unimaginably huge array of peoples.

Looking at the old river
From the opposite banks
Of a yellow ribbon

Like reading an ancient scroll—
Pictographs of man's flailing
Against the eddies
Of oft told histories . . .

LI BAI, TANG DYNASTY,
8TH CENTURY

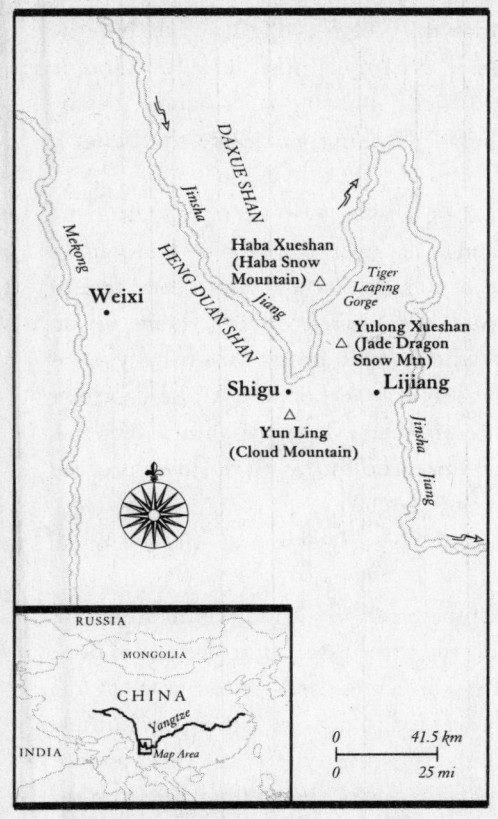

Prelude

About a thousand miles downstream from the Yangtze's source—after it has performed nearly a quarter of its journey from the mountains to the sea—the river executes a most remarkable hairpin bend. Within the space of just a few hundred yards, a river that for hundreds of miles had been pouring relentlessly and indisputably southward slams head-on into a massif of limestone, ricochets and cannonades off it and then promptly thunders headlong back up to the north.

It is difficult to think of any other world-class river that does such a thing. The Nile performs a flirtatious little wiggle through the

north of Sudan. The Lena engages in a long, slow curve near Ya-
kutsk. No one can pretend that the Volga is die-straight, nor the
upper reaches of the Ganges, nor even the Rhine. The Rio Grande
has a "great bend," but like all these other big-river bends, it is by
Chinese standards laughably small. Nothing looks like the Yangtze
in northern Yunnan.

The sheer sharpness of the turn is what is so peculiarly dramatic
about it—the sudden whirl-on-a-sixpence, turn-on-a-dime, now-
you-see-it-now-you-don't kind of a back flip, a riparian *volte-face* of
epic dimensions. It is so dramatically obvious that it shows up on
even the smallest-scale maps—whole-world projections usually manage to display it: it shows up as a strange notch, a kink, a curious
indentation in the passage of great waters. It seems almost artificial,
as though some great deity had once said to this river alone: proceed
thus far in this direction, and no farther.

They call it the Great Bend at Shigu Town, and the fate of all
China has long depended on it.

For the sake of what the Chinese call the Middle Kingdom, it is
just as well that the river makes the turn it does. For had it not done
so, had it been permitted to flow on southward—as a glance at any
map will show that it probably wanted to do—then it is certain there
would never have been an entity that westerners call the Yangtze.
There would never have been a river deserving of the name that the
Chinese use: Chang Jiang, the Long River, or just Jiang, *The* River.

Had there been no bend, and had the waters been allowed to flow
on, they would have passed inexorably, inevitably and quite tragically away from and out of China. They would have left the continent for the Pacific not in the huge embayment known as the East
China Sea, but via the almost insignificant and palm- and karst-
ringed inlet called the Gulf of Tonkin. They would have spilled from
the land not in the great delta on which has been built the great city
of Shanghai, but on the much smaller stretch of mud and shingle
where man created the very much lesser twin cities of Hanoi and
Haiphong.

But for the presence of the singular geological oddity at Shigu, the Yangtze would have flowed on down into what is now the valley of the Red River. Instead of joining the sea two thousand miles later at Shanghai, this river would have dribbled lazily and insignificantly where the treacly mess of the Red River does today; it would have been, for most of its foreshortened length, a river—sister to the Mekong—in the country that is these days called Vietnam.

And China would be left without the Yangtze. The tributaries that today join the Yangtze would have flowed elsewhere, probably never joining forces with a great mother-stream and making an attempt at mightiness. There still would be some big rivers in China's heartland—the Yellow River would flow on unaffected, as would the Pearl. But had not the limestone massif intervened at Shigu, there would be nothing so unimaginably vast as the river that slices through the nation's heart today. A China without such an immense torrent at its heart is almost impossible to contemplate.

And yet, but for this one event, this single happenstance at Shigu, it could so easily have been so. A map will show the evidence: it is incontrovertible—the Yangtze would have ended its days in undistinguished fashion. Palm-oil jungles would take the place of container ports, muddy villages instead of pagodas and palaces, small market towns instead of giant industrial cities.

The fate and condition of a China made riverless by such an event would be profoundly and unutterably different from the complicated, ancient, infuriating and unashamedly powerful China with which the rest of the world has to deal today. Which is why I have always found it odd that the little town of Shigu in Yunnan is by and large undistinguished, unvisited and unknown—a place that, if famed at all, wins its repute not for its remarkable geology, but for a long forgotten battle in which an invading Tibetan army loses to a local people whose menfolk carry falcons, keep parrots as household pets and leave all their major decisions to the women.

Fascinating though this all may be, what Shigu should by rights be known for is the miracle of geography that took place there, and that allowed China to become watered by and divided by and unified by the most important river in the world.

There is naturally a rational explanation for the Great Bend. The sudden diversion of the river at Shigu is simply the work of tectonics, a geomorphological happenstance called river-capture, and more specifically, the work of the terrifyingly powerful and ten-million-year-long event known as the Miocene Orogeny. In China, though, rational explanation often bows before legend, and it does so impressively at Shigu. Children are taught in school that what happened in Shigu is the work not so much of tectonics, but of an emperor who was called Yü the Great, lived four thousand years ago and was so exercised by the thought of this mighty stream pouring out of China, and of the leaching of good Chinese earth out into the realms of the Annamese barbarians, that he set a huge mountain down at Shigu and blocked the river at its exit.

The hill Da Yü chose for this purpose is called Yun Ling, Cloud Mountain. It exists today, looming over the little town. One early summer's day, as I was halfway through a long journey upriver, I took an afternoon to clamber up its flanks and to gaze down at the bend it creates. I was quite alone. Few others bother to walk the hill: it is not very high, it offers no spectacular sport, and from all aspects it looks ordinary enough, with little to single it out from the chaotic jumble of hills that make up this part of the Empire.

But some—especially if they have hold of a map that shows what this mountain does, how it shapes the course of the river that skids up against its impregnable northern slopes—could build a plausible and persuasive case for Cloud Mountain being quite the most important mountain in the world. Its very existence, they would argue, whether it was created by tectonics, or by a long dead emperor, quite simply and profoundly allowed both the Yangtze and China to be. Cloud Mountain caused the Yangtze to exist; and given the central role that the Yangtze has for aeons played in the creation of China, one can say without risk of too strong contradiction that it caused China to exist as well.

The hill is pretty, with a deceptively soft aspect, and when I walked up it the lower slopes were covered with rhododendrons in bloom, and with camellias and stunted camphor trees. It has, all told, a gentle ordinariness about it. But like so much in China, this is a cunning deceit: for in the formidable story of the Long River, and in the only marginally less formidable story of the Middle Kingdom, Yunnan's modest-looking Cloud Mountain plays an unsung but most extraordinary part.

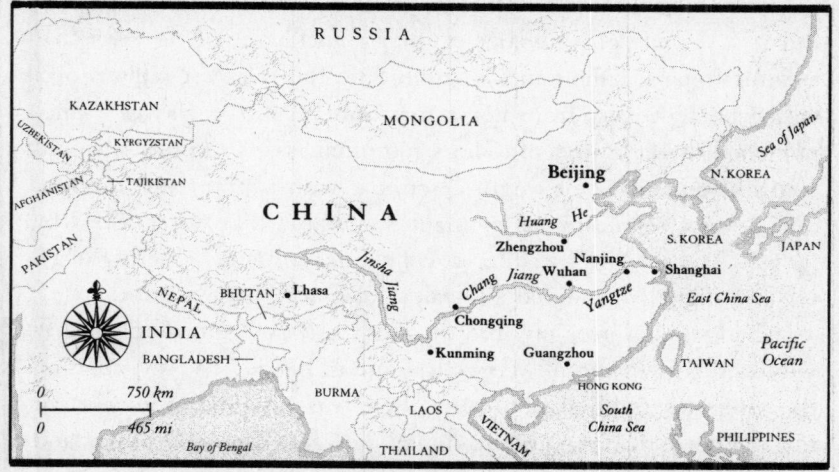

I

The Plan

"Welcome!" spoke the computer, with a tinny amiability that took the chill off the early morning. "You have mail!"

Duly, and robotlike, I then performed the slight mouse movements of finger and thumb that are all that is necessary these days to retrieve inbound electronic letters, and found in an instant the morning's mass of post. Most of it was routine, letters that I wouldn't bother with for an hour or so. But one did seem at first blush more intriguing—a note from someone I clearly did not know, someone who signed himself or herself with the rather unattractive sobriquet of *Lima Bean.* Peruvian? Surely not. I settled for the likelihood of an American correspondent, someone who was probably from the Middle West.

Everything that follows had its origins in this letter, leading as it did to a cascade of peculiar electronic coincidences. A journey that eventually passed thousands of miles into the remotest regions of a China far, far away from home first came about by way of a phenomenon that admirers of today's communications revolution would heartily applaud. Some might describe it with appropriate grandiloquence: as a serendipitous moment, something that was grasped by happy chance while speeding down the information superhighway. Or as a digitally rendered equivalent of Once Upon a Time.

I had walked groggily into my study one cold morning in early winter, the first mug of Maxwell House in hand. I had switched on the computer and looked to see if there was anything of interest for me. I hoped so: even in the digital universe one still wakes and hopes for letters. The tinny *Welcome,* the jaunty *You Have Mail,* caused as always that telltale quickening of the heart. "All long for mail," Auden wrote, "for who can bear to feel himself forgotten?" So with a couple of keystrokes I told the computer to display the note from Mr. or Mrs. or Ms. Lima Bean, and within seconds this uninvited stranger's words were tumbling onto the cathode tube before me.

They seemed to be asking for my advice about Hong Kong.

I could guess why. Some months before I had been asked to write up a list, on a sort of electronic self-portrait-cum-census-form, of what I considered at the time to be things that interested me. My response had been rather glib, and in retrospect not a little pretentious. Borrowing a line from Jorge Luis Borges, I said that I liked *hourglasses, maps, eighteenth century typography, the roots of words, the taste of coffee, the prose of Robert Louis Stevenson—and Hong Kong.* This last I had added to the blind sage's list, and it was this last that prompted Lima Bean's brief letter.

"Dear Sir," it said, or something to that effect, "I am about to go with my husband on our first-ever journey to Hong Kong. Since you say you are interested in the place, could you give us some hints on where to go, what to do, what to see. . . . We are late middle-aged, we think of ourselves as bright, and quite adventurous. . . . We leave next week." The writer lived in northern Illinois. She confessed to rarely having ventured farther afield than Boston.

I replied instantly and almost unthinkingly, in the way that electronic mail tempts us to do. A swift tap on the Write a Reply button, then a few hastily chosen suggestions—the name of a temple near Sai Kung, my membership number at the China Club, my son's phone number on Lamma Island, the titles of a couple of good books—followed by a swift tap on Send Reply, and it was done. I returned to whatever work I was planning to do, and promptly forgot all about the exchange.

Two months later, on the afternoon of a day when I had returned from a trip abroad, a bulky package came in the mail, express, special delivery. It was postmarked Chicago. The return address was unfamiliar; but since it was unlikely that the Unabomber would have any interest in me, I unwrapped the parcel, though gingerly. It turned out to be a copy of the fifth edition of Sherman Lee's classic *History of Far Eastern Art,* expensively produced by a tony Fifth Avenue art house. The jacket was nicely culturally agnostic, balancing Japanese art and Chinese art with equal weight by showing a Momoyama period screen painting and a Sung dynasty handscroll side by side. It was very elegant: the perfect temptation, no doubt, for the impulsive buyer of this kind of hundred-dollar book.

I flipped through it for a while, stopping occasionally to look at color plates of places I knew—temple gardens in Kyoto, a fresco at Borobudur, an elephantine sandstone Buddha in China's Shanxi province. Then a handwritten note fell out: it was from someone called Andrea, thanking me for the advice I had offered her and her husband all those weeks before.

They apologized for what seemed an unconscionable delay in expressing their gratitude, the note began. They had had an unforgettable time: the China Club was wonderful, the Austin Coates book* was unforgettable, my son's phone number was always busy. The enclosed was the very least way they could express their gratitude. Enjoy.

I was astonished. For what had taken me perhaps three minutes' thought—all this? I flipped through some more pages, pleased at the generosity of strangers—and then, quite suddenly, I stopped. For there before me was a reproduction, in black and white, and spread across the upper half of two pages, of what I knew to be a remarkable work of Chinese art. And more than that: I knew, the very moment I saw it, that this was a creation that, in some way or other, was going to change my life.

It was part of a picture by a Qing dynasty court painter named Wang Hui—part of it only, because the entire thing, if unrolled, would measure fifty-three feet from end to end. It was called *Wen Li Chang Jiang—the Ten thousand li Yangtze.*† It had been painted in about 1680. It was a fanciful ink and pastel realization of the entire course of the Yangtze River—which the Chinese generally called Chang Jiang, the Long River, or simply Jiang, *The* River.

Every mile of the stream, every town along its banks, every tributary, every rapid, every rockpool, everything from the mouth to the mountains was said to be there, in a more or less recognizable form. It was very beautiful, even in this fragment—the delicate brush strokes of more than three centuries before had produced pagodas, sailing junks, mountains, tree-covered rock pillars, reeds, fishermen, ancient city walls. . . . Even had I not been grateful for the book, I was hugely glad to be seeing the picture. For—and herein lies the

---

* *Myself a Mandarin,* required reading for anyone bound for Hong Kong.
† The phrase "ten thousand *li*" is widely used in China to describe an entity—most notably the Great Wall—that is known for its extreme length. The phrase is not meant to be taken literally—just as well considering the *li*'s notorious flexibility as a unit of measure: an uphill *li* being longer than a downhill *li,* a Shanghai *li* being shorter than a Chengdu *li.* But the Yangtze benefits from a happy arithmetical accident: the early western railway builders in China fixed a firm definition onto the unit, making one *li* equivalent to precisely 25/58ths of an English mile. Since the Yangtze measures 3964 miles from source to sea, Wang Hui might consider his fancy vindicated: his ten-thousand-*li* river is 9200 *li* from end to end—near enough.

most important of the cascade of coincidences—the river of the painting was the river at the center of my world.

For the very day that the book came so unexpectedly and so pleasingly in the mail was the day that I had returned from China, and, more specifically, from the river itself. And I had made the journey along the river purely and simply because I had been casting about trying to work out how best to write a book about it.

I had been fascinated by the Yangtze for many years—at least since the mid-1980s, when I first went to live in Hong Kong. I remember vividly the first time I saw it. I had traveled out to the colony by train, all the way from Liverpool Street to Kowloon, and although our various expresses had thundered over some fine rivers on the way (the Volga, the Ob, the Yenisei) and even though we had crossed the Huang He, the Yellow River, which I knew they called China's Sorrow because of the huge amount of heartland she ripped out to sea each year—despite all of these mighty crossings, nothing quite prepared me for the thundering roar of the bridge that took the train from Hanyang to Wuchang, across the vast brown winding-cloth that, to my unlettered English mind, was still known as the Yangtze Kiang.

One moment there were the lights of a city, and then came the rumble, rumble, rumble of the bridge girders and iron railway ties, and there was blackness below, and just nothing. It was like roaring on a railway in outer space. Once in a while a firefly of a light sped by underneath, or there was a line of little lights, some red, some green; and as my eyes grew accustomed to the gloom I could see the glint of rushing water, lit by the umbery sliver of soot-polluted moon. The dark and pinpricked river swept by below for minute after minute until suddenly, with a great relieving gush of silence, the girders dropped away, the rails became welded and seamless once again, and the lights of the steel mills of Wuchang turned sepia night into orange morning. We were past the Yangtze now: and though it was not apparent in the night we were in a different geography, in almost another country, and among quite another people.

Some geographers and writers like to think of the river as a sort of waistline, a silk ribbon that cinches China quite decidedly into two. Above the waist are the brain and the heart and soul of China, a land that is home to the tall, pale-skinned, wheat-eating, Mandarin-speaking, reclusive and conservative peoples who are the true heirs to their Middle Kingdom's five thousand years of uninterrupted history. Below the river-waist, on the other hand, are the country's muscles and sinews: the stocky, darker, more flamboyant, rice-eating peoples who speak in the furiously complicated coastal dialects, the men and women whose energies and acumen and cunning—and cooking—have spread the goods and words of China to the world beyond.

I could see nothing of this, of course, from my seat on the Shanghai Down Express. But I had been to Hong Kong before, and I had been to many of China's northern towns as well, and had been only too aware there was a certain facile truth about the geographers' theories: in summary, and superficially, one can readily observe that Northerners don't like rice, and they don't like Southerners, and the Yangtze is as convenient a line as any to draw between them.

And yet there was a paradox, too—in that the river that separates the nation also manages to unite it. The Yangtze divides the country in two by its sheer and barely bridgeable width. But at the same time and on another level it also manages to weld the country into one, at least in part by virtue of its vast and barely imaginable length. All Chinese, whether they are from Hainan Island in the far south, or Mohe in Manchuria in the far north, or whether they live in Kashgar in remotest Turkestan, or on the Korean borderland near the lake at the summit of Mt. Paektu—all Chinese have a feeling of ownership for and kinship with their Long River. It is all China's river—a sacred icon revered and respected by all.

All Chinese know they are fed by the Yangtze and flooded by the Yangtze; they know the river is their country's gateway and its major highway; they write poems about it and sing songs to it, they fight battles on its banks, they sign treaties on its shores, they draw water for fishing and washing and making power, they dump rubbish in it, they drown babies in it, they scatter ashes in it and pollute it with coal and sulphur and naphtha and the excretion and decay of every animal known, and of humans too. They respect it, fear it, welcome it, run from it, hate it and love it. More than any other river in the world—more even the Nile, which also cradles an entire country and nurtures a civilization—the Yangtze is a mother-river. It is the symbolic heart of the country, and at the very center, both literally and figuratively and spiritually, of the country through which it so ponderously and so hugely flows.

If the Yangtze valley were to be a country it would be the second most populous in the world, after India. Out of all the people in the world, one in twelve lives in the river's watershed. There are almost 500 million people whose homes and workplaces are scattered along the miles of river cliffs and mud banks between the Tibetan Plateau and the East China Sea. And although two other rivers, the Nile and the Amazon, are marginally longer, their importance—social, economic, even cultural—is almost nothing by comparison.

The Mississippi-Missouri might seem a real rival, for length, power, industrial might; and yet there is a signal difference, for Old Glory exerts none of the popular unifying power over America that the Yangtze does for China. A man in San Francisco feels precious little for the river that he or his ancestors might once have crossed to get to his present home; by contrast a man in Canton knows only too well the power and the might of the river that he or his forebears crossed in their *sampan* or their *wupan* to bring him eventually from the heartland to the coast.

Even from where I lived down on that southern coast, a thousand miles away, it is impossible to be unaware of the Yangtze's presence, of the import of this slumbering dragon of a river. It has a commanding existence, a lowering geographical reality. It was easy to be captivated by its power and stern visage: and for many years before the morning when I first gazed down at Wang Hui's masterpiece, I had indeed been captivated, quite truly. I had wanted to write about the Yangtze almost from the first moment I caught sight of it.

• • •

But if the kernel of an idea of writing an account of this great river was there, then how best exactly to write it remained a problem. Except that as I studied the picture before me that day, and looked ever more closely, an idea occurred to me. Something about the picture seemed unusual—something about its construction, its composition. It was something that hinted at a way to explore the river, a way to write the book. Perhaps, I thought, if I could actually find his picture, if I could see the original, the full-size version of the fragment that was so tantalizingly displayed in Sherman Lee's great book—if I could see the entire thing in its pristine state, then it might provide the clue. But how to see the picture? Where exactly was it?

The caption gave the name: *H. C. Weng Collection, New Hampshire.* A couple of phone calls—one to the publisher, another to the Department of Asian Art at the Metropolitan Museum of Art—brought a further name, Wan-go Weng, and the vague thought from one of the Metropolitan's staff that he did indeed live in New Hampshire, quite probably near a university town. But as to exactly where, infinite regrets, no idea.

I had once visited Dartmouth College, near the town of Hanover, and I had a hunch this might be the place. I called directory information and my luck was in: there was indeed a listing for Weng, W. G. Within moments I had Mr. Weng on the line, his barely accented Chinese voice thin, educated, precise, cheerful. I introduced myself, first in poor Chinese to suggest some credentials, then in English.

Yes, he said, he had the picture. It was one of his most precious possessions. It was locked away in a bank vault. He took it out every few years, to gaze at it, just as handscroll paintings are meant to be gazed at. Would I like to see it? He could easily take it out of the bank on a Friday evening, in time for a weekend when I might be free. He suggested a Sunday a week or so after Christmas. Would I come in midafternoon? "You are English, yes?" He gave a courteous little giggle of pleasure. "Teatime, yes? We'll see you for tea. I've no doubt we will have a lot of snow by then. I will send you a map. You must take care driving in the weather we have."

Wan-go Weng and his wife lived at the end of a rutted lane in the low hills above the Connecticut River valley. Their house was new, made of warm polished pale woods like pine and butternut, and it was well insulated against the bitter cold that in these parts lasts long into the spring. Mr. Weng came to the door—a slight, kindly-looking figure, he smiled easily and often. He led me indoors, through an airy living room on whose walls hung a number of small ink-brush drawings. There was a spare elegance about the place, everything tidy and bright and clean, everything chosen for a purpose, no clutter.

"I have the scroll," he said, and pointed to a neat cherry-wood box, maybe two feet long and eight inches wide and deep, sitting on the kitchen table. "We'll look at it in a moment. But first it's important to know how I came to get it. Part of the magic of a handscroll is in its history—in how many hands it has scrolled through, if you will. Best only to see the picture when you know its story."

Wang Hui had been one, perhaps the most distinguished, of the famous Four Wangs, the painters who won the unstinting patronage of the Chinese courts in the late Ming and early Qing dynasties. He was born in 1632—the same year as Vermeer and Christopher Wren—and he died in 1717. He was a contemporary of Rembrandt, Velázquez, Frans Hals; and though his art did not appear in the West until long after his death, the first exports from China—most notably tea—did make their appearance at about this time in England. The craze for chinoiserie, which would before long make such classical and orthodox and Confucian styles as Wang's all the rage in modish houses of London and Paris, was to erupt during his lifetime—not that he ever knew.

His best-known commission came in 1691, when the second Qing emperor, Kangxi, demanded that he accompany the court on a seventy-day Imperial Progress, an official tour through the southern and eastern provinces of the country. Wang painted like a man possessed: he produced no fewer than twelve handscrolls, recording faithfully—for he was a keenly traditional painter of the no-frills Confucian school—all the minutiae of court life and country habits. And he brought the same painstaking approach, rather dry and fussy by some accounts, to his triumphal painting of the Long River.

He completed this sometime around the end of the seventeenth century, and there is some suggestion—though no documentation to prove—that he gave it to a Court official for safekeeping. When he, and later the mandarin, died, the box, the silk wrapping cloth, and the tightly rolled painting inside were passed to a succession of wise men. The only one of these to have a personal link with Wan-go Weng was the latter's great-great-grandfather, who owned it during the opening years of the twentieth century.

This man, though a Han Chinese in the Manchu court, had once been tutor to two of the child-emperors. For his troubles he had been appointed a mandarin of the First Rank: he was allowed the distinction of wearing a violet robe,* a hat with a scarlet button on top, and a peacock feather. His great-great-grandson knows of him as an austere, Confucian, conservative figure—one of the few men in Court who stood firmly against those appeasers who wanted to treat with the Japanese. He would brook no nonsense from the invaders: he represented the unflinching spirit of China at her apogee.

But it was not long before the combined effects of Japanese and the barbarian intervention in China—to say nothing of Communism and the civil war—sapped the energies of such proud figures as this. China's Empire was ebbing its way toward extinction, the mandarinate along with it. It was during these turbulent times that the then-young Mr. Weng was given charge of the painting: during the dreadful and chaotic days in 1949, when the Communists and the Nationalists were slugging it out for control, it was one of the few connections, it seemed to him, with the courtly and stable dignity of China's past. He was in Shanghai at the time, and he was planning

---

* Yellow, the quintessential Chinese Imperial color, was only allowed to be worn by the Emperor and Princes of the Blood Royal.

to flee to the United States. It was vital, his family said, that he take Wang Hui's picture with him.

The tale would have had more derring-do about it had the young Mr. Weng managed to escape from the Communist armies with the cherry-wood box under his arm, hidden under a cloak, his only possession. But in fact the box, along with his other luggage, went in a crate, deep in the hold of a President Lines freighter that sailed out of the Whangpoo and out of the mouth of the Yangtze and across the Pacific.

He, in more of a hurry than his bags, came out just ahead of Mao's troops by flying on the very last North West Airlines turbo-prop flight to leave China in November 1949. He reached New York via airfields in Tokyo, an Aleutian island, Anchorage, Edmonton and Minneapolis. The freighter steaming across the ocean duly docked somewhere on New York's Lower West Side. Mr. Weng was eventually reunited with his boxes and with the picture, and Wang Hui's *Wen Li Chang Jiang* has never been out of America since.

This history all duly recited, we went over to the dining-room table, which was now brilliant in the late afternoon sun. Mr. Weng, with steady and delicate movements, unfastened the two tiny ivory hasps that kept the box lid shut. Inside was what looked like a bolt of gray silk: it too was fastened with ties of ivory and white cotton, which Mr. Weng undid, his hands shaking a little.

It is rare indeed that we can ever touch a work of art that is as old as three hundred years. Pictures of great age and value are invariably guarded and protected—those on public display generally well, those in private hands usually jealously. They are suspended beyond our grasp, high, unreachable, beyond molestation. Or like some sculptures they may be put behind a little fence, or a tracery of velvet ropes, or with a discreet sign that warns Don't Touch. But Chinese handscrolls had quite a different purpose.

They were meant to be touched. They were never meant for mere public display. Rather, they were specifically offered to give both visual and tactile pleasure to the owner, at home, in private. They were all part of Confucian civility: with his books and his pipes and his wine—and his paintings—a Chinese man of former times could indulge himself of an evening with a sensual experience of the highest order. As we were doing now. I watched as Mr. Weng unrolled the beginning of the painting, and I felt the same electric thrill at the sensation as civilized old Chinese men must have felt through dozens of decades before.

The paper was soft, faintly spongy, like parchment, and it stayed quite flat on the table even though it had been tightly rolled for the last five years. It had a small bamboo stiffener at the end, and as he pulled it out toward the right—the picture itself remaining unrolled to the left—he laid it over the table edge, just in case there was a tendency for the paper to spring back. But there was none: it stayed just where it was, and so he unrolled, and unrolled, and watched slowly as, one by one, and as though appearing through a summer sea-mist of the purest white, small objects—junks and fishing boats! I began to identify—began to appear on the paper.

They were black. Some were triangular, some elongate. In one or two of them small figures could be made out, men in wide conical hats peering intently downward. We were on the ocean, near the coast. Mr. Weng unrolled some more—the fast-forming but still slender roll at the right beginning to swell, the mother roll on the left diminishing very slightly.

Low cliffs then came into view, one with a pagoda, nine stories high, perhaps a monument to some vainglorious Chinese duke. Then came more cliffs, a city wall, two low and tree-fringed banks of what was now clearly a river, coming together out of nowhere, and moving in a rough parallel to the left. There was a patch of color, a dab of yellowish brown pastel on a small curved roof in a village in the foreground. "Shanghai!" said Mr. Weng. "Small place, back then."

And so, inch by inch and mile by mile, we journeyed up the Long River of three centuries before. It was a little like watching a film, or seeing the countryside through a long lens with which the director would execute a slow and lazy pan, downstream to upstream. Occasionally Mr. Weng would see something that he thought he recognized. "Must be Nanking!" he'd say. "There's the triangle at Chunking, the junction where the Japs used to bomb! You read Han Suyin? Terrifying place to be, Chungking." (Mr. Weng had a tendency to use the old names, the names that were in use in China at the time he had fled. I thought it helped him cling to the China that had been his home: to talk of Nanjing and Chongqing would be to talk of another country, which in a sense Mao's China had become.)

We passed the representation of what might have been the town that is now called Yichang—though all we could see was a mere hamlet, a few huts huddled behind a low wall. This, I thought, was probably where the great new dam, the subject of so much present-day controversy, was going to be built. Mr. Weng had told me he had studied hydrology, and I imagined he might hold a view on the dam, as most people did: but no, he had all the tact and circumspection of the careful scholar and ventured no opinion. "I have studied it in detail," was all he said as we passed the site by. "It is a most complicated issue."

Some Chinese scroll paintings are adorned with annotations by the artist, the better to help identify the succession of locales. But Wang Hui had done no such thing, and we had to guess at the more fancifully named formations that slid before our eyes. Was this pile of rock, deep in the Three Gorges, Wang's representation of what all China knew as the *Military Books* formation? Could the sinuously formed limestone cliff pictured here be what they called the *Ox Lung and Horse Liver*? It was difficult to tell, from this at least, what had prompted China's mariners to imagine once that the strata had been shaped like a pile of volumes, or a dish of umbles.

Steadily we journeyed upriver, and steadily upriver the stream narrowed. The drawing became rather more fanciful as—we must presume—the territory became steadily more unfamiliar to Wang Hui, and it was replaced by the more imaginary river that legend and anecdote had settled inside the artist's grizzled head. How far he had traveled we do not know. We know he completed his Progress, and that great journey must have taken him to a number of places along the course of the Long River—no emperor could avoid passing by, so central was it to dynastic China's topography. But whether the painter traveled as far along it as his scroll implies, we have no knowledge.

Some places to which he may well not have traveled did seem to be there, however—or at least they seemed recognizable. Shigu's Great Bend, for example, appeared to be represented—Mr. Weng and I turned our heads this way and that to convince ourselves that one length of delicate tracery was indeed the hairpin turn, despite being hidden on the painting among wildly imagined precipices and waterfalls and mist-shrouded temples with their ever-watching monks. We couldn't be sure. After all, Shigu was getting on for two thousand miles away from country in which the painter lived and where he would have felt comfortable and secure: few Chinese in those days went any farther west from the capital than the Red Basin of Sichuan. They only imagined the wilderness, the terrifying monsters, the godless savagery that stretched beyond.

And then the source, the headwaters—unknown, unvisited and so imagined also. Fifty-three linear feet after those first few fishing boats had appeared bobbing in the East China Sea, so the river-picture came to its end in a swirl of spray and mist and cloudy heavens. A few last peaks were dotted through the snow-folds of the clouds, like nunataks on snow, tiny black triangles against the blankness.

There was an intentional symmetry here: the peaks were there to echo the mainsails of the junks on the estuary waves. Just as the boats would be fewer and fewer as we went away from land, so the mountaintops would grow smaller and less distinct as the artist's mind closed into the clouds. And so then there was nothing—just an expanse of white emptiness, the unsullied heavens from which the river had first come.

But though the painting was now quite done, the scroll itself was not quite ended. I pushed my chair away from the table. Mr. Weng stopped me. "No, don't stop. There's more," he said. "This is what I really want to show you. Carry on. You'll get to it soon."

What Mr. Weng had wanted me to see was the artist's colophon, and all the writings that had followed it down the decades. It is a common feature of Chinese handscroll pictures that the last few feet of mulberry paper—the part of the sheet nearest to the core when the painting is wound up—are left blank. The emptiness is first for the painter himself to write a brief but elegant few lines of explanation. Three hundred years ago Wang Hui had done so—his orthodoxy demanded it—and he had written many vertical lines of characters, telling how long the work had taken him, the cities he had visited, the places he liked best. He dated it and signed it, and then sealed it with his chop, in scarlet ink.

Next to his writings were lines from others who next owned the painting—perhaps a high Court official who had kept it until the 1720s, next to whoever had it until 1760, then another in 1790, another in the early nineteenth century—and so on and on, essay succeeding essay succeeding poem succeeding poem, different interpretations, different expressions of joy, different offerings from the centuries.

The final one in the series had been written in this century, by Wan-go Weng's great-great-grandfather. It had been sealed with what I supposed to be the magisterial impression of the Reign Year of Aisin-Gioro Pu Yi—the forlorn, childish, and Hollywood-memorialized Last Emperor of China.

But now what would happen? What would Weng himself write when it became his turn? And who would write after him? His children live in California, and their ability to write the kind of calligraphy necessary for so venerable a document is limited, to say the least. Wang Hui—long dead maybe, but his presence nonetheless haunting all who ever owned his work—might have to face the possibility that his painting, so long in the hands of Chinese and so long in the orbit of the Court, might now have to remain overseas, beyond the Chinese Pale, and that it might one day perhaps even come into the possession of a barbarian. Not a prospect to please, not at all.

I liked to imagine Wan-go Weng trying to salvage the situation. I liked to think of him taking the painting from its vault once in a while, trying to pluck up the courage to add his own writing to the colophon. How would he prepare? Would he take his inkstone and grind the finest and blackest ink, and select the most graceful and finest-pointed from a selection of badger-hair brushes? Would he then hold it vertically, heavy with its new load of black fluid, above the next blank space on the mulberry paper? And then would he wait, his hand poised, steady, unwavering?

What to write? he would wonder. And then, once content was composed, how best to write? Should it be with long sweeping characters, or in figures that were small, tidy, and precise? And let alone what he should do—could he do it, could he write an epigraph that was as elegant in style and expression as that of his great-great-grandfather, or of the succession of mandarins who had gone before? Would whatever he managed to write have the poetry, the rhythm, and the spare economy that was appropriate to a picture of such antiquity and to a Yangtze river that demands and deserves such greatness?

I fancy—though I never inquired—that his courage in such situations would invariably fail him. His brush would hover above the empty paper, paper that almost cried out to be marked indelibly by the owner's ink. But that very indelibility was what made it all so intimidating—and on each occasion, so I supposed, he would eventually replace the brush on its stand, clean the ink from its stone, roll the painting up again and put it back in its silken wrappings, and then in its box. Maybe later, he would say to himself, maybe when I'm eighty, ninety, or when I am back in China for good. It was, it seemed to me, an exquisite kind of dilemma, a kind of mind-torture that only China, with her perverse ways, could invent.

After I had said my good-byes that first evening and had begun the drive down through the dark and the snow, I realized that Mr. Weng, though he may not yet have solved his own problem with the river, had indeed and unwittingly solved mine. As I thought about it, I realized I knew exactly now how I would tackle—and how I should tackle, indeed how I *must* tackle—the story of the Yangtze. It was the thought of the written colophon, which I had almost been too impatient to see, that had given me the essential clue.

The painting, which we had slowly rolled open on that dining table, had offered us, as it had offered all those who had seen it in the past, a steady and stately progression through the river as geography, as *place*. But the writings that followed it, the letters and poems that came from a long line of owners and borrowers, had then offered us, and all who likewise had viewed it before, a steady progression through experience, through *time*. Now, I realized, I could and should combine those two journeys: I could make my own exploration of the river not simply an inquiry into Chinese geography—but also an excursion through Chinese history.

If I were to travel upstream along the river, going as we had that snowy teatime, I would be able not just to travel deep inward, into the Chinese heartland; I could also travel at the same moment ever backward into the Chinese saga. For that was a feature of the Yangtze which only began to occur to me on the drive home: that the river's history, or much of it, made a rough-and-ready parallel with its progress as a river. As the river flowed, so had China flowed as well.

The riverside cities that lay close to the sea, for instance, tended to be the cities that had been affected by more modern times. The towns and villages that lay up in the headwater hills, on the other hand, were ancient, or had lain untouched and unspoiled for centuries. Upstream was ancient; downstream was more modern. Downstream was today; upstream was yesterday.

I thought on. This uniqueness of the Yangtze, if indeed it was a true uniqueness and not a feature common to all great rivers, had much to do with foreigners, and with the remarkable interfering role that they played in the recent history of China. It had come about in part at least because the western penetration of China, which had been such a feature of China's eighteenth- and nineteenth-century history, had largely involved the Yangtze as a means of achieving that penetration. The cities that were easiest of access—by foreign gunboats, by traders, by missionaries—had naturally seen more foreign influence. Those that were more distant, more difficult to reach, had been left relatively untouched—by both foreigners and, to a lesser extent, by the Chinese themselves.

It was an imperfect argument, I could see. Other rivers shared something of the same kind: downstream means *now*, upstream means *before* on streams other than this. Cairo is a more up-to-date city than Khartoum; Belém has more skyscrapers than Iquitos—judging from such observations as these one could imagine that by traveling up all giant rivers one could venture backward in much the same way. And yet—the Yangtze seemed, in this special context, *more so*. And the more I thought about the Yangtze's peculiar position in the story of China—a peculiarity that came about to a measurable extent because of the influence of foreigners of one kind and another on the making and unmaking of China—so this approach became ever more tempting. It had a compelling logic, an almost tidy elegance about it.

I could begin at the twenty-first-century world of the shipping lanes and the radar-controlled approaches to the spectacularly modern city of Shanghai; and I could end among the peaks and isolated villages of a China that had probably not changed in five thousand years. Moreover, something hugely important had just been disclosed, making the argument even more potent. Some new research had just been completed at universities in both America and China, and from the sketchy details that had been made public the finds seemed to show that the original Chinese men—the *ur*-Chinese— had lived *in the Yangtze valley*.

The conventional view had long been that China's civilization had grown up along the valley of the Yellow River. In terms of the events in human evolution of a few hundred thousand years ago this may well still be true; but the new work related to events of very much more than a million years ago. Discoveries that were said to be shaking the anthropological world to its very foundations showed beyond too much doubt that the first prehuman hominid animals to arrive in Asia from Africa—from where by common consent all mankind has sprung—had first settled down in caves not on the Yellow River, but on the south side of the Yangtze. A cave no more than a dozen miles from the Three Gorges had lately been identified—and this, more than anywhere else so far discovered or known, was where the vast saga of China had seemingly all begun. The Yangtze, in other words, was by this reckoning the true anthropological cradle of the immense entity that we now call not just China, but all Asia—an irresistibly persuasive argument, if one was needed, for me to make this journey in this very way.

A voyage downstream would be a transport forward, into the present; but a journey upstream would be a voyage back into the whole spectrum of the past—to the recent, the middle and now the far, far distant aeons of unrecorded time. By relating the story of the river, I could relate after a fashion the entire story of China. And that, surely, was the way to go. Making one continuum, even though as ragged and unruly as the river itself, out of all China's vast reaches of space and history.

It did seem ideal. I stopped my car at a pay phone somewhere in the forests of Vermont. It was now pitch dark and very cold, and a snowstorm was swirling down from Canada. I called Wan-go Weng to tell him what I had decided, and to thank him for the inspiration. He said he thought the approach would probably work, though as a thesis it could be picked full of holes. But he had been thinking too, he said. There was something more he had wanted to say. And if I hadn't called, he would have written. He would have said just three things: *when you travel on the Yangtze—remember the painting; don't condemn; and only wonder.*

It sounded a little ominous, like a warning. I asked him to explain, but all he would say was that I should call him when I came back from China, and tell him how the river was.

It now remained to make a proper plan. Three months before my meeting with Mr. Weng, when I had been vaguely pondering how best to tackle the river, I had flown to China to have a look around, taking a scouting trip on a downstream cruise ship that was attempting rather less than successfully to make passage through the Three Gorges, from Chongqing to Wuhan.* On board I had met a member

---

* There had been all kinds of problems. The ships owned by the company had all been built in East Germany for the Volga trade and drew three feet more than was

of the crew, a young Chinese woman who, it seemed to me, could be an ideal companion for any long expedition. I will call her Li Xiaodi. Like many younger Chinese she also had an English name, Lily.

Lily had never been out of China, but she spoke the perfect and perfectly enunciated English that is taught in the country's better metropolitan universities (in her case, Shanghai's International Studies University). Her Chinese was classic *putonghua*—the so-called common speech—unaccented Mandarin, the kind of language that ought to be comprehensible in most of the Lower Yangtze basin. This was important for me: despite the best efforts of a small army of teachers, my spoken Chinese remained of a kind that the most charitable critic would call halting. (Not long before I had called over a waitress in a Chinese restaurant and had attempted to ask her for pepper and salt. She had responded by sitting down and asking me in English whether she had understood me properly: had I really wanted to come to her restaurant, as she was certain I had suggested, for a discussion on *how to acquire a passport?*)

When I first met Lily it was not, however, her linguistic ability that most impressed me. It was, as a navy man might say, the cut of her jib. She was, for a start, extraordinarily tall. Her back was ramrod straight, her jaw was set firm, her eyes managed to be at the same time kindly, piercing and demanding. She looked the very antithesis of the demure and sometimes coquettish waif that many westerners wrongly suppose young Chinese women to be. This woman looked tough: well-tempered, unyielding.

And toughness, I knew, would be very necessary for a journey like the one I had in mind. It was not so much a need for physical toughness—though with the Yangtze headwaters being on a cold and desolate plateau at around eighteen thousand feet, a certain stubborn endurance would be helpful. Rather there would inevitably be

<hr />

permissible in this unusually low-water autumn. So a journey that normally took three days took five, and involved two boats and a daylong bus journey. The following day the same bus, performing the same portage, crashed, killing three passengers.

occasions—many occasions, I imagined—when a trip like this would run head-on into a wall of stultifying, impenetrable and incomprehensible official opposition. Someone would be needed to ensure that all such opposition was swiftly and surely overcome.

No easy task. There is perhaps no one more mulish—not even a Bengali *babu,* a figure who since Kipling's day has been legendary all round the East for his techniques of inventive obstructionism—than a middle-ranking Chinese cadre who tells a foreigner that he cannot, or may not, or will not do something. A journey to somewhere as outlandish as the headwaters of the Yangtze passes across territories in which foreigners have at best only a questionable right to travel— and I knew that in consequence we would encounter at least one, and possibly scores of humorless young men who would try, by fiat or trickery, to stop us. An ally with a rugged and unwearying inflexibility in dealing with such men, an ally who would never take a Chinese "no" for an answer, someone who could stare down a Chinese *babu* and not be the first to blink—for a venture like this, such a person would be an absolute essential.

Lily, I felt at my very first sight of her, would prove an ally of heroic stature. Her height alone, and the set of her jaw, would cause even the sternest bully boy from the Public Security Bureau to shake in his boots. She had been born into an army family in Dalian in south Manchuria—by repute the meanest, hardest city in China. Her father, unwilling to be parted from her, had won permission to take her with him through all his subsequent army postings, and she lived in a succession of barracks from Heilongjiang to Hainan for the first fifteen years of her life, exposing her to a regime that mixed unremitting discipline with unshakable pride. The years of army life, and the rigors of a Manchurian upbringing, had certainly left their marks on her. She was now thirty-two—married, divorced, with one son left behind in Dalian, being looked after by her own mother. There was a icy determination to her, a ruthlessness that, for the circumstances I had in mind at least, I admired. And I was as certain as I could be, from the two weeks I had spent talking to her on that river cruise that, if ever I did manage to make this journey, she could be the ideal companion: when matters became too trying she would brook no nonsense, give no quarter, take no prisoners.

I wrote to her in Shanghai, where the cruise company had its head office, to see if she might be interested. At first she was reluctant, unsure of her ability: *It will be difficult, I do not think I would be competent.* More letters followed, and as the winter advanced and I explained the idea, she began to understand the possibilities. *I am quite intrigued. . . . I doubt if such an opportunity would ever come my way again.* A small practical doubt then crept into her mind: *I have only a month of holiday owing to me—but I have been looking at the map; surely to reach the headwaters will take very much longer. . . . I might have to risk my job.* Finally, as winter became spring, she melted: *I have decided to come with you. . . . it is so difficult to get good travel gear here in China, so please bring me some sturdy boots, size 39, and a cold-weather jacket in a good fresh color. I am mentally prepared for the venture. . . . I just hope that I will be able to deal with any problems.*

I wrote her one final note, making certain that she would be able to come. *Don't worry,* she replied. *I am a woman of great self-confidence. I do not want to rely on others. I have my own way of doing things. Once decided, nobody can make me change my mind.* That, I thought, was the clincher. She, like no one else, could probably make this journey work.

It remained then only to get hold of some walking and camping gear, and a selection of good maps and charts.

I had hoped at first that I might get hold of some of the classic charts made by the British Admiralty—once the most accurate and most elegant ever made. Sedulously observant Royal Naval cartographers had been drawing maps of the Yangtze ever since Lord Macartney had been grudgingly permitted to sail along a few miles of the river in 1793. A second British expedition to China in 1816 under Lord Amherst had also resulted in some diligent mapmaking, and by the time of the First Opium War thirty years later, the river's mouth had been almost as well charted as the Thames, the Hooghly or the Hudson. The British tradition of making fine river maps continued well into the twentieth century—perhaps, I fancied, they would still be made, and still be of use.

I found a nautical chart agency in New York that stocked them—
they had the Royal Navy charts of the Yangtze all the way up to
Yichang, the city just downstream of the Three Gorges, 940 miles
above the sea. But, the store owner warned me darkly, the maps'
accuracy was no longer guaranteed, the data no longer reliable. Communism had put paid to free movement on the river since 1949, and
the only extensive surveys since had been made by the Chinese, and
their figures were kept broadly secret. Royal Naval survey vessels
could no longer bustle along in the river's deeps and shallows, sounding and dredging by turns as they once were wont to do. But I
bought the maps anyway, for sentimental reasons—they were very
lovely, and I didn't mind too much if the depths were off by a
fathom or two, or the distances wrong by the odd cable.

I also managed to find, in a secondhand bookstore, a 1954 copy of
The Admiralty Pilot for the Yangtze—it was one of the great series of
books that, bound in their distinctive and official-looking dark-blue
weatherproof covers, describe in minute detail the coastlines of the
entire world. These books are biblical in their authority and they
display, to the delight of landlubbers, a fine dramatic economy in
their prose style when talking about such matters as whirlpools and
tide-rips or the dangers of Cape Horn. The *Yangtze Pilot* has been
out of print since 1954: Communism had put paid to attempts to
keep it timely and accurate too, and so the Admiralty scrapped it.
There was a rather pathetic *cri de coeur*, I thought, penned inside one
of its covers: civilian mariners making passage along the river could
perhaps help, the surveyors pleaded, by writing in with any new
information on any sightings of freshly formed sandbanks or other
hazards to navigation. "A form (H.102) on which to render this
information, can be obtained *gratis* from Creechbarrow House,
Taunton, Somerset. . . ."

But while nautical charts require visits by ships with echo sound-
ers and tallow-ended lead lines, topographical maps are easier to
find: satellites and high-flying aircraft perform most of the necessary
functions for those who want no more than hills, rivers and roads. So
there were plenty of maps available for the Chinese countryside on

either bank of the river. No tourist map was worth having; but eleven of the huge sheets of the U.S. Defense Mapping Agency's Tactical Pilotage Chart series covered the entire river at a scale of 1:500,000, or about eight miles to the inch, and they were to prove useful, if occasionally frustrating. The smaller four-miles-to-the-inch Joint Operations Graphics sheets, which American troops use when planning for war, cover the same ground—and, indeed, the entire world land surface—with a terrifying degree of accuracy.

The TPCs were easy to get: a toll-free number in Maryland, four dollars a sheet, credit cards accepted. The JOG sheets were more severely restricted, at least in theory. To have any chance of acquiring them I was obliged, starting a full six months before I was due to leave, to go through the curiously empty ritual of threatening a lawsuit under the Freedom of Information Act. This was the only way—an almost foolproof and face-saving device, I was told—with which to unlock all kinds of government documents, these maps included, from the grip of the censors.

A young paralegal was assigned by the Defense Department's chief counsel to shepherd my request through the bureaucracy. The guiding principle of her task, she explained to me later, was President Clinton's pronounced doctrine that *unless a specific statutory prohibition existed, forbidding the release of any map, the map could and should be made public*. Maps of remote areas of western China are supposed to be top-secret—but were there specific laws forbidding their release? To find that out was the young woman's appointed task.

The Pentagon, makers and prime users of the maps, took a disinterested view of the impending lawsuit, and passed the buck. The matter went to the Department of State, who objected strenuously. What if the maps fell into the hands of the Taiwanese? an official wanted to know. No matter, retorted my young helper—is there a *specific written order* forbidding the release of the maps? The State Department had to admit there was not, so far as they knew. It was up to the Central Intelligence Agency, and then the White House and the National Security Council, to have the final say. Officials in both these agencies tried equally hard to block the release. The Chinese, they said, should not be allowed to know how well America had mapped their country. No matter, said my paralegal once again—is there a *specific written prohibition?* No, said the NSC, there was not. No, said the CIA, there was not.

And that was that. A formal letter arrived the next day saying the "releasability status of the maps had been determined positively." The young woman telephoned to say it had been the most difficult and stimulating Freedom of Information Act case for which she had ever been responsible. "I've learned a lot," she said. To celebrate her victory she had decided to waive all charges—I would have to pay none of her own legal fees, and none of the charges for the maps themselves. And a week later a buff official envelope arrived, enclosing two dozen astonishingly detailed maps of the far Upper Yangtze—maps of a scale and a supposed accuracy that would enable American and allied air and ground forces to go to war there. I felt a strange sense of privilege holding them in my hands: few others could have ever seen them; and had I made the request in almost any other country—Britain included—there is little hope that I would ever have acquired them. The Clinton White House, I thought, had some admirable qualities.

My only concern on having the maps was that the Chinese (who restrict their own maps with understandable severity) might, if they found these on me, either confiscate them for their own use or regard me with the gravest suspicion for possessing them. *Don't worry— they'll think you're a spy whether you have maps or not,* Lily wrote reassuringly when I mentioned them. *Where we're going, any round-eye is thought to be up to no good.*

After that all was simple. My days were dominated by the delights of rummaging around in camping stores for gear: I made myself popular indeed with the owners of a new and at the time not very successful shop close to the Appalachian Trail in Kent, Connecticut, by buying a new Kelty rucksack, a good sleeping bag guaranteed to give comfort at minus twenty degrees, an inflatable sleeping pad, a new down ski jacket (in the "good fresh color" of bright red for Lily), two new pairs of Vasquez boots, innumerable pairs of socks, two tiny flashlights, a spare Silva compass, fingerless gloves, two sets of Ex Officio dry-in-an-hour shirts and trousers, a his and hers set of Oakley high-altitude sunglasses and a pair of smart telescopic German walking canes (which proved entirely useless for anything except driving away wild dogs in Tibet).

To this collection I added my own Leica M6 camera, a Sony microcassette recorder with a remote-control switch, a tiny short-wave radio receiver and my own home-grown first-aid kit with its assortment of hypodermic syringes, morphine, painkillers and broad-spectrum antibiotics—all obtained from friendly doctors who go in for expedition medicine and don't trouble with such niceties as prescriptions. Two bottles of SPF 45 sunblock, some equally strong lip salve (I had been warned that the summer sun in Qinghai province could sear the lips from a camel), insect repellent and a trusted and battered hip flask made up the pack, which, when fully tamped down, weighed a quite acceptable fifty pounds.

I hoisted it onto my back, whistled down a taxi to Kennedy, and twenty hours later was through customs at Hong Kong's Kai Tak Airport. Two days later still, having made a series of complicated arrangements by telephone and having received a somewhat dubious series of assurances, having a new six-month multiple-entry "F" class China visa stamped in my passport and a few wads of American dollars tucked into various waterproof pockets around my person, I stepped onto a boat.

I had a rendezvous arranged at a very precise point in the East China Sea. It was at position 31°03.5′ N, 122°23.2′ E. What was there, according to the charts, was known to China coast mariners, and now to me, as the Chang Jiang Kou Lanby—the Yangtze Entrance Large Automatic Navigation Buoy. Given fair winds and calm seas I expected to arrive at this point, or thereabouts, in three days' time.

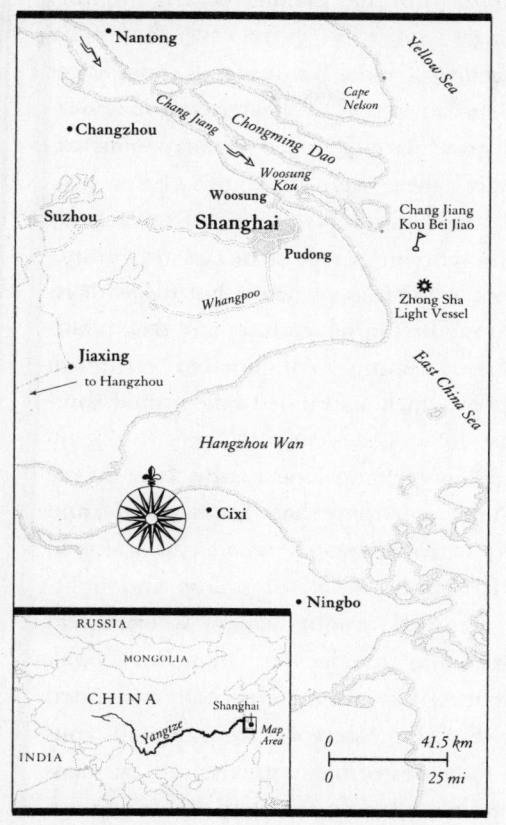

2

The
Mouth,
Open
Wide

The bridge telegraph clanged backward to "Stop all engines," the roar
of our cathedral of diesels promptly softened to a low burble, the
rusty white ship lost headway and hissed to a halt. The world then
fell silent. We rocked listlessly on an invisible swell. The air was
heavy, without movement. Stripped of the breeze of our own making, it became quickly very hot and sultry, and with no relief coming
through the punkah louvers, the cabins became unbearable. The
decks were scalding too, except where we could find shade—but
even though the midmorning sky seemed brassy and bright, the glare
was without focus and there was neither sun nor shadows, so dark

places were hard to find. We drifted in the current, rocking slightly, waiting for something to happen.

I stood at the bow and looked for China. But it was as though we had come to rest inside a cloud made of sweltering cotton wool. Everything was a featureless gray glare, stripped of any points of reference. There was no horizon, there were no landmarks or sea-marks, and it was difficult even to see the waves, though I could hear them splashing untidily on the scorching iron of our plates below. The East China Sea is not known for frets or haars: but it has days like this of boiling-porridge invisibility, in which haze and dew point and temperature and a warm sea-mist combine to create a nondimensional world, a place in which a stranded sailor could well go mad.

We had already passed the Chang Jiang Kou Lanby. It is a sort of cut-down lightship—not long ago there had been a real ship anchored here, bright scarlet, with the words *Ch'ang Jiang Light Ship* in white on the hull. It had been full of sailors and light keepers and wick trimmers, men who might wave a welcome or a farewell to a vessel that passed and sounded her siren. But China has taken advantage of automation like almost everybody else, and the distant markers of her busiest waterway are now all run automatically, by computers, their performance monitored by men high in darkened and air-conditioned shoreside towers, dozens of miles away.

Nonetheless, this massive buoy, fifteen feet above water and weighing a thousand tons or more, had a certain shabby romance about it, marking as it did the place where the great inbound ships leave the ocean proper, and begin their entry to China. So as we passed I took due note of its bright red hull, its white light tower, the muffled sound of its bronze bell. At the same time the master was given new orders by radio: we were to make a further five miles west, heave to and await fresh instructions.

This new spot, a glance at the charts suggested, seemed to be where one is supposed to pick up a Yangtze River pilot. Back in the old days—people who knew the old Shanghai use the phrase frequently—the river pilots used to be swashbuckling fellows, and they had a table permanently reserved for them in the bay window of the Shanghai Club. They alone could take vessels up and down the hazardous waters between here and the docks by the city Bund,* and they commanded prestige and high wages. But these are less dashing times, and the relevant portolanos, the blue volumes of *China Sea Pilot*—Oxford-dark from the Admiralty, Cambridge-light from the Pentagon—are a little vague as to their haunts today. London gave the right latitude and longitude and said that a boat "from which two or three pilots may embark" was generally to be found within a mile or so of it. Washington's navigation instructions said the pilots would lurk in perhaps two places, one of them about four miles north of the closest lighthouse, the other three miles south. But where we were now bobbing and rolling there was no pilot boat, no buoy, no lighthouse: nothing. And so we waited, the static from the bridge radio dull and irritating, like frying fat.

Then with sudden urgency this static was interrupted. A voice in Chinese greeted our ship by name. It broke into English. "Our Inspection Cruiser Number Two is now coming to your starboard quarter. Kindly board your passenger to our port bow. We will arrive in three minutes. Please get ready. Please attend."

It was time to say farewell. I said my thanks to the captain who had given me the ride this far—he was bound for other ports far away—and I ran to the poop, where a gang of sailors were uncoiling a rope ladder. On the horizon was a small black-and-white boat, its bows rearing up as it headed toward us at speed. It came closer and closer, then its prow dropped as it cut back power and it sidled slowly in and up to the dangling rope. From the foremast the boat was flying the blue-and-white burgee of the Yangtze Harbor Super-

---

* Bunds—waterfront roads—exist in the foreign settlements all along the Yangtze, as well as in Calcutta. But in Hong Kong the road was named the Praya, a linguistic infection prompted by the closeness of Macau, which was run by the Portuguese.

intendency, and from the stern, the red, five-starred flag of the People's Republic. Two young Chinese sailors were standing on the foredeck and with them, waving up at me, was Lily.

"They're certain you're a spy!" was the first thing she shouted. "All very irregular, us meeting out here." She grinned wickedly as she helped me down from the swinging ladder and watched me lug my rucksack onto the bridge. "You'll never know *what* I had to do to persuade them to allow you on board." She said no more, but stowed my bags under a table. All was Bristol-fashion within a minute: the sailors then let go fore and aft, and the two boats parted company.

Our siren gave a yelp, and the rusty white transport that had brought me here replied with three blasts on her horn. Her screws began to thresh up the green water, and with her rudder set hard to starboard, she started to push sedately away to the northeast. The Inspection Cruiser Number Two—the *Shu-in Lo*—then set her own course due west, right into the mouth of the Long River. She was making for the point that is customarily regarded as marking the Yangtze River's outward end—the proper starting point for the long upstream journey.

There was still no sign of land. The bridge radar showed a fuzzy image ahead on either side, but though I squinted hard, I could see nothing except the brown-gray blur where sea met sky. We chugged inward, twisting this way and that to avoid shallows. After a while we slowed again, and ahead of us, alone in the emptiness, was another very large buoy.

It was smaller than the Gateway Buoy, but if the satellite navigator's readout was correct, then it had an importance all its own. The cruiser captain started pointing at it, jabbing his finger and shouting, *"Zhong Sha! Zhong Sha!"* It was just as I thought, confirmed by the list of lights on the chart table: this was what the world's mariners agreed was the position of the mouth of the Yangtze River, the place where estuary encounters ocean. It is marked by twenty tons of floating and barnacle-crusted metal, a white flashing lamp, a bell and a somewhat prosaic name: Zhong Sha, or Middle Sand Light.

It was swiftly evident, too, that this structure did lie more in a river than on the sea. The tide was slack—we had organized our rendezvous with the inspection cruiser while the waters were as quiet as possible, just in case. But the waters here, only a little farther west, were not quiet at all—they were streaming hard against the great buoy, their force tilting her a good five degrees from the vertical. A rich coffee-colored wake, murkier than the color of the ocean behind, stretched fifty feet from the buoy's downstream side. Up close I could hear the bubbling and chuckling of the water rushing past, doing two knots at the very least. For a moment I thought the buoy itself was moving at two knots, towed by some underwater force, perhaps a shark. But then I realized what it was: even out here, where there was no land visible and no evidence that land was anywhere near, the river, *the* River, was running.

And running with waters that had flowed a very long way indeed. The generally accepted length is 3964 miles (6378 kilometers, and nearly ten thousand Chinese *li*): the waters have seeped and trickled and gurgled and foamed and roared and slowed and sidled and lumbered all the way here from Tibet—almost from China's faraway frontier with India. This urgent brown stream, heavy with silt particles that even now were drifting down to the seabed and making fresh land below us, was bringing soil all the way from the Himalayas, and leaving it here on the floor of the East China Sea.

Blue ice had thickened and shattered the granites of summits, ice-milk streams had emerged from distant glaciers, crystals of mica had glinted in salmon-rich headwaters, and all had merged with other sands and muds and gravels, and had flowed down from the plateaus for hundreds upon hundreds of miles before casting itself down here, fifty feet below on a dark ocean floor in the upper tropics, beneath the shadowless iron of a rusting light buoy.

There was nothing languid in the transfer, nothing casual about the way that these waters flowed and slowed and deposited their long-hauled baggage. Like China herself, the river here seemed to be surging along, forging robustly out into the ocean, making new Chinese territory with deliberate purpose, even so far from shore. Hydrologists suggest she journeys outward on a prodigious scale: 1.2 million cubic feet of water gush from the Yangtze's mouth every second, and more than twice that amount each August and September, when the snowfields have melted back and the summer rains have dumped still more water into her seven hundred or so furious tributaries. Each year a total of 244 cubic *miles* of water slide out from what the radar insists is the river mouth: a veritable planet of water, of which each side is as long as the distance from New York to Washington, or from Oxford to Amsterdam.

The Yangtze journeys hugely, and she travels heavily. The same science that produces the figures for her flow calculates that her waters pick up and carry 500 million tons of assorted alluvium every year, and dump 300 million of those tons onto the seabed. (The rest stays, left inland—a swamp here, a drying patch there, a new cliff or a swelling eyot.) The result is that the Yangtze has a formidable delta, pushing itself out to sea at the quite respectable rate of 25 yards a year. All to be tilled and cropped by the rice farmers of China's easterly province of Jiangsu, of course—fortunate men indeed. The gradual abrasion of faraway mountains keeps on giving them brand-new territory, two and a half inches more of it every single day.

This steady eastward expansion has over the centuries given eastern China a comfortable, corpulent profile, so that on the map it seems puffed up like a pouter pigeon, or a diner out—though rather more Pickwick than Falstaff. The place where the Yangtze pushes outward to cause it all is deceptive, however: the great notch that looks as though it should be the Yangtze's embouchure was once fed by three huge branches of the river, with the fourth in its present channel. But silt and sand choked the three southerly streams, and the accelerated flow in the northern branch favored and deepened that one. In the seventh century the last of the southern delta streams was closed for good, and the Yangtze has been flowing along its present course, as a single, vastly wide river, for the thirteen subsequent centuries. The gaping mouth below provides a coastline for the old ports of Ningbo and Hangzhou; but it is, by the Yangtze's standards, quite dry.

As we moved hesitantly through the mist, so evidence of land slowly started to appear. Two white butterflies, a dragonfly. Flotsam on the water—fragments of Styrofoam, pieces of lunch containers from some distant city. A carcass, probably pig. I very much hoped it was pig, and turned back quickly to make sure, but it was lost in our wake. Then the riverbanks began to come into view—the mist and hum of coastal China at long last, even if only vaguely in the distance, first on the starboard beam, then off to port.

A hundred years ago almost every piece of this land had a recognizably English name—the Royal Navy surveyed these coasts well—and so once I might have been able to pick out Saddle Island, Parker Island and House Island, Drinkwater Point and, marking the northern entrance to the river, Cape Nelson.* But these names have all now vanished from the charts: the islands are called now what they have in fact been called for thousands of years—Chenqian, Shengsi and Heng Sha. Drinkwater is now simply Dong Jiao, East Point. As for the hero of Trafalgar, his promontory (not visible from here, since the estuary is fifty miles wide) has long since been changed back to its rightful, if more prosaic title: Chang Jiang Kou Bei Jiao— Long River Gateway, North Cape.

As the islands started to close in, so too, did the ships. A thousand ships pass in and out of the Yangtze estuary every day. In any river entrance their presence would be carefully noted, for safety's sake; in

---

* The efforts of foreign hydrographers were once memorialized along the entire Chinese coastline, from Charlotte Point (near the frontier with today's North Korea) via Shovel-Nosed Shark Island and the Bear and Cubs (outside what was then called Ningpo), Crocodile Island and the Three Chimneys (by the former Foochow), the Cape of Good Hope and the Asses Ears (near the former Amoy), Cape Bastion (China's most southerly point) to Nightingale or Merryman's Island, in the Gulf of Tonkin. But since the 1950s these names have generally vanished. They went not only because of communism's crusading zeal: the admiralties in London and Washington realized quite quickly that the Chinese had already named everything, and had inscribed the names on their own charts, hundreds of years before any foreign nation had even started to build ships.

Chinese waters they are noted, and watched, for the security of the State as well. Captain Zhu, master of Inspection Cruiser Number Two, swept the horizon with his glasses. "Anyone who looks unusual, we go and see him," he said. "And if very unusual, we turn to"—and he jabbed his finger off to port, to where a dark gray corvette was speeding past, a ship armed with two obvious guns, one for'ard, the other aft, and with a forest of radio aerials grouped around her mast—"the Chinese Navy. She guards our river. Just in case."

Captain Zhu looked about fifty, was slightly overweight and sweated a lot. His face was marked, for me anyway, by a single long hair that extended from a mole on his chin, curving as it did so. It looked like a wire that had been stripped for connection to a plug: I wanted it to be half-sheathed in red plastic. It was considered bad luck to cut it, Lily explained. The captain did not wear a uniform— just a yellowed cotton sleeveless singlet, a pair of ragged blue pants and sneakers. He laughed as he warmed to his theme, that of securing the nation.

"You are a spy? We think all *lao wai* are wanting to know too many things about China. Why you are so curious? We are not curious about you." The bridge clerk, alerted by this exchange, hurriedly wrote my name into the ship's log—an exercise book with a red flag gummed onto the cover.

The captain swept his glasses along a fairway that was now becoming quite crowded with vessels. Some of the ships passed close enough, and I could read their names on the stern. There was an ore carrier from Australia, bringing iron from Mount Newman to the steel mills at Baoshan. There were a couple of squat oil tankers, Panama-registered, lying slow and sluggish in the water, their anchor nostrils flaring just above the surface. Three Indian bulk carriers, their plates streaked with rust, new names written over the old, lumbered out to sea.

A Russian reefer registered in Vladivostok was speeding in more jauntily, probably in ballast. Perhaps, I thought, she was coming to collect a cargo of pork. A wild surmise perhaps—but one that stemmed from a strange journey I had made during a planning trip a few weeks beforehand. I had booked a flight from Canton to Turkestan and was somewhat surprised to find that I was not boarding a Chinese aircraft, but an old Ilyushin dressed in Aeroflot colors, and with an Aeroflot crew. I asked the captain why—what was a Russian plane doing flying a domestic Chinese route?

He said it was a simple barter deal: Russia had too many planes and China too few, and China had—I asked him to repeat this—too many pigs and Russia not enough. So for every round-trip plane journey between Canton and Ürümqi—the Russians providing the plane and the crew, the Chinese the fuel and the food—Moscow charged the Chinese government twenty railway boxcars of pork. Some of the animals went to Moscow by the Trans-Siberian Railway, others, the captain had said, by ship. "Down the Yangtze," I remembered him saying. "They have many pigs in that valley there."

A buzz of smaller boats wove their way dangerously among the slow-moving cargo vessels. Many were fishing boats, and to judge from the huge silver arc lights that were suspended on bamboo poles from their bridge wings, they were off to hunt for cuttlefish, at night. Astronauts have reported seeing a diamond-dust twinkle on the black ink of the sea out here: scores of cuttlefish boats out at night on the waters between China and Korea. These passing craft would have been members of that little fleet, probably utterly ignorant that they were visible (unlike the much more frequently touted Great Wall, which can't be seen) from outer space.

The river went on narrowing, steadily. On the right now was a low and treeless bulk of mud-and-misery known as Chongming Dao, the Tongue of the Yangtze—so called because on the maps it does look just like a lolling tongue, poised halfway between the open jaws of the river. It had once been a place of banishment, like Sakhalin, and the men sent there did little but build dikes to protect the island and their prison from being inundated. During the Cultural

Revolution a Shanghainese poet whose daughter I know well was sent there to prepare the land for raising pigs.* Now, thanks to the labors of men like him and his predecessors, the island is quite fertile: a million people live on Chongming Island, farming rice, raising ducks, planting cotton.

On the left—and here the total river width was now down to about ten miles—I could just see the first buildings, the first evidence of real human settlement. There were the usual constructions of a coastline: a chimney or two, a cluster of radio masts, a water tower, barracks. Then, after another mile, a tall building, maybe a block of workers' flats.

No pagodas, though. I had very much doubted that I would see a pagoda on this coast—the people who live here, on the drying mud-flats of the estuary, have long been isolated from the mainstream Chinese and from their customs. They are darker, almost Malay in their appearance, a little like the aboriginals who are to be found in central Taiwan. These never were a pagoda-building people; and any hopes I might have had for spying a graceful structure of nine slightly fluted stories, with upcurved eaves, a delicate spire and arched windows overgrown with kudzu, and from which I could imagine some Tang duke gazing out toward the ocean in the moon-light—all such hopes were quite in vain.

These people lived on mud; they paddled their *sampans* down a labyrinth of small canals, they contentedly raised ducks and rice and they fished for squid. An early guide warns Europeans that the mud-people "are not altogether free from piratical tendencies." But then came civilization, of a kind: someone came and built a factory, and slapped up some modern hulk of cement and iron. This was about all I could see—mud and gray reinforced cement. There was

---

* He was released in 1975 but was never allowed to publish his poems again and died in 1980. His daughter insists his heart was broken.

certainly precious little drama about this particular approach to China—this was indeed no Verrazano Narrows, no Pool of London. Captain Zhu saw me looking at the coast. "Soon there will be a golf club there," he spat. "A country club for rich Shanghai people." He didn't sound too pleased.

We were into a fairway now. The marker buoys came more regularly, and most of the ever increasing armada of ships seemed to be obeying rules of the road in the dredged channels—the inbound vessels were sticking to the right, the outbound to the left. A radar tower reared above the brilliant yellow of a rapeseed field, its thumbnail-shaped scanner turning languidly, noting all the ships passing underneath, missing nothing. But the river was starting to look crowded, dangerously so. I mentioned it to the captain.

"They say it's the most dangerous approach in the world," he replied, cheerfully. "I've seen some foreign masters freeze, just stop their ships, not knowing what to do. Coming in for the first time can be quite terrifying. Even with a pilot aboard. There are sandbanks that pop up out of nowhere. Whirlpools.

"The tide is terribly erratic. You can get a flood a thousand miles away and it sends a surge of water down the Yangtze and *poof,* it blows the tide back in its tracks. There are wrecks everywhere. You see a mast in the water and there's no buoy marking it and you think, My God! what if I hadn't seen it? What if there hadn't been anything poking up out of the water? What if I'd just sailed into it?"

Lily nodded. She said she had once worked for a man who had a ship-breaking business a few miles upriver. She was still interested, and had made it her business to know all about the wrecks in the Yangtze mouth. One of her boss's ships, a thirty-year-old bulk carrier that he had bought for scrap in Manila and was having towed to his breakers' yard, had capsized in the river just the week before. One of the tug captains was said to have been drunk, and had no idea where he was going.

"I know the ship! I know it!" exclaimed Zhu, warming to the

task. "It was a big one—twelve thousand tons. It hit the side of a sandbank and just turned over. Right over there." He pointed toward a patch of sludge-colored river a mile off our starboard beam. "Now—do you see a wreck buoy, one of the green ones? No—not a thing. No one's gotten round to marking it. There's nothing to tell anything's there. Only a few people know about it. But the fact is there's a great big ship lying down there, in just three fathoms of water. So easy to hit it. It'd rip the bottom from a tanker, just like a sushi knife! Very dangerous!

"And there's more! Not just the wrecks and the sand. There's all the traffic. They have wrecks in Calcutta, on the Hooghly. Lots of sand there, too. What's the big bank there—the St. James's Bank? That's a bad one, I remember. I went up the Hooghly once. They have a Bund there, don't they? Just like us. But they don't have the traffic. Who wants to go to Calcutta, after all?

"But here—what do they say officially—a thousand ships a day? That's only the ones with radios and radar reflectors. There are thousands more that have no marks at all, no lights, nothing. You try to keep out of their way, you run into a sandbank and, *bang*. Look— see if there's a red flag up on the bar there. There usually is at this time of day. That's the signal station, where they keep an eye on things. That'll tell you how bad the traffic is."

Sure enough, two miles ahead and waving lazily in the hot breeze, was an enormous flag. The *Admiralty Pilot* explains: "When the number of junks manoeuvring in the channel at Wusong Kou is such as to make navigation difficult, a red flag shall be hoisted." And as if to underscore the flag's warning, there were scores of black dots on the waters ahead, like a vast floating business of flies. Some were large ships that moved slowly across my field of view; the others, the smaller vessels, darted almost furtively back and forth on their appointed business.

They dart where once they glided. The junks on nearly all the reaches of the Lower Yangtze have motors these days, not sails. It is a rare delight to see the distinctive shape of a classic Chinese junk— the peaked lugsail with its die-straight luff and sinuous leech and

with the heavy bamboo battens jutting from the edges. But the be-
wildering variety of craft that scuttle between the riverbanks today
performs much the same functions as the sailing junks did half a
century ago—there are almost as many different designs of power
vessels as there were of the old and much loved sailing junks. Captain Zhu had a book of charts on the bridge that showed silhouettes
of the different types—and at the back of the book, on pages that
were less well-thumbed, were silhouettes of sailing junks as well.

Scores of subtly different designs were to be found on the pages,
dozens of sizes, boats bent to innumerable tasks, a nautical bestiary.
Flipping through the pages was like seeing a shadow play, the boats
the cut-paper figures from a Javan *wayang* show. There were outlines of the long, low cotton boats from Chongming, which take raw
cotton out to the markets of Shanghai, and return with what is
politely called night soil, still the principal fertilizer on the great
tonguelike mudflat. There were silhouettes of the pig boats also from
Chongming, but larger and fatter and with a bulk that was easy to
recognize. They had to be sturdy, since their business was with pigs*
taken to market, people brought back. There were pictures of ice
carriers that transport blocks frozen in the fields in midwinter—and
which are kept insulated through the warmth of early spring by
ingenious arrangements of straw and soil. There were broad-beamed
fish carriers, made stoutly of pine to weather the estuary's storms and
heavy seas and tide rips. It is said that the game of mah-jongg was
invented by the crew of a Ningbo fish-carrying junk, who believed
that by making up a game on which they had to concentrate their
minds they might forget a discomfort which they couldn't understand, which we now know as seasickness.

But you don't see too many of these special craft. More often than
not the smaller boats on this reach of the estuary would be the tiny
stern-poled (and sailless) *sampans,* so called because they are made of

---

* And excessively bulky pigs at that: Chongming Dao pig farmers were once notorious through all China for injecting their market-bound carcasses with water, to
increase the weight and the market price.

three pieces of wood, compared with the five of the *wupans*—and on the day I arrived they seemed to be everywhere. I knew that once in a while one might see one of the larger vessels—like a long-distance coastal trading junk, or one of the special light-wood junks built so they can ride up and over the deadly bore that sweeps down into the funnel of Hangzhou Bay, on the far side of the Yangtze herself. But on this morning I saw neither of these bigger craft. Still, with all the activity that I could see from where I stood on deck, it was small wonder that the red warning flag was flying. Small wonder, too, that inspection cruisers like this one patrol the river ceaselessly, helping, watching, guarding.

On the left side—technically the right bank of the river, reckoned from the point of view of the water flowing downstream—there was a sudden burst of industry. Cooling towers exhaled tall florets of white cloud, cranes swung containers up from the decks of waiting ships, black rubbery umbilical cords sucked oil from waiting tankers, there was what appeared to be a mine building with two winding wheels rotating at speed, an array of great chimneys with strobe lights and with typhoon gantries bolted up their sides, to keep them standing in the storm winds of midsummer. In the distance, ranks of skyscrapers marched across the horizon. I could see the glint of the sun on hundreds of windshields as trucks and cars waited for a steam train to chuff by and let their drivers pass. The land was well established: the city was now beginning.

And Wusong Kou, where the flag was flying, was where it all really starts. True, the Gateway is the technical beginning or the technical end of the river; but Wusong Kou is the place that anyone with any sense of the romantic, anyone with any sense of history, regards as the terminus of the river proper. The Chinese know it by this name: the world's mariners, however, know it by a slight variation, by a name that is as familiar to their rollicking community as is Blood Alley or the Liver Building or Dundalk Docks.

This place, with its scarlet warning flag and its lighthouse and the twenty-foot dial of what looks like a clock, but is in fact the Whangpoo River Tide Gauge, is the spot where all vessels bound for

Shanghai—which means most of the ships found in the estuary—turn left. It is, depending on your perspective, the beginning of the Yangtze proper, or the true end of a trick across a long, long sea. This spot on the river, formally marked by just a single red canister buoy, is known as the Woosung Bar.

A century ago Tennyson planted an image that has lasted longest: the bar as a place of danger and melancholy, where sailors wave their farewells, where the pilots wait to steer a mariner home. Crossing the Bar is an event: leaving, you pass from still waters into swells; returning, you take one last risk, since at the bar the sea has one last chance to toy with you, and toss you over in the foam. But if you do make it past—and on a gale-swept day the waves and spindrift on a river bar can make for a terrifying sight, and perilous navigation—then you are home, safe and sound.

The Woosung Bar is more benign, however, than anything Tennyson had in mind. It marks the spot where one river, the Whangpoo, meets the Yangtze.* The meeting is as calm as the meeting of most rivers: there is no line of breakers, no cloud of spume. It is not a dangerous place—but it is, and long has been, a wretched nuisance. It once caused great friction between East and West. It exercised the minds and pens of diplomats for scores of years. And all because a great tongue of Whangpoo mud and sand oozes endlessly out onto the bed of the Yangtze and, because the Yangtze waters are pushed and pulled back and forth by tide and flood, the

---

* Given that bars are created whenever one moving body of water meets another—when a river meets the ocean, or a lake, or when a river meets another river—it should be added that there is technically a second Yangtze bar, at the place where the river meets the sea, and which Victorian hydrographers named the Fairy Flats. It is two miles wide, and at one time it limited river traffic to ships drawing less than eighteen feet. On a stormy day it can be a furious place—Tennyson would have loved it. But nowadays it no longer really exists—not as a hazard to navigation. In 1935 the Whangpoo Conservancy Board embarked on a scheme to dredge five million tons of mud away from it each year: a channel through Fairy Flats, twenty-seven feet deep at least, is now permanently guaranteed.

mud stays more or less where it is, thickening all the time. The estuary is generally about fifty feet deep: at the Woosung Bar it shallows in places to no more than about twelve. The shallowing was a nineteenth-century cause célèbre.

The problem was never noticed by the Chinese of a century ago: they glided serenely up and down the rivers on sailing junks that drew ten feet, or even five. But when the foreign traders began to arrive, in iron ships that customarily drew twenty feet or more, they were in for some unpleasant surprises. Perhaps their leadsmen may have warned them in time: often they did not. A river that until the 1850s had been alive with moving traffic was, twenty years later, suddenly replete with barbarian vessels stopped dead in the water and hopelessly stuck.

Some had been stranded on their way in. Others, seemingly luckier, managed to get in, but then went to load themselves at the wharves with tons of rhubarb and tea and bolts of silk and sacks of rice—and then found they were drawing too much, that the bar would not let them get out. The local Lloyd's agent duly sent the cables home to London, warning of delay and demurrage. "The *Travancore* sailed out with the mails but was unable to cross the bar, and spent a whole day unloading her cargo into lighters to lessen her load. . . ." "I beg to report that the *Australia* was detained for five days at Woosung. . . ." "The French mail-steamer *Provence* was unable to reach Shanghae at all. . . ." It made a nonsense of the river as a trading route. The great artery of China, as barkers had already long been advertising the Yangtze, suddenly had a bad case of sclerosis.

By the mid-1870s merchants, weary of having their ships pinned by sand, began to lose their tempers. They wrote angry letters: the State of the Woosung Bar, which sounds today like a Gilbert and Sullivan ditty, became a heated talking point in the coffeehouses of Cheapside and the bars on the Fulton Street waterfront.

An august-sounding body known as the Association for the Protection of Commercial Interests as Respects Wrecked and Damaged Property wrote to Lord Granville at the Foreign Office: the Bar, they

said, is "an impediment to shipping . . . a cause for great anxiety."
It could be cleared, the technical people had advised the Association,
without more than ordinary difficulty, and with no extravagant ex-
pense. Indeed it could, agreed Vice-Admiral Charles Shadwell, writing from his cabin on HMS *Iron Duke* in Hong Kong harbor.
Chinese coolies could move the mud by hand, he said; their labor
was very cheap. There was, in short, no practical reason why the Bar
could not be cleared, and navigation allowed to move freely. It
merely needed one thing: for "the superior authorities at Peking" to
give their permission.

But there, it turned out, was the rub. Peking, as it was called in
the documents of the day, didn't seem to give a fig about the Bar.
Haughty, aloof, unaware of all matters considered beneath their dignity, the Manchus in the Forbidden City paid no official attention to
the wails of the red-haired, long-nosed *Uitlanders*. Privately they
must have been delighted. What buffoons these foreigners were, indeed! Nothing much had changed, it seemed, since 1793, when Lord
Macartney had tried in vain to cajole and flatter the Emperor of the
day, and had been sent away with a flea in his ear. The diplomat had
offered to the Celestial Throne the very best goods that Britain had
ever made in an effort to win permission to do business, and to be
recognized. But the Emperor was not remotely interested. The gifts
were regarded as items of tribute from a respectful liege. Some boxes
were never even opened. Macartney was asked to go home.

And the Emperor of eight decades later was similarly unbothered
by the travails and demands of the foreign merchants. The dignity of
the Long River, the Throne implied by its silence, was not to be
sullied by such vulgarities as dredging, just because the barbarians
wanted it so. Despite torrents of letters that passed between ambassadors and ministers and high dignitaries of the Manchu Court, nothing was done. "You should do all that you properly can to induce the
Chinese government," wrote Lord Granville to his man on the spot,
"to take steps for improving the condition on the bar." "I have sent
three identic letter to the Prince," wrote the Earl of Derby. But it did
no good. Prince Kung, the mandarin who was in charge of the

Tsungli Yamen—the Office of the General Administration of the Affairs of Different Countries—did not even deign to reply.

It was not until the eve of the Revolution that was to end the rule of the emperors and princes that this impasse was ended. It was 1905: the Manchus were on their last legs and knew it, and in part because of weakness, in part as a placatory gesture that might work for their survival, they gave permission to the foreigners to begin their work. A Dutchman named de Rijke, an expert on the polders back home, was the first to bring in the dredging engines. By 1910 he had completed the first channel through the Bar. When the first Chinese president, the foreign-educated Sun Yat-sen, came home to China in 1912 he entered via the Yangtze—and he sailed symbolically to Shanghai through the foreign-engineered channel. In 1937—just in time for the Japanese war, as it happened—the entire length of the Whangpoo was finally dredged, so that ships drawing twenty-eight feet could pass all the way from the Pacific Ocean, along the estuary of the Yangtze, up into the Whangpoo and right up to the wharves on the Bund.

The perils of the sands lessened, then vanished altogether. Shanghai duly took her place as one of the world's great trading cities, and the Yangtze made good on her promise to become a huge highway into the very heart of China. Yet had the Manchus remained in control in Beijing, it might never have been so. As a symbol of Chinese Imperial intransigence clashing head-on with western mercantile realism—or, viewed another way, as a symbol of ancient and home-grown pride clashing with an alien culture of greed—the sixty-year saga of the State of the Woosung Bar has few equals.

Yet the foreigners were not motivated merely by avarice. To those who knew its geography and its importance, the Yangtze was the principal gateway into the mysterious heart of the Middle Kingdom, the choicest place for the West's wholesale penetration of China. If major surgery was required to bring China to heel, then Woosung was the place where the anesthesiologist should first sink his needle. When Sir George Balfour of the Madras Artillery arrived in 1843 to take up the post of Britain's first consul to Shanghai, then nothing but a muddy, steamy village, he recognized and declared at once its strategic importance: "There our navy can float, and by our ships, our power can be seen and, if necessary, promptly felt. Our policy is the thorough command of this great river."

A command that it would only be possible fully to exercise if the Woosung Bar was gone. It took almost a century to remove it. And then a little more than a decade later the British and all other foreign navies were banished from the river, for all time. Seen in this context, as a device for keeping the foreigners at bay, the Chinese intransigence over the matter has a shrewdness all of its own.

I watched the echo sounder as we passed over the Bar's submerged relics. It barely registered a change—the channel dug by the Dutchmen almost a century ago was nearly as deep as the river fairway. What had exercised so many minds for so many years was now quite invisible, utterly lacking in significance. And the red canister buoy that bobbed off our port beam—that, too, had an insignificance about it that belied its symbolism. For the buoy was Mile Zero for mariners sailing beyond, and into the Yangtze proper. The Zhong Sha light, now twenty miles behind us, was where the sea ended and the estuary began; the red Woosung buoy was where the estuary ended, and the Long River got under way. Captain Zhu sounded his siren and turned his little ship smartly to port. We passed out of the slight chop of the Yangtze proper and, once inside the curving breakwater, into the black and doubtless poisonously anoxic waters of the Whangpoo.

A squadron of Chinese ships—destroyers, frigates and corvettes—was moored on the left bank. They looked, I thought, decidedly unprepared either for the protection of China's maritime frontier or for war. Laundry was dangling from the stern of each craft, straw hats were perched on some of the after guns and the sailors were mooching about idly, smoking in the warming sun. Had these been British or American vessels the men would have been busily chipping paint, greasing bearings, polishing brass or holystoning the decks: here they looked as though they were on holiday, or else dying from boredom.

But it was a timely encounter, as it happened, and I gazed with interest at the ships through my binoculars. The headlines that I had seen in the Hong Kong papers just a few days before had all been about the Chinese Navy, and what a new and belligerent mood its admirals seemed to have adopted. There had been a lot of concern about China's high-handed attitude, so called, toward a group of low atolls called the Spratly Islands that lay close to the Vietnamese coast, and toward another group known as the Paracels, which lay even nearer.

For years the sovereignty of these islands, and of a low reef called the Macclesfield Bank, had been at the center of a smoldering dispute. Vietnam had laid an ancient claim, as had (complicating matters hugely) the Philippines, Malaysia and Taiwan. In the case of the Spratly Islands, the tiny state of Brunei—hardly the world's most imperially minded state, even though its ruler was said to be the planet's richest man—had advanced a claim as well. But Beijing had airily ignored them all. Successive governments had stated flatly that the islands were historically and by geographical logic Chinese, and any official maps you buy of China inside China show a curved dotted line extending from Shanghai south and returning north to a point near Hainan, and encompassing every atoll and reef and skerry in the South China Sea. All, says China, are Chinese.

In recent years Beijing has stated these claims rather more robustly, and shortly before my arrival at Woosung the Chinese Navy had installed a detachment of the Chinese Army, who would build a small base on one of the rocks. Now, as I arrived in Shanghai, the Chinese government was publicly defying anyone to try to move it. This had led neighbor nations to complain about Chinese "hegemony"—a popular word in the East, and hitherto much used by countries like Nepal and Sikkim in connection with India. Now it was China's turn, and everyone was becoming exercised about what they saw as a revival of the country's ancient imperialistic ambitions and suchlike. The role of the Chinese Navy in the mechanics of it all had suddenly become a hot topic.

To underline the alarmist talk there had been suggestions in the Hong Kong papers and magazines that this newly boisterous navy might be about to order an aircraft carrier, no less, and moor it down on Hainan Island, close to the disputed islands.* Such a mighty ship, it was said, would give China what naval people call "blue-water capability"—the wherewithal to project her power across thousands of miles of ocean. Many of China's neighbors, as well as strategically minded analysts in Washington, were starting to fret publicly about her doing such a thing.

So it was in the context of all such superheated disputations that I found myself gazing at this clutch of some of China's most modern warships. Everything seemed sleepy and halfhearted about them. As we cruised slowly alongside it looked pretty unlikely that these sailors at least were getting into the business of flexing their maritime muscles, or that they or their officers entertained the kind of ambitions that were causing such alarm elsewhere. There didn't seem much eagerness about them, lazing as they were in the late-morning sun. It reminded me that the Chinese had invented gunpowder for use in fireworks, and yet had never thought of using it for war. It looked much the same for these half dozen ships—they had been constructed just for the show, and not to menace, perhaps not even to fight.

We steered in to land now. Soon a gang of greasy-looking Chinese men on the quay were securing our hawsers to the bollards. Four men in uniform were waiting, and they waved up at me, indicating their relief at seeing, at last, the foreigner for whom they had been asked to wait. I said good-bye to the captain. "They've come to take you away," he said, and didn't laugh. And then I walked down the metal gangplank, stepping over a pile of rotting fish. Lily came with me. "Nothing to worry about. Just routine."

One of the men was Immigration—he took my passport and neatly impressed a bright red chop on it, giving me sanction to stay six months. Another was Health, and he made me affirm that I had no illnesses worth mentioning. His form had a line saying "Describe the country you last visited," and when I came to China in the early days I would write juvenile things like "hilly, green, rainy," or "fine

---

* They already had the deck of an old Australian carrier, stripped off the hull and bolted onto an aerodrome runway near Beijing, where it was used for practice.

beaches, strong women." But as he was looking on this time I simply wrote "United States," and handed it over.

Customs proffered the usual form asking me how many bicycles and sewing machines I had, and the brand name of my camera. But then he took the form, crumpled it up in his hand and, with a sweeping gesture, tossed it into the water. "No need these days," he announced. "Waste of time."

The fourth man turned out to be the official with whom Lily had arranged the venture—a Mr. Zhang Zu Long. I thanked him profusely. "They didn't want you to do this, the people in Shanghai," he said. "But they are very conservative. I told them they must indulge in up-to-date thinking. Anyone who is interested in my station is welcome." He indicated a ten-story building behind the fish market, a structure festooned with radar scanners and satellite dishes and radio aerials. "I am very proud of it. You must come and see."

His card offered an impossibly long description: he was Master of the Woosung Supervision Station of the Shanghai Harbor Superintendency Administration of the People's Republic of China, Shanghai Bureau of Maritime Safety of the Superintendency of the Ministry of Communications. He gave me tea, showed me the Chinese charts of the Yangtze—stamped "Secret" on every page—and then took me upstairs, to a darkened room at the top of the building. There was a double door, an air lock. Inside three men peered intently at a bank of color computer screens and whispered occasionally into microphones.

"These are the air-traffic controllers of the sea," said Mr. Zhang, with a chortle. "They run the most up-to-date harbor control system in the world. It makes me very proud."

The Germans supplied the computers, the Chinese made everything else themselves. Every one of the ships coming along the Lower Yangtze that day, and every single vessel turning into or out of the Whangpoo, was tracked on radar. Computers assessed all the tracks, the speeds and the directions, and calculated who might collide with whom, and what changes needed to be made to ensure they didn't. It was the operators' job to tell the skippers what the computers wanted. All of the operators were Chinese. One spoke English, another Greek, the third Russian, and they used these languages, and more often Chinese, to talk to the watch officers on the ships that passed below. Mr. Chen, a man of about twenty-five who spoke impeccable English, was talking to an Indian bulk carrier, just now mooring at Baoshan. "Bringing coal up from Calcutta," he said. "Then coming to Shanghai to take—what is it?—wolfram and antimony ore, back to India. Typical. I have to watch him in and out. Make sure he doesn't hit anything.

"The computers make it very easy. It really is like air-traffic control. Twelve hours on, twelve hours off. Very intense. But fine job, don't you agree?

"This is bringing Shanghai into the next century, I think. Soon—not very long, I am sure—it will be the finest port in the world. It will pass Hong Kong, Singapore. This system is going to help. We will win! That I guarantee."

Mr. Zhang patted him on the shoulder, and ushered me out from the dark, and down the stairs. Soon I was stepping gingerly over the rotten fishheads on the dockside once again, this time making my way to what I hoped might be the Woosung railway station. I needed to get to Shanghai, and for purely historical reasons the train seemed the best bet.

For this was the third reason for Woosung's fame. This might now be the site of China's first computerized port; but a century and a quarter before, doubtless confirming Mr. Zhang's view that his city had long been in the vanguard of China's modernization, Woosung was the site of the country's first, and as it happens very short-lived, steam railway.

It was Jardine, Matheson & Co. who built it. This hardly surprising: the firm whose mercantile empire still remains a potent force in the Far East was instrumental—via such devices as railway making and shipbuilding—in opening up China to foreign commerce. (Its contacts back in London were such as to influence governments: it is still said today, and not entirely unfairly, that the British Foreign Secretary, Lord Palmerston, suggested the prosecution of the First Opium War—with the cession of Hong Kong the most notable corollary to Britain's military success—mainly to keep the Jardines opium trade in business.) But the construction of this first modest permanent way over the twelve modest miles that separated Woosung from Shanghai proved a difficult and, eventually, unhappy experience for the firm: it showed how deeply suspicious China was then of anything—no matter how obviously beneficial—that was fashioned by barbarian hands.

Since the 1850s Jardines and other foreign firms doing business in China had suggested building railways. It was part of the mood of the moment: Britain had started its own first commercial train service back in 1825, and railways now crisscrossed the island from Cornwall to Cromarty. In America, too, tracks were being laid as fast as the Pennsylvania steel mills could forge them. And yet by 1869, the year when thousands of laborers—Chinese laborers, no less—brought the Central Pacific metals to Utah and spiked them together with the rails from the Union Pacific in Omaha, and so knitted the country into one—by that same year not one single mile of railway had been laid in China. India was at the same time tottering under the weight of iron and brass; but China was still a nation of post roads and canals and bucolic inefficiency.

Jardines, in a hurry to make money, thought all of this a nonsense. China was, in their view, woefully out of step with the rest of the world. In letter after letter the firm kept beseeching the Manchus to make way for the modern. But the Court maintained an unyielding hauteur, turning down request after request, just as they had done to the merchants who wanted progress made on the Woosung Bar. Besides, the Chinese said in one letter, which I once saw in the Jardines archive, "railways would only be beneficial to China if undertaken by the Chinese themselves, and constructed under their own management."

There was only one thing for it, so the westerners thought. Displaying the combination of mercantile acumen and bare-faced cheek that (perhaps in part because it is so *Chinese*) continues to infuriate Beijing today, the firm decided to go ahead anyway, and in secret.* There was some hesitation—the first steps were taken in 1865, abandoned two years later and then revived in 1872. But finally the company had taken into their confidence the Shanghai city *taotai*—the official, appointed by the mandarinate, who was essentially the local mayor. The scheme, the foreigners thought, was bound to succeed.

The subterfuge had many elements and strategies. The company first had its Shanghai land agent buy up sections of real estate north of Shanghai, saying they were planning to build nothing more threatening than a horse road. At the same time they set up a London-based company, the Woosung Road Co. Ltd., and purchased a number of tiny steam railway engines made by a British firm called Ransomes and Rapier. The firm then quietly and surreptitiously laid a few miles of track, trusting that the *taotai*—who by now had been so taken into confidence that he had been persuaded to buy some W.R.Co. shares—would not step in to prevent it.

The rails, once unveiled, were just thirty inches apart—a little more than half the width of the railways that were then being built all across Britain and America. The trains made by Ransomes were small as well—they looked like models, the kind of engines that were found in amusement parks. The carriages, too, were child-sized, and open to the elements. The whole idea was to construct a railway that was on the one hand relatively inexpensive and on the other, and rather more important, would not terrify the Chinese public—to whom the idea of a foreign-made fire-breathing iron monster rushing about on iron tracks would be unsettling, to say the least. Nor could Jardines be accused of ostentation: nothing the com-

---

* Much the same atmosphere of suspicion and secrecy surrounded the construction of the first telegraph cable, which also came into China via Woosung. A Danish company built it, but was told that the infernal cable could not touch any part of the Celestial Empire, but had to be landed on a hulk, moored out in the river. The Danes ignored this and paid the cable secretly out along the Whangpoo, bringing it ashore at night, in a hut. It was some while before the Court found out, by which time the telegraph's value had been indisputably proven.

pany was doing on the Woosung road would or could be allowed in any way to challenge the supremacy of grandeur that was embodied in the Emperor or his appointed representatives.

The railway service duly opened with only reserved fanfare on June 30, 1876. The trains—pulled by a Ransomes engine appropriately called the Pioneer—were known locally as "devil's carriages," and for many weeks no one would ride in them. Slowly, though, their convenience and economy caught on—187,000 people were counted as having ridden during the first year of operation.

The business would have continued to flourish, no doubt, had not disaster struck: in October 1877 a Chinese man was hit by a train and killed—whether it was suicide, murder, contrived misfortune or just a simple accident was never made clear. Jardines promptly compensated the family; but the Qing court in faraway Beijing then heard about the line (their *taotai* having carelessly omitted to inform them), complained that it had been built without permission and demanded that it be taken over by the government. Besides, the officials said, the railway was clearly a dangerous invention: the public, now back to being frightened by this evil monster, was in mortal fear.

And so a few months later, with a silk merchant acting as intermediary between the court and the barbarian merchants, the line was sold for a quarter of a million Shanghai taels. A court-appointed company took over the running of the little line for a day or so, and then, presumably as planned, the Qing officials shut the operation down, ordered the lines torn up within a few days and then shipped everything—rails, carriages, signals and the little toy trains—across the sea to Formosa.

Their people, they said, felt that fiery iron dragons—no matter how modestly sized—disturbed the essential harmony of the Empire. A temple to the Queen of Heaven was to be built on the site of the terminus—a proper propitiation, it was felt, to a deity whose tranquillity had been insulted by the foreigners. It was to be twenty more years before Woosung and Shanghai were connected by rail again— by which time China was on the verge of building (and not by its own devices, but with the help of the British, Americans, Russians,

Germans and French) one of the biggest railway systems in the world. The mood by then had changed, profoundly. Fiery iron monsters now rumble across every province of the People's Republic—except for Tibet—and, far from disturbing celestial harmony, they are as essential to the well-being of the nation as rice and air. But that was not how matters were viewed in the China of the 1870s: back then in Woosung railways were foreign, they were unsettling and for the while at least they were not to be.

Nor, as it happened, was a railway for me in Woosung a century and a quarter later. Try as I might to find my way through the back streets by the docks, and try as I might to get to the station where it had all begun, I managed to get myself utterly and hopelessly lost. It had been a long day—up before dawn, transferring from ship to ship, rocking and lumbering up the estuary—and so when a red Toyota taxi stopped and the driver asked if I wanted a ride, and when I considered the trials of finding the station and then dealing with the complexities of buying a ticket, I uttered my cowardly agreement.

I loaded my rucksack into the back of the car, Lily and I wedged ourselves behind a formidable wall of Perspex security shield, which even Shanghainese taxis claim they need these days, and, with the radio blaring a noisy Foochow pop song, we headed past the Baoshan steel mills—and into the city. I told the driver to take us to a gateway beside the old Russian Consulate on Whangpoo Road. There was a ship docked behind it, I knew, in a cabin aboard which I had an invitation to sleep.

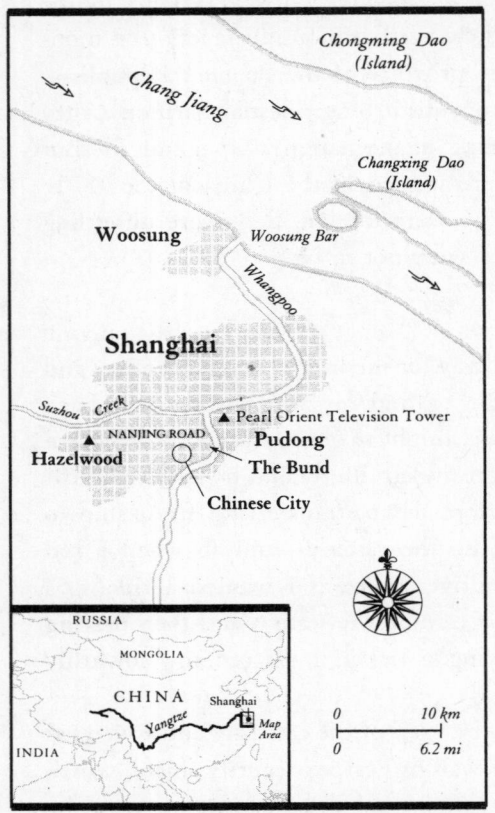

3

The City
Without
a Past

The tiny patch of brilliant green—it looked tinier, somewhat
shrunken from when I had seen it last, five years before—lay half
hidden behind a grove of London plane trees. There were shrub-
beries, a croquet lawn, the tattered leavings of a tennis net, a rusty
roller with a dried-out wooden handle. The sharp scent of boxwood,
of damp moss, of old pinecones. At the center of the gardens a squat
country house with a copper roof, dormer windows and ten Doric
columns on the second floor. In places—the shadow of an old brass
plate, the outline of iron letters on a garden gate—relics of what they
called the place half a century ago: Hazelwood.

I had always liked the house. As a creation of the mid-thirties, it reeked of solid Home Counties suburbia, Betjeman country, although its creator insisted it was art deco and had it done up in canary yellow. It had been built as the residence of the *taipan* of Swires—or Butterfield & Swire, as it was known more precisely—the great British business house that along with its rival Jardine, Matheson & Co. once dominated trading in and around China. Swires ran China Navigation (C.N.Co.) one of the greatest shipping lines that worked the Yangtze. The grand men who were chosen to manage the firm for four- or five-year stints in Shanghai were immensely well looked after, treated like diplomats, or like the suzerains that in this peculiar hothouse of a city they invariably turned out to be. This house was part of the package.

I liked the house in part because what it represented—mercantile confidence, colonial swagger, a certain rigorous high-mindedness—and in part because of who designed the building: Clough Williams-Ellis, one of Britain's more eccentric architects, and a man I had known a little. In the remote corner of north Wales where he lived, he cut a striking figure, not least by wearing plus fours with canary yellow socks and a cravat. His wife was a Strachey—his own bohemian air may have been half derived from his association with Bloomsbury—and he helped edit her anthologies of science fiction.

Architecture was his love, and eternal warfare against those he called "the Philistines" his self-appointed mission. With a view to creating beauty wherever he might, he designed buildings in almost every corner of the world. The quarry workers' tenement he inherited was turned into a house of fantasy and delight. He created an entire village near his home—and so fantastic did it turn out that it was later to become world-famous as the set for a cult television show.* He designed a baroque chapel in Hertfordshire and a Tudor castle on the Wye. He rebuilt the center of one of Ireland's prettiest towns. He designed Lloyd George's tomb. And he designed—though he never visited—two properties for Swires in China: the *taipan*'s house in the port city of Tientsin and this house in Shanghai, Hazel-

---

* *The Prisoner,* with Patrick McGoohan.

wood. What he would have thought of the old place now, sitting in the midst of so much modern philistinism—for modern Shanghai is nothing if not a philistine metropolis—is not hard to imagine.

Whenever I found myself in these parts I would always come and pay homage to the house and through it, to old Clough: I thought of the place rather as a friend, a place I could hold on to, or as somewhere that, in this most crowded and jostling of cities, I could get my bearings.

Once it was a home, comfortable, well set, with four tennis courts and a raked gravel drive. It was much the same kind of house as you might have visited for a Saturday lunchtime gin in genteel suburbs like Camberley or Virginia Water, or perhaps White Plains or Grosse Point—except that this was Shanghai, the most iniquitous town in the world, a cruel, mercenary city of white-hot passions and ice-cold hearts.

Not that those who lived at Hazelwood seemed party to any obvious iniquity, nor any cruelty or passion. You could remember what they looked like: the Swires men invariably tall, with square jaws, neat moustaches, kitted out in yellow cardigans and cavalry twill; the women matronly, competent, handsome, with the deep voices of the hockey field. (The first resident was the redoubtably square-jawed N. S. Brown, known to his staff, less than kindly, as Night Soil Brown.)

You could remember the innocent sounds, as well: the crunch of gravel as tires pulled in under the porte cochere, a sudden burst of laughter from the grass court, the patient clicking of the pruning shears by the matron with the trug of roses, the music drifting lazily from a wireless in the drawing room. The Chinese *amah* calling to the children to come inside for tea.

But these days what once was Hazelwood is just a small hotel, the Xinguo Bingguan, the Prosperous Kingdom Guest House. It was confiscated from Swires in the 1950s, like almost all the assets and property of the city's foreigners. Nowadays there is a glossy brochure: "Inside the Xing Guo Hotel the scenery is beautiful and peaceful. Big trees with exuberant foliage are alive with melodious birds. Fragrant wafts of flowers in full blossom breeze about. Several villas in European style are enrapped by the greenery. . . ."

What was once the main bedroom of the house, the one where the *taipan* slept and which had the french windows leading onto the terrace, and a view over the south lawn, has now been made into what they call a suite. The proprietors—the local government, a city ward in fact—will take sixty-five American dollars for each night you stay there, and they will charge it to your credit card. You are assured of privacy, just as the lairds of Hazelwood once were: the house is quite invisible behind the high brick walls that insulate it from the people and the traffic on Avenue Haig and Avenue Joffre and Rue Cardinal Mercier, and Bubbling Well Road, as the streets around were then known.

It was indeed made to be quite hidden from all of the city, amid which it nestled, secretly. It had been designed as a private house for one of Shanghai's most powerful foreign figures, a man who wanted a place tucked away from the bustle and the sin, a place where you could forget the existence of the city's 668 brothels and the calls for drinks at the longest bar in the world and the assorted terrors of Blood Alley—and for all the time he lived there, and for decades afterward, Hazelwood was private indeed.

But things have lately changed in Shanghai, and Hazelwood's splendid seclusion has gone. The privet hedges and the plane trees may still be there. But now, from another angle, an entirely new one, the house has recently become eminently and rather dramatically visible. A great new building has just gone up, one that dominates the city skyline and provides a place from which to gaze down on this and on all the old jumble of structures from Shanghai's extraordinary past.

It is impossible to miss: I saw it the very instant that I drew back the curtains of my cabin, and I almost jumped with surprise. The boat on which I was staying was moored at the northern end of the city reach, just downstream of the old Russian Consulate, at the place where the Whangpoo makes the final turn of the S-bend that once dictated where Shanghai was first built. My cabin faced south, and so the view was impeccable—directly down the river. The huge walls of old Imperial Shanghai ran down the Bund to the right. The suspension wires of the new Yangpu bridge—the second of two—glinted ahead in the distance. But on the left, bathed in white searchlight glare and winking with dozens of anticollision lights, rose the extraordinary, unexpected, bright-red-tinted and breathtakingly ugly Oriental Pearl Television Tower, the tallest and, for the time being, unarguably the most vulgar structure in the East.

The Oriental Pearl Tower is a mongrel of a thing, a high-technology fantasy by an architect who was commissioned merely to build something that was defiantly and symbolically Twenty-first Century. It stands, perhaps with deliberately revisionist cheek, on top of the very spot where Jardines once had their main Pudong wharves and warehouses. It is 1535 feet high, all legs and bulbs and pods and needles; it looks like an insect. It is not unimpressive: those who see it for the first time gasp, for it quite dwarfs every other building in Shanghai by both its scale and its bellowing chutzpah.

At night it looks as though it is about to take off. ("I wish it would," muttered Lily, who at first thought it a very disagreeable addition to the city's skyline.) By day it stands suspended above the hurrying crowds, looking dark and vaguely menacing, half lighthouse, half gibbet. It is of course suggestive of tomorrow, but at the same time it somehow seems to be a warning of tomorrow. Some people who see it shudder: it is so huge, it went up so quickly* and on close inspection it is so badly made. And indeed, by being so gigantic, so hurriedly done and so shoddily put together it does manage to symbolize—in more ways than its makers know—the realities of the fast-growing new city that sprawls around and beneath it. But that is not why I found it so menacing a structure: I think it was the fact that it

* When funds ran low the city government created a private company to run the tower, and floated shares on the Shanghai Stock Exchange. Hotel rooms inside the larger pearls will produce, the owners trust, enough of a profit to keep the investors—the Shanghai public—at least happy enough not to want to storm the structure and tear it down.

combined its sheer ugliness with its utter domination of the view. How, I kept wondering to myself, could city fathers with any sense of civic pride have permitted such a thing?

A deliriously proud citizen named Mr. Su took me to the top of the monster. According to his thickly laminated business card, he was its Vice General Manager, and I gathered from his ceaseless chatter that his task was for him a labor of love—he adored both his building and all of new Shanghai. As we stepped from the elevator, he spread wide his arms and began to point out grand and new and ever more glittering structures that were rising around the city on every side, down amid a forest of construction cranes. For a while I happily ignored him: I was content to peer down through the gray-blue haze of factory smoke and car exhausts until I found the tiny landmark patch of green that was Hazelwood, far away to the west. I spent some while gazing fondly down and across at it, getting my bearings in a way I had never imagined possible. It was infinitely more pleasurable to do this, to shut out Mr. Su's unending drumbeat of statistics and notable achievements and, in a poignant sort of way, to savor the connection and reflect on the dissonance between Clough's old house down there and this new colossus on top of which we were standing.

But eventually Mr. Su became less easy to ignore. He moved away from the windows, invited me into another elevator, took us up a few floors, then down a few more, along a corridor and onto an escalator until I was quite comprehensively disorientated. He had by now stopped talking of the changes that were being wrought down in the city, bubbling away instead with explanations of the specific architectural details of his own building. He did so at a great clip, shouting all the while, like a circus barker.

"The symbol of this city is—what? The pearl. Pearl of the Orient, yes? Well, look at this: how many pearls you see?"

We seemed to be standing now near one of the tower's three elephantine legs, and I saw he was waving pictures before me, jabbing at each of them with his finger.

"Look at Seattle. Only one pearl at the top. Look at Moscow.

Look at Toronto—bigger than us, yes—but how many pearls? One, just one.

"Now look up, look at ours."

And I looked, and halfway up the closest leg was a thirty-foot sphere of red glass, like a thrombosis.

"Er—a pearl?" I ventured, hesitantly.

"Yes—exactly." He looked amazed at my insight. "And look—there's another, and another."

One pearl, so-called, on each of the three legs. One immense sphere—another pearl, I should say—where the three legs joined. Then five more smaller globule-pearls, each sixty feet in diameter, up along the main shaft. Another truly massive one at the top of this shaft, then a smaller one farther up on a subsidiary and narrower shaft, after which was the spire and on top of this the television antennae.

"Eleven pearls. Eleven! How's that for a symbol? We wanted to be different, and we wanted to make a statement about who we are. So we truly are the Pearl of the Orient now, don't you think?"

Lily was stifling her laughter at all of this—though I rather sensed she was changing her mind about the tower now that we had taken this tour; she had nudged me at one point and said that the building was making her feel "quite proud"—but there was no stopping Mr. Su. "Come into the elevator. We go to the topmost pearl. The most private room in Shanghai. Here you will get away from everything. You want to hold a secret meeting, you hold it here, in full view of everyone—but no one can get here. You understand?"

Men in red uniforms stood as elevator doors opened and shut, girls in red uniforms took their positions on red carpets inside the lifts, red light filtered in through the red glass. ("Canadian, imported specially. Far too expensive. The old buildings here only ever had blue glass, or clear glass, so we are much better, yes?") There was a fiery anger to the inside of the tower, a furnace feeling that was not much relieved when finally we arrived inside the sphere—the pearl—at the top of Shanghai. The place was still plastery with makings, workers scurrying around hammering and drilling and tightening things, and there was sawdust on the red carpet. The light that filtered in was tinted rose.

"One thousand three hundred of your feet up in the air," announced Mr. Su happily. "Still not quite the top, but this is as far as guests can go. Here we will have conferences, honeymoons. Who knows?" He giggled amiably. "Very private."

As private as Hazelwood once had been, I thought. There it stood, five miles away across the hazy plain of mud over which the early Shanghai had been settled. Five miles separated us, and sixty or seventy years—which was just about all the real history that Shanghai ever had.

Technically the city actually is quite old: there are suggestions that a fishing village existed on the site in 200 B.C., and it was given its present name—which means simply "above the sea"—in A.D. 900. But it never amounted to much, and compared with its neighbor cities—places like the then-called Soochow and Hangchow and Ningpo—it was generally ignored. It had a modest wall, three miles around, built more to protect the inhabitants from Japanese pirates than to give itself airs. The wall was unusual in that it was round—most Chinese walled cities are square—and its outline, surrounding what was once called the Chinese City, or the Native City, is still plainly visible on maps.

At ground level, the wall is less easy to spot: the curving road can just be made out, and beyond it the streets are narrower and grubbier. The laundry hung out to dry from one house touches the clothes poles suspended from the house opposite. There are rats everywhere, despite posters advertising incentives—cash, rice, cheap radios—for carcasses handed in to the local street committee chairman. Tiny stalls sell joss sticks and spices and plastic shoes, and there are more open-air restaurants—a dignified term to describe a scurvy-looking man presiding over a wok filled with dark and ominously bubbling and hissing fat—than elsewhere in the city. Generally, though, the relict part of Shanghai's old quarter is dull and charmless, with an unhealthy feeling, and when I suggested to Lily that we might linger there and perhaps take dinner, she made a face and refused point-blank.

The city's real history—the history that has made her so notorious a place—began at the end of the eighteenth century: this was when the East India Company, spurred on by the reports of missionaries who had seen it, began to take an earnest mercantile interest. What the company officers in Calcutta liked about Shanghai—what was then, as now, the city's crucial advantage—was her prime location.

Shanghai was no isolated trading port like Canton or Macau, merely suspended on the underbelly of China, cut off from the vastness of the Empire by ranges of hills and linked to it only by moody and irritatingly short rivers. Shanghai, rather, was at the downstream end of the Yangtze, a river that, though then quite unexplored by foreigners, clearly penetrated deep into the heartland of the nation.

The distinction is an important one, and it has implications today for the future of, among other places, Hong Kong. All of the southern entrepôts, of which Hong Kong is the best-known, are in truth little more than gateways to the south of China. Circumstance has forced them to become gateways to all of China. But a glance at any map will show they are not really gateways to China at all—they are simply gateways to south China. For eighteenth- and nineteenth-century merchants eager to win permission to trade with the vast Chinese Empire, any gateway was good enough—even entryways as limited in access as the southern port cities.

Shanghai, however, is linked intimately with the entire country: no hills, no barrier of any kind, separates the port from the interior. A journey from Tibet to Shanghai is merely long: it is not, as the Yangtze herself so perfectly illustrates, impossible. And so, both when the East India ships first recognized that fact and today (and in the future), this city on the Yangtze is an entrance- and an exitway for all of China. (This is a reality that was recognized too late, one might argue, in the haphazard process by which Britain settled her colonies in the East. How might matters have turned out if Shanghai had been the colony, not Hong Kong?)

The crews of the East Indiamen who visited the Shanghai of the beginning of the nineteenth century had only to glance at the cargoes in the Yangtze junks moored out in the roadsteads to know that this modest city should, one day, be the principal port for all of China. The bills of lading preserved today speak of bolts of silk, bags of green and black tea, sacks of bean cake, tobacco, camel wool, porcelain, noodles, liquid indigo, musk, rhubarb, lily flowers, nutgalls, fans, ginseng, mulberry paper, bamboo shoots, books, the hides of strange and exotic beasts, cuttlefish, straw hats, rice, varnish, dried fish, tung oil, safflower—all China, settled in the junks' holds. So in 1830 the company plucked up the courage to send in a ship, the *Lord Amherst,* to ask the local *taotai* for permission to trade: they were sent away with orders never to be so impertinent again.

But all had changed a decade later. Under the combined malignities of Patna opium and Lord Armstrong's heavy guns—a story that belongs to a later chapter, as it culminated in solemn ceremonies held farther up the river—China caved in to the West's demands and conceded that the foreign devils could indeed have permission to trade—not only in Shanghai, but in the other four so-called treaty ports of Canton, Amoy, Foochow and Ningpo as well. From 1843 onward they could trade and, moreover, their traders could live in these same five cities and could enjoy the extraordinary privilege known as extraterritoriality, as if they were diplomats in an embassy, or crewmen aboard a ship on the high seas.

So within the British fiefdom that was to grow up beneath the British flag beside the Soochow Creek, British policemen (actually Sikhs, recruited in and imported from the Punjab) enforced British law.* Within the French Concession, which lounged defiant and insular to its south, policemen from Vietnam did much the same. Such Chinese authority as prevailed in the rest of Shanghai—in the native quarter, for instance—was to these mercantile Europeans an exotic irrelevance. The newcomers were men beyond the reach of local law, and beyond the constraining reach of the mores of their homelands. Bad behavior, unsupervised by home, could henceforth begin.

And, whether justified or not, it is bad behavior for which Shang-

---

* It was actually the American Henry Wolcott's Stars and Stripes that flew first in Shanghai, because the British took a while to acquire a flagpole.

hai is still best known. On the mudflats that stretched between where the Oriental Pearl Tower now stands and where Hazelwood still languishes were all the worst imaginings of a West unleashed, a concentrated essence of wantonness that made Shanghai one of the most memorably sinful cities in creation, a place that—so faded memory and modern journalism have it—may have been founded on godowns but was irretrievably grounded in Gomorrah.

For a few dozen copper cash you could have a nine-year-old child of either sex perform any act you wished. Brothels the size of factories operated with total impunity. Opium divans were as common as teahouses. You are drunk on absinthe, and you run over a Chinese coolie in the street? Four hundred dollars paid to his friend, or to his mother, and the problem evaporated. Trouble with one of the locals—perhaps he was impertinent, or your servants didn't care for him? A trifling sum paid in Mexican eagle-headed dollars would secure the services of a man with a meat cleaver who would slice through the tendons of the offender's shoulder, so he would never again be able to lift a box or a sack, or even his arm.

Shanghai was, if you believed its reputation, a dreadful place. Yes, most people—or at least the foreigners, and the rich Chinese who had evolved from the class of men called compradors, the businessmen's go-betweens—enjoyed themselves, or believed they did. This was a city where one could dance all night, go riding (on especially small Mongolian ponies, which raced vigorously at the track) at dawn, work all day and begin a new round of parties that evening without ever feeling weary. "I used to gamble, gamble, gamble oh, till five o'clock in the morning," noted one Shanghailander, a middle-aged gentlewoman transplanted from the innocence of Sussex. "Then I would go home, have a bath, get into jodhpurs, go down to the race-course, ride my ponies. . . ."

During the twenties and the thirties, Shanghai's salad days, there were the delights provided by the caravans of White Russian girls who had been evicted from their homeland by the Bolsheviks, and proved the finest and most accommodating of whores, pandering agnostically to the needs of either Devils or Celestials, while operating under the guise of what were peculiarly Shanghainese professions—artiste, *entraîneuse,* taxi dancer. (The less attractive, or less young, took to walking hopefully beneath the plane trees of Avenue Joffre.) Teenage boys would seduce their parents' Chinese maids, knowing no complaint was possible, nor would ever be entertained. Auden and Isherwood took a close look at gay Shanghai and found much to their liking—amid a Chinese community for which, as Lily would constantly remind me when we talked of such louche happenings, homosexuality was then (as now in most of China) regarded as an illness for which treatment was possible, and which was confined, it was firmly believed, almost wholly to men of the decadent West.

More workaday needs were catered for as well. Your parrot's toenails growing too long, or your fox terrier's coat too bushy? The Shanghai Pet Store at the corner of Dixwell and Bubbling Well Roads would oblige. Handmade silk *directoire* knickers? Consult Messrs. Ying Tai on Yates Road, or any of the other lingerie shops on what the locals called Petticoat Lane. The Kiddy Shop for your child's dungarees, Godfrey & Company for decent beef, Miss Maisie at La Donna Bella could do marvelous things with one's hair, and Madame Soloha's clairvoyance service often proved effective, though rarely for placing bets on the horses.

In the concessions where the foreigners lived there were four dairies, two dog hospitals, three expert masseuses, two furriers, a saddler. Whiteway & Laidlaw was the big department store, better regarded than the Sincere Company or Wing On. Kelly and Walsh supplied books and copies of the latest English and American magazines. And there was always Ramsey & Company on Nanking Road, who could supply you with enough gin to float a battleship, and a pretty decent claret for when one of your tennis partners from Frenchtown brought her husband round to dinner: moreover, it would all be delivered, and given to you on tick.

I once came across a small dictionary of pidgin, which offered something of the tone of the place. The pidgin itself (the word is said to be a corruption of "business," so the excuse is that this is the Oriental version of business English) sounds from this distance like a cruel joke, with its *no b'long ploppers* (this is not right) and *my catchee chows* (I'm going to eat) and *pay my look-sees* (let me look at it). But it is in the English equivalents, as laid out in the dictionary, that one can more properly hear the attitude of the times. *Never mind,* reads the book, irritably. *Tell him. I don't want that. Let me look at it. Upstairs! I don't want. Get me a ricksha. Fetch quickly. Give Master the letter. Tell him to come in the morning. Get the coolie. Give me two. No overcharging! Is the bargain settled? That will do.*

It would certainly not do in Shanghai if you didn't belong to a club. A club was a vital institution for the expatriate world, and in Shanghai the clubs, like most in the East, were made to appear grander than they actually were by their rigidly exclusionary policies—no vulgar salesmen, no shopkeepers, only the grandest of men who had associations with trade, and no one with the vaguest hint of Asian blood. Behind their grand façades, however, was bland normality: the *taipans* (the company chiefs) and the griffins (the fresh-faced newcomers to the East) merely drank, played cards or billiards, slept, nattered, or read. (Not too much reading, though: the Shanghai Club, with its famous forty-seven-yard-long bar, spent $16,240 on drinks in 1870, and only $72 on books.) The Shanghai Club was on the Bund, and still stands; so was the Concordia for Germans, and the Masonic. There were the grand and agreeably social sporting clubs—the Rowing Club, the Midge Sailing Club, the Cricket Club. As soon as Britain's first consul, George Balfour, had officially opened his mission in 1843, he set about overseeing the building of the most important sporting body of all, the Race Club. It built beside a huge track that after 1949 was deemed large enough a space to be converted to Shanghai People's Park, and of which a part has in more recent years been made into the city's monumental new People's Square.

Everything in Shanghai in those days—the only days people talked about, until very recently—took place at a run: there was no time for languid contemplation in a city where everyone needed to make money in fistfuls, where no one trusted anyone else, where it was always feared that the next deal would go to the next man if you did not attend to your business. Rich men had two bodyguards—one Chinese, the other Russian—and each would watch the other for signs of disloyalty. There was a rigid hierarchy of distaste, as well: the English merchants looked down on everyone, the Indians and the Eurasians were despised by the English and the Chinese; the Sikhs were despised by the Parsi businessmen; the coolies were despised by the Sikhs. "Chop, chop!" you'd scream at the ricksha boy, and you'd clip him round the ears if he didn't go fast enough.

And all the while, below the glitter and the meretricious glamour of the place, so its rottenness seethed and grew. The poor would come to beg on Nanking Road and be shooed away by the guards. The ricksha boys had the thinnest shoulders you'd ever see—you knew they were hungry and would live for thirty years at best. Lorries would growl around the International Settlement on chilly winter mornings, taking away the bodies of those who had died of starvation and cold during the night. A banker might be so rich that he would (like one Joseph Hsia, who later moved to Hong Kong) have a gold smelter in his back garden: but outside his front door there would invariably be a gaunt Chinese, dressed in rags, shivering and hungry. Some of the rich were kindly; most, in this ice-cold metropolis, were anything but.

And yet what made Shanghai so appealing to the foreigners who first settled there was an attitude among the local people that might well have prompted gentler sentiments than these. For unlike in the rest of China, where the barbarian foreigners were regarded by the Chinese with a deep and abiding contempt—after all, the inherent superiority of the Chinese was, and still remains, central to the national psyche—early settlers in Shanghai wrote of their distinct impression that they were, well, almost *liked*.

Few foreigners would go so far as to say the Shanghai Chinese admired or respected them—there was a general acceptance that a people with five thousand years of uninterrupted civilization behind them had some right to hauteur. One might not agree with it, one might try to ignore, skulking behind one's own mock-superior airs—the club's exclusionary policies, frequent reminders of who had won the Opium Wars, or of who had sacked the Summer Palace up in Beijing. But it was always there, and it would be a wise expatriate who would try not to fight it.

Yet in Shanghai there seemed less need to fight. It was always thought that here the subterranean hostility had abated somewhat, that the Shanghainese "were little afflicted," as one writer put it, "with that peculiarly passionate hatred of the pale-eyed and fair-haired beings which was so widespread among the Cantonese." They seemed more open-minded here, more willing to adapt to foreign ways, more tolerant of the devils from across the water. The Shanghainese learned, happily and willingly, and masking their disdain, from the foreigners. And within this distinction lies the root, undoubtedly, of the future success of the city. Her location on the Yangtze is her greatest boon; her people, unique in all China (and speaking the ugliest of languages, a discordant mélange of Mandarin and Cantonese spoken by no one outside the Yangtze delta), are her greatest asset.

For while sin is at the core of Shanghai's reputation, the more sober reality—what allowed the city to survive and to prosper, and what made it less of a Gomorrah than it seems—was its unashamed and freebooting mercantilism. This was a city in which the trader was absolute king, a city (perhaps the last in the world) that was created by and for and utterly dominated by the demands of the merchant. Shanghai was a place so dedicated in its commitment to commerce that Hong Kong seemed by comparison a dreamy city of poets and philosophers. Shanghai was a place founded in the traditions of Genoa and Venice. It was guided by the same kind of aggressive self-interest that was invented by the Germans of the Hanseatic League—with the Rhenish traders of fourteenth-century North Europe replaced by the Britons and the Frenchmen and the Americans who came to China in the nineteenth. True, the merchant of Shanghai played, and he played hard and fast and loose, and there are those who will say he became unshackled from his moral guide-wires in doing so: that is one side of Shanghai's story, and the more titillating one for today's palates. But

he also worked, and traded, conducting business on a breathtaking
scale: the legacy of that side of the city is what remains. And this is
what a place like Hazelwood stood for, or stands for today: the memory of sin on the city's surface, but the reality of sturdily respectable—
or at least sturdily profitable—commerce underneath.

I walked down what used to be Avenue Joffre one spring evening to
see something of that legacy at work. I was coming back from taking
a stroll around what is left of Hazelwood's lawns, and I headed east,
toward the winking towers on the Whangpoo. The avenue is now
Huaihai Road, and though its name gives it stout revolutionary credentials,* and though for many years it was as dull and gray as ditch
water, it is now one of the liveliest of streets in any city, a Chinese
version of the Ginza.

Colored lights were strung in arches along its length. Small dress
shops, tiny Japanese restaurants, sports cars parked outside nightclubs
with their ubiquitous neon lure, the flickering Kara-OK signs, smart-
looking cafés with names like Los Angeles and the wrongly spelled
Cordon Blue. The street was choked with people—mostly young,
nearly all Chinese: the Europeans stay on the six-mile strip of Nanjing Road, a few blocks north, where the prices are higher, the shops
are open later and there is a McDonald's. Huaihai Road is by contrast
a purely Chinese affair: the shops, the bars, the discos all Chinese-
owned, the customers all from the suburbs and the tiny city streets
called *hutongs* and the tower blocks of flats nearby.

As we were passing one particularly glossy-looking bar, Lily suddenly beckoned to me: three girls were sitting together at a window
table, each nursing a can of Coca-Cola. One girl was talking on a
mobile telephone; there were three pagers on the table, each beside a
pack of Marlboros.

"Prostitutes!" said Lily. "Can tell them a mile off."

---

* It commemorates the second great campaign of the 1949 revolution, when Mao's
soldiers advanced from the Huai River to the sea, and were thus poised to take
Shanghai.

We sat down with them. None of the three spoke English, nor had any of them ever had a western client. The girl with the phone said her name was Xiao-an—Little Serenity—and she charged four hundred *renminbi* for an hour with a man. Did the police bother her? "They are often our best customers," she said, and the three exploded in laughter. She was not a Shanghainese—she had come down from the far north, after hearing how good the money could be. She thought she would stay in Shanghai a year, and then go back home to Harbin in Manchuria and set up a karaoke club of her own. "This is a good life," she said. "Shanghai must be like your New York, I think."

Outside the window I could see two policemen, who must have been only too aware what was going on. Indeed there were a lot of police in Shanghai: at every crossing one stood on a plinth, directing traffic.

I spoke to one of them: he was unarmed (although Lily kept insisting that all Chinese policemen did keep side arms under their shirts), but he did have a radio, and he would be able to get brother officers within thirty seconds if any motorist broke the law. Shanghai seemed to me one of the most aggressively policed of Chinese cities. Maybe it has to be: maybe the old habits of lawlessness—this was a gangland city, after all—have not yet died. Something of the sin remains.

And older citizens are brought in to help regulate matters too: old men with tattered red and green flags stand at every intersection to make sure people don't jaywalk, and that cyclists don't ride against red lights. Equally venerable men and women are employed by shops to advise innocents on how best to get onto an escalator, or how to find their way among the maze of stalls and corridors. "There was no unemployment in Shanghai under the old-style Communists," one old man remarked to me. "And there isn't any now, under the new ones. Everyone here works. Everyone here makes money, everyone makes his contribution to seeing that the city keeps going."*

This ancient directed me around a corner, to Joyful Undertaking

---

* The old man was deluded. Official, but unpublished, figures say that there were 300,000 unemployed in the city in 1996.

Street (where I tried to explain to an uncomprehending Lily why a joyful undertaker would be hard to find) and the old pink building where the Communists first met in July 1921. It used to be a girls' school: now a museum, a shrine for the Shanghai faithful. Pictures of a young-looking Mao were on the wall, ranged beside those of the other twelve delegates at that first gathering. But I noticed that of this group, eight are dignified with full-page pictures in the brochure on sale in the foyer for a couple of *renminbi.* The others—an augury of things to come—have small and out-of-focus snapshots, and explanations in the rubric that they either had left or had been expelled from the Party, or, *horribile dictu,* had gone over to the Japanese.

We wandered idly through the school halls, looking at various icons of Imperial cruelty. A ticket that gave a worker in a capitalist tram-factory permission to spend only two minutes in the bathroom particularly exercised Lily—it made her so angry, in fact, that she immediately developed a spectacular nosebleed and had to be looked after by the crone who ran the place. The woman kept soothing Lily by saying how her red blood was a symbol of her socialist purity—she looked witheringly up at me while she delivered this homily—and demanded that Lily sign the visitors' book in blood. "It is a symbol," she kept saying. "A sign. I am very proud to know you." Lily, as perplexed as most modern young Chinese about the realities of Marxist-Leninism, made an excuse, signed the book in ink, and we hurried back out into the lights of Huaihai Road.

There, under one spreading tree a number of elderly ladies had set up ear-cleaning stalls. Nearby, younger masseuses offered to twist and pummel the tip of one of your fingers, promising thereby to make you feel younger and more active for the night ahead. Beside them was a man selling crickets' cages, and another offering steaming buns, ten *jiao* each. This was China still, no matter the neon, the mobile phones and beepers, and no matter the distinctive rumble I could hear beneath them—a Manhattan-like rumble—of the brand-new subway trains rolling their passengers home.

The subways—one line is now ready, six more are to be opened before the end of the century—are already changing the lives of the millions who live here. One example came home to me especially vividly. A few years before I had been making a film in which I examined in some detail the life of a young Hong Kong bank worker, and of his opposite number in Shanghai. It was, back in 1988, a brutal comparison.

The Hong Kong man spoke English, had a huge flat, drove a two-year-old Toyota, worked in a vast air-conditioned skyscraper, took annual holidays in Thailand and California. His Shanghai counterpart, Ge Guo-hong, was a clever, rather intense young man who did exactly the same work for the same bank, but in a cramped and ancient office that stood not far from where I was now walking. He told me, rather sullenly, that he spent three hours in a dirty bus each day traveling to and from work, standing—never sitting; he could never find an empty seat—in the hot and muggy air. He lived in a tiny one-room flat five floors up—no elevator, of course—and his wife worked in a factory: their combined earnings were such that neither had ever had a holiday. His life, he said, was not good.

I looked for him on this new journey, but in vain. I found where his old flat had been, but it had been demolished, and a hotel was being built on the site by a South Korean company. A shopkeeper who had appeared in the film remembered him, though rather vaguely. The last definite news was from two years before, when he heard that Ge's wife was living with relations across the river in Poodong, and had for a while worked as a waitress in the French-owned Sofitel on Nanjing Road, where she had been trying to learn how to speak French in the process. Had Mr. Ge still worked at the bank, I reflected, and had he still lived in his old district, he would now be able to travel to his office in one of the new air-conditioned subway trains, and his journey—a trip that beforehand would have taken him ninety miserable minutes each way—would take him only nine minutes, and would cost no more.

His old office block had been knocked down six months before, and the bank is now housed on the tenth and eleventh floor of a skyscraper overlooking the Whangpoo, a building that is every bit as glittering as its parent in Hong Kong. When I went there and asked for Mr. Ge, an ancient Chinese man operating an abacus at the back of the room, and who spoke impeccable English, said the name to himself over and over again. "Ge Guo-hong. Ge Guo-hong." He then turned to me and, in the rueful tones of an Oxford lodge porter, said: "Sorry, old man—the name doesn't ring a bell with me."

But then I found one of his friends, a man who worked in the bank's computer department. It turned out that Mr. Ge was away from Shanghai and had been for "some years." He was on special leave, studying at a university in Philadelphia. He was getting a doctorate and a command of English, and quite possibly a green card. There was more to it than that. The friend explained:

"It was all to do with the film. You made it? You may not realize, but you changed his life in a very big way. Mr. Ge was ashamed by what he saw when you compared his life with that Mr. Wong, or whatever his name was. He became determined to do better than the man in Hong Kong. We all saw the film. The office people sent a copy up from Hong Kong—we looked at the tape time after time. We all felt the same way: we thought it was quite wrong that the Hong Kong people, who are not in any way as clever as we are, should do better than us.

"So he has gone, sort of as our ambassador. He will come back, and he will be a great success. We will show those southern people how poor they really are!"

I asked the young man what he thought of the new Shanghai, symbolized by the Pearl Tower he could see from his window.

"I like the new Shanghai," he said. "But that thing? I try not to look at it. It's not the kind of symbol I want to see. I am very proud of this city. But that—that looks, how to say it in English?—somewhat vulgar." "Tacky!" chimed in another man, who said he had been to San Francisco, and who knew American slang. "Yes, that's it—tacky."

The bank's office is at the southern end of a half-mile stretch of castellated Imperial architecture that offers the world the best-known face of Shanghai. We have to thank a prescient *taotai* for its existence, however, and not the foreigners who built it. When the first settlements were being delineated—the Americans to the north of Suzhou creek, the British in twenty-three muddy acres to its south—the Chinese laid down a rule: to preserve the rights of coolies who used the towpath to track their grain boats up the Whangpoo and toward the Yangtze, no foreign building would be allowed within thirty feet of the river itself. So a line of stakes were driven in at the water's edge, and a wide road was created between the river and the new city. This was an esplanade to which the British gave the Persian name: the Bund.

The scale of the walkway was titanic. It was more like a seafront than a riverfront: a stretch of open land positively demanding that a slew of imposing buildings be built to march along its length. The great consulates and clubs and commercial houses all competed to oblige: the Hongkong & Shanghai Bank, the Yokohama Specie Bank, Jardines, the Shanghai Club, the British Consulate, the Chartered Bank, Butterfield & Swire, Victor Sassoon's Cathay Hotel, and the immense Maritime Custom House, with its tower clock that played a fair version of the chimes of faraway Big Ben, or by some accounts, the clock on Westminster Abbey, and which in any case the Shanghailanders, as the expatriate community liked to be known, called Big Ching.

There may have been one or two touches of charm—the Chinese passersby liked to stroke the paws of the Hongkong Bank's bronze lions, rendering them golden and thus more prosperous-looking— but the stretch of buildings looks, in truth, pretty gloomy. There is a mausoleum-like quality to the architecture, the buildings all heavy and solemn, faced in grayish Ningpo stone and overdesigned, made to look ponderous, imposing and grand. It was as though someone had taken the Woolworth Building from lower Broadway, cloned it several times, and then set it down unsuitably in Cannes, in place of the Carlton Hotel. You look at the Bund today, close your eyes and wonder what might have been, and then open them to find these gaunt memorials to the British. What dismay!

The Chinese seem to have a disdainful view of these once grand structures, though for other reasons, born more of nationalistic pride than the questioning of architectural taste. So there is now a Kentucky Fried Chicken outlet unsuitably placed in the basement of the old Shanghai Club building, and a Citibank automatic teller machine stands outside the Cathay Hotel—it worked perfectly, and I was able to get depressing news of my available balance back in New York in no more than half a minute. Thus are the great monuments to empire being rendered prosaic, and brought down to earth.

However, since foreign tourists like to come and see the buildings, and since they have tended to come at night when traffic on the normally congested Bund is lighter, the city authorities have begun to urge the managers of the string of buildings to illuminate them, to show them off. They may do so only for two hours, the power bill being so high—but when they turn on the switches at about nine each evening, the great buildings do gleam briefly with some sense of their old glory, bathed in the glare of battalions of golden and pink and green arc lights.

I took a boat cruise along the Whangpoo one evening and watched enthralled as the banks of lights came on one by one—first the old consulate, then the bank, then the club. Some buildings remained dark until the very last moment. Whoever, for instance, is now in the old Jardines building (quite probably the Jiangsu Animal By-Products Import and Export Corporation, which has its tenancy hinted at by a dirty iron plate on the wall), clearly likes to keep its electricity bills down to a minimum, and for several moments there was a dark gap in the façade, like a broken tooth. But then the lights flickered on there as well, and for a while the entire serrated wall of stone appeared on fire, a last hurrah for the West's Imperial memory.

Lily was with me, gazing over at the buildings slipping by. Flashbulbs popped from hundreds of watchers on the Bund—people taking pictures of our passing boat, not of the structures at which we were encouraged to look. The photographers were mostly standing in what is now called Whangpoo Park, and Lily pointed to it contemptuously. "That's where you put up the sign No Dogs or Chinese. Remember? But now you are gone, and now it is full of Chinese. Dogs too, I expect."

I argued with her. There had never been any such sign, I said.* The British knew only too well the disadvantages of such impertinence. The story of the sign was a myth, part romantic conceit, part an instance of the Communists' revisionist history of Shanghai, in which all foreigners were regarded as having exploited the place, and having cordially loathed the Chinese among whom they lived. Nothing could be further from the truth, I said—though frankly, of the last point, I wasn't wholly convinced myself.

Lily wasn't listening, and she continued, overexcited. "Look at your ridiculous buildings. They're not pretty, not grand. Not useful. We do them up in colored lights to make them look foolish. They are caricatures. Like circus performers. That's how we think of you now. We dress your great buildings in colored lights to show everyone how ridiculous you were."

The boat had stopped in the river now. We were beside the Custom House—whose clock was indeed chiming familiarly, and no longer playing "The East Is Red" as it had during the Cultural Revolution and for some years afterward. Then we were turning around to port, and as the Bund began to edge away behind us, so the new buildings of Poodong were coming into view once more. The gigantic monstrosity of the Pearl Tower, of course, and half a dozen other skyscrapers, their summits topped with the currently fashionable syringelike architectural conceits that gave them extra height at little

---

* Academics continue to pore over the saga. A study in the *China Quarterly* showed that in 1903 Regulation Number 1 on the notice board of what was then called the Recreation Ground said, "No dogs or bicycles are admitted," and Regulation Number 5, several inches below, read, "No Chinese are admitted, except servants in attendance upon foreigners." That was as close as dog ever came to Chinaman—close enough, though, for the mythmakers (the first of whom was an American journalist named Putnam Weale, who wrote a novel in 1914 mentioning the supposed sign).

extra cost. There were huge neon signs for Hitachi and Samsung; behind us the last sign on the Bund, the French Bund, was for Nescafé. The two big new bridges were lit up as well, and in the distance I could see the lights of traffic streaming by on the new elevated *périphérique,* four lanes wide, two months open, and already crammed with traffic that its planners had underestimated, grossly. This was the new Shanghai ahead: the old, festooned in its brief moment of pastel brilliance, lay on the far side of the boat.

Perhaps Lily was right. Perhaps this was how the Chinese wanted to remember us—as greedy buffoons, as vulgar and immoral intruders who were responsible for giving their city its aura of decadence, dissipation and decay. Perhaps that is why they had been demolishing the inner city so ruthlessly, so wantonly—tearing down the Frenchtown houses that had once been brothels, pounding into rubble the old White Russian mansions on the Avenue Joffre, making libraries out of clubs, hotels out of *taipans'* houses, fast-food restaurants where once the city's great and good had feasted at a more leisured pace. The Bund, left as it was and lit so extravagantly, was just a caricature of the Shanghai that had been left behind.

The fine new skyscrapers and the glass-and-steel department stores and the great new public buildings—in People's Square particularly—now give Shanghai the appearance she wants and craves. She wants her image, like her self-image, to be one of determined progress and a historyless modernity. Cities like Tokyo and Seoul, which have such an appearance today, owe it largely to war and foreign bombers that smashed and burned most of the old buildings with cordite, high explosive and shrapnel. But the physical Shanghai suffered little from war, even when the Japanese invaded and occupied the place, and certainly when the Communists took the city over.*

So she has had to destroy her past on her own. It is generally

---

* Mao's revolutionary troops entered on Wednesday, May 25, 1949, without any break in the city routine, except that an insomniac radio listener noted that Beethoven's Fifth Symphony was played over and over again during the night. When morning came the Communists were in firm control.

accepted that 1990 was the year when this all began: before that, the fortunes of the city were essentially controlled by the Communist masters in Beijing. For more than forty years the city was imprisoned in dust and decay, a bag of bones, a collection of relics of the loathed occupants of old. But in 1990 the brakes were taken off: Shanghai was told by the Communist leadership that she could rebuild herself, make something of herself, present herself as a showcase of the new China. And she started to do so with a vengeance—and as she did her population (for many years static at about 13 million) began to rise, newcomers attracted by the old magnetism, but this time a magnetism that had patriotically Chinese, and not foreign, characteristics.

There can be little doubt that Shanghai is soon going to occupy an exalted place in twenty-first-century China—and a position that, I would guess, may be very much more exalted in China than that occupied by today's Hong Kong, or by its fast-growing neighbor along the Pearl River, Canton. The Shanghainese have a masonic solidarity about them, a grim determination, a ruthlessness that inspires fear and respect throughout all China. Now that they have been unshackled, they have a much greater potential—and many more friends and allies—than their country cousins in the south.

Say "Shanghainese" to a man in Chengdu, or Xi'an, or Harbin, or Beijing, and he will curl his lips in mock terror. Say "Cantonese" before a similar audience, and the listener will curl his lips—but in disdain. The Cantonese—"rice-eating monkeys," a Beijing friend remarked to me once—are ill regarded by just about all their brother Chinese. They have performed economically so well, it is widely thought, merely and solely because of the benign invigilation of the British, who kept them cozy and secure and colonized for a century and a half.

"Who are the really smart Chinese in Hong Kong anyway?" asked Lily, who detests the Cantonese. "They are the Shanghainese businessmen who went there after the revolution. All the really big fellows in Hong Kong are from Shanghai. Everyone in China knows that. And they'll come back—they're coming back here now—now there's money to be made and kept on the Yangtze. You see.

"The Pearl River has no real future. At least, not compared with this. The British are leaving anyway. The Yangtze is everything. It means so much to China. What does the Pearl River mean? Pah! Not a thing! And you know, what the people here are doing, they're doing on their own. They learned from you, the foreigners. The Shanghainese are not too proud to learn, that's always true. But what they are doing now, they are doing without any help.

"Did anyone help build that tower?" she asked, jerking her thumb toward the floodlit monster. "Everyone said it would be impossible, that we'd need to bring in foreign experts. But not at all. We did it ourselves."

I reminded her that when we were up at the top of the tower she had been laughing unkindly at the ludicrously hyperbolic Mr. Su, mocking his evident love affair with the insect structure. She brushed my remark away, carelessly.

"Okay, okay—I may not like it. I admit that it is terribly ugly. And you may not understand this—but in a strange way I'm proud of it. I'm proud because it is homemade, like all of Shanghai's success today."

I nodded sympathetically. But she had her dander up, and her face was flushed. She wasn't quite finished.

"You know what? This tower—it says to me that we Chinese are on the inside. We are running the place. We make the decisions. You foreign people are on the outside. At long last. And that is as it should be."

We took dinner that night in a small underground café called Judy's Place. It was the kind of noisy and bustling spot where expatriates like to come and feel briefly at home. It was not much different from places in Manila and Djakarta and in the less restricted parts of the Middle East. The waitresses were all Chinese students, pretty young women doing time to learn English and make a few *renminbi* as tips.

The expats were there in their scores, drinking Bass and Corona and San Miguel, giving their Chinese girlfriends strange cocktails with erotic names, wolfing down hamburgers or bowls of chili.

There were all the usual signs pinned up on the tribal notice board: the Hash House Harriers were meeting next day, someone wanted a secondhand mountain bike, a fourth person was wanted to shoot snipe up in Liaoning province in Manchuria. There was a leaving sale of white-wood furniture from Ikea.

On the night we were there, the noisiest table—and there were some noisy tables—was hosted by a handsome young Briton. He was the son of a governor of the Bank of England, as it happened, and he was the current foreign representative of Butterfield & Swire. He was a man in direct line of succession from old Night Soil Brown, the first of the tenants at Hazelwood.

But compared with his predecessors of half a century ago this young man presides over very little—which is perhaps why so many of his evenings are spent boisterously with the professional expatriate set, and not taking part, as his predecessors once had, in the grander task of the running of Shanghai. His company, still big and important and rich, does not trade as it did along the Yangtze anymore. It has no boats. Nor indeed does it have access to Hazelwood—unless any of its staff wish to pay sixty-five dollars a night to sleep in the old *taipan*'s bedroom. There is no office on the Bund. The firm makes such money as it can—it acts as the agent for Volvo motor cars and is involved in joint ventures, making paint, selling insurance. Most of the Volvos are bought by newly rich Chinese—and indeed, the senior representative of Swires these days is a Chinese. Once, in Hazelwood days, any Chinese employees were merely there as compradors; now—in the days of the Oriental Pearl Tower—the Chinese are the bosses.

For much of the twentieth century, Shanghai may have essentially belonged to Britons like this young man in Judy's Place, and to foreign firms like the one for whom he works. But in general those men and their firms made a bad show of it. The locals learned from them what they could, and they then discarded what was of little worth—including most of what these westerners thought of as their colorful and cheerful past, and then most of the westerners themselves. The Shanghai of the twenty-first century, now so forcefully shunning all that history, casting it away like so much baggage, is indisputably and irrevocably Chinese—just as once, long before the barbarians came in their tall sailing ships, it used to be. The wheel has come full circle as, in China, it always seems to do. The foreigners turned out to be only temporary kings, at best.

When I came back to the ship that night it was raining hard. The sentry outside the naval base was standing ramrod straight beneath a steel umbrella, not flinching when occasional gusts of wind blew water on his face. No Foreigners Allowed Beyond This Point, read a warning sign, but Lily gripped my arm and pushed me through. She had a pass. The sentry stared fixedly ahead.

The boat on which I was staying was a cruise vessel, detached for the off-season from its usual work on the Upper Yangtze. It was owned by a Chinese man who lived in New York, and he had generously offered to let me sleep in one of the staterooms while I did my work in the city. This night the boat was all but deserted, and it was silent and brilliantly lit. Security around these wharves is tremendous: a Chinese wanting to leave his country could scale the razor wire and be on a foreign-bound ship. Like the Soviets in the old days, the Chinese authorities keep their borders closed tight, and this, technically speaking, was a border too.

I had been on this quayside once before, when Queen Elizabeth, who had been touring China, was about to make her farewell and board the royal yacht *Britannia* for the voyage home.* The yacht was moored alongside where my ship, the *Princess Jeannie*, was berthed and as a Royal Marine band played sea shanties and anthems, so the lights along the Bund were switched on. The Chinese president of the day was an old war hero named Yang Shangkun, and I remem-

---

* The trip, the first to China by a reigning British monarch, had not been a success, and there was much fodder for the tabloid press. Prince Philip, the Queen's prickly consort, had remarked tactlessly to a Scottish student in Xian that if he stayed much longer he would risk getting "slitty eyes." One paper thereafter referred to him as "The Great Wally of China."

ber that he shook my hand, very affably. It was a grand evening, a moment when the old, dead Shanghai came briefly alive, stirred in her sleep.

Nowadays the city is fully awake all the time. All night there are lights, cars, crowds, the sounds of distant music and shouting, the sirens of vessels passing by on their way to and from the sea. Our ship's arc lights blazed down on the water, and for a fathom or so the Whangpoo had a kind of translucence to it, the blackness rubbed briefly away. Lily and I were gazing down at it, looking halfheartedly for fish, when a body bobbed gently into view.

It was that of a man in his thirties. He was floating face up, fully clothed, and his eyes were open. His would not be the first body I saw on this voyage, nor would it be the most disturbing: but the image of his face staring up at me through the waters was one I carried for many days. How he had died, how he had come to be in the waters, whom he had left behind—these were questions I could never answer. But as to notifying the police, or trying to haul the body out—Lily gave a dismissive wave.

"You see them all the time," she said. "And you'll see worse. The river is a cemetery for those who can't afford a proper burial. Just let him be. He'll just drift out to sea, and that'll be an end to him."

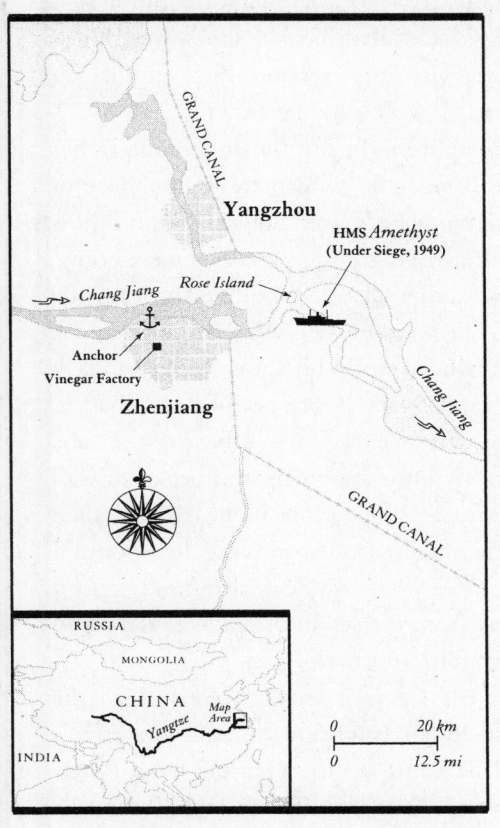

4

The First
Reach

Shanghai was already slipping well astern as the old Russian-built
hydrofoil—one of the fleet of well-rusted craft used for high-speed
journeying on the lower reaches of the river—crunched and clanked
herself into cruising gear. We lurched uncomfortably for a few moments in the wake of a passing tanker—a stained and battered Ban-
gladeshi ship, registered in Chittagong. Then the sponsons began to
bite into the black waters of the Whangpoo and we started to accel-
erate noisily, our engines belching an oily, feltlike smoke. Soon, and
with a thin and chilly rain falling, we were speeding along ahead of a
half-mile wake of fudge-colored foam. By the time we were out in
the open reaches of the Yangtze itself and had turned sharply to the

left to start the four-hour run upstream to Zhenjiang, the hostess—a plump teenage girl in a gray skirt, Cuban-heeled shoes, and knee-stockings so tight they left purple rings around the tops of her calves—was calling for requests. It was karaoke time.

Lily asked for a song she thought might suit the occasion, a rather soothing number called *"Zhu ni ping an,"* which translates more or less as "Good Wishes for Arriving Safe and Sound." Our fellow passengers, who all seemed to know where the two of us were going, thought this was an ideal choice and applauded loudly. But it turned out to be a rather odd choice. The woman who sang the song on the boat's television screen was shown, inexplicably, attempting to teach it to a group of deaf children, and so the entire performance had to be conducted in sign language. The scene was so affecting that one young woman passenger promptly burst into tears and began to wail about how terrible it must be for a child to lose its hearing. It then became impossible to hear the singer, rather proving her point. I promptly gave up on karaoke, after what had been admittedly only a brief experiment. I turned away from the set and tried as best I could to gaze out of the craft's grimy little portholes.

Plover Point, Dove's Nest, the Centaur Buoy: according to the sailing directions there was so much Englishness about the river's reaches here we could as well be going up the Hamble from Portsmouth. But no: at Fushan, half an hour into the journey, there was supposed to be—though in this rain I couldn't see it—a ruined pagoda, the first in China, and, according to the *Admiralty Pilot,* "a small fort resembling a martello tower." And then at Jiangyin, where the river's banks close in and for the first time I had the feeling that we were on a river and no longer in its estuary, there was supposed to be on the left "a walled town, quadrilateral in form, the sides of the square each being about one mile long. In it is a tall and prominent pagoda and the town is surrounded by a moat, which is joined to waterways leading southwestward to the Grand Canal."

There, in the bald sentence of a navigator's log, lay a first hint of the delights and terrors of Imperial China. I could close my eyes, blot out the wailing from the television and imagine what Chiang-yin—

as it was known to foreigners half a century ago—must have been like before the Communist revolution. The mandarin in his chair, the citizens kowtowing before him, the scholars in their buttoned silk coats and white slippers and their spotless spats, the women with their bound feet, the prisoners fettered into their wooden neckblock constraints called *cangues,* the pigs running pell-mell through a market filled with spices from India and Arabia. Marco Polo, who (if he had come to China at all: some scholars say he didn't) crossed the river just a few miles ahead, would have recognized a dozen cities that were exactly like the navigator's description of what is now Jiangyin.

And as lately as half a century ago there were walls around most cities, with gates that were slammed shut at night, and a barbican and a water gate with a lockable iron grid. All over China Proper— the official term for the eighteen provinces of Qing dynasty China that lay east of the upper reaches of the Yangtze and well south of the Gobi desert, and which omitted Manchuria, Xinjiang, Tibet and Mongolia—were sedate, well-ordered cities, the kind of place that Gladys Aylward first saw when she found her way to Wang-ching, and to *The Inn of the Sixth Happiness*—or rather, when Ingrid Bergman saw it from her mule, after her ten days' ride from Tientsin.

But how many such delights remain? How many of these exquisite conceits of urban design escaped from Japanese bombs, or from Communist central planning? What happened to them all? Squinting through the drizzle in the direction of Jiangyin, I could see a low and rather crude pagoda down by the mud of the foreshore: it was overgrown with grass, which sprouted in bunches from its upper stories. But as to a wall or a moat or a barbican tower—all gone, or else overwhelmed by the mean piles of workers' flats and their factories, all spewing smoke as thick as lava. Black coils of it lay hanging in the wet air, too thick and heavy to be blown away.

Maybe there was a wall still, if the Japanese hadn't blown it down. But if it did still exist it would be covered with foot-thick layers of oily dust. No one would have cherished it, or have shown any pleasure in what it once had meant to the city—of how it once had defined and delineated what was to become a typically Chinese center of order. Now all that defined the limits of a city like Jiangyin was the rule of the local police, and the range of the urban rat catchers.

The karaoke was making my head spin. I walked out to the afterdeck of the speeding hydrofoil, feeling fresher with the rain whistling past my head at twenty knots. Up here it was prettier. The banks were lined in parts with Cunningham firs, from which the Foochow junkmen used to make their masts. There were groves of cinnamon and camphor trees, stands of bamboo that shrouded the more isolated farmhouses from the winter winds, and Japanese cedars and maidenhair trees on the low hills marking the sites of graves. Industry and communism may have changed the face of China—but there was still something immutable, even here.

There was one other passenger up on deck, a young woman who, in spite of the stinging drizzle, had decided to come up for air.

"You'll soon smell the place we're going to," she remarked without introduction. "Smelliest city in China." She stood at the port-side rail and sniffed deeply. "There!" she exclaimed with delight. "Don't you get it?"

I confessed that I didn't. But I was no stranger to olfactory humiliation. Once I had been sailing on a small boat running westward across the Indian Ocean, and after two months at sea, the yacht's cat had taken to standing with her head held high, just like this woman's, sniffing intently from the boat's side. Nellie, the cat was called, and she would take in the air like a student of wine—savoring it before letting it out, trying to catch even the faintest whiff. One morning she went suddenly quite wild, waving her tail like a cat possessed. I could not smell a thing except the sea. But the skipper said the cat could: it was Madagascar, rather more than two hundred miles away.

We were still eighty miles from our destination of Zhenjiang, and this woman claimed to be able to smell it. "Famous for vinegar," she said, and she gave me a card I could use as an introduction, in case I wanted to see. She was apparently a lawyer, and probably quite well known in town.

A low hill, more a tumulus than a mountain, rose on the right bank—*the first hill in China,* I wrote in my diary, *the most easterly extension of the mountains that eventually make the Three Gorges.* And as we swept around and below it, so in swept the smell—the unmistakable pungent and sour tang of brown rice vinegar, wafting down the river in the rain. "It even sinks into the stones of the place," said Lily. "They say people who come from Zhenjiang can be picked out wherever they go in China. They walk into a room and there is a chorus: 'Hey, you from Zhenjiang!' They hate it."

As soon as we docked I rushed to the factory. It was a Saturday and the plant was closing early, but the lawyer's card worked a treat. The gate was pushed back, the already struck company flags (one Chinese, one American—this was a joint venture, it turned out) were raised again on their poles. Within moments—and after battling my way upstairs through fumes so heavy that I felt as though I was somehow inside a vinaigrette dressing—I was brought to the office of the Chief Vinegar Manager, Dr. Yu Kehua, a man with a face so long and pinched and lips so thin and wrinkled that he looked as if he had been sipping the stuff since the cradle.

But Dr. Yu was courteous to a fault. He quickly arranged tea, postponed a meeting with his wife, summoned in a secretary who was on the point of leaving for his weekend, found a number of scholarly books for me, trundled a blackboard in from another room and—all this at one o'clock on a wet Saturday—proceeded to give me a brief but seminal lecture on the Role of Vinegar in Chinese Society.

He had a framed piece of calligraphy hanging over his desk, a reminder: There Are Seven Necessities in Chinese Life, it warned: Firewood. Rice. Oil. Salt. Soybean Sauce. Vinegar. Tea. *Without these, people cannot survive.*

Dr. Yu saw my look. "We have been making this particular necessity here since 1840," he said. "Vinegar is essential—it provides the contrast that is so important in all Chinese cooking. The balance. The yin and yang, you know all about that, yes? We like to think what we make is the best in China. It is certainly the most famous. We have a certain notoriety here." He lowered his voice. "They even say *we smell*."

He then got to his feet, went over to the board and began to explain matters at a clip. It was like a school chemistry lesson: how the water was mixed with polished sticky rice and allowed to ferment, how a bacterium called *Acetobacter* then made the alcohol react with oxygen in the air, how acetic acid formed, how the liquid was then flavored with secret herbs and spices, how it was all then aged and casked, bottled and sold. He quoted from a brochure: "Sour without tasting puckery, fragrant smell with sweet taste, strong color and tasty, stronger fragrance after storage."

Lily had been listening to this, occasionally shaking her head. Finally she blurted out: "But Dr. Yu, with respect, I have heard some criticism of your vinegar. I have heard that the gourmets think it is not so good, that the vinegar from Panpu is rather better."

Dr. Yu snorted with derision. "That old fool Yuan Mei! I know his book. Very famous Qing dynasty cookbook—he said that Zhenjiang vinegar wasn't sharp enough, didn't have the right *penzhi,* the right balance between fragrance and sourness.

"Well look at our awards! Gold medals, year after year for eighty years. Eighty! The Golden Plum award. The Paris award. The Hong Kong award. Many other people believe ours is the best. Not Panpu city vinegar. That is weak, limpid, no good.

"And you know what? Now we are not just a state company, now we are a joint venture, we have to be competitive. Before, if you had said the Panpu vinegar is better, I would have shrugged my shoulder and said—no matter. Now I am stung by what you say. We have to be better. Our American partner insists we make money. We have to tell all the world to buy our vinegars, no one else's."

A vein on Dr. Yu's right temple was pulsing angrily. I thought I should try to calm him. Who was the American partner? I asked.

"She is Chinese lady, lives in New York I think. Or San Francisco. One of those places. She is very strong, very demanding. Things are different now. I must defend our vinegar or she will be upset. I must put to rest that bad story by Yuan Mei. Old fool that he was. Our products are the best. Come see."

A whirlwind tour ensued. Strong young men, stripped to the waist (and delayed from heading off for their weekends as well), were raking trays of glutinous brown rice. Porcelain vats were bubbling with fermenting vinegar water. I was taken through warm halls of towers—some steel, some bamboo, some pottery—where the vinegar was aged. There were long bottling plants, with battalions of bottles standing silent on their racks. Smaller rooms for hand-wrapping the more costly bottles. A warehouse, with boxes of the company products arranged in long ranks, many of them bearing the old-fashioned spelling—Chinkiang—of the town where we were, Zhenjiang. So there was plain Chinkiang Vinegar, Ginger Vinegar, Ancient Well-Matured Vinegar, Chinkiang Soy Sauce, Pickled Radish, Pickled Chinkiang Coriander Heart, Pagoda-Shaped Vegetable, Sweet Gourd Pickle. "Fifteen thousand tons of vinegar each year," said Dr. Yu as we left. He was calmer now. "Three thousand tons of soy sauce. Seven thousand tons of pickles. Here—take some." He pressed bottles of vinegar into our hands, and gave me a large drum of Pagoda-Shaped Vegetable. "You taste. You will find we are the best!"

As the iron gates slid shut behind us, and the flags were lowered once again, I told Lily she had been brilliant, if rather forward. "I couldn't let him get away with it," she explained. "This is the new China. He had to rise to the bait. And he did. Quite well, I thought. He's the new breed of businessman. Such a change from the old cadres of the past. 'Eating vinegar,' they say—jealousy. That's what he feels. Competition, I suppose. A bit like your West, I imagine, yes?" She held up the sleeve of her shirt, sniffed it and made a face. She leaned over to me and did the same. "Now we both smell. Everyone will know just where we've been."

· · ·

Zhenjiang is—or rather was, during its more glorious days in the Sung dynasty, between the tenth and the thirteenth centuries—one of the great crossing points of the eastern world, for this is where the East's greatest river intersected with the world's greatest canal. The Grand Canal, which still lays claim to being the longest man-made waterway, was built during the Sui and Tang dynasties, mostly during the seventh century. While the Yangtze wanders in these parts from east to west, the Canal spears directly north and south. The two waterways intersect at right angles. The Canal enters the river from the south a few miles below Zhenjiang, and it leaves for the north at a point on the far bank almost directly opposite the city.

Five hundred years ago, the waters around Zhenjiang (the name means "guarding the River," and there was once a huge military garrison) would have been busier than almost anywhere else on the Yangtze. Up- and downstream commercial traffic, dominated by the huge wooden trading junks whose descendants are the great iron barges of today, would have mingled with the smaller and lighter but nonetheless important junks and skiffs that were involved in the supply and military business for which the canal had been built. Marco Polo, in the thirteenth century, noted the frantic activity on the waterways: this was a place, he said, that "lived for commerce."

Lily and I walked down what was called Small Jetty Street, aiming for the precise spot on the dockside where Polo was said to have stepped ashore. The street itself had much of the charm of old China—it was cobbled, and there were well-worn stone steps, and every few yards an old stone archway. Behind one of these was a tall Buddhist stupa, which the locals said was eight hundred years old. It didn't look it: I suspected that, like so many relics in China, this one had been far too exuberantly restored far too often, and it was in fact almost modern.

We reached the river, an opaque gray and chocolate-colored flood with oil rings in the eddies, and clumps of refuse bobbing on the wavelets. When Lord Macartney came here in November 1793—he was the first foreign ambassador to try to pry open China's locked doors to trade, and he failed, signally—this stretch of the river was called the Blue River: his diarist noted, as well he might, that the name was rather ill suited, since the water's color was in fact quite similar that of the ocher-and-umber sludge of the Yellow River; which they had seen only a few days before. "The waves rolled like the sea," he said of the crossing (Macartney's expedition, which was traveling southward on the Grand Canal, had to cross the Yangtze with the rest of the southbound Imperial traffic), "and porpoises are said to be sometimes seen leaping amongst them."

There was a fisherman sitting in a rickety-looking boat by the quay. He was puffing gently on a bamboo pipe, a smoldering nut of tobacco in its tiny brass bowl. I reminded Lily about the porpoises and the lovely little white dolphins, the *baiji,* once so common in the Yangtze and now said to be almost extinct. What did this man know about them? She shouted a question down to him.

At first he said nothing, but then as if by way of answer he slowly got up, walked to a locked box near the prow of his boat, and pulled from it a huge and tangled mess of fishing line that jangled and clanked with its several pounds of rusty ironmongery. He shook it at me, almost angrily, inviting me to take a look. But I knew what it was, instantly: this was an example of the very device that had put the pathetic little Yangtze dolphin into such grave danger: it was called a rolling hook trawl, and it was every bit as vicious a device as it appeared. It didn't just catch fish: it snared them, hurt them and killed them.

The Chinese once revered the Yangtze dolphin—five-foot-long, silvery-colored, bottled-nosed creatures that, it is said, have resisted evolution for twenty million years. Poets of the time were amazed at how gentle the creatures were, how they smiled and whistled, how they stood up in the water, breast-fed their young, seemed anthropomorphically charming. Dolphins appealed mightily to the mythmaking mind of the ancient Chinese. They called them "Yangtze Goddesses," and the Song dynasty poets had a ready legend for their creation: it involved a slave maiden who was being ferried across the river by a sex-starved boatman. He tried to rape her, she jumped into the water to preserve her dignity, God took pity on her and turned her into a white dolphin-goddess, while the boatman was tossed into the river and turned into a black finless porpoise which, also still found in the river today, is known in Chinese as a "Yangtze Pig." But whether Goddess or Pig, these two cetaceans are both in dire danger today—the industrial filth of the river being one reason, the invention of the cruel rolling hook trawls another.

Up until the late 1950s fishermen regarded the animals as simply too godlike to catch. If one turned up in their nets, they let it free. That was the rule, obeyed by all. But in 1958 Mao Zedong inaugurated the Great Leap Forward and declared that there were no more Heavenly Emperors and Dragon Kings: nothing was too revered for inclusion in the great maw of China's great Communist enginework. Overnight, whatever protection with which history and myth had invested the Yangtze dolphin was peremptorily stripped away. As one Hong Kong journalist put it, almost overnight "the Goddess of the Yangtze became lunch."

Catching the animals turned out to be ridiculously easy, quite literally like shooting fish in a barrel. The rolling hook trawl was invented to make it easier still: on each line were scores of eight-inch iron hooks, set two or three inches apart. This line was trawled from behind a boat like the one that now bobbing beside us. When a dolphin was snagged on one hook, it panicked, thrashed violently around and, instead of freeing itself (as might happen had there been only one hook), was promptly caught on a neighboring hook and then by more and more until it was raked with slashes and cuts and was eventually dragged from the river bleeding to death from a thousand cuts. *Baiji* meat became swiftly abundant, and was to be found in the riverside markets costing only a few cents a pound. Leather factories opened to make goods from what little unslashed *baiji* skin was salvaged. *Baiji* oil was found to have magical healing properties for people with skin problems. And as the new trade flourished, so the number of dolphins in the river dropped dramatically, a tragedy for Chinese wildlife that makes the sad saga of the giant panda seem a triumph by comparison.

Now there are said by biologists to be only 100 *baiji* left in the entire river, maybe 150. Did the fisherman feel responsible? I asked. He nodded, and he did indeed look contrite. I let him explain. "Back in the sixties we needed to eat. I took a lot of the dolphins out, and I sold them, or took the meat for my family. It didn't matter that we had once called them goddesses. We didn't care.

"But then as the years went by they became more and more difficult to find. We all"—and here he gestured to the other fishermen, who had gathered their skiffs around his and were listening to him, nodding themselves—"we all slowly realized what was happening. We knew we were wiping them out. We were killing them off, and by doing so we were helping to kill the river. And soon our attitude changed. Every time a *baiji* came out, cut to pieces by the hooks, we felt we had lost a little more. So we stopped using these rolling hooks. We went back to nets. And if we ever find a *baiji*— and I haven't seen one for six or seven years now—we throw it back. It's the rule again.

"Yangtze fishermen have good hearts, you know. We love this river. We love the fish. We love the dolphin and we revere her. But back then—back then it was very different. It was very difficult. Mao did some terrible things. We had to eat. We thought we had no choice. It was the dolphins, or it was our children. Which would you choose?"

Lily and I walked silently back up the worn old stairway. I could tell she was cross with me. A few days before, in talking to her about the well-publicized lack of fish and wildlife in China's greatest river, I had made some remarks about how it all seemed due to greed and to China's utter and contemptuous disregard for her environment. Perhaps some of this was true. But what this old fisherman had said rang true as well. It seemed something of an explanation, and a very sad one at that. Lily looked balefully at me from time to time. I made a silent vow as we tramped on upward, something to the effect that judgments about China should not be lightly made. So I mumbled an apology, and Lily grinned.

At the top of Small Jetty Street was a redbrick wall, much pitted with age. Behind it, on a small hillock, was the Zhenjiang Museum—a complex of rather ugly redbrick Victorian structures that had once been the British Consulate. Since 1861 this city had been a treaty port, a place where foreigners had been leased a concession in which to trade. The newcomers had been energetic: they built a waterworks and generating station—and, just as in Shanghai and the then Nanking and the forty-five other cities that were eventually to become treaty ports, they built clubs and courts (for both law and tennis) and established a newspaper. The quasi-western infrastructure wasn't quite enough, however, to assuage the boredom of those who lived and worked there. "I went to the silent street for a breath of air," wrote a Scandinavian called Rasmussen, who lived in Zhenjiang for many years, "and walked up and down the Bund, three hundred paces one way and three hundred paces back. To get a little change I walked up and down the only cross street to the south gate of the Concession, two hundred paces one way and two hundred paces back."

Britain, Germany, France and Austro-Hungary set up consulates in Zhenjiang. Jardines and Swires had their hulks moored in midriver, a terminal for their steamers; and Standard Oil of New York—Socony Vacuum, which was later to become Mobil Oil, and a company with formidably strong connections in Old China—had a farm of oil storage tanks. Japan put paid to most of this bustle and the relative comfort and prosperity when it captured the city in 1937; later, the Communists managed to finish it off. Few outsiders have lived in Zhenjiang since: the only foreigners I heard about while we were there were a couple of Algerians said to be working in a talcum powder factory.

Behind the consulate walls, I had been told, lay a relic that would stir the hearts of any English schoolboy of my generation. I had wanted—for many years, in fact—to see it if in fact it was there: the anchor of the famous and (so all Britons of the time had been told) heroic Royal Naval vessel HMS *Amethyst.*

I told Lily what I wanted, and suggested we might go to the museum to ask where the anchor might be found. She translated the vessel's name to herself—"*Amethyst,* how to say?"—and then suddenly snorted with mock annoyance.

"I know the ship. Of course! We call it the *Imperial Make-Trouble-Vessel,* what is the name? *Purple Stone Hero,* yes, that's it! We defeated it! All Chinese know the story. You came as pirates and we made you run! You were forced to leave a part of your precious ship behind, here in Zhenjiang. You destroyed a passenger ship on your way out. Killed many people. Yes, I had forgotten. We will find the piece you left behind here as proof. The anchor—you're right! It was a great humiliation for your *precious* British Empire."

I reeled slightly from this unexpected onslaught. Not that Lily was entirely correct. Nor entirely wrong, for that matter. The facts—or at least, the facts as presented to us as schoolchildren—had cast the whole affair in a very different light.

His Majesty's Ship *Amethyst* was a sloop-cum-frigate of 1500 tons, and in 1949—an exceptionally dangerous year, considering the vicious civil war going on between the Kuomintang and the Communists—she was assigned to a task on the Yangtze. It was nothing new for a foreign warship: for nearly a hundred years the slew of treaties that had been imposed on the war-weakened China had given a number of foreign countries—Britain, America, France and Italy among them—certain rights on the river. They were allowed to steam their gunboats and corvettes and destroyers and frigates along every navigable mile of the river—the 1600 miles between the red buoy at Woosung and the rapids at Pingshan in Sichuan—and with all guns locked and loaded, for the purposes of protecting their own trade, their own interests and their own citizens.

By today's standards it was a bizarre arrangement—as outlandish and unimaginable as, say, letting Japanese warships patrol today's Mississippi to protect a Honda plant in Hannibal, or allowing Chinese gunboats to sidle among the punts on the Isis to look out for the interests of Beijing students up at Oxford University. But in the late nineteenth century the Chinese were too debilitated and powerless to prevent such high-handedness. It was an arrangement that had gone hand in hand with the similarly bizarre concept of extraterritoriality—by which foreign citizens in the concession areas of China's treaty ports could be judged only by their own courts, and not be subject to Chinese law. The concept, which became shortened to the word "extrality," is something the sheer strangeness of which should not be forgotten. It led, among other things, to the creation of the Yangtze Patrol of the United States Navy and the Royal Navy's equally famous Yangtze Flotilla—to which, in the spring of 1949, HMS *Amethyst* was temporarily assigned.

In that year the Chinese capital was the city of Nanjing, known then as Nanking: it lies on the south side of the Yangtze a few miles above Zhenjiang, and was indeed to be our next upriver destination. All the major foreign countries that had postwar diplomatic relations with China maintained embassies in Nanjing: the Americans did, and so did the British. As China's capital the city was naturally a prime target for capture by the Communists. In March 1949 the Foreign Office in London sensed that with the recent stunning successes of General Zhu De's People's Liberation Army, matters were deteriorating rapidly. To help raise the morale of the British, and indeed all the rest of the local foreign community, and to prepare for a possible evacuation, a warship was needed: an urgent signal was sent to Hong Kong, and in return the Navy's Commander in Chief Far East Station sent the *Amethyst*.

The little ship passed the red buoy at Woosung on April 19, 1949, and on the next day approached the section of the river where the Communists were known to be massing. Her captain ordered up precautions: large Union Jacks were to be draped over the ship's side, the guns were to be armed and trained, speed was to be increased to sixteen knots. The ship was officially neutral, and should not attract any hostile fire. But this was China, a country in an unpredictable mood. As she passed Low Island, near the end of a long north-south reach in the river, there was a sudden crackle of rifle fire from the shore. The captain ordered his gunners to train and aim. Then rifle fire was followed, more ominously, by the zoom and whine of shell fire as a shore battery opened up. Huge splashes of water erupted off the starboard beam. Fifteen rounds were fired—none hit the British ship. On the bridge the officers made caustic remarks about poor Communist marksmanship. As *Amethyst* rounded the bend and began to head due west along the river's muddy, duck-filled Kou-an Reach, the final leg on the way to Zhenjiang, so the order was piped: "Hands relax action stations." The danger, it was thought, was over.

The sun was rising into a cloudless midmorning sky as the ship drew abreast of Rose Island. She was now at reduced speed, her guns trained fore and aft. No one aboard suspected a thing—when suddenly, without any warning, without any cries or flags or bugle blow, a shell flashed across the ship's topmast. The captain ordered "Action stations" once more, and demanded speed. The telegraphs clanged urgently, the motors began to roar. And then, in an instant, the Communists found their aim. Three shells slammed into the ship and exploded: one hit the wheelhouse, turning it into a maelstrom of splintered steel and wood and trapping the coxswain against the wheel, pulling it—and the ship—hard over to port.

The wounded vessel was now racing directly toward the thick mud of Rose Island. The captain ordered "Hard a-starboard," trying desperately to correct the course and prevent his ship's running aground. At the same time he ordered his guns to open fire. But almost at the very same instant two more shells hit the ship: the bridge detonated in a ball of fire, and everyone in or near it was killed or terribly wounded. The captain was mortally injured, and would live on for two agonizing days. The Chinese pilot had the back of his head blown off, killed instantly. Another man was blinded when a shell fragment took his entire eye out. The ship's Number One took a piece of shrapnel the size of a matchbox: it tore through his lungs and lodged in his liver. This man, Weston, though bleeding heavily and barely able to speak, took command: he had to watch in impotent horror as the ship slid steadily into the mudflats and then stopped, dead, stuck fast, right in the gun sights of the Communist batteries. He managed to croak one urgent Flash signal to the commander in chief in Hong Kong: "Under heavy fire. Am aground in approx. position 31 degrees 10 minutes North 119 degrees 50 minutes East. Large number of casualties."*

General Zhu's men showed no mercy. Shell after shell tore into the ship, and within minutes the deck was an inferno, littered with dead and wounded men. The ship's power was cut, the radio was out, the sick bay suffered a direct hit, the aft gun turret was ruined, the depth-charge store was penetrated by an armor-piercing shell and *Amethyst*'s TNT went up in a roar. Injured men lay untended among the flames, and if not burned by the fires they were hit by splinters from new shell bursts. For more than an hour the ship shuddered and shook under the barrage: Weston gave the order to evacuate—though not totally abandon—the vessel. A steaming party was to be left on board, as were volunteers to help tend the wounded. The rest swam or took life rafts to shore—under withering hail of machine-gun fire, which killed further numbers of the terrified men. Those who made it set themselves up in the underbrush, watched and waited. The plan was to reboard the ship at nightfall, repair her, refloat her and get away. The Communists stopped shelling shortly before noon, and the river fell quiet.

The *Amethyst* remained where she was, critically wounded, immobilized and impotent, for the next 101 days—a neutral ship held hostage to a foreign revolution's fortune, a symbol of the unfamiliar new demands of what was being called the Cold War.† Everyone in Britain knew about her: just as with the American hostages who were held in postrevolutionary Iran some thirty years later, this was a drama that enthralled the nation. Not a day passed without the broadcast of some scrap of information on the helpless ship. Not a Briton lived who did not care about the trapped vessel and her helpless crew.

As it turned out, however, neither the ship nor the crew turned out

---

* His position was wrong by about seventy-five miles. But he can hardly be blamed: his charts were torn to pieces and soaked in officers' blood.
† So named by George Orwell, only four years before.

quite as helpless as was thought. Slowly but eventually, the engines were repaired, as was her steering mechanism. And when everyone involved realized that negotiations with the Communists were going nowhere, it was decided, during the unbearable heat of the last days of that July, that the ship would try to escape. She would try to make her way downriver under the cover of darkness, and to break out from under the very gun sights of Zhu De's batteries.

All manner of precautions were taken for the run. Mattresses and awnings and hammocks were arranged along the ship's sides to make her look as different as possible from usual. She rearranged her lights, showing green over red, masquerading as a civilian vessel, a merchantman. The crew were told that talking above a whisper was forbidden; smoking was banned; no one could use the intercom, certainly not the radio. To preserve the silence that was vitally necessary for the break-out moment it was decided that the anchor could not be raised in the normal way—the chain's rattling passage up the hawse pipe would make a din certain to awaken every Communist battery from Zhenjiang to Shanghai. Instead it was decided to knock the pin from one of the half-shackles that held together the lengths of anchor chain, and to let the chain fall into the water—vertically, with thick grease on all and any of the ship's surfaces that it might touch. This, it was said, was the anchor I might see behind the old consulate's red-brick wall.

At 10 P.M. on the hot and moonless night of Saturday, July 30, the bosun knocked out the pin on the anchor chain, the ship gunned her engines and steamed out into the night. Twenty miles downriver she was spotted, gunfire rang out, and she was hit—though not badly. Someone sent a signal to the C-M-C in Hong Kong. The admiral was hosting a dinner party, and a toast was drunk—"To HMS *Amethyst* and all who sail in her."

More signals came in to headquarters during the night. "Halfway," said one. "Hundred up," another (a cricketing term, to which the admiral replied with the same metaphor: "A magnificent century!"). A junk unexpectedly crossed into the path of the fleeing and unlit ship: the bridge officers waited, sickened, for the awful crunch of smashed wood and the cries of drowning fishermen. There was nothing they could have done. Many must have died. But the *Amethyst* could not afford to stop. It raced on, now doing an unheard-of twenty-two knots.

At dawn they passed under the searchlights of Woosung Fort, where another Communist battery stood on the right bank, just where the Whangpoo entered the Yangtze. The searchlights briefly glanced off the hull—everyone on board holding his breath—and then moved on. *Amethyst* kept roaring onward: "Everything you've got!" the bridge telegraphed down to the engine room. "Damage to engines accepted."

And then finally, there in the dim light of morning, and resting under a plume of smoke on the wide gray waters of the outer Yangtze estuary, the spotters on the bow of *Amethyst* saw the familiar outline of her sister ship, the destroyer HMS *Concord*. The signal was flashed by Aldis lamp: "Fancy meeting you again." It was now beyond doubt that HMS *Amethyst*—after 101 days in captivity, and with 23 of her crew dead and 31 missing—had at long last broken free.

No one is quite sure how the Chinese in Zhenjiang reacted to the escape. It is said that divers were sent down and located the anchor—still attached to its several tons of chain—and pulled it from the river. They paraded it around town as a spoil of battle, a trophy that their men had wrested bravely from a fleeing imperial coward. How many of the locals accepted the story is anyone's guess; but it was not to be too much longer before the city of Zhenjiang had been swept clear of all its foreign residents, and the old British Consulate had turned into a revolutionary museum: it is said the Communists dumped the relic there, in the gardens. Some guidebooks mention it: but when I asked—and when Lily asked—no one could be sure either what it was, or where it was.

(It is a most baffling habit of most Chinese—this mute insistence that *they do not know where anything is*. You ask an ancient who has lived all of his long life in Zhenjiang, Where is the old British Consulate?, as I did—and he will shake his head, wave you away with his hand, professing no clue, having no interest. Asking for the anchor itself produced still more puzzled refusal. No, never heard of it. *Purple Stone Hero?* Not anywhere here. *Doesn't ring a bell with me, old man.*)

I handed over one *yuan* to a woman behind the museum gate's guichet, and inquired whether the anchor might be inside. No, she said, definitely not. There is no such thing as an anchor anywhere here. The cadre standing inside the gate said much the same: there were plenty of Song dynasty pots and pans, but no anchor from a barbarian war vessel. "You have wasted your time," he said, and laughed bitterly.

Just then a young Chinese woman came down the stairs. She had been reading a novel—the museum had few visitors—and was chewing on a sweet called Sugared Cow Skin. She offered me one. She smiled warmly.

"I heard there was an anchor here. But it is buried in grass, I think. Besides, they are doing some demolition work. Come with me."

And we followed her up a hillock, through one of the archways, past a flight of stone steps that must have once seen processions of clerks and second secretaries and consuls bearing the intelligences of the world from one empire to another. We came out onto a newly flattened area of wrecked brickwork, where one of the seven buildings had recently been flattened. Behind it was a small slope, covered with jungle. The girl pointed to it.

"There, I think. Use a knife, if you have one," she cried, and went off, back to her novel and her bag of Sugared Cow Skins.

Thick laurel bushes had infested the hillside, and the branches slashed at my legs as I waded through to the edge of the cliff. And there, burdened by growth but unmistakably nautical, was the anchor—four feet tall, its shank covered in some kind of cracked poultice, its ring solid, a half-shackle with a pin hanging loosely from it. The anchor's crown was firmly cemented to the ground, and the flukes rose sharp and spadelike into the surrounding bushes. It looked half a century old—but it had been built well, and it was neither rusty nor broken. The Admiralty commissioned its iron to last.

A small notice, half illegible from dirt and growth, was mounted in front. I rubbed away the grime, and read: this was the anchor from the foreign imperial war vessel *Purple Stone Hero,* "captured in the seventh month of 1949 by heroic members of the People's Liberation Army after the ship had made a cowardly run away down the Long River to the sea."

But was it? Since coming back, and poring over the pictures, I have begun to wonder. I have started to have doubts.

The anchor in Zhenjiang is a much smaller device than that normally used to hold a warship. Its design is that of a fisherman's anchor, made specifically to hold a little craft. It is most certainly not the standard Admiralty Pattern Stockless Anchor, with which pictures show *Amethyst*'s bows to have been equipped. My guess is that the Chinese have actually duped us, and themselves—not, one might say, for the first time. What stands among the undergrowth in Zhenjiang may well actually be another anchor, perhaps from one of the vessel's whalers—perhaps, indeed, a British anchor, and so a symbol of the treachery. But my guess is that the real half ton of iron, together with all its chains—that which was so silently slipped on the night of the getaway—remains buried in the Yangtze mud, even today. It might have been a good idea to raise it, but it was in all likelihood far too heavy and far too sunk for even the bitterest Chinese to try to recover it and put it on show. A lesser substitute had to do.

I imagined it might be tempting to cross the river and make a pilgrimage to Yangzhou, where there are temples and gardens, and supposedly the most beautiful women in China. So I went over on the chugging car ferry, and found as I had rather anticipated that it was filled with tourists and their buses; but when I saw two noble Mongolian camels locked up in a paddock for the benefit of sightseers, and that their keeper had left them so ragged and hungry that their humps had withered and fallen across their sides like empty shopping bags, I stormed off and went looking for the Grand Canal instead.

But that too turned out to be an infinitely depressing thing. It may be long (1554 miles) and ancient (fully 2500 years, if one accepts that the first of its links was built in the fifth century B.C.). It may be noble and wondrous, a triumph of Tang dynasty engineering and perseverance, and a celebration of the technology of earlier times as well.* But it is now filthy dirty, its congestion makes it irredeemably ugly, it is choked with rubbish and human leavings, and it is so industrialized as to have any hint of romance hammer-pressed out of it. What remains of it, even in a supposedly picturesque place like Yangzhou, seems so ruined and broken as to be barely a canal; and it is certainly, for all of its miles, anything but grand. Canals are in general fascinating memorials to commerce and civil engineering: it is a shame indeed that this, the greatest of them all, has fallen so very far from grace.

It was in part because I found both the camels and the canal so depressing that I decided to leave Yangzhou to its infestation of tourists. Back on the muddy flats of the riverbank I found a junk whose owner was willing to sail us back across the river for a few *jiao,* and within half an hour of bumping over the grayish waves Lily and I were happily back on the wet stone steps of the Zhenjiang dock. There was a sudden shout of recognition: it was the fisherman who had been showing us his collection of rolling hooks earlier in the day. He had been working all day mending a net, and since he looked cold and tired I suggested that he come and have a bottle of beer at a local bar. He puffed on his bamboo pipe, and showed Lily how to do the same. We ended up the best of temporary friends, and he gave me the name of a friend he said I should look up in Nanjing: it was another fisherman, just in case I wanted more stories about dolphins.

There was one small pilgrimage I had to make before I left Zhenjiang. At the turn of the century Mr. and Mrs. Absalom Sydenstricker,

---

* At one time the project's overseer was a peculiarly cruel man named Ma Shumou, better known as Mahu, the Barbarous One. He was said to have eaten a steamed two-year-old child each day he worked on the Canal—and to this day naughty children are warned by their mothers to behave, "or else Mahu will get you!"

Presbyterian missionaries from West Virginia, had brought up a child there, a child who later studied in Shanghai and Lynchburg, Virginia, and went on to write novels under the name John Hedges.

But John was in fact a girl-child, named Pearl, who later married another missionary named John Buck; and it was under the name Pearl S. Buck that she wrote most famously, and under which name she won the Nobel Prize for Literature in 1938. The woman who wrote *The Good Earth,* the creator of Wang Lung and his slave-wife and their rise and fall through the vicissitudes of famine and locusts and war and concubinage, lived for fifteen formative years in a house in Zhenjiang. It is now a radio factory, and since Pearl Buck has been restored to a tepid kind of official favor—she was officially prevented from coming to China in 1972—it stands open to the public, occasionally.

No one knew where it was, naturally. I approached a dozen people and gave them Pearl Buck's Chinese name, or the Chinese title of her best-known book, and I still I got blank looks on all sides—a reflection, no doubt, of my lamentable pronunciation. Lily then asked where the Zhenjiang Number One Radio Factory was, got directions in an instant, and we walked up another cobbled street to where it sat on a hilltop—and beside the plant itself was a small two-story house behind a high barbed-wire fence: The Home of Pearl S. Buck, said a wooden plaque, Winner of the Nobel Prize for Literature.

The house was shut, naturally. But a woman lived there, and through the wire I managed to persuade her to open both the gate and the front door to the house. "But"—she spluttered, and I knew what was coming next—"her private rooms are locked and"—and both Lily and I joined in the mantra chorus that inevitably followed, as burp follows noodles—"*the man with the key is not here.*"

So I used my Citibank card, which had previously been so useful in Shanghai for showing me my balance on the Bund. I twisted and turned it in the lock, and within twenty seconds was in the lady's bedroom. Pearl Buck slept hard, on a plain mahogany bed, and she kept her clothes in a plain mahogany cupboard. Everything about her part of the house, indeed, was plain and unadorned, with a Shakerite austerity. But then there was a room devoted to, of all places, Tempe, Arizona, with which Zhenjiang has lately become affiliated, as a sister city. So there was a Kachina doll, a basketball signed by some of Tempe's tallest, and countless photographs of Tempe worthies shaking hands with smiling officials from Zhenjiang while paying homage, as I did, to the city's best-known daughter. There was no connection at all between Miss Buck and the city of Tempe: but the Chinese, still officially irritated at the writer for her implacable anticommunism, seemingly thought it quite reasonable to herd all western tributaries, whether they came from Arizona or the Appalachians, into the same building. Some say that the house was actually never the Sydenstrickers' at all, and that the authorities are playing a joke on Pearl Buck's memory, on the Arizonans and on us today. To the Chinese, it must not be forgotten, we are all alike, and can well afford to be the butt of their little amusements.

I pulled her bedroom door behind me until it locked, gave the old woman five *yuan* to compensate for her initial shock at and later complicity with my housebreaking, and walked away from the radio factory, Pearl Buck's home or not. I flagged down a taxi, piled in our bags and asked him to take us to Nanjing.

It turned out to be a slightly eccentric journey, though nothing particularly unusual for the adventurous universe in which Chinese taxicabs like to operate. In this case the man offered to give us the ride to Nanjing at half price if we in return would agree to let him cross the Yangtze once again to pick up one of his relations, an elderly man who lived on the outskirts of Yangzhou. This meant we would have to board the car ferry one more time, and that we would have to approach Nanjing by driving on the river's north shore, not the south. But all this seemed of little moment, and I readily agreed. The driver was very happy. I rather liked the little car ferry, anyway, and I stood happily in a thin evening drizzle, watching the lights of Zhenjiang prick on in the gathering gloom.

It seemed that I was drawing away from the city and from one very small enigma—the minor mystery of what exactly was the long forgotten piece of Royal Naval hardware that lay behind the bushes in the consulate garden. Later that night, once I had taken a long hot shower in the hotel in Nanjing, I found with some gratitude that I was leaving behind something else: the pervasive sharp-sour smell of the medal-winning, first-class, internationally renowned and copiously produced Zhenjiang Brown Rice Vinegar.

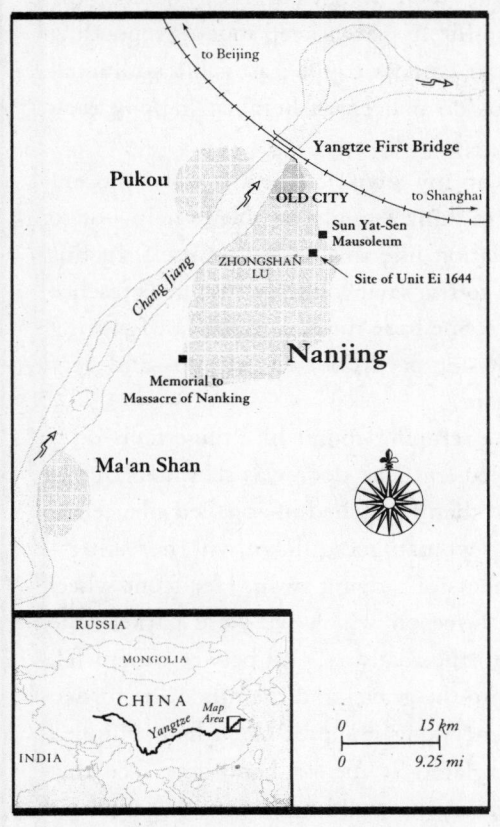

5

City of
Victims

On the outskirts of Nanjing I knocked a young woman off her bicycle.
She was wearing a long white linen skirt and she fell with the slow
grace of a ballerina, managing perfectly to preserve her dignity. It
was all, without a doubt, my fault.

Moments before our driver had been pulled over by the police.
The routine that ensued was to become a familiar one: an officer
with a flag leaps from behind a bush, waves us to a halt, mentions
some alleged infraction; the driver is persuaded to cross the road and
discuss matters with a group of well-fed-looking colleague-officers,
a not insubstantial sum in folding money changes hands, the first
policeman is told to return the license, drop his red flag and

let us proceed, whereupon he then wedges himself behind the bush once again. Thus does traffic in China keep moving smoothly; thus does the small corps of car owners pay a reasonable additional tax for the privilege; and thus do policemen lie abed happily each night.

During these early days of my own journey I was innocent enough and arrogant enough to think I might be able to help—or to object or argue—when a situation like this presented itself. In this instance, Lily warned me not to try, saying sternly that my presence would only complicate matters. She bade me stay in the car. Ignoring her advice I opened the right-side back door to get out—and very nearly killed the young woman.

There was a sudden cry, a scraping sound like fingernails on a blackboard, and a sickening crunch. The door was slammed rudely and forcefully back on me and then I watched in appalled silence the slow-motion image of a young woman going down with her skittering bicycle, like the last moments of a dying swan. Her front wheel headed downward from the levee on which we were parked, the other wheel swerved back into the roadway, and between them fell the woman, sinking slowly onto the gravel and the mud. She turned her head around fast so that her long mane of black hair whipped around behind her, and she glared at me—a handsome face that looked at once perplexed that anyone could not know that Chinese cyclists rode close to cars and that is how it was and always had been and how foolish of anyone to open a door without looking, and angry that she was about to be hurt, perhaps, and also that in front of a carful of strangers she was going to fall over and tumble and show her legs and worse, and lose her dignity and face and the elegant comeliness with which she evidently tried to ride her bicycle every day.

Gravity did its powerful work, and I thought the woman would steadily and inevitably succumb. But instead she fought for all she was worth, and as she fell so her legs twisted this way and that, and her arms did the same, and she stared ahead and around with such concentration that, by the kind of miracle no foreigner could ever manage, she did eventually stop the great black confection of iron and rubber that I recognized as a Flying Pigeon brand bicycle from falling anymore, and she managed to halt its forward progress and its downward progress and its tipping and skidding as well, and she managed to stop herself falling too—she just sank, caught her balance and her breath and her dignity, and stopped, in a crumpled mass of white linen, lying between two upright wheels and in a cloud of dust.

With a sudden weary sag of her shoulders she remounted the saddle, looked back at me in silent fury once more, straightened her wheels, shook her head in defiance of that gravity and momentum and the baleful influence of the foreigner who had initiated all this, and shakily, nervously, bumpily and then with ever growing confidence she resumed her ride, joining in with the uncaring rows of other cyclists and merging among them, anonymous and dignified once again. She gave me one last look—a beautiful face framed by a marvel of hair, her white blouse slightly off one shoulder but still crisp and fresh, her long white skirt a little crumpled and with a small smudge of dust down one side. She looked glorious, I thought, newly arisen from what could have been the wreckage of her day, and riding serenely off into the afternoon sun.

Rising from wreckage of one kind and another has been a perennial occupation for the city of Nanjing. Very few places in China have soared and plummeted with such fantastic and tragic recklessness. The city was the glorious capital of some dynasties, and then remaindered as a dusty and provincial backwater for others. There was, as in many Chinese cities of long history, at least one of those tragedies that scholars later term an "incident": this came in 1927, when Nationalist troops killed seven foreigners, and a force of foreign gunboats sent to retaliate shelled and killed twice as many Chinese. But there had been more terrible tragedies too: during late Qing times, for example—for the eleven years between March 1853 and July 1864—the city became the headquarters of a notorious sect of power-hungry fanatics, the Taipings, whose resistance was eventually destroyed (along with most of the city) after a siege partly staged by a foreign-led mercenary army, and whose leader was driven to suicide (it is said) by swallowing gold.* This most traumatic of events was sandwiched between two other humiliations: ten years before the arrival of the Taiping rebels, the city had been forced to bow low before one group of barbarians, the British; and seventy years after the Taipings, Nanjing became an epicenter of mayhem and cruelty at the hands of another group, the Japanese.

It is a city that, more than almost any other in China, has fully deserved the doleful and all-too-common description that you will read in all Chinese history books, a sentence that appears in one guise or other, referring to some such place in some such time at the hands of some such madness: *its population was greatly reduced, its trade destroyed, and many of its beautiful, historic buildings and part of its walls, reduced to ruins.* Nanjing has had, in other words, a horribly checkered past.

And yet on the surface you would never know it. Her present is blandly prosperous. Her image is relentlessly upbeat. It seems as though under the Communists the city of Nanjing has been urged, cajoled, *made* to rise from all that has gone before. Perhaps because of her past glories she has had money spent on her, she has come in for the caring attention of the central government, and has been persuaded to shake herself free of the more wretched side of her history. And she has gone along with the country's perceived wishes: she has washed off the dust and grime and, even if she is slightly crumpled from all of her trials, she looks well enough now, and quite presentable. Which is what the country seems to want for its most shabbily treated town.

---

* The Taiping Rebellion, led by a man named Hong Xiuquan who believed himself the younger brother of Jesus Christ, is thought today to have been the most destructive war of all time: twenty million people are said to have died during its fourteen years. Frederick Townsend Ward, an American, and Charles "Chinese" Gordon, a Briton who later died a hero in Khartoum, led the Chinese Ever-Victorious Army in successfully defending Shanghai from the Taiping onslaught.

For whenever I told a Chinese that I was planning to go up the Yangtze and stop awhile at Nanjing, they would invariably say what they would never say if I admitted I was off to somewhere more pedestrian, like Harbin or Changsha or Canton: "Oh, really? Nanjing! How nice! How lucky you are!" one man said. "Lovely city!" said another. One elderly man in New York became dreamy eyed and hinted at romance, muttering a nostalgic formula: "The flower boats! Taking your ease under the shade of a weeping willow, listening to a pretty little singsong girl . . . ah, that was the life. . . . What a fine, fine place!" This old man knew what had happened to the city through the years; but he seemed to be caught up like everyone else in the earnestness with which the rest of China seems to be trying to reinvent Nanjing. "One of the most interesting cities in our country—truly," said Lily. "All of us are very proud of Nanjing—of the way her people have risen above all their sufferings."

That evening as we drove in from Yangzhou—having passed the still angry cyclist—the first view was the one that seemed most apt, a panorama that showed off Nanjing's newness and her determined effort to be modern. We crossed the river not by ferry, as we had been forced to do at Zhenjiang, but on a vast bridge—the bridge that is closest to the river mouth, and one of the longest, heaviest, ugliest, most graceless triumphs of engineering built to cross a river anywhere in the world. It has a magnificence to it, though: it is solid and imperturbable looking, lined with ranks of the five-bulbed egg-lamps that have been a ubiquitous feature of the Chinese landscape since 1949—and which were probably made in the first factory in the first Chinese soviet ever created. The bridge has four buff concrete towers, two at each end, with triple-flamed beacons on top; and on the landward side of each of these, two collections of heroic statues, one in memory of those who built the bridge, the other in honor of all of those who harbor socialist sympathies around the world.

Until I read the inscription I was rather puzzled by this second statue. It seemed a little odd to have the entrance to Nanjing memorialized by a very white cement statue of a group of people led by an obviously very black man. He was looking joyous and defiant and—

given the hearty (although heartily denied) Chinese dislike for their black brethren—very irrelevant. Or certainly discordant. There was a woman running a food stall on the other side of the road: I asked her what she thought.

"Of what?" she grunted. "That statue? Wonderful, I think." But what, I pressed, of having a black man leading the group? She squinted up at it, disbelief written over her face.

"Black? Black? My word—yes! I suppose he is. Would you believe I never noticed. Working on this very spot night and day for the last eight years. Eight years! I know those statues like my own bed. It never occurred to me that man might be black. Of course I can see he is now. He couldn't be anything else."

And she wrinkled her nose, as if there was a nasty smell in the air. Which, this being Nanjing—producer of lead, zinc, dolomite, iron, televisions, cars, clocks, watches and, to judge from the huge flames I could see gushing up from refinery towers all around, petroleum products in abundance—there probably was. Time was when Nanjing was the world's great producer of a soft silk called pongee: this, not an industry known for its smell, has now all but vanished.

Building the bridge had been extraordinarily difficult. The Yangtze is for most of its length an almost impossible river for an engineer to deal with—it is very fast, very deep, it is given to eccentric turbulences and cruel unpredictability, and it rises and falls to a degree that most bridge foundations would find fatally punishing. In Nanjing, the range of water levels is particularly complicated, for not only is the river narrow enough for the outflow to vary hugely with the seasons, but it is also close enough to the sea for the effects of tides to be noticed still. (They say you can feel these effects as far away as Datong, a full 350 miles upstream, though the ocean's practical effects on shipping are of no real importance above Wuhu, 289 miles from the ocean. And it is here at Nanjing, 50 miles below Wuhu, where the river is said to start being properly tidal.)

The Yangtze at Nanjing is on average eighteen feet higher in July than it is in January; and at high tide it is nearly four feet higher than that—so the buttresses and columns designed to support the

20,000-foot-long, twin-deck, four-lane-roadway-above-two-track-railway* bridge have to withstand the river's current, the sea's tides, the estuary's bores and a range in water height that is unknown on any river elsewhere on the planet.

The problem was first approached in 1958, when the Chinese realized that they must end the nonsense and delay of having to use ferryboats to get their railway passengers and freight across the great river. The Russians, masters of river bridging at the time, were asked for advice, and then assistance—they eventually agreed to provide a design, as well as technical help and the right kind of steel. But shortly thereafter political relations with Moscow went into a tailspin and their engineers were hauled back home—insisting anyway that no bridge could be constructed over so wide and wayward a river for at least another three hundred miles upstream.

They hadn't realized just who they were talking to. The China of the late 1950s was a country intoxicated with the madness of her Great Leap Forward, a people suffused with a barely rational pride and determination, and a nation whose technical institutes were filled with engineers who insisted they could manage the building of this bridge, however difficult, quite alone. It took them eight years, and it required the total reorganization of the Chinese steel industry to provide the necessary bars and girders. But they did it. At the end of 1968, when the whole world was in the midst of revolutionary ferment and when China was starting her own, the Yangtze First Bridge was formally and proudly opened. The Chinese way, it must have seemed back then, was capable of achieving almost anything: the bridge may be ugly and graceless, but it works, and thus far it has shown few signs that it is about to fall down.

---

* It is possible, through judicious use of skeleton keys or a credit card, to open the locked steel door that leads from a staircase in one of the bridge towers, out onto the forbidden railway deck. There can be few more unforgettable sights of raw industrial majesty than this—an endlessly vanishing abyss of iron latticework, the thundering of the trucks speeding overhead, the roaring of the swirling waters streaming by below, and then an express train, its headlights burning brilliantly, rushing toward you at full tilt.

I had the address of one man in Nanjing, an Italian who worked for a truck-assembly joint venture and who had lived in the same hotel—in fact the same hotel room—for the previous eight years. I telephoned him. *Come immediately, prontissimo!* he demanded, and he gave me the address of the Jinling Hotel, thirty-six storeys, locally owned and, by all standards, a five-star establishment. It was in the center of town, at the junction of four avenues each named Zhong Shan (North, South and so on), in honor of Sun Yat-sen.

Every town in China has something—a main street, a boulevard, an esplanade, a mighty building, a bund—that is named after Sun Yat-sen: Zhong Shan is the Mandarin rendering of a name that is essentially romanized Cantonese—the Christian, Western-educated Father of Modern China having been, in an irony that most Chinese would prefer to forget, a Southerner. For Nanjing to have four streets named after the great man is no surprise: it was in this city that he set up his first capital, and it is on the outskirts of this city that, after his death in 1925 at only fifty-nine, he was buried. The mausoleum, tricked out in pale blue tile, is probably the city's principal place of pilgrimage—a place of respectful comfort for the mainlanders, though for the more raucous Taiwanese who visit it has recently become a kind of Oriental Graceland, a shrine to another fallen king, and every bit as vulgar, with its souvenir stalls and hawkers, as the shrine in Tennessee.

Giancarlo was standing alone in the Jinling's vast marble lobby when we arrived. He was a tall Turinese in his early sixties, with gray hair like wire wool, big teeth discolored by years of smoking strong Craven "A" cigarettes and a nose as big as a small rodent. He wore a loudly checked sport jacket and a yellow cravat. He had the booming and eternally genial voice of an expatriate who was happy tonight because, for one marginally less tedious evening than most, he was about to meet a fellow wanderer, someone who might know the name of his country's latest prime minister or some news from the FIFA Cup or the Tour de France, and who might join him later for an espresso or a glass of grappa—of which, he added, he had ample supplies in his room.

" 'Ow are you, Meester Simmon?" he boomed from twenty paces. "I 'ave cheap room for you. I also 'ave deener, which I, Giancarlo, will cook for you. You come now, please, immediate, immediate. You will drop your bags 'ere. Giancarlo will look after everything. You will 'ave wonderful time, yes?"

Eight years in the same hotel room in China can do strange things to a man. Giancarlo Barolo had clearly gone a little mad: after years in which his natural Piedmontese exuberance had been dismissed as eccentricity and had struck few sparks in either the hotel or his office, he decided to go for broke, to play his role as caricature. So he now swept waitresses off their feet and planted blizzards of tiny kisses on their cheeks, he rushed wildly into kitchens throwing startled Chinese chefs away from their woks and commandeering the stoves himself, he complained loudly about wines and demanded his own, he sat down with startled lone foreign businessmen to enjoy, if briefly, their company, he made endlessly long telephone calls to distant half-forgotten friends around the world, and each night at nine—this night being no different—he retired to his double room, which is furnished with a few paintings and carpets, and listened to Verdi and Rossini, and tried to forget.

Before I met him on this journey, it had never been entirely clear why he had stayed for so long. He does not speak Chinese, nor does he like China very much. He has no particular loyalty to the truck-making firm he works for, nor has he ambitions for the factory his eight years here have helped create. He loathes banquets, speeches, local food: he has had one marriage and two failed love affairs, and he doubts if he will have another.

Night after night we watched him do his routine—frightening waitresses, dismissing chefs, summoning managers, retching after tasting the local wines—except after sipping one particular Chinese red wine, a merlot, which he claimed was as good as any of the younger Antinoris. We usually said good night to him, exhausted by the performance, no later than nine each night. Behind the bluster and the braggadocio was loneliness, of course: what secret back home had compelled this man to bury himself in the wilds of central

China? Who knows, any more than they knew what had really compelled celebrated westerners like the forger-scholar Edmund Backhouse to become a recluse in Beijing, or the botanist Joseph Rock to go on his ceaseless explorations in Yunnan, or the Good Man in Africa to stay for so long and so good in Africa and to choose the expatriate life with its constant frisson of solitary danger? Giancarlo seemed a picture of sadness blanketed in an enigma, but nonetheless living under the guise of being a character, a good chap, *knows the scene old boy, knows simply everyone.* He was being laughed at, and knew it, and yet was unable, despite his good humor, to laugh back.

But he had a certain wisdom, and he knew Nanjing well, which is why I had sought him out. The bluster irritated me: I wanted him to be serious for a moment. He obliged one evening before dinner, when we were alone. We talked about Shanghai, a city he disliked with a passion. I said how it seemed to me unique in being a city that didn't have any real history, that it was a city without roots of any substance, except for those few years when it was a fishing village and the brief period when it was inhabited by noisy and truculent foreigners.

"This is very different, you know," he replied. "Here is nothing else but history, you know," he said. "Nanjing is a little like your Irish city, Belfast is it? Looks new on the surface—all this *gleeter,* like this hotel, the shops, the pretty girls. It looks like Hong Kong, yes? But below is very different, you can feel it when you stay here long. The people here are all trapped by their city's past. And very bad past it has had. Sadder than most places. The people here look as if they have forgotten, but in fact they never can. They are very old-fashioned people. Very conservative. So very different from Shanghai.

"You say you are going up the Yangtze and seeing if you can go backward in time? Well, coming here you have stepped back a hundred years. At least. Maybe getting on for four hundred years, back to the end of the Ming. It may not look like it. But you have. Like a living museum, Nanjing. This is why I don't like it—and at the same time it is perhaps why I do like it too. Italy is much the same in some ways. Great cities are often trapped by their past—particularly when it is a past filled with tragedy. I find that not good, and yet very good.

It makes the people keep their feet on the ground. Shanghai—I spit at it! Hateful place! Here—well, there is something I like, just a bit."

And that was as near as he came to offering an explanation. Lily came in just then, and the moment was gone. Giancarlo winked at me, stood up and kissed her noisily, and began his routine. He bellowed at the waiter: "This garbage, you are calling it chicken? I, Giancarlo, will come cook something good for my friends. They will not eat this rubbish food. So you please, most kind, get out of my way, *prontissimo*!"

I had come to Nanjing armed with an old Japanese guidebook, and I had done so very much on purpose.

Not long after Karl Baedeker and John Murray had uncovered the delights of Europe and published them in pocket-sized compendiums in Leipzig and London, so a Japanese nobleman, Baron Gotō—and for far less amiable reasons—began to do much the same for Asia, in Tokyo. By today's standards Gotō was not a very laudable figure: he was a keen believer in Japan's right to expand and to rule the lesser peoples of Asia, he had been a fairly brutal civil administrator of Formosa during her early years as a Japanese colony, and he had come to China to run the South Manchurian Railway. But his colonial attitudes aside (and what Briton can decry colonial attitudes?), he did inspire editors and writers to produce excellent guidebooks. The small red volumes published between 1908 and 1920 under the colophon of the Imperial Japanese Government Railways remain masterly.

Not, however, just as guides. Certainly, on one level the books offer hugely detailed, highly accurate, prettily designed and compact *tours d'horizon*—they remain undeniably useful, even nearly a century on. But they also offer, unwittingly—and this is why I had decided to stuff them into my rucksack back in New York—an unexpected window on the Japanese mind, a revealing look at the way that Japan then regarded her neighbor states across the sea. Each of the books deals in detail with peoples (Koreans, Manchurians, Formosans and, most particularly, the Chinese) whom the Japanese considered then, and perhaps still consider today, to be amusing, colorful, interesting—but grossly inferior. Given time, Japanese readers of these volumes must have thought, each would be right for the plucking.

I had with me Volume IV. Its chapter on Nanjing can be seen, in hindsight, as offering the first lip-smacking, appetite-whetting accounts of a city that the Japanese were soon to brutalize like few others, anywhere. Baron Gotō's tidy little book must have seemed to the sterner souls in the Japanese army rather like a menu card in a fancy Roppongi restaurant: oh come ye sons of Nippon, some might have heard its siren call, and feast yourselves on this! Beneath the come-hither of it all, a sneering tone is audible, if faintly.

> *Encircled by these cyclopean walls, the city has been planned on a most magnificent scale, no unworthy capital of a great empire. . . . Before the coming of the Taiping rebels there existed tolerably good roads and drainage. . . . The Taipings made dreadful havoc everywhere and scarcely anything had been done by way of repairs, until the recent introduction of the new regime . . . which is now making roads and repairing the drainage, burning up all the garbage and filth. Carp and mandarin-fish are caught in the Yangtze-kiang, and are of a very fine flavour. The Flower Boats in the Chin-hwai-ho contain chairs, tables and quilts, food and liquor as well as singing girls. . . . There is a club, the Hwa-Ying, established by the Japanese and Chinese together.*

Such was the beguiling image of Nanjing—pools filled with succulent carp, boatfuls of pretty flower girls, a walled capital of great beauty—in the autumn and early winter of 1937. It was a treasure that such unworthies as mere Chinese should not be allowed to keep. Japan's ambitions in China—which she had stoutly denied throughout her annexation of Manchuria, and her installation of Pu Yi as the puppet emperor—were by now nakedly apparent. In July she had instigated the Marco Polo Bridge incident, which many see as the true origin of the Pacific War. By August she was occupying Beijing and Tianjin. In November she landed troops in Hangzhou Bay, and she took Shanghai with extraordinary violence but without so much as an official murmur from the League of Nations, the spokesman for the outside world; and now, come December, her soldiers were racing toward Nanjing, which for the past ten years had been the capital of the Chinese Republic.

Chiang Kai-shek was wily enough to know what would happen. He fled up along the Yangtze to Wuhan and Chongqing, declaring each a new capital in turn. Foreign ambassadors did much the same, pleading not unreasonably that they needed to be wherever the nation's heads of state and government presided and resided. Only the ragged remains of Chiang's Nanjing garrison, together with a few hundred foreigners and half a million wretched civilians, were left to face the music. Chiang had left Nanjing, the city that Baron Gotō's writers had called, in their oily way, "one of the most interesting in China," in the hands of an incompetent scoundrel of a general, a former warlord. And he fled too, when six divisions, containing 120,000 well-trained Japanese soldiers, began to bear down on the walls of his city.

The battle for the land south of the Yangtze was well fought: Chinese soldiers in Jiangyin and Zhenjiang fought bravely, but hopelessly. The tanks and field pieces and planes of the Japanese advanced along the river's right bank, day by ghastly day. By December 6, 1937, their troops were surrounding Nanjing on three sides—and the river that streamed below the city walls on the fourth, the west side, was about to be crossed by General Matsui Iwane's soldiers, who were also advancing on the river's left bank.

Mitsubishi bombers began to pound the city nightly: casualties were terrible. But the Chinese, even leaderless, fought on doughtily. Japanese losses rose stubbornly. There was hand-to-hand fighting in the suburbs—down where Lily and I had driven, where I had knocked the young woman from her bicycle—soldiers from the armies of the two competing tiger-states had fought with bayonets and bare hands, the victims broken and dying amid the rubble and the backyard paddies. One unit of the Chinese Army did manage to break out from within the walls—which were, at 21 miles long, 40 feet high, and dating from the Ming dynasty, at the time one of the grandest sets of city walls to be found anywhere in China, a wonder of the Eastern world—and do battle with the onrushing armies. But it was all, inevitably, to no avail.

On the evening of Monday, December 13, 1937, General Matsui entered through the great eastern gates of Nanjing's wall and proceeded to unleash one of the most horrifying episodes of soldierly excess in modern times. It has since become known as the Rape of Nanking—but rape was only a part of it. This was cruelty on an epic scale, the settling of unspoken scores and the uncollaring of decades of blind hatred, one race for the other.

Thousands tried first to flee across the river, to swim to safety. But the river in December is cold and swirling with residual autumn currents, and the pace of the swimmers was slow: machine gunners raked them with bullets, and hundreds, maybe thousands, drowned. One Japanese, Masuda Rokusuke, reckoned later he had shot five hundred, at least. But after this, as terrible an atrocity as it would have been alone, the Japanese turned their attention to the hundreds of thousands who remained behind.

They performed a formal gate-opening ceremony and then commenced their butchery. *Katazukeru* was one word for it: tidying up. *Shori*—treatment—was another. Missionaries and doctors and foreign businessmen and -women stood in horror as the terror unfolded and then went on and on and on, for six terrible weeks. Japanese soldiers treated the soldiers and civilians they had pinioned in Nanjing as animals, available for every act of barbarism and butchery it is possible to imagine. The Tokyo War Crimes Tribunal said later that 200,000 men were slaughtered, and 20,000 women raped.

Children were used for bayonet practice. Women were raped repeatedly by dozens of soldiers standing in line, one after another. Old people were buried alive. Contests were held to see how many heads could be cut off with a single sword blade—the winner claimed 106, and his victory made headlines in the Tokyo press. Women had sharpened bamboo poles thrust deep into their vaginas. Men were lashed between the poles of bullock carts and made to pull away booty looted from the stores, then shot or burned to death. The Japanese hacked and sliced and filleted and butchered and battered and burned their way through an unprotected civilian people. They lined them up and machine-gunned them to death. They herded them into ruined buildings and doused them with paraffin and torched them. They humiliated them in every way imaginable, and most unimaginable ways as well.

Soldiers staked their victims out on the wrecked ground and knifed them and raped them and then took snapshots of one another doing so, and sent the films off to shops in Shanghai to be developed and sent back home to Japan to demonstrate how they had *taught the Chinese a thing or two*. They did what they did with swagger and brute pride: they had caught the Chinese, from whose loins they had once sprung, and taken them down a peg or two, or more. They had brought the mighty Celestials low, had showed them who were the masters now.

Lily and I spent a stunned afternoon wandering around the museum to this horror show. Its compound is in a distant suburb, and its buildings are ugly, though better maintained than most state-funded operations. There is a rock garden, with names of victims, and a large concrete building with an inscription over the main entrance: Victims, 300,000. There are sandboxes filled with skulls and bones, said to be those of murdered and tortured Chinese.

The Massacre Museum was built not to demonstrate a horror that must never be permitted to happen again, but, according to a notice on the wall, "to commemorate the victory of the Chinese people in the anti-Japanese war . . . to educate the people . . . to promote friendship between the Japanese and Chinese people. . . ." Lily and I were as dazed and quiet as all the others who came, even though the tour buses from which they spilled made us think they would be noisy and would behave like tourists, gawking and insensitive. Instead, everyone came here well prepared to be shocked, and they saw it all, and they duly were. Rooms after rooms of black-and-white pictures (not grainy or out of focus or the hasty work of surreptitious spies, but well-posed, well-composed studies)—snaps, for the wife and children back in Sapporo and Kagoshima and Tokyo—of man behaving with the utmost incivility and depravity toward his fellow man . . . and woman.

One of the display cabinets held a roll call of the International Relief Committee, a body set up in a hurry in response to the terrible happenings. There was John Rabe of Siemens, J. M. Hanson from the Texas Oil Company, J. V. Pickering of Standard Vacuum, Ivor Mackay from Swires, the Rev. W. P. Mills of the Presbyterian Mission, E. Sperling of the Shanghai Insurance Company—such comfortable, suburban names, having to deal with such horrors. They set up a number of encampments that they called "safety zones,"* where terrified civilians could take sanctuary from the marauders. But time and again the Japanese stormed into the zones anyway and took young men away, adding them to the steadily rising toll of victims. Afterward the committee members wrote a report; nine years later they gave evidence to the War Crimes Tribunal. They did their best: but against the awful power of the Japanese army, it was little enough.

And against the awful power of Japanese disbelief, their story still has not been properly told in Japan itself. For years there was no mention of it; history books spoke not a word of the atrocities, and merely praised Japan's action in ultimately liberating Asian countries from foreign—or rather, Western—domination. School history books spoke of the Japanese Army's "advances" into China, rather than its "invasion." The terrible happenings in Nanjing were summarized with surgical succinctness: "In December Japanese troops

---

* Unlike most of the treaty ports, Nanjing never had a formal foreign concession area where the victims might have sought sanctuary. The 1858 agreement that added Nanjing to the growing list of ports was not actually taken up until 1899, because of the frightful devastation of the city caused by the Taiping Rebellion. But the land suggested for a concession, which lay outside the city walls and on the banks of the Yangtze, was swampy, malarial and more unpleasant even than the Shanghai waterfront. The foreigners never took the offer up.

occupied Nanjing. At this time [explains a footnote] Japanese troops were reported to have killed many Chinese, including civilians, and Japan was the target of international criticism."

As late as 1991, senior Japanese officials were insisting that the story of the Rape of Nanking was all invention, that spiteful and humiliated Chinese were telling lies to besmirch the reputation of their innocent neighbor. Only in 1995 did a Japanese prime minister make a first formal apology: but there was still plenty of opposition to his doing so, and scepticism continues among many Japanese that they might be capable of such a thing.

The museum—which has captions in Japanese, and a book of condolence and a room where Japanese visitors could leave their gifts and their apologies—was in the process of expanding. There were cranes and backhoes all around, piles of gravel, bags of cement. More sculptures are being added in the garden, more rooms being built above and below ground, the further to remind the world of what happens when a people go mad for blood.

There was a small cinema in the complex, and every few minutes a film was shown. One might think that a film of a massacre would merely appeal to a voyeuristic streak in all our natures; but watching the Chinese—and a few Japanese, amazingly—who sat on those hard metal chairs and watched in rapt and sad attention the images of life being squeezed and burned and choked and stabbed out of so many victims, I felt that it was something else, something very different from mere voyeurism, that had brought them all there. There was a sense of shame, a sense of awful incredulity, that man might be capable of such things.

There was a sense, too, undeniable, that *in their attitude to the Chinese, the Japanese were somehow different*. True, they were cruel beyond belief to the alien others with whom they dealt in the Pacific War—to the Burmese, the Filipinos, the Malays, the Americans and the British. But to the Chinese it was always much, much worse. They were terrible to the Koreans: they were pathologically inhuman to the Chinese, and the Chinese never have forgotten, and never will forget.

· · ·

Yet it was not as if the Rape was the end of the atrocities in Nanjing. The Japanese did something far more terrible for the next six years, in a compound only half a mile from our hotel.

For some years it has been known that the Japanese occupation troops in China had set up a huge biological experimentation camp at a place called Pingshan, near Harbin in Manchuria. I had been there once: it had been called Unit 731, and what was left of it, in the squalid outskirts of a cold and windy industrial town, was a most unutterably depressing place. There was a small museum among the coal heaps, showing photographs of some of the victims who had been experimented upon, who had been given ghastly diseases while they were still alive, and observed in the throes of their agonizing deaths. The fields where women had been crucified naked and left soaked in winter to freeze and have their frostbitten limbs plunged later into boiling water were still there. The stakes to which men were tied while bombs containing typhus bacilli were exploded near them, they remained as well. Tables where men had been injected with gasoline, or horse urine, or prussic acid, and where children had been dissected alive . . . The Japanese, commanded by a man named Ishii, had not regarded their prisoners as humans at all—they called them *maruta,* logs of wood. And on a wooden log you may perform any indignity you like.

Shortly before I left for the Yangtze a new book was published, telling in great detail the story of another camp, but this time in Nanjing. Called Unit Ei 1644, it was commanded by a general named Masuda Tomosada. It was just as terrible a place as Pingshan, set down next to an old hospital on Zhong Shan Road East, close to the old Ming Palace, which was then and still is now a museum. Of the Japanese compound—the ten-foot walls, electrified fences, a four-story research annex—there remains no evidence. Lily and I went to the exact address, but all we found was a shopping arcade and a car showroom. There was a black Rolls-Royce car on display, a 1993 Silver Spur. The salesman was asking for three million *yuan*—

but warned that taxes would amount to another million, at the very least. "I have been trying to sell it for a year. Business is a little slow. I can't say why."

The Rolls-Royce in China was known as a Lao-si Lai-si, its closest phonetic equivalent. There were two others in the city, the salesman said, one owned by the head of Nanjing Petrochemical Corporation, the other parked in the basement of our hotel. But perhaps if I wasn't interested in the Rolls-Royce, I might care for a Ferrari? I asked if he knew that he was selling his cars on the site of an old Japanese death camp, and all he said was that in Japan "they have many of these cars. Very rich people, the Japanese."

Next door Lily ran into a man she knew from the time she lived in Nanjing. He ran a hairdressing salon, his own business, and he was doing very well. He had no idea that he was blow-drying and coiffing where once Japanese technicians had murdered scores of people, all in the so-called interests of biological science. He shuddered theatrically. "Their hair is very different from ours. You can always tell a Japanese girl by her haircut. Much neater. Much tidier."

The Japanese had also been tidy in the way they organized their camp. They had called the captured citizens of the Chinese capital *zaimoku*—lumber—and no indignity was too great for them either. The *lumber storage unit* was on the top floor of the research building. Prisoners, brought to what they had thought was a prison hospital, were fed copiously and nutritiously in a refectory on the floor below as they were prepared for the coming experiments. Then they were taken upstairs to what the guards called *the rooms that did not open*. White-coated technicians were brought in to the room—interpreters told the prisoners that they were doctors, would give them injections to cure their ailments. But the injections were of bizarrely horrific substances, with names as sinister sounding as their effects: nitrile prussiate, cyanide hydric, arsenite, acetone, crystallized blowfish poison, and the distilled venoms of cobras, habu snakes and a vile reptile called an amagasu. The scientists watched unemotionally as the victims choked and screamed toward paralysis and spasm, and in most cases, death. If not dead by chemical, then—since they were now hopelessly contaminated and useless for further work—by a bullet in the head, and quick incineration in the camp furnace.

The Japanese bred fleas in Nanjing, too, which they infected with a variety of bacilli and had released in distant parts of China, experimenting once again on the possible effectiveness of biological warfare. They manufactured phials of anthrax and plague and paratyphoid, all designed to be used in poisoning wells and rivers. Plague was proudly referred to as *a Nanjing speciality.*

The experiments continued for six years. The Zhong Shan East Road camp had been set up on April 18, 1939, as the Central China Anti-Epidemic Water Supply Unit. It was closed, in a frantic hurry, in the early days of August 1945. The remaining "lumber" was murdered and burned. The files were destroyed, the buildings were leveled. General Masuda fled home to Japan. He was detained by the Americans and, it has subsequently been revealed, he exchanged the information he had on this grotesque biology for immunity from prosecution. None of those involved in this terrible trade were tried: the world may have loathed what they had done, but eagerly accepted the data from all their terrible tests. It was one of the uglier examples of the end retroactively justifying the means—particularly since the means were carried out by Orientals, and not by those living in the supposedly civilized West.

General Masuda died when his motorcycle hit a truck east of Tokyo, in 1952. He is remembered a little among the old people of Nanjing; but it goes without saying that neither he, nor any other Japanese, is missed.

But as to why all these things happened—no one then or since has come up with any kind of acceptable answer.

As Lily came away from the film at the Massacre Museum she said she had found it difficult to breathe, she was so horrified. Her chest had tightened in a way she had never experienced before.

"Why did they kill all those civilians, those innocent people? Why couldn't they just kill the Chinese soldiers? There seems to have been no point in it! I really cannot bring myself to like the Japanese, you know." The gifts in a glass cabinet—plastic flowers, a child's painting, bottles of sake—seemed to her tawdry, puny, and not sincere enough. Only one thing cheered her: the surrender table, which had a room to itself, and around which Chiang Kai-shek had made the Japanese sit on child-sized chairs, so that their stature appeared as diminished as they deserved.

I asked her about the grudging, half-hearted apologies that had been occasionally wrested from the Japanese, now that the war has faded somewhat by time. She thought for a moment.

"I cannot believe we will not meet them again one day. I think one day they will have to answer for what they did. They were powerful then. But we are becoming more so now. We will get our own back for all this, I think. I hope." I have heard Chinese say many times that they believe that if they ever do go to war, serious war, it will one day be against the Japanese, against the detested "little people." From the strength of feeling in Nanjing, a feeling that is so strong and palpable it infects the very air, I can well believe it. One day, the city seems to be constantly murmuring, *we will teach those little people a lesson.*

Outside what remains of the city's western wall is a small stream, polluted now, but still overhung with the sycamores shipped in from France. It leads into the Yangtze itself, disgorging beside an island where the port has been built, and from which the Yangtze steamers leave. I had bought tickets on an evening boat upriver: we made our way along the little stream, which is called the Chin-huai, and tried hard to conjure up memories of this as one of China's epicenters of erotic delight.

For the Chin-huai was where the famous flower boats were moored. They had lovely names—*Lady Sincerity, Laughing Peach Blossom, Singing Fragrance, Iris Pavilion.* Some were large—ten yards long, and with room for parties. Most were tiny, with room for only one singsong girl, and for her customer.

On a summer's evening you might stroll northward under the trees as we were doing now, the city walls looming to the right, the sentries patrolling silently up above, the ships' sirens echoing mournfully from the great river nearby. Moored in the stream would be the little boats, a paper lantern lit in the stern of each and, underneath and dressed in bright silks, the singsong girl herself. She would have a fan on which were written the names of the songs she could perform: you would pay one hundred copper cash for her to perform three of these, in her high-pitched voice, while two old men would provide strings and timps. There would be a low bed, a *kang,* and if you liked each other you could hire her entire boat for the evening, on payment of just four Mexican silver dollars, the currency of the time. The old men would be dismissed; standing forlorn on the riverbanks they would cast you off, after which you would drift downriver while the girl sang more songs for you, and then gently extinguished the paper lantern with a brief puff from between her delicate lips. . . .

I was awakened from this pleasant reverie by a Chinese soldier. He had a submachine gun slung over his shoulder and was demanding to see my passport. We had reached the end of the Chin-huai stream, and the area ahead, on the far side of a crudely built brick wall, was controlled by the military. But only very informally: after I had showed my documents, I was waved through, and within minutes a group of sailors who were working stacking sandbags—for everyone was expecting the Yangtze to flood, as the radio had warned of excessively rapid snowmelt up near the headwaters, in Tibet—stopped and offered me tea. Their official task, they explained, was to guard a boat that was used by Party leaders whenever they came to Nanjing. Chairman Mao had used it many times on the river: perhaps I might like to see it?

I had to walk along a dangerous arrangement of planks balanced on breeze blocks, because all the normal entranceways to the dock were flooded: the river was rising very fast now, and ports upstream were reporting damage, warning that some dikes were in danger of breaking. Mao's pleasure palace is called the *Jiang Han 56*—the Han River No. 56—though in Mao's time it had been called *The East Is Red Number One*. For nearly twenty years it had been his private yacht. He first used it when he swam in the Yangtze in 1956. He would do so again ten years later in an act that—as a sign of his rebellion against the wishes of the Party elders—essentially signaled the start of the Cultural Revolution.

It was not a pretty boat, and it was furnished poorly, though the stained sofas looked comfortably roomy. There was a lot of chrome and molded plastic. The wood furnishings reminded me of those you would see on the set of a low-budget sixties television show—Dick Van Dyke's living room sprang to mind, or Mr. Wilson's house in *Dennis the Menace*. A clock, broken, had sun-ray spikes. The main lounge had one of its walls entirely covered with the kind of wallpaper you used to be able to buy in cheap Scandinavian shops, a blown-up photograph of life-sized birch trees offering the illusion of being beside a forest. On another wall was a picture of Bora Bora.

In every room soldiers lay asleep in their underwear, though they got up and saluted groggily when I looked in. One of them, an officer, showed me the cabin where Fidel Castro had once stayed and said Kim Il Sung had been aboard many times. He then took me to a larger room occupied for a week by the Ceauşescus. I doubt if they had much fun. Mao's private stateroom, across the corridor, had a pair of giant armchairs and a huge bed, but little else. The kitchens were dirty, with bamboo buckets full of rice, and thermos flasks waiting to be filled with hot water for tea. Perhaps it had been more luxurious when Mao was its Great Helmsman: today it hardly looked suited for its role as China's royal yacht.

I had one final mission in Nanjing. I had left it until last in deference to what I thought were Lily's increasingly strident nationalist sympathies. Close to where the evening steamer was due to depart was, I had been told, a memorial marking the site of the city's—and perhaps of China's—greatest political humiliation. It had taken place in August 1842. Although this rather accelerated the pace of my backward progress through history (so far in voyaging from Shanghai I had passed back sixty years, to 1937, which was roughly what I had expected), I had always known that this was going to happen: the historical aspect of this journey was only approximate, at best. And while I felt reasonably comfortable in paying only slight attention here to the Nanking Incident of 1927, and the Taiping Rebellion of the 1860s, it was impossible to ignore either the Japanese assault of 1937 or, as in this last excursion, the signing of the Treaty of Nanking in 1842. I told Lily this is what I wanted to see. "Oh my God," she wailed. "Your bloody British Empire again!"

The memorial was tucked away off a side street, not far from the old British Embassy (which is now a seedy two-star hotel and from where a local businessman was trying to sell debentures in a new golf club, at $20,000 apiece). It is in a tiny temple known as the Jing Hui Shi, which was made famous five centuries before when Cheng Ho, the country's most famous explorer, stayed there before he took off on his famous sailing trip to Mogadishu.* It is now called simply the Nanjing Treaty Museum, and it is looked after by an elderly lady named Mrs. Chen.

"How nice to see a foreigner here," she said chirpily when I walked in, banging my head on the low doorway. "Even the British are welcome here now. This is all just—history." She took two *yuan* from me, and made as if to add some further comment, but whispered that she would say it later. She picked up the telephone and spoke in a low voice to someone on the other end.

The treaty was signed on August 29, 1842, in the captain's cabin on the man-of-war HMS *Cornwallis,* moored a quarter of a mile offshore. It had come about after British soldiers, fresh from a mili-

---

* Where he captured a giraffe and brought it back for the Emperor of the day to see. Cheng Ho is still revered as China's equivalent of Columbus, or Magellan; but in fact he was not properly Chinese, being a Muslim from a minority tribe, as well as a eunuch.

tary success in Zhenjiang, from where we had just come, had established themselves in a commanding position outside the Nanjing city walls. That was August 5: the local Qing dynasty leadership—charged with plenipotentiary permissions from the Emperor Daoguang's court in Beijing—agreed to negotiate. A seasoned diplomat named Sir Henry Pottinger had been appointed by Lord Palmerston to negotiate for the British and bring to an end the two years of tiresome skirmishing that have since been dignified as the First Opium War. (His predecessor, Charles Elliot, had been summarily sacked by Palmerston for a variety of supposed offenses—one being his choice of settling in Hong Kong, which the British prime minister described scathingly, and with a stunning lack of prescience, as merely "a barren island with hardly a house upon it.")

At the beginning of the second week of August, Sir Henry Pottinger entered the little Jing Hui temple and seated himself at a hastily set up conference table. On the other side, resplendent in his purple robes and scarlet-buttoned cap, was a Manchu mandarin named Qiyang. For two weeks these two, and their attendant advisers and translators, worked out an agreement that would change China's history for all time. The resulting treaty would force the Celestials to open themselves up to commerce with the barbarians—a term that was formally used in this treaty, and would be for another ten years. It would also begin the dismemberment of the Chinese nation—and spark the wider ambitions of the still slumbering island-nation nearby.

The Treaty's full text, written in elegant calligraphy, can be read on one of the walls of the small museum. Any visiting Chinese—and there are not many visitors at all, so tiny and tucked away is the place (I found it odd that they keep it open at all)—may read all of the twelve clauses, and realize how humiliating it must have been then, and how eager the Chinese are to rid themselves of the humiliation today.

The second clause was the most unpalatable of all. "The Island of Hong Kong shall be possessed in perpetuity by Her Majesty Queen Victoria and her successors, and shall be ruled as they see fit." There were other matters: five treaty ports to be opened, $21 million to be paid in compensation for burned opium and other indignities,* the establishment of a customs service with fair duties levied on goods, the formal abandonment of phrases like "petition" and "beg" in all further communications between the two courts. But they were as nothing compared to the savagery of having to give up an island, part of the most ancient empire on earth. It was a bitter pill for Daoguang to swallow then. Over subsequent years other morsels fell to other nations—Manchuria and Liaoning and Shandong and even the Summer Palace in Beijing itself, and the bitterness and isolation of China increased, and she retreated to her lonely contemplation of nobler times of old, and of her hopes of nobler times to come.

Mrs. Chen came up to us, telling Lily to stop tutting and clicking her tongue. "It is not this man's fault," she said, kindly, looking at me. "Besides—" only she was interrupted by a bespectacled, cheerful-looking old man who introduced himself as Professor Wang, director of the Nanjing Relics Bureau.

"Besides, Mrs. Chen," he said, drawing himself up for a lecture, "all this humiliation is about to be ended now—isn't it? Now we have almost everything back. Manchuria is ours again. Shandong was taken back from the Germans. The Russians were kicked out. So were the Japanese—the hateful Japanese. The Portuguese are leaving Macau.

"Now all that remains are you people, the British. And very soon now you will go. Your Mrs. Thatcher knew that she could not defend the Pottinger treaty. She knew that Hong Kong could not be held for ever. So you are having to give up and go home.

"Once you have done that we will have all of China back. Maybe Taiwan, too. It will be a glorious day for us. Then the treaty signed here will just be a relic—of no importance. People will not forget. But they will never let it happen again."

Professor Wang let that sink in, then smiled broadly at Lily,

---

* The compensation was paid in silver, sixty-five tons of it arriving on a ship at Portsmouth in 1842 and being taken promptly to the Royal Mint.

sighed with pleased relief and suggested that Mrs. Chen pour us all cups of tea. "Now we must be friends. But equal friends. Not like before. We Chinese are at least the equal of you now, don't you agree? At the very least, equal."

We waited in the gathering gloom for our 9 P.M. boat to Jiujiang, and other points upstream. Kathleen, an American woman I knew vaguely who taught at one of the universities in Nanjing, had come to see us off. She was from Connecticut and was in love with China, didn't much want to go home. She taught English to a class of about forty students. That day they had been reading *Tess of the D'Urbervilles.*

I had been telling her of the conversation with Professor Wang, and I remarked that he—like many Chinese these days—seemed to have been much more candid with me, much more forceful and direct than used to be the case. Perhaps, I said, he was displaying something of the country's new self-confidence, a new belief in itself.

"I'm not so sure," she said. Some things were still only discussed behind veils, she went on, were talked about only with great embarrassment. Sex, for instance.

"Only today it happened. I have a student called Nancy, twenty-one, beautiful, perfect English. I had asked her to précis the book. She got to the bit where Alec D'Urberville rapes Tess when she is sleeping in the wood. The rape that led to the child, near the start of the story. Well, Nancy was telling the class how Alec had taken her for a ride, how they had gotten lost, how they had to stop in the wood.

"Nancy paused in the story here. 'And then?' I asked. She blushed. She didn't want to say it. And then finally she came out with it.

" 'Alec,' she said, 'was then *very rude to her.*'

"I was amazed, for a moment. Then I asked her what she meant—rude? But she wouldn't say, and just hung her head. That wasn't rude—that was rape! I yelled. I suppose I was a bit too

American about it—trying to force the issue. But she wouldn't talk about it, and nor would anyone else in the class."

Lily said: "That's Nanjing for you—very conservative place. Very conservative people."

"I'll say," said Kathleen. "It was even worse when I started talking about homosexuality. I thought I'd go for broke. I told them it exists everywhere—in China as well as everywhere else. I told them there were gay prostitutes on the pedestrian bridge near the Shin Jie gate, near your hotel. They just wouldn't believe it.

"They said that there are hardly any homosexuals in China, and that I wasn't to import my ideas about them, please."

Lily stood up. "We must get on board now," she said. Her mood, changeable at the best of times, had suddenly hardened. I was afraid I knew what was coming.

"The students are right, you know," she said. "There really is no homosexuality here—except for some ill people. It is a disease, a mental disease. Something that can be cured. It is quite disgusting. Americans allow it. We do not. I can't blame them for not wanting to talk about it.

"But Tess and the rape. That's different. That's just Nanjing people. Nancy was a very typical girl. People in Shanghai wouldn't feel the same. Rape is a very sensitive subject here. I am sure you both know that."

The boat's siren sounded. Thanks be, I muttered to myself. The last thing I wanted to be caught in the midst of was a fight between a stridently and vocally modern American woman and my tough-as-nails companion. *The Clash of Two Civilizations* had nothing on a full-blown argument between these two. I said my farewells to Kathleen, who rolled her eyes heavenward. Lily and I joined the throng, feeding ourselves into the huge crush of people at the gangplank like a slab of beef going into a mincer.

"Soldiers go first!" scolded a woman guard, harshly. That was always the way: Let the Soldiers Pass First, said a notice board. They Make Great Sacrifices for Our Nation.

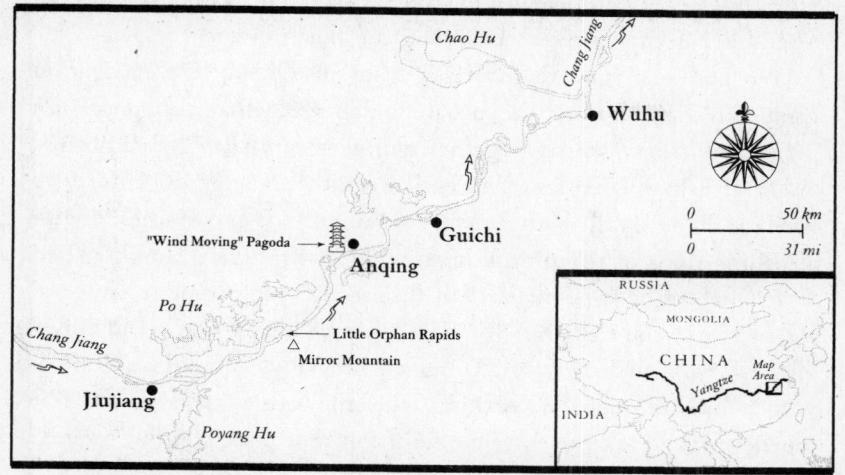

6

Rising Waters

The last traces of the evening sun were glimmering from behind the purple clouds of factory smoke as the *Jiang Han 18* edged gingerly out into the swollen stream. A long freight train rumbled over the bridge behind, its wagons heaped high with coal for plants and smelters on the north bank. The ferry from Pukou, its lower decks crammed with passengers and bicycles, was sweeping around the harbor buoy. An old man in a string vest standing beside me on the *Jiang Han*'s second deck was pissing happily over the side of the boat; as he buttoned the fly on his khaki shorts so he spat down into the river, thirty feet below, for good measure. The clock on the Nanjing Ship Terminal then struck—or clanked—a tinny and discordant nine times: we were leaving exactly on schedule, with just over six hundred passengers jammed among the hot ironwork below.

We had managed to secure a cabin just below the navigation bridge. It had cost us: the usual double price that foreigners are invariably obliged to pay, together with a twenty-*yuan* bribe. But the alternatives had been less than enticing: either a huge dormitory, its sizzling floors awash with dubious-looking fluids and crammed with a jostling mass of shouting humanity, or a third-class bunkhouse in which twelve beds—four tiers of three—provided some measure of serenity and comfort. But for only twenty dollars one could travel second-class—first-class still being an officially forbidden phrase—with a lockable door, a working fan, and beds with curtains. The journey was to take twenty-five hours: at that price comfort seemed very good value.

"More like thirty hours, this trip," said Captain Wu De Yin, when I went up to the bridge. "The flooding this year seems very bad. The stream is quite fast. Downstream we came along like a rocket. But upstream we are having to fight every inch of the way."

Captain Wu had been on the Yangtze since he was eleven—more than forty years. He had once worked on the *Kunlun,* the boat that was now used to take tourists along the Yangtze and which was mistakenly said by its American charterers to have been used by Chairman Mao. "Zhou Enlai, yes," he said. "Mao, never, I'm sad to say." He pointed respectfully to a small photograph of Mao that bobbed on a string from a bulkhead pipe, a talisman. All long-distance travelers in China had them, Mao or Zhou and sometimes both, together with a length of red cloth that fluttered in the wind: they doubled as Saint Christophers and as a visible sign of faith in the Party.

Captain Wu had left the *Kunlun* with honors ten years before, and for the last decade had worked on the scheduled passenger boats like ours, shuttling between Nanjing and Wuhan. This is what one might call the upper reach of the Lower Yangtze—and journeying in these waters always sorely tried his nerves.

"Everyone imagines the Yangtze is only difficult in the Gorges," he said, lighting a cigarette. "But this river—pah!—it is always difficult. Always. It changes every day, every hour. One moment there is clear water and then—pah!—there is a whirlpool that will suck you in and turn you round and before you know it, you're heading for a rock, or a cliff.

"You have to treat it like your enemy. It is a real battle, going up this river. I will show you in the morning. But even now you can hear it—just listen."

And I cocked an ear to hear something above the deep-throated roaring of the engines, and below the cries of a legion of off-key singers in a crew cabin behind us. After a few seconds there was a sort of iron hiccup in the rhythm of the diesels, a squeal of distant chains, and the boat seemed to lurch slightly from the port side. I staggered. The captain did not. For a moment or two longer the boat resumed her smooth progress, and then there came another battering, this time from starboard. There was second squawk of industrial pain from below, another sound of tortured metal, another lurch.

"See what I mean? All you can see ahead is the night. It looks quite calm. But below us the river is doing strange things. I can never say I know it. I know the ports, the destinations. I know the bridges, and all the lights. But the water—wah!—it is a strange beast. I should get paid more than I do!" He said he was paid about 6000 *yuan* a month, around $700.

Before turning in I stood on the bridge wing, gazing out into the inky blackness. It was a warm and humid late spring night, and rivulets of condensation ran down the steel plates. In the distance there was the glow of factory furnaces, each a silent indication of China's strength. But from down below came an unsteady gurgling roar as the river coursed by our hull—a reminder that the river was stronger still and, as all who live along her banks know full well, that she would be able to snuff out all those distant fires and a great deal else besides, with no more than a summertime shrug of her giant shoulders.

This stretch of the river suffers terribly from floods. Later on I would find out that what was at that moment swirling below our hull was reported to be a memorably bad flood: it was said that 1500 people were killed and hundreds of millions more were "affected." Patriotic television films would show heroic soldiers gallantly fighting to secure dikes and dams along thousands of miles of brimming streams. But however destructive the 1995 floods, they were as mere wettings compared with what the Chinese believe to have been one of the worst natural calamities of all time: the Central China Flood of 1931. The wild and wayward Yangtze, as usual, was to blame.

Except that the blame can be apportioned much more fundamentally than this. China is a country that is doubly and uniquely cursed, both by her climate and her topography.

Her cross section, for example, is dramatically unlike any other on earth. China's western side is universally high—an immense mélange of contorted geologies that involve the Himalayas, the Tibetan Plateau, and the great mountain ranges of Sichuan, Yunnan and Gansu. Her eastern side, on the other hand, is flat and alluvial and slides muddily and morosely down into the sea. The country in between is far from a smoothly inclined plane, of course, but the difference in altitude between her western provinces and the sea is so vast—involving four and a half miles of vertical drop—and the trend of the slope so unremitting that anything which falls onto her western side, be it snow, hail, torrential rain or the slow gray drizzle of a Wuhan autumn afternoon, will roll naturally and inevitably down to the east.

Her two greatest rivers, the Yellow River and the Yangtze, flow in precisely that direction—west to east. They take this runoff from the high Himalayas and the other ranges and then, capturing river after river after river along the way—all of which do just the same, scouring their source mountains for every drop of water they can find—they cascade the entire collected rainfall from tens of thousands of square and high-altitude miles down into the earth-stained waters of the East China Sea.

But the configuration of China's surface is not the only factor. It is eccentric, certainly, like one half of a temple roof. Nonetheless, it could have offered the country a hydraulically manageable situation, were it not for four additional curses.

The first is that China receives a very great deal of rain each year—far more, per square mile, than Europe or the Americas, and in places, as much as the record-holding villages of Assam. Second, nearly all of this precipitation falls in the topographically chaotic west and the south of the country—the principal reason, as it happens, that rice is the crop of choice grown in the wet warm south, and wheat the staple in the dry and cool north. (The dividing line, the so-called wheat-rice line, almost precisely parallels the track of the Yangtze.)

Third, this substantial and geographically concentrated rainfall is intensely seasonal—the summer monsoon dominates southwestern China's weather system, just as it dominates the northern part of the India against which China abuts. This is a very odd combination: in very few regions around the world is rain concentrated both by place *and* by time. It is not in India, for instance. It is not in the Amazon valley. Nor is it anywhere in Europe. But in China, savagely, more or less all of it falls in one place, and more or less all of it falls in one four-month period, between June and September.

Fourth, and as if the other reasons were not enough, the rain falls just when the summer sun begins warming things up—things that include, crucially, the snows and glaciers of China's western mountains. These start to melt, and to produce their own torrents of eastbound water, at exactly the time the rains come.

The coincidence of these four factors—each of which, like St. John's Four Horsemen, is an agent of potential destruction—produces results that are often quite literally apocalyptic. Every summer and all of a sudden, gigantic quantities of water begin to course down each of the tributary streams of China's two main river systems. Some comes from the melting ice and snow. Some comes from the torrential monsoonal rains. But all goes eventually to the same two places.

In the north of the country the Huang He, the Yellow River, swells rapidly and enormously. It collects additional waters from its two main feeder streams, and it wrenches millions more tons of loess out of China's heartland and carries them swiftly out to the delta, and the sea.* Not for nothing is this river known colloquially as China's Sorrow, or The Unmanageable.

But the Yellow River's history of flooding, while spectacular, has rarely been as catastrophic as the Yangtze's. The Yangtze is nearly a sixth as long again as the Yellow, and rages through hundreds more miles of mountainous and well-watered land. It has in addition very many more tributaries—about seven hundred in total, and among them are formidable rivers like the Yalong, the Min, the Jialing, the Han Shui, the Wu and the Yuan. Each of these deserves to be ranked among the world's biggest rivers itself, but in this context they are mere contributors to the Yangtze and to its huge engorgement.

Furthermore, unlike the Yellow River, the Yangtze flows through a part of China that is itself rained upon during the monsoon season—meaning that to whatever mass of waters it has collected from the hills and the tributaries, still more is added from the rain that simply falls upon the river's surface as it sidles languidly through the lower stages.

The results are invariably stupendous, occasionally disastrous and, more often than seems fair, catastrophic. In 1871, the river at one point rose—and quite suddenly—by no less than 275 feet. A little above where I was sailing this night, places exist where the average summertime rise is 70 feet, year after year; and painted on the rocky walls and on cliffs and poles and riverside buildings all along the way are the ragged white numerals—once in feet, now in meters—showing the possible range of the water. At Jiujiang, which we were due to reach after a day's hard sailing, there was said to be a plaque record-

---

* In places it is more like a river of syrup than of water: in some tributaries 30 percent of its bulk is silt, compared with only 0.2 percent for the Yangtze.

ing the level on the fateful August 19, 1931: the river rose 53 feet, 7 inches above normal, and inundated everything for miles around.

During that summer, in addition to all the normal mountain monsoons and snowmelts, calamitous rains fell along the entire length of the middle and Lower Yangtze. Storms raged all over these very lowlands through which I was now steaming—lowlands that begin at the foot of a mountain range five hundred miles ahead and extend to the ocean that now lay three hundred miles behind. This extraordinary amount of water was dumped into a river that had already been swollen massively by the melting of the Tibetan snowfields and was, moreover, about to get huge shock infusions of storm water from its mightiest tributaries.

The results were that the Yangtze, at precisely the point where I was now rumbling through the night, first rose to 30 feet above its present level and then, no fewer than six times in quick succession, was jolted by great storm bores as the new tributary waters kicked in.

The tributary bores are no joke. In a bad-flood year a grotesquely swollen Min River, for example, discharges itself into the Yangtze and produces a ten-foot tidal wave, which sweeps down and along the river for days. Another bloated river like the Jialing disgorges its water in the same way but a few days later, or earlier, depending on the weather near its own source; this causes another tidal wave to rush out into the great river—and so on and so on. Before long an aerial view of the Yangtze would show it overflowing its banks for hundreds of miles, and then those broken banks and inundated villages and towns being buffeted by successive new water pulses, each a few days or so apart. In 1931 there was no slow inundation: it was rapid flooding, followed by episodes of total immersion, then a brief relief, then total immersion once again, five more times.

The consequences of what the history books now record as the Central China Flood were staggering, the figures numbing and barely credible. More than 140,000 people drowned. Twenty-eight million people were affected—forty million by some estimates. Seventy thousand square miles of central China were submerged—as much land area as in all of New York state, New Jersey and Connecticut combined, or all of England and most of Scotland. Twelve million people had to migrate or leave their ruined homes—twice that number, according to the more doom-laden reports. Two billion dollars in losses—and those are 1931 figures, when the average family earnings in China were just a fistful of cents in copper cash—were directly attributable to the flooding. Some streets in cities like Wuhan, two days sailing away from me this night, were under nine feet of water, others under twenty feet. The city remained awash for four months. Fields nearby, not protected by dikes, were thirty feet under. Nanjing was under water for six weeks.

And though this was the worst for many years, floods like it had happened before, and others like it would happen again. The country's formidably well-annotated history records more than one thousand major inundations in the last two thousand years. Catastrophes on the Yangtze alone seemed to have occurred roughly every fifty years. Even if one disregards Chinese record keeping—which is unwise, since the Courts kept scrupulous watch over their Empire—and relies only on the records of the British-run Imperial Maritime Customs, the regularity of disaster is obvious: the 1931 floods were preceded by terrible calamities in 1896 and 1870, and even higher river levels were seen in 1949, 1954 and on my own journey, in 1995.

The inevitability of such happenings has annealed and anesthetized the national psyche. The Chinese have long been accustomed to a mute subservience to nature. A glance at almost any classical Chinese painting—with its tiny and peripheral figures of men surrounded and dominated by mountains and waterfalls, clouds and trees—indicates the state of mind, with its stoic acceptance of the overarching gigantism of the world, the puny insignificance of man. A European painting on the other hand is invariably very different in all respects: man or his creations lie usually at the center. Nature is peripheral, portrayed as background, or barely noted at all, and if it is, is usually seen as gentle, pastoral, merely pretty.

A phlegmatic acceptance of this insignificance, of powerlessness when set against the alternating benevolent and minatory cycles of nature, is an immutable part of the Chinese peasant's psychological makeup. Of course, all mankind acknowledges reality. Most peoples have variations on our own "Man proposes but God disposes." But in China it is said with far greater dramatic flourish: "Heaven nourishes," goes the Celestials' equivalent, "and Heaven destroys." Acceptance is all, it seems. Once in a while things have become so desperate that the supposed benevolence of the supervising gods was invoked: in 1788 the Emperor Qianlong had nine iron oxen forged and submerged in the rising river. The act, he declared, should propitiate the guardians of the stream since, according to the cumbersome cosmology of the day, the sea submits to iron, the ox belongs to the earth, and so a herd of iron oxen should be able to suppress a flood. But it didn't, and the floods of the summer of 1788 were devastating—and records from later times consistently show that prayer has rarely managed to halt or slow a rising Chinese river. The yin and the yang are in constant operation in the matter of China's wayward waterways; here is every advance countered by a setback, there are the years of too little followed by the months of too much. The entire history of China seems patterned like this, the Yangtze simply a paradigm.

Not that all the drama of 1931 seemed so tragic—particularly for the foreigners living in the region. Newspapers reported how the businessmen in the flooded treaty ports went to work in newly bought *sampans,* lazing in overstuffed armchairs that coolies had mounted in the stern, reading the morning paper. Police *sampans* cruised along the flooded roads, Browning machine guns mounted in swivels on their bows. Wuhan had a fire brigade boat equipped with a siren and painted a properly searing shade of red. A boat-shuttle service operated between the westerners' offices on the Hankou Bund and the racecourse—where the bar still operated, even though the horses did not.

A notice went up at the Jardines office forbidding employees from mooring their boats on the roof and tying them to the firm's chimneys. The post office set up floating substations, and canceled their stamps with a mark still highly valued by philatelists. A junk floated into the gardens of the Hankou Club, and when the waters went down it remained. It was later mounted on four pillars of concrete, a memorial to the barely credible height that the waters had reached.*

It was left to Chiang Kai-shek's new and untested government—just three years old, and based in Nanjing—to deal with the mess. The Flood Relief Commission's three-hundred-page report, issued when the waters had gone down and the fields had been sown again with rice and tobacco and cotton, refers wearily to the fact that workers, set to rebuilding the damaged dikes, "had to be protected against Communists and bandits." Another page—nowadays it reads like agitprop—has references to the depredations of "the Reds." Politics intruded in 1931, as often before and always afterward, conspiring to make a trying situation a very great deal more so.

Measures to try to control China's disastrous floods have been an recurrent feature of her history. As early as the second century B.C., letters were written referring to China's five "harmful influences"—flood, drought, unseasonable weathers, pestilence, and insects: of these, a second-century duke wrote, floods are by far the worst. His correspondent agreed: the consequences of water gone awry could be profound—though he went rather further than most. "Running wild, it injures men. When it injures men there is great distress among them. In great distress they treat the laws lightly. Laws being treated lightly it is difficult to maintain order. Good order lapsing, filial piety disappears. And when people have lost filial piety, they are no longer submissive."

The notion that flooding might stimulate insubordinate behavior may seem a peculiarly Chinese rationale—but it did sufficiently alarm the mandarinate that the Court took very seriously the problem of taming the Empire's wild rivers. More than two thousand years ago there were documents that specified how to build and repair dikes, how to muster corvées of workers to maintain them,

---

* It was actually a Shanghai junk, brought down by a local British businessman who was eager to show off. But no local boatman could, or would, work so alien a craft—which is why it found its way, uselessly, into the club gardens. It disappeared during the anti-Japanese war.

how many baskets, spades, earth-tamping devices and carts to assign
to each water conservancy office; if ever the maturity of Chinese
civilization were in doubt, the record of her attitude to her waterways would provide more than ample confirmation of its antiquity.

So dikes were built, for thousands of miles along the most vulnerable riverbanks. They were not always built sturdily enough—those
that broke too often, and let the waters escape, were known as *dou-fu*
dikes—the word is rendered in English as "tofu," the jellylike bean
curd with which they were compared. From the Yangtze, well-diked
sluiceways were also constructed to carry off excess water from the
main river and dribble it into a number of retention basins, as well as
into two gigantic lakes that, quite fortuitously, spread to the south of
the river—Dongting Lake, near Wuhan, and Poyang Lake, a little to
the south of where we were steaming now.

In the low-water period of the winter and early spring, these
lakes—especially Dongting—shrink dramatically. What in the summertime is a great expanse of water, often as much as 3000 square
miles, is in winter reduced to a sandy marsh, like a huge inland
delta. People move back onto this newly exposed land: rice paddies
are hastily built, straw huts go up, little farms oversee vast flocks of
swans, geese and ducks. And then, come June, the river rises once
again, the lake re-creates itself, and, with dispatch born of centuries
of experience, the temporary farmers move out and site themselves
back on high ground to wait out the season.

Ships ply the deeper channels of both lakes—in fact, thanks to an
astonishing achievement of canal building and diversion that dates
back to the third century B.C., a system of waterways passing through
Dongting Lake allows ships to pass from the Yangtze all the way
south to Canton. Only small ships, admittedly (and the railway from
Wuhan now parallels the route, taking most of the north-south cargoes); but as a piece of hydraulic engineering, the Qin dynasty's extraordinary Miracle Canal, as it is still known, was truly a Panama of
its day.*

---

* The Qin—or Ch'in—dynasty was the origin of the English word "China."

Dikes and retention basins improved as the centuries wore on—the former became higher and stronger, the latter larger and more numerous. After the 1931 catastrophe formidable efforts were made to try and solve the problem forever; dikes were built and new diversion schemes were constructed that could deal with the so-called hundred-year floods, as well as with the more modest disasters in between. The Flood Relief Commission, eager to show the ability of the Nationalist government, wrote that "the amount of earthwork done by this army of laborers would have built a dike two meters high and two meters thick, long enough to encircle the earth at its equator."

Work was still going on twenty years later, despite the anti-Japanese war, the Civil War, Mao's revolution. In 1951 a huge new retention basin was finished upstream at Jinjiang. It had mile-long cement spillways, hundreds of lock gates, seemingly endless concrete canals. Three years later the monsoon storms lashed down, the snowmelt was huge, and the Yangtze rose again—brimming as high as it had in 1931, and then higher still as shock wave after shock wave came with the joining of the tributary floods. But the Jinjiang locks all opened in proper time, the commission's earth-girdling chain of new dikes all held—and after a week of anxious, rain-sodden nights and days, the Yangtze's level began to fall. What could have been a more terrible calamity had been averted. Old Emperor Yü the Great, who legend said had begun all this river taming four thousand years before, would have been well pleased.

I slept well in the little cabin. Lily did too, and she was still deeply asleep when the dim morning light filtered in. It was raining hard, and when I went up on deck I heard a group of fellow passengers worrying out loud about the grim possibilities of rising waters at their various destinations. But it seemed I hadn't missed much of importance along the river during the night: the only thing was that at Datong, the captain said, he had seen the earthworks for the new bridge. We had also passed the town of Wuhu, where there was the very last vague hint of influence from the ocean tides: this now was the Yangtze pure and simple, its flow unaffected by anything except the rain and the melting snows, still far away.

After a breakfast down in the ship's grubby little shop, with rice *congee* and deep-fried strips of dough called oilsticks that are far from my favorite way of jump starting the day, I went back out on deck to take the morning air, and to see if the river had risen much. Sure enough it had: buildings beside the river were now standing in several feet of muddy water, and at one point I could see a convoy of trucks, half-submerged themselves, driving along a water-lapped riverside road, taking people and their cattle up to higher ground.

But also as I watched I saw by chance two examples of perhaps the most emblematic of all the ancients' river remedies. Pagodas, quite rare in the lower reaches, had been erected by the score by Ming and early Qing viceroys in the more flood-prone regions. They were built there to propitiate gods, to persuade them not to permit floods—but also from which to spot the floods at a distance if the deities were, as so often, unrelenting. On this damp morning here were a couple of them, in quick succession.

The first was on the river's right bank, outside the wretched-looking little town of Guichi, where we stopped for five minutes. The pagoda was a forlorn thing, too—seven stories, rotting masonry, a tottering cupola and tufts of greenery sprouting from its windows. Perhaps, I thought sourly, its abandonment was due to the existence of one of the country's newer pagodas, a steel and wire temple to a replacement religion, for Guichi's modern skyline is now dominated by a brand-new telecommunications tower, and through one of the old pagoda's ragged windows I could see men working on it and the blue sputterings of a welding torch.

The ship slid home beside an old pontoon, with much screeching of rust against rust. Six passengers disembarked: they were from Taiwan, and one of them had told me they were bound for the sacred mountain of Jiuhua, some few hours' bus journey away.

"Most times it's Koreans who get off here," remarked one of the crew, a man I had met on the bridge the night before. He was squinting down into the drizzle. "It was a Korean monk who made the mountain famous, you know. He set up a monastery on the top, back in the old days. So in August they come in their hundreds, celebrating his birthday. The whole boat reeks of *kimchi.*"

The Guichi pagoda may not have been a very fine specimen, but half an hour later, and on the opposite shore, one of the finest pagodas in all China swept into view: the famous Wind Moving Pagoda of Anqing. It is said to sway in the wind; it was built in 1570; and it has eight sides and, uncommonly, eight stories—most pagodas having an odd number, usually five, seven, or nine.

The junkmen on the Yangtze are said to revere the Anqing pagoda. In the old days the walls of the city were arranged in the outline of a junk with the pagoda at the center, rising like a mast. On the gates of the fort outside are the flukes of a gigantic grapnel anchor: the fishermen believe that if these are ever removed, the city will drift away downstream and vanish forever.

They also believe that the pagoda is the king of all other pagodas in the world—including those built later in Japan and Korea, and also of the stupas in Thailand and India and the chortens in Tibet. During the autumn moon festival, it is said, the pagodas all come to pay homage to their monarch. Priests praying in the upper storeys say that on the choppy waters of the Yangtze below, the images of the thousands of other pagodas can be seen flickering in the moonlight—transported reflections of the world's tributary temples, all paying their brief annual respects. No junk or other ship dares pass the river during these nighttime hours, for fear of disturbing the reflections.

Among the stones of the pagoda's basement there is said to be a tomb containing the heart of a fallen Chinese warrior. The structure's topmost pinnacle holds a strange confection of bells, which ring in even the most gentle breeze. And in rougher winds—the winter gales especially—the whole whitewashed structure leans back and forth, the bells shaking noisily, warning the citizens below of a coming storm.

I had with me a photograph of the town taken during the 1931 floods, which showed the pagoda standing, its skirts dipping deep into the river, a sailing junk passing gracefully below. The *Admiralty Pilot* of 1953 has a picture of it, too—it is a major navigation mark, vital for the masters of all passing ships. In this photograph the structure towers above a neat arrangement of curl-topped roofs and fortress walls, a classic illustration of China.

Today, however, matters have changed a lot. The pagoda still towers nobly, the fort's roofs are still untouched—but all around them are cindery blocks of godowns and office buildings, cranes and iron wharves. In the background, dominating the skyline far more obviously than the pagoda itself, is a huge cone-shaped stain of oily smoke, belching blackly from an unseen chimney and drifting high above the entire town. The ruin of modern China is a sorry thing to see, and in Anqing more so than in many places. What had gone before had been so very, very lovely.

And much vanishes still that is not so easy to see. The animal and fish life of the Yangtze, for example, has been ruined by pollution and greed: the building of great hydroelectric projects upstream is doing yet more damage, and the whole world says it is alarmed about the fate of cetaceans and sturgeons that once were abundant in the river, but which are now fast dying out. In the waters between Anqing and Wuhu, for example, there were until quite recently thousands of specimens of the Yangtze alligator, *Alligator sinensis*—a miniature version of the familiar reptile, with a black stripe along its side. Three thousand years ago the local warlords used to make battle drums from its skin, since the hide was said to remain taut in rain or summer heat. In more recent times, the river's toxins have probably claimed more alligators than the drum makers ever did. Local quacks also sell alligator skins and heads—a big skin goes for two hundred *yuan,* a small head for twenty—as a sexual stimulant (ground alligator head allowing for semiperpetual erection, it is said). There are thought to be fewer than a couple hundred of the beasts left—more or less the same number as the surviving *baiji* a little farther downstream—and one wildlife organization has declared that the Yangtze alligator is in fact now wholly extinct.

• • •

An hour past Anqing and the mood on the ship's bridge suddenly became tense. We were due to negotiate a narrow pass in the river. There was a steep cliff on the port side, a reedy islet to starboard, the shallow and whirling channel in between. The islet is known as the Little Orphan, and the cliff the Mirror Mountain, and legends concerning drowned children and turtles and capsizing rescuers abound. The radio operator in Jiujiang had called to caution Captain Wu that the whirlpools of the so-called *chow-chow* waters here by Mirror Mountain were exceptionally bad, that the floods were causing the river to race at a dozen feet a second, and that it might not be possible for our slow and deep-draft ship even to pass that day.

Captain Wu put on a shirt, stubbed out his cigarette. Lookouts were posted on the bridge wings, and a detail stood to beside the anchor chains. The engineers were asked for full power, and the steersman called for quiet on the bridge.

The cliff loomed ahead and to our left. The channel ahead was clearly visible—huge whorls of muddy water sucking and gulping as they spun down toward us. The marshes waited patiently to our starboard, eager for us to strand. Fifty years ago the invading Japanese had been checked here by a boom: a dozen junks were arranged in line abreast above the rapid, with bamboo hawsers and chains connecting them. A siege cannon had been placed on top of the mountain. Any Japanese ships that made it through the choppy waters had to negotiate the guns and the barrier ahead, and for a while, all of them turned back. But only, the Chinese shake their heads and sadly admit, for a while.

We seemed first to steer in quite the wrong direction, heading directly for the cliff. At the last moment, when the great limestone walls seemed ready to smash into our bows, the captain whispered an instruction, the vessel heeled hard to starboard and we lurched back into the full force of the stream. We then were kicked from side to side as though on a bronco, and for a moment it seemed just as likely that we would plow into the reeds and be stuck in mud for the day.

But then another huge wave crashed into us and knocked us back into the channel, just as Captain Wu, I supposed, had calculated. A few more knocks, a host of lesser crashes, a roar of thick black smoke from the funnel as the engines were gunned hard—and we were through. The reach widened, the waters calmed.

Fifty years ago a band of naked men would have tracked our boat along the Little Orphan Channel. They would have been bending low in the mud, pulling to a drumbeat and an ancient song, straining against the bamboo ropes that would have been fastened to our mast. But trackers were rare men in the China of today: it would be a few hundred miles farther upstream before I had any chance of encountering them. Big engines did the heavy hauling in these parts these days, and on a dangerous day like this, when the stream was running high, it was probably just as well. Trackers died in accidents by the score: the work was dangerous, damp, dirty and cold.

The flooding did seem to be spreading farther and farther afield on both sides of the river. A line of trees, half-submerged, marked where the river's bank had been a week ago: a new one, changing by the hour, now lay scores of feet beyond. Nonetheless I had a sneaking feeling that these floods were actually not as terrible as the radio was endlessly telling us.

It was just a hunch. I had no evidence to support it—other than the ubiquity and the relentlessness of information to the contrary. Yes, I could see that the waters were high. But I had seen them this high before, on earlier visits to the river, and there hadn't been all this fuss before. There didn't seem to be a feeling of disaster in the air—there didn't seem, from this vantage point, to be a catastrophe that was at all related to the dire headlines that I saw each day in the *China Daily,* or to the grim-faced announcements made on the evening television news. We didn't see refugees at the little ports, nor were there more than the average number of drowned bodies bobbing down our stream each day. No ruined houses swirling in the stream, no shards of shattered timber, no shaking thunderstorms, no embarked battalions or patrol vessels, no bags of rice or sand, no Red Cross officials anywhere. There was no panic, nothing more than a vaguely concerned equanimity. Perhaps it was fatalism. Perhaps this is how the Chinese always behave in a crisis. Or perhaps, the skeptic gnawing away inside me thought, this flood was not so terrible as it was made to seem.

I had one good reason, and only one, for my doubts. Five hundred miles ahead of where the *Jiang Han 18* was sailing, the Chinese were starting to build the greatest flood control mechanism of all time—a giant dam, the biggest in the world, that would block the Yangtze just below the famous Three Gorges. Its primary actual purpose was to generate lots and lots of electricity; its primary stated purpose, on the other hand, and according to the propagandists in Beijing, was "to control the river and prevent the recurrence of the devastating floods of the past."

The whole world seemed implacably set against the building of the dam. Almost everyone of influence and knowledge appeared to have good reason to oppose its construction. Big dams generally were seen as outdated and environmentally irresponsible totems, wasteful symbols of national pride. This one, for a score of reasons, was even worse than most. The World Bank was against it. The Americans were against it. Almost no one had sympathy for the Chinese case. But—if central China were to be devastated by another flood, thus proving the Yangtze to be an uncontrollable monster—then perhaps, just perhaps, this lack of sympathy might begin to turn. That, I unpleasantly suspected, was what the Chinese might be thinking.

This year was crucial, a year when the fund raising for the almost unbelievably costly dam was at its most energetic stage. So it was not beyond the bounds of possibility that the Chinese leadership might have thought a hostile outside world could be persuaded to take some kind of pity and begin to think anew about the wisdom of building the brute. The Chinese Communists have a proven capacity for lying on an epic scale—and to lie about the size of a summertime flood was not wholly beyond their range of mendacity. The bigger the lie, after all. So were they telling the truth? Or were they exaggerating matters, the better to make their case for the immense project, one in which so much national, ideological and political face was involved? It was an intriguing thought, at the very least.

It had in any case now stopped raining, and through the pale blue haze I could see that hills were rising in the distance—mountain ranges, a whisper of the terrain of the coming western lands. On the flanks of the nearer hills grew the one crop for which this part of China had once been famous all around the world, and which once gave the Yangtze the bulk of her downstream cargoes. Around the bend ahead, past the entrance to Poyang Lake, was the town of Jiujiang, a place that was known only a few years ago—and to some specialists, still even now—for the pure and elegant excellence of her tea.

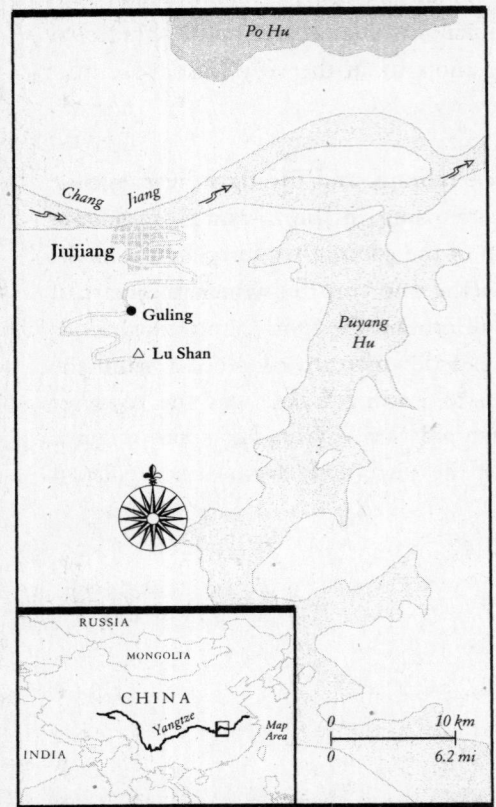

7

Crushed,
Torn and
Curled

Considering the immense damage that the British once did to China, and all of it essentially perpetrated in the hot pursuit of tea, it is not too surprising to find that it is well-nigh impossible to get today what most Britons would consider a decent cup of the stuff anywhere in the People's Republic.

You can of course always get Earl Grey at the Portman Hotel in Shanghai, or Lapsang souchong at the White Swan in Canton—but these are teas imported from India, and they will cost you five dollars a pot. In a city like Jiujiang, once the epicenter of an industry that had half a world bent in mute submission, it is about as pointless to ask for a cup of oolong or keemun or orange pekoe as it would be to demand a plate of scones and clotted cream. The damage that the British did to China's body politic was echoed in the damage they did to her tea business—more so, in truth, because while the former recovered and survived, the latter was more or less done to death.

At the Jiujiang Hotel that night, it not only appeared impossible to get any tea: there also wasn't any food. The boat was late—because of the floods, Captain Wu kept insisting—and we finally disembarked at midnight and found a broken-down taxi. As it limped along with us to what all agreed was the best hotel, we still had high hopes for a substantial dinner. The Jiujiang was after all a spanking new hotel, tricked out impressively in chrome and polished marble. It had fake columns six feet wide, colored fountains playing outside and in, a doorman who wore the uniform of some steamy Latin republic—a mauve shako, a long heliotrope jacket in velvet with gold epaulets and the yellow stripes of a master sergeant—and a small battalion of scarlet-coated little girls who stood behind a reception desk so long that the girls at one end had to telephone to speak to colleagues at the other.

"Welcome to our new Jiujiang Hotel," said one of them, as I approached her for rooms. She bowed low. "We offer five-star comfort and extreme luxury for all our honored foreign guests." It was a memorized speech, but good. She smiled, and pushed a "foreigners' registration form" at me. She tried to give another to Lily, who sniffed haughtily, said something curt, and flashed her Chinese identity card. The girl blushed and handed her instead the much smaller form that Chinese are required to sign. "Smaller card, smaller price," she said, with a winsome grin. The cost of a room for a Chinese citizen was ten dollars. For me, three times as much.

Right then, I said, as I handed over the deposit monies. Food.

"Oh dear," said the girl. She telephoned her friend at the far end of the desk, and both shook their heads as if connected by an invisible string.

"No food here. All the cooks gone home. They leave at eight, to have their dinner."

"Not even a cup of tea?" I wailed, in mock disgust. But I was too tired to argue. They must have seen my dismay, for they kept up a continual bright banter all the time I was checking in, and while the man in the shako wrestled gamely with our two rucksacks, trying and failing repeatedly to load them onto his velveted back.

"President Jiang Zemin was here last week," said the girl, conversationally. I stopped in my tracks.

"You mean—the president of China?" I asked. She nodded.

"He came here, to this hotel?" I had turned to listen, and I must have looked incredulous, for she nodded vigorously for emphasis.

"Certainly he did. And you know how much he spent? Four hundred thousand *yuan*—just two days he was here. *Four hundred thousand.* Can you believe it?"

I couldn't. Nor could I really believe she was telling me this. This was the kind of information only imparted in whispers in the old days and never, never mentioned to foreigners.

"Look—I show you the bill we made up." She waved a long sheet of paper at me. "Bodyguards, secretaries, members of the Central Committee. They took two whole floors. They came in on Tuesday, and they left on Thursday."

I asked why. Why would the president of the People's Republic come to a tired old onetime tea port halfway up the Yangtze? It wasn't as though he was running for elected office and needed to secure the votes in Jiangxi province (although with more than 25 million of them, they would be handy to have in the event China ever became a democracy).

"Yes, I can answer that, too," replied the girl, eagerly. She would go far, this young woman. She was really good. "You know the dam they are building up at Sanxia—the Three Gorges. Well, a million and a quarter people are going to have to move out, you know? President Jiang was here because he wants to suggest to the mayor of Jiujiang that quite a lot of them should move here. To this city. I think it is about two hundred thousand. They will come here in a number of stages. We heard them talking about it weeks ago. Our mayor wasn't sure it was a good idea. So the President came down from Beijing to tell him it was.

"So they had their talks, and I hear they've decided exactly where they're going to put them, where they're going to live. Beijing's going to give some money to the city to build some houses, over near Binjiang Road, on the Yangtze, on the riverside. Plenty of room there. It'll be good for the city. There's no life here. It'll be good to have a few more people."

The would-be Nicaraguan master sergeant, who had finally managed to get the two rucksacks over his epaulets and was perspiring heavily from the effort, ushered us into the lift. I asked the girl why it was that she knew so much, and why she was talking so much. I propped the elevator door ajar.

"The odd thing is—the main owner of this hotel is actually a journalist," she said. "He used to work for the *Renmin Wenbao*. He still writes stories, in fact. But he thought it was better to run a hotel. He bought sixty percent of it. But he talks news all the time. It's part of life here—he makes me take an interest in everyone who comes to stay here. It is much more interesting. You will meet him tomorrow, I think. He will confirm all that I am saying."

I made notes of this rather unexpected exchange and then climbed into the lumpy bed. No matter how grand hotel reception halls may be in China, the carpets upstairs are always stained and the beds are always lumpy. I was too tired to care: it must have been about one o'clock by the time I fell asleep.

Some time later, however, I was awakened by a noise. There was someone knocking at my door, softly but insistently. I looked at my watch: it was just before two. Well accustomed to the sensual thrills in Eastern hotels that begin with a soft tap from outside, I tiptoed over to the door and with an expectant flourish threw it open.

Two of the reception girls stood there, together with a crisp young man who was wheeling a small trolley laden with food. Lily was standing there too, a towel draped around her. They had, prudently, gone to her room first.

"They've been to their homes and cooked for us," she explained. "They thought we looked hungry, and they knew we were disappointed. So look—noodles! beef! beer! These Jiujiang people are wonderful, yes?"

And I had to agree. The young man was in charge of the hotel's food, and he had been telephoned at home. He in turn had roused his mother and asked her to prepare something for two strangers who had come in late from the Nanjing steamer. The girls had set the trays. They would accept no money, and they only apologized that everything had taken so long, and that perhaps they had awakened me.

As they were leaving, one of the girls suddenly made as if she had remembered something, and produced from her pocket a set of utensils wrapped in a napkin.

"Knife and fork," she announced proudly. "In case you no good at *kuai-zi*. Many foreign guests prefer these." She gave them to me, bowed slightly and smiled, and then quietly backed out of the door.

On my table were a bowl of wheat noodles, a plate of stir-fried beef and garlic, a small orange, a much ablated bar of gritty Chinese chocolate and a tall bottle of the local beer with its label glued upside down. There was also, in deference to the plea I thought had gone unheard (and also, I liked to think, in deference to where we were), a pale little bamboo box with a line of four characters that I recognized in an instant: Yun Wu Lu Cha—Lushan Misty Clouds Green Tea. The city's most famous product of old, the seven-times-processed tea, once reserved as a gift for emperors, and still to be found here, even at two in the morning.

Wen Zi-jian, the hotel's owner-manager—who said he had indeed once been a reporter but who was reluctant to explain how on a journalist's salary he had managed to collect enough cash to finance buying part of a hotel—arranged a car for us the next day. He stood alongside his man in the extravagant shako and waved us off. No need to pay the bill now, he said—settle everything when you leave town. He would arrange tickets on the next upstream boat—although perhaps we would like to ride in his car, as he was going to

Wuhan himself in a day or so? Mr. Wen was a most accommodating man, and his hotel a little gem. But we said no—we preferred to go by ship. We would talk about it over dinner, maybe, when we got back from our excursion to tea country.

The Lushan road began to slope steeply upward within yards. Jiujiang's suburbs—or at least the untidy mess of thatched huts, army- and police-barrack blocks and filling stations that passes for suburbia in most of China—clung onto the roadside like moss, but soon gave way to fields of corn and huddles of banana palms. Before long the straight road began to wind and then to curve in hairpins as we clawed our way up the side of the mountain. Lily, who said she had never been in a car for more than two hours at a stretch, began to look green, and closed her eyes—a shame, since the clumps of banana trees soon gave way to peach trees in blossom, and to long stands of azalea bushes.

It was easy to see why the Europeans used to flock to Lushan. It had the same kind of appeal as Indian hill stations like Simla, or Ooty, or Kodikanal, or Murree—cool where below is hot, blue where below is brown, crisp where below is soggy, and above all, somewhat like home where below is wholly like abroad. They had come up here for holidays, and some had built summer homes here—small limestone bungalows with a living room and two bedrooms and a hut outside the scullery where the maid or the *amah* might stay.

The big companies had built villas here—Chiang Kai-shek had built one too, and named it after his wife, Mei-ling—and most of these are now hotels. There are sanitariums, where the old or the sick can take advantage of the cool, clear air; and there is a botanical garden, designed by a Briton in 1934, and brimming with an orderly wilderness of around four thousand kinds of native plants. And there are the memorable views and sights—the peaks up on the Guling ridge that they call the Five Old Men, the Cave of the Immortals, the Single Drop Spring from which one might drink and be guaranteed eternal life.

Long before it had attracted China's expatriate community,

Lushan had drawn painters and poets and contemplative souls, too. It was a place to get away and reflect, to pause, to write, to compose lines of poetry. Li Bai, the most famous of the Tang poets, visited often and wrote poems that all Chinese children know by heart; and Mao Zedong came here for the more prosaic reasons of state, and he came away having written poems that are still quoted today, and for reasons of poetry, not state.

The Yangtze plain was below, and it fell away behind us, and before long the river itself came into view—a brown swathe of winding-cloth, more than a mile wide, stretching far into the hazes of two horizons. It seemed then that when afloat on its surface, pinioned between the buoys of the navigation channel, or when walking on a bund beside its banks, the river looks merely immense: but from up here, half a mile up on the flanks of a mountain, the Yangtze looked like a primary feature of the planet, as much a part of the visible fabric of things as the canals on Mars, or the rings around Saturn. It was so dominant a feature of the land, and of so important and self-regarding a land, that one could see exactly why the Chinese had only one name for it. Other bodies of flowing water might be called *this* river or *that* stream or *those* brooks; from up here it did seem quite right that what wound terrifyingly below, erasing all thoughts of others, was properly called in these parts just *Jiang*. *The* River. Nothing more.

The driver thought he could sneak us past the town barrier without paying, but he was wrong. After eighteen miles of hairpins the road straightened and we came to a massive cement gate, adorned with lions and dragons. There was a metal pole, raised, with an ugly-looking youth in a powder-blue uniform standing idly beside it. We passed by, but he yelled and cursed as we did, and so the driver stopped in mute obedience. The thug in pale blue demanded thirty *yuan* for the privilege of entering the village of Guling, a part of Lushan town: Guling had been made into a provincial park, he said, and the buildings needed to be maintained.

"Buildings that *you people* built," he snarled, once he saw he was dealing with a foreigner. "You didn't make them so good. They keep falling down. Who is to pay for the repairs? Thirty *yuan* is cheap."

Lushan is known throughout China for three reasons. For tea, for pleasure and for politics. And in particular, in the latter category, for the events that took place in the Guling People's Theatre during one week in the summer of Lushan's most celebrated and infamous year—1959.

The story of tea, however, which in its own way becomes enmeshed in the other two strands of Lushan's fame, began almost exactly three hundred years before. It was in 1657 that bags of it were first offered for sale at Garway's Coffee House in London. Historians like to think that coffee, cocoa and tea all actually arrived in London and were first sampled five years before, in 1652: but in the lore of the tea industry, 1657 is said to be when the fabric of English social and commercial life began to include as an essential significant quantities of this hot brown infusion. The year marked by this development in the drinking habits of the infant British Empire also saw, and as a direct result, the beginning of the end for the existence of the infinitely older Empire of China.

The tea plant that did it all is a potentially massive piece of botany. It is a kind of camellia that if allowed will happily grow up to sixty feet high: but in the tea gardens of China and elsewhere it is pruned and punished until it keeps itself to a stunted three- or four-foot bush, easy for the pickers to reach around. All camellias belong to the Theacea family, whose 240 species include a mere 7—*Camellia sinensis* among them, tea proper—that are amenable to infusion. Eighty are more obviously familiar as the garden camellias that, with their pink and white flowers and glossy green leaves, decorate herbaceous borders all around the temperate world.

All of the Theacea, whether big or small tea plants or red or cream floral bushes, came first from western China. They were brought to the outside world by the great plant hunters of the eighteenth and nineteenth centuries*: but not, significantly, until then. In 1657 none of this—words like "Theacea," *"Camellia"* or even "tea"—was known to the excited patrons of Garway's. Back then no one had the first idea how the leaves in their new drink were grown, or what or exactly where they came from. They knew only that they liked the brew, that it was mildly stimulating, and that it was a better bet for imbibing than the two customary choices in the London of the day, dirty water or alcohol. At their coffeehouse counters and to the servants who entered their withdrawing rooms, they became accustomed to asking for it using the pronunciation *tay,* which was perhaps their version of the Chinese word *"cha."*

As well they might. The hessian bags on offer in Mr. Garway's emporium did in fact all come from China, and more specifically, from Canton. They came via Lisbon and Amsterdam, for the Portuguese and the Dutch had rights to trade in Canton—albeit under the strict supervision of the Court. Commerce with outsiders was for the Chinese an unnecessary vulgarism. The rights to indulge in it were granted simply as a boon to barbarians who had a need for Chinese goods. The dynasts of the Qing deluded themselves into believing that they, on the other hand, needed nothing from outside.

It did not take long for the British East India Company to get involved in the tea trade and to try to convince the Chinese otherwise. In 1669, the supercargoes on company ships were buying cases of Chinese tea in Java—where it was cultivated, as it was in Japan- and Formosa. By 1686, they were purchasing it in Canton itself. Such was the rocketing demand for the leaf in England (and so huge were the tax revenues that the British government found it could earn by levying duty both at home and on the tea exported to their colonies, like North America) that the company made huge profits. Its agents began to buy so many tons of tea from the Canton merchants that it established a near monopoly, bitterly contested by other foreigners. A new generation of ships—the magnificent tea clippers—were built in yards

---

* Including the Moravian Jesuit missionary named Kame, the Latinized version of whose name is memorialized in the genus.

in London and all around the English coast to supply the huge demand: they would speed home from the China coast with hundreds of tons of tea aboard, and with additional tons of Chinese porcelain for ballast.*

But before long an embarrassing question arose: how exactly were the Chinese to be paid for all this tea? In the early days they had been happy to accept copper, one of the few minerals in which the Empire was then deficient. They would also accept gold, though they preferred silver. Yet by the middle of the eighteenth century the demand for tea had swollen to such a level that London, already near bankrupted by its European wars, found it could no longer afford to pay in metal of any kind. The company men offered paper money, but the Chinese were disdainful. They said they had no use for such stuff and distrusted it, viewing it quite sensibly as merely a promise of payment made by men quite probably unreliable. To the Chinese, it was just a new piece of foreign devilry.

Caught in a money trap, men can do terrible things. The British were caught, and terrible things they promptly did—deciding as an act of East India Company policy that the tea trade with Canton should in future be balanced by selling the Chinese the one commodity that the peasantry appeared, urgently, to need—the dried, fermented, and pressed juice of the head of the Indian white poppy: opium.

This drug had been declared illegal by China in 1729. Growing, supplying or smoking it was ultimately to become a capital offense. But it was an identifiable need, a popular craving, and once Britain had identified it as such, so the purveyors—and in the early days the monopoly belonged to the company—exploited the craving to the hilt. Patna and Benares and the other great opium-growing centers in India began to produce the flat brown cakes or four-pound can-

---

* The company shipmasters' need for stability at sea—which they achieved by stowing the light cases of tea (and bolts of silk) on top, the heavy crates of china underneath as kentledge—led unintentionally to a passion for chinoiserie in England and America that flourishes to this day.

nonballs of pressed opium by the hundreds: sixty tons in 1776, three hundred in 1790. It was then but a short trip to take it from Calcutta to Canton—opium ships ran a virtual shuttle service in the summer, running the drug from Indian godown to Chinese godown and selling at an incredible profit.

Chinese tea was sold to the British for sixty dollars a ton. For the same amount of money the Chinese merchants could buy just half a box of the opium—one layer from a standard Patna box, with twenty four-pound balls sealed in pitch and sewn up in a gunnysack. It was, from the British point of view, a perfect trade—a true license to print money. And while the East India Company made the first good money, its own monopoly was eventually weakened and broken—after which time magnificent baronies grew up in London, headed by men who could count their cash ten thousand miles away from where their dirty trade was done, and who were making profits quite as fast and as furiously as do the cocaine bosses of Colombia three centuries later.

There was a signal difference between then and now, however. While the Colombians are today condemned all around the world, firms in Victorian times, like Jardine, Matheson & Co. and their main rivals Lancelot Dent and Company, the American firm of Russell & Co., a lone British entrepreneur named Innes and the Parsi trader Heerjeebhoy Rustomjee, were all handsomely and officially rewarded for their business—of which opium dealing produced the greatest profit. They were able to accumulate an impressive storehouse, one that in many cases is maintained today, of respectability, political power, influence and official honors.*

---

* Jardines, which went on virtually to create Hong Kong, and which still plays a dominant role in business in the territory, is understandably weary of being pilloried for the role it once played in the selling of "foreign mud." It has to be said that some in the firm's ranks objected at the time—Donald Matheson, for example, grew so distressed at the social and medical effects of the drug that he resigned from the firm. He was a rarity, however, and China to this day has not quite forgiven the company, delivering a sharp rebuke from time to time, just to keep it on its toes.

The almost fantastic cascade of political consequences of the opium trade, and China's attempts to ban it and thus curb the westerners' profiteering, are well known. They included two vicious wars between Britain and China, any number of manifestly unequal treaties that were then imposed on the vanquished Chinese (such as that signed back on HMS *Cornwallis,* moored in mid-Yangtze off Nanjing in 1842), the cession of Hong Kong to Britain, the steady slicing away of China (the Shandong peninsula going to Germany, Port Arthur to Russia, the Manchurian railway concession to Japan, Port Edward to Britain, and so on), its invasion by soldiers from Europe, the Americas, and Japan, the fall of the Manchu dynasty, the fall of the Republic, the creation of the People's Republic. It is by no means stretching things to say that the opium trade led more or less directly to the dropping of the atomic bomb as well—for once the Japanese had found themselves able to defeat the war-weakened Chinese at battle, to annex Manchuria and to invade and occupy fully half of the Empire, so they found an increasing confidence in their own belief that they should rule the Pacific, and began promptly to try to do so, overrunning Malaya and Burma, bombing Pearl Harbor.

And if all in the name of opium, then all in the name of tea. The Chinese sent other products, too—rhubarb and silk and the kentledge-ballast of which porcelain was the main part. But tea was what the fuss was really all about, and opium was needed to pay for it. Never, at least in this context, was there a more appropriate metaphor than a tempest in a teacup.

But there was one further complication, and an unkind irony it was. The very Chinese tea industry whose existence sparked all of this was itself eventually consumed and virtually destroyed by those who had been its greatest patrons. The British all but ruined China, and on the way they set about ruining its tea business with a vengeance, too.

This happened because of a chance discovery that was made in 1820 by the new commissioner of Cooch Behar in India—the finding of a plant, not seen before. The new commissioner sent samples of it down to Calcutta, where it was received by a young and ambitious

Dane named Nathaniel Wallich, who had just been appointed botanist to the Government of India. He suspected what was later confirmed in London: the plant was *Camellia sinenis,* the tea tree, and it grew in abundance in Assam. It was not, however, used by any of the locals as an infusion. No Indian of the time drank tea. That was all to change, drastically.

Tea, it was realized by the British, would grow as well in the hills of eastern India as it already did in the hills of western China. From the British colonists' point of view this presented a perfect opportunity. For India was their territory, and they could henceforth grow their crop on what they believed to be their land. In less than thirty years from Wallich's identification, tea plants were being cultivated and processed in India on a prodigious scale, on sprawling plantations, their managements British, their factories equipped with English machinery and European efficiency. A new industry had been established. A new subculture, that of the planter-*wallah,* had been created.

In all those places where Englishmen ruled—Assam, Darjeeling, Bengal, Burma, Ceylon—the very same plants that were being farmed so secretly and primitively across the border in Yunnan and Sichuan were being made to turn out twice as much tea in a third of the time for a quarter the cost of labor. Where the Yangtze valley had for all history been the capital of tea, it was now, thanks to the foreigners, the turn of the valley of the Brahmaputra.

The Chinese monopoly—until that time broken only by Japan, Formosa and some enterprising Javans—was now ripped asunder. The Yangtze treaty ports—Jiujiang down below me here, and Hankou just a day's sailing upstream—continued to be important bases for tea sales only for another few years. By the time the Suez Canal was opened to traffic in 1869, it made sound commercial sense for Europe to buy all its teas from India. They were cheaper, of better quality, and they were rushed to the London markets with dispatch. From henceforth what was called in the drawing room "China tea" was to be a product of the tea industry of the Indian Empire, and all profit was to be made by the English traders and all taxes paid to the

English Crown. The China tea industry was brought back to the condition it had been in before the Portuguese traders first came to Canton: it was in business to supply just the Emperor and his people.

Our driver had a screw-topped jar beside him, half-filled with what he called his tea. This was a pale green tepid liquid that lay on top of an inch-thick and occasionally swirling sediment of coarse green leaves. Every so often the driver would unscrew the lid, take a swig— at an angle that just prevented any leaves getting in his mouth—then set the jar down again to settle. Every couple of hours he would take the opportunity to replenish the jar with boiling water, from one of the elephantine thermos flasks that are a modern Chinese ubiquity: the strength of the infusion would diminish steadily, until at the end of the day his jar looked as though it held old pond water from which a layer of even older spinach had precipitated. He sipped away at it nonethless, though I suspect more out of habit than delight.

Every driver in China is similarly equipped. As well as every officer worker, every policeman in his booth, every hotel receptionist, every bank clerk, probably every airline pilot too. You peer over the counter in a shop, or at a currency exchange, or in a government office, and as like as not one of the clerks who is awake will be sipping on a jar of tea. Not an elegant porcelain cup with its domed lid slightly off center; not a tiny faience beaker of iron-tea that you get in fancy Chaozhou restaurants; but a glass jar, by Kilner, Mason or old Nescafé, and with a rusty old lid, screwed down tight. The Chinese tea ceremony that was has come to a pretty pass. The old reverence for what used to be called the "froth of the liquid jade" has been denatured to a point of unrecognizability. Tea drinking in China today is no more than "watering the ox."

As with the ceremonial and romance, so with the business. I had asked on every street corner down below for the address of the Jiujiang Tea Company, from whose wharves thousands of cases of oolongs and pekoes and souchongs had once been placed on the waiting clippers for London. But the company was nowhere to be found, and the only remark I heard was a disdainful "red tea—no good" from a grizzled ancient who remembered when the town did still export a fair amount of the stuff, back in the thirties.

Red tea is what the Chinese call black tea, and they loathe it. It is what, generally speaking, westerners drink. Black tea is what has vanished from the Chinese scene, and good riddance to it, most Chinese seem to say.

It used to be said—a myth, I suspect—that black tea was the result of the first reaction of a Chinese tea merchant on being told that the foreign devils, the Portuguese in Canton, actually wanted to buy tea. He had no reason to suppose barbarians could appreciate anything of good quality, so he took the meanest-looking sticks and twigs and leathery leaves and stuffed them in bags and dropped them into the hold of a Europe-bound ship. By journey's end in Lisbon they had rotted and turned black—but the Europeans liked the infusion that resulted, and they demanded more. The Chinese were happy to oblige. They were happy to supply Europe with the leavings of their own green tea crop, letting it mature and ferment over the period of long ocean crossing.

There is a measure of truth to the story. Black tea (the Chinese call it red because of the color of the infusion; we call it black because of the color of the leaves) is nothing more than green tea that has undergone processing, heating and fermenting.

The most commonly accepted process for making modern tea is known as CTC—in which the tea leaves plucked from the bushes (two-leaves-and-a-bud, the same formula taught to tea pickers whether they are in Sri Lanka or on the hills beside the Yangtze) are first *crushed,* to release their aromas and their more potent alkaloid chemicals;* then *torn,* to pop their leaf cells; and finally *curled,* so that the surface area available for fermentation is expanded.

Crushed, torn and curled tea leaves are then gently withered, roasted, dried and finally packaged—sometimes in the process scented with bergamot (as in Earl Grey) or rope tar (as in Lapsang

---

* Like theine, tea's weak equivalent of the caffeine in coffee.

souchong). The craft of tea making is as infinitely subtle and complicated a business as the making of wine—and the steady advance of
crush-tear-curl machines, which are to be found in all tea factories
from Nepal to Nairobi, is deplored by those who think they know. It
brings mechanized mediocrity, they say, to a once original little universe of good taste.

But in any case little such machinery is available anymore in
China. For although a small amount of the half-processed, half-
fermented tea known as oolong is made here, almost all the tea sold
within and exported from China is green tea—tea that is picked and
steam-blasted and then dried without being allowed to ferment at all.
Green tea is raw tea, or in some senses dead tea. Whether it is good
or not depends almost totally on the quality of the leaf, and not
nearly so much on the quality of the processing. Lushan Misty
Clouds Green Tea was famous throughout China because of where it
came from—because of the legends about the fullness of the bushes,
the youth and beauty of the women who picked it, the roll call of all
the Courts that drank it—not, to any great extent, on how it was
made.

And so it was with a sense of mounting excitement that I eventually tracked down the gate to the Lushan Tea Research Institute. It
had taken us two hours of patient searching along the butterfly-filled
lanes of the hilltop—past caves and waterfalls and beside cliffs that
loomed high over the whorls of the distant Yangtze—before I found
what I wanted. It was three in the afternoon, pleasantly warm, the
air filled with scents of late spring—an appropriate time I thought to
see the Lushan Institute, the cosmic center of whatever was left of
the world of Chinese tea.

"Go away!" was the first thing anybody said. "This place has
nothing to do with tea."

Three policemen were sprawled on the sun-dappled grass outside
a decrepit mansion. One of them, the man who had shouted, got to
his feet and starting swinging a black-metal billy club. "Electric tip,"
warned Lily. She had pointed out clubs like this before, back in
Shanghai. They had batteries and a coil inside, and were used for

crowd control. They could inflict a nasty shock if the policeman didn't like you.

I pointed to the brass plaque on the gate outside. "Not here," said the guard. "Next door."

We walked next door, to a small outhouse of a building that was connected to the old mansion by a low corridor. It seemed empty, except that in one office on the second floor we found one old woman asleep at her desk. Was this the research institute? we asked. No, she said. Over the road. We crossed the lane to a third building, Grecian style, overlooking gardens. There was a receptionist here. Tea institute? we said. Not here, she replied. Over the road. Building on the left. The very building, as it happened, from which we had been ejected in the first place.

The policemen were still there, and this time they lay mutely as we marched past them. This building turned out to be empty too, although there was a poster showing a young woman picking tea on a misty hillside, which augured well. We peered into each office on all three of the floors. It had been a foreign-built club, by the look of things, perhaps a summertime chummery. There was no one there. On the way down the back staircase, however, we met a man— middle-aged, smoking, sandals, a querulous look on his long and lugubrious face. He appeared to have been woken up, and he rubbed his eyes with surprise on seeing us.

Tea institute, we asked again? "Yes, yes," he said, in a tone of sleepy exasperation. "This is the place. Come to my office, building across the road. I will telephone." He picked up an old black Bakelite telephone and bellowed into it, assuming that I wouldn't understand. "Ling! Wake up, Ling!" he said. "There's a blessed foreigner here. Round up everybody. Go to the meeting room!"

Five minutes later and we were sitting in his office on pink polyester-ruched armchairs in a room furnished like a schoolroom. The lugubrious man, who introduced himself as Dr. Ye, had by now assembled three equally sleepy-looking men, one of whom was Ling. The door kept opening to admit latecomers. None looked very good-tempered. A very old woman came in staggering under the weight of a huge iron kettle and did the rounds of the room, filling everyone's beakers with well-boiled tea. Most people lit cigarettes and sat staring at me. It was ten minutes before everyone was assembled, and then Dr. Ye looked across, waiting for a question.

I said something about how sad it was that China's tea industry had withered away. Maybe—maybe this august research institute was going to breathe new life into it, I ventured, hopefully. There was a long pause.

"Rice," said Dr. Ye eventually. It was not exactly what I had been expecting.

"Come again?" I inquired.

"Rice. Jiujiang is a big rice exporting town." He looked around him. There were nods of approval, then silence again. One man was already falling asleep, his cigarette dangling dangerously.

I tried to focus Dr. Ye's mind. "But wasn't this a big tea city, once upon a time?" There was a further long pause, broken only by snoring. His next declaration made me start.

"They employ virgin girls," he said. "They used to pierce their tongues with needles. They were the best."

This conversation was generating a sort of strange fog, although through it I could discern small dark objects that did seem to relate to tea, if peripherally. I had once heard an old story to the effect that the finest Lushan teas were picked only by virgin girls, and that the green leaves were sent by courier to the Emperor himself. Why the girls pricked their tongues with needles was never clear, and Dr. Ye did not choose to enlighten me.

"We have developed a machine for picking." He let this remark hang in the smoky air. So this is where the conversation was going. It did have a certain time-lapse logic about it. Rice had supplanted tea as the region's major export; once virgin girls were used to pick the two-leaves-and-a-bud, and now the scientists of the Lushan Institute—these sleepy, bad-tempered men assembled here, perhaps— had developed a tea-plucking machine.

If this was so, it was a clear breakthrough. The Georgians once tried to put a modified hedge-cutter to lop the leaves in their Caucasus foothills; and the Japanese made something that looked like a pelican. But both were disasters. Only humans—young, agile, and willing to work for a pittance—could pick tea properly. That was a reality the industry had been living with for hundreds of years, though the dreamers continued to dream.

"Really," I said, suddenly interested. "Can I see it? Where is it?"

Dr. Ye's knees suddenly started to vibrate in a most curious way, as though they were seismograph needles recording a distant earthquake. Several men closed their eyes—meaning that, with the number already asleep, the whole room looked to be at prayer. But Dr. Ye, left alone to answer the question, looked uneasy.

"It is not here," he replied. Where is it? I asked.

"Nanchang," he said.

Had he a picture of it?

"The film is being developed."

A paper I could glance at? An article?

"It is in the office, but"—and he brightened—"there is no key!"

So I tried to press him on what else the Lushan Institute did.

"We have one hundred people here," he replied. His knees had stopped shaking. The quake was past. He said with evident pride: "They spread the knowledge of tea."

The room fell silent again, except for some gentle snoring in a corner. So could I see some people picking tea? I asked. "It is not the season," said Dr. Ye, and laughed gently. Then—could I perhaps look in on the processing plant? "So sorry. It is being cleaned. Maintenance time."

The tea I was drinking today—the tea in the big kettle which the aged woman was bringing around again, weaving her way unsteadily between the sprawled feet of the snoozing ancients—was this Lushan Misty Clouds Green Tea?

"I don't know," said Dr. Ye. "I think we don't have any. Maybe at the shop."

Lily rolled her eyes, and suggested that we leave. We were learning little. We stood up. Immediately the room came alive, the men rubbing their eyes, lighting fresh cigarettes, smiling.

Dr. Ye led us out. "We are so glad you could come. May we have your business card please. You are interested in investing here, maybe?"

In the car I laughed, but Lily erupted. "This kind of thing makes me *really* ashamed of China, you know. That you should see such people. They are *idiots*. These *fucking cadres*." I hadn't heard her employ such colorful language before: I was starting to enjoy this. There was no stopping her now.

"Old Communists, useless old men who get put into jobs like this where they do nothing, *nothing*. They just sit around and talk and smoke all day, and get paid fat salaries and live in nice houses. You think it's your fault that there's no China tea industry? Well maybe it is—but it is also half the fault of idiots like that.

"You know, the sad thing is—there really is good tea here. Look at the hills, look at the weather. They could make it famous around the world. But I'll bet you can't get Lushan tea in your Macy's or your Bloomingdale's? You should be able to—but you can't, and it's because of idiots like these.

"You know the solution? Make it private. Everything that is state run is useless. Everything that is private is better."

She brightened suddenly. "I have an idea. Why not come and live here and run the tea business in Lushan?" She was joking, but only half. "You could be happy. You would make money. You would be living in a lovely place. The old British houses would make you comfortable, make you feel you were at home. And you could make people have work here. You could bring it back to life."

She said later she had thought better of it; and I in turn told Lily about those old army couples who had stayed on in some of the Indian hill stations, long after the end of British India, and how wretchedly most of their stories turned out. I doubt if anyone from the old China days had ever wanted to stay on in Lushan, even if the Communists had agreed. It might still have the look of a colonial hill station, it might have the cool pine-tree smell of a hill station and on a crisp late afternoon like this it might look and feel a little like Perthshire in September, or Vermont in October. But only a little, in truth: just a little below the surface it still was China, very much so.

Each time I mentioned Lushan to Lily in the weeks that followed she bristled at the memory. "Awful men!" she would say. "Their wretched machine. Of course they never made one. Cheats and liars, all of them. Pah!"

At the People's Theatre, on the road that led from the institute back up to Guling, there was no mistaking the town's Chineseness. There was a car park full of buses, a huge crowd of people, cross-faced girls with small plastic megaphones, tour leaders with yellow flags urging elderly men and women to follow, to hurry up, step lively! and not lag behind. They were all here today—twenty thousand like them come every day of the year, it is said—to see where some of the most momentous decisions of the Communist leadership were made.

Within this ugly little building with its three entrance arches, which looked like the kind of cinema-turned-bingo-hall that is found in blighted industrial suburbs in the English Midlands, China's oldest and most powerful men met, fell out and argued and fought, and performed acts, signed papers and changed policies that affected—and usually for the worse—the lives of tens of millions of Chinese people. The most notable decisions were those taken in early July 1959, during what has been called High Noon at Lushan. Nearly all of the pictures that were on display for the benefit of the tourists—most of whom were brought here in buses by their work units: there were groups of several hundred from a steel factory in Wuhan on this day—were taken during that unseemly week of brawling. It was a week when the rulers of China took decisions that can rightly be said to have provided, for millions, hell's foundations.

1959 was the second year of the Great Leap Forward. So it was a time when some kind of an evaluation could be made of Chairman Mao's bold plan to increase, drastically, China's agricultural and industrial production. His plan had been radical, and in many senses, bizarre: it had called for the establishment of giant agricultural communes, for the transfer of millions of city dwellers to work on grandiose irrigation projects, for the building of tens of thousands of "backyard furnaces" that would turn steelmaking into a nationwide cottage industry and swell production. People were told to hand in their pots and pans for melting; communal feeding halls were set up as household kitchens vanished. Society underwent a profound change, with unanticipated and often haphazard consequences, and all in the vain hope of elevating the world's most populous nation into the international premier league.

The Great Leap Forward was an unmitigated disaster—perhaps the most searing indictment of a command economy since Stalin had forced collectivization on the Ukraine in the thirties. Anyone with any insight who gathered in Lushan that summer, for the eighth plenum of the Communist Party Central Committee, knew that it was a disaster—or at the very least that it was going badly wrong. But hardly anyone had the courage or the folly to say so—no one, that is, except for a tiny group of moderates led by the ill-educated but shrewd bulldog of a defense minister, a man who has since been pilloried and victimized into legend, Peng Dehuai. Peng alone felt able to say that what was going on was madness; and in a letter sent from his cool bungalow at one side of Guling to Mao's compound on the other, he told him so.

Given the cruel imperium that was beginning to grip Mao's rule, the result was predictable. The Chairman began by admitting to some mistakes—though in his own defense said that Lenin and Marx had made errors too, but were brilliant and invincible nonetheless—and tried to give the impression of flexibility. It was merely a feint: for the rest of the Lushan meeting Mao tore into Peng and those few men who dared support him—with the result that when all trooped down from the hills at the end of that July, Peng was out of a job, the People's Liberation Army (PLA) was firmly under the hand of Mao, and Peng himself was dispatched into a six-year political exile in a slum on the outskirts of Beijing, sweeping his own floors and carrying out his own night soil, reduced from a hero to a scapegoat in the blink of an eye.

If it was possible to make a connection in Lushan between the growing of tea and the eventual collapse of Imperial China, so it turns out also to be possible, and also in Lushan, to construct a filigree of connections between the angry exchanges in the People's Theatre in 1959 and the terrors that were unleashed in Beijing by Mao and his supporters seven years later that came to be known as the Cultural Revolution. The connections might seem tenuous, only half visible: but unlike the saga of tea and opium and war and treaties, where the links are mostly commercial, political, western and obvious, those that link Peng's sacking and the start of the madness of 1966 are very Chinese, relying as they do to deliver their force on hints, allusions, literature and legend. It is a complicated story, but it is one that has Lushan as its backdrop, and manages to be of huge importance in the history of the country.

Peng Dehuai had found himself in trouble simply because he had told the truth. Doubtless he saw himself as a martyr, though he left no written record saying so. But the deputy mayor of Beijing, a noted and brilliant Chinese historian, party propagandist and occasional essayist named Wu Han, essentially said as much in an article in the *People's Daily* shortly after the Lushan meeting, alluding in well-turned historical phrasings to all that had happened. Wu did not mention Peng by name. Instead, he used his stature as a historian to reprise a famous and often told story from the Ming dynasty: that of the summary sacking and imprisonment, in February 1566, of a devout, honest and well-loved court official named Hai Rui.

Hai, who worked for the Board of Revenue, had sent a minute to the Emperor, accusing him of extravagance, banditry and corruption—all of which was evidently true. The Emperor was duly outraged, sacked and fettered Hai—and then suddenly died himself. Hai was released, and then went and did more or less the same thing twice more in his checkered life—he was impeached and dismissed by the governor of Suzhou, whom he had similarly accused, and then he was censured for calling for the introduction of the death penalty for corruption. Hai was too righteous for his own good, perhaps—a prophet without honor in his own time.

Wu Han had been studying Hai Rui, and had already published one article about Hai's decision to stand up for right against the Ming Emperor. This had appeared in the *People's Daily* on the eve of the Lushan meeting, and it is more than possible that Peng read it. He may even have been inspired by it. But the more important article came after Peng had been sacked. It was a lengthy essay about the sacking of Hai in which he was called "a man of courage for all times," someone who refused to be intimidated. The Emperor, on the other hand, was "self-opinionated and unreceptive to criticism," a man "craving vainly for immortality." To any Chinese skilled in reading between the lines of ideographs, the allusion was clear: yet another good man had been sacked for standing up for right, and a tyrant was in power, behaving as a classical demagogue.

Two years later Wu developed the theme of this now celebrated article into a full-length play, *The Dismissal of Hai Rui from Office*. It was staged in a Communist Party theater in Beijing, and it was also published in book form. The idea, lèse-majesté that it obviously was, was being broadcast far and wide. But—was it real criticism, thinly veiled? Was it a red herring? Why was Wu himself not arrested and humiliated for daring to speak out? Scholars still wrestle with such matters: theses tumble from the presses, their authors poring over the bones of the Lushan encounter and all that stemmed from it.

They do so because the echoes of Lushan and the allusive saga of Hai Rui reverberated down the years, most strongly in 1965. It was then that Mao moved to secure absolute control over the PLA, and in that same year Mao's wife, Jiang Qing, had her colleague Yao Wenyuan attack Wu Han's by now infamous play. Yao, Mao's wife and Mao himself were at long last saying: thus far and no further. Those who dared to compare Mao's energetic running of China with the behavior of a vain and corrupt Ming emperor were, in essence, the new enemy. China must be purged of them, and of all who dared to think like them. Those foolish people who agreed with Wu Han were people who would have agreed with Peng Dehuai; those who condemned Peng and stood alongside Mao would be safe. For the remainder—who knew?

This, then, was the very beginning of what would swiftly become the Great Proletarian Cultural Revolution, a ten-year nightmare that changed the face of the country, horribly and terrifyingly, forever. Tender and elegant though the essays of the seven-year interregnum may have been, they hid the realities of a mighty power struggle that had been going on ever since the Lushan meeting, and which penetrated to the very core of the new China. As usual, what took place in the Middle Kingdom was hidden, at least at first, by the obsequies and curlicues of history and literature. What began with a brief display of plays and poems ended with the deaths of millions in thousands of prisons, and in limitless acres of mud and dirt.

It also saw the end of Peng Dehuai's life. He was arrested by Red Guards at the beginning of the Cultural Revolution, fell ill in prison, was denied any treatment for his ailments. He died in pain eight years later, but four years would pass before his family was told. His victimization, which began at Lushan, continued with all the special bitterness that a revolution can employ only when its chooses that to further its ideals it must consume its own children.*

It was early evening and growing cool by the time we were back down from the hills. Mr. Wen, the manager of the hotel, was waiting for us in his cavernous marble lobby. Good to his word, he had two tickets for the night steamer to Wuhan, and he now gave us a ride down to the riverside. He asked us again to join him on his drive to the city—the road journey would take five hours, while we would have to be aboard the ship for twelve. But he seemed to understand when I said we wanted to go on the ship.

---

* Wu Han was arrested and brutalized, and died within three years. Yao Wenyuan, who wrote the attack on Wu Han's play, went on to become one of the infamous Gang of Four, a steersman of the Cultural Revolution. Once Mao had died he, Mao's widow and their two colleagues were arrested and put on trial: Yao was sentenced to eighteen years in prison.

"You come to love the river after a while," he said. "Whenever I do this drive and I go round a curve and there the river is—I feel that I'm back with a friend. It grips your mind somehow. It is always there in the background. It is part of our lives. So I'll think of you when I am driving. In fact I'll envy you, I think."

He stood on the quay as men lifted the hawsers from the oily bollards and he waved to us. The ship boomed her own three blasts of farewell and edged out into the fairway. The setting sun glimmered its watery way down behind the hills ahead, and within moments Jiujiang was just a smoky smudge astern, its lights swallowed up in the gathering gloom. Somewhere below a karaoke session had begun.

Dark came upon us swiftly. I stood on the deck as we washed steadily through the seamless blackness and listened to the news on the BBC—reception in the Yangtze valley is clear as crystal. They were reporting the Chinese floods, using words like "devastating" and "catastrophe." But here the channel buoys winked, the radars swept the unseen banks, the ship moved steadily upstream, this night as every night. The Yangtze seemed her late-springtime self, fast, full and deep.

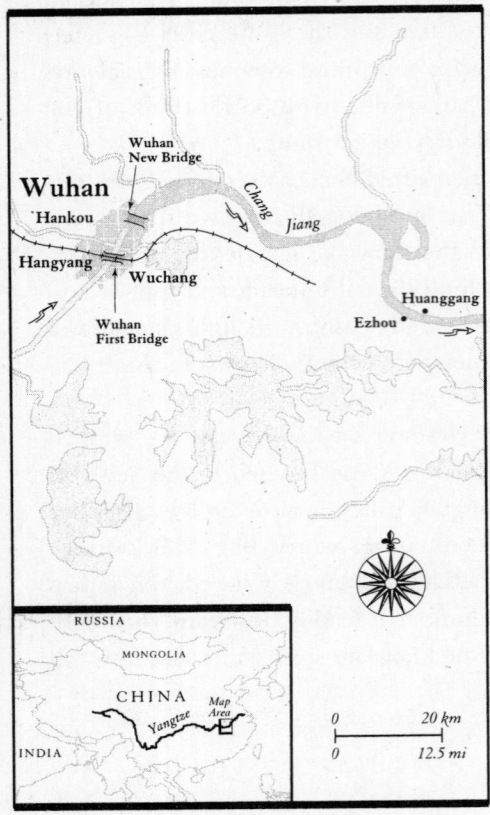

Wuhan
Wuhan
New Bridge
Hankou
Chang
Jiang
Hangyang
Wuchang
Huanggang
Ezhou
Wuhan
First Bridge

RUSSIA
MONGOLIA
CHINA
Yangtze
Map Area
INDIA

0   20 km
0   12.5 mi

8

Swimming

I was awakened the next morning at first light by the noise of passengers chattering excitedly out on deck, calling to one another to come and see something in the river. When I emerged sleepily from my cabin I could see them pointing into the middle distance. Some had cameras and binoculars—we had private cabins once again, so our neighbors were fairly well-to-do—and were busily snapping away.

At first I assumed that it was a body. We had already spotted four of them, two on the journey from Nanjing, floating with the stream. Pigs, I had at first supposed, except that on closer inspection they soon turned out to be the carcasses of children, and of those whose sex I could judge, girls. It was a particularly distressing sight, and I wasn't very eager to gawk at yet another floating testament to the tyranny of the country's birth-control policy, certainly not this early in the morning. But then Lily put on her spectacles, spotted what it was that everyone was looking at and called to me to come.

"Swimmers!" she cried. "People—swimming across the river."

Were this almost any other country in the world, and almost any other river, the fact would barely raise an eyebrow. Dawn on a late spring Sunday might seem a generally eccentric time to go for a dip, but the simple fact of river swimming—across the Mississippi, say, or the Volga—would hardly bring slumbering passengers tearing up from their beds. But this, here, was something different.

The Chinese can by nature be an incurious and in many ways a barely competitive people. The fact that one lives beside a great river, for example, would not seem to the average Chinese a good reason for immersing oneself in it and thrashing across to the far side. What, this average Chinese would say, is the point?

And then too, not only would the exercise here be pointless, it would be very dangerous as well. The Yangtze is a peculiarly treacherous river in which to swim for almost all of its 3964 miles. It is very wide, very deep, and its currents are very fast. It is a viciously capricious, freakish stream—even in these middle reaches, where the banks are flat and covered with violets. The ragged patterns of violent upwellings and depth-plumbing vortices that are known to shipmasters as flower water and chow-chow water can render the most powerful swimmer powerless. There are also water snakes of an uncommonly poisonous kind, and in the vicinity of Wuhan, where these morning swimmers appeared, the waters are known to be afflicted by snails that carry schistosomes, wormy parasites that can wreak havoc in the human bloodstream.* Farmers working on the banks keep well away from the water or wear heavy boots. So why should anyone be out swimming?

Through the gloom I could see dozens of them, arranged in

---

* Causing the blood ailment bilharzia, which British soldiers working on the Yangtze, and on the Nile, liked to call "Billy Harris."

groups. A small armada of little boats led the way—one boat, sometimes two, leading each group of swimmers. Each craft had a red flag fluttering from a tall bamboo spar and one or two young men sitting in the stern, who were shouting exhortations to those splashing through the waters behind. Swim faster! Head this way! Watch out for this eddy! Steer clear of that balk of lumber!

One group, larger than most, passed close to our steamer. It was led by a pair of boats from which rose a celebration arch made of red balloons. There were twenty swimmers in the formation, most young men, perhaps three women. They swam steadily downstream, their arms shoveling the brown waters in near unison. The current swept them along fast, and as their stake-boats evidently guided them past the more treacherous stretches, it looked as though it could have been rather good fun. Like Olympic synchronized swimmers, the men and women wore expressions mixing determination and rapture with fixed smiles and gritted teeth, but with the hint of amazing and powerful things going on underwater, out of sight.

As the lead boat passed by, a young man held up a banner for us to read: "Hankou Number 16 Iron Foundry. To the Eternal Glory of Comrade Mao." Now the reason for the swim became instantly clear: it all had to do with politics, and with reminiscence and the symbolism and sanctity of ancient deeds. And, more important still, it was because the three cities that make up the gigantic conurbation of Wuhan can rightly be said to be, in a historical sense, the most significant in modern China.

For Mao Zedong had swum this river and, precisely because of Wuhan's historical uniqueness, at this very place. One of the ship's bridge officers promptly realized what was going on, and announced over the public address system that today's swim was in commemoration of Mao's. The loyal Wuhan people, he said, performed this act of fealty each midsummer. What was going on today was a dress rehearsal for the real thing, due to take place in a month or so, when men and women who worked in factories and offices all around would come to the Yangtze to race in teams, to see who might come closest to the natatory ideals set by the late Great Helmsman.

Mao loved to swim: he saw it as an elemental kind of sport, where man's energy and wiles could be pitted against the brute strength of nature. It was June 1956 when the Chairman embarked on his first swimming expedition on the Yangtze: he did so to pit himself, symbolically, against brute strengths of quite another variety. He swam to demonstrate, as publicly as he could, his personal frustration, and protest.

The People's Republic that he had fashioned was at the time less than seven years old, but already was running into all manner of trouble. Mao's reforms, as he saw things, were being slowed by the turgid pace of the bureaucracy, there were signs of real opposition to him in some of the cities,* the party elders were squabbling openly and were not always giving Mao the credit for the revolution that he had so keenly engineered.

Some of the mistakes were clearly his own. Mao had made a grave error, for instance, by so naïvely permitting a sudden measure of intellectual freedom—the movement that grew up in the wake of his repeated declarations to "let a hundred flowers bloom." It had rapidly gotten out of hand—and it had to be summarily put down, as it was, with Stalinist robustness.

But the revolution also seemed to have lost its head of steam for vaguer and more puzzling reasons. The nation's enthusiasm needed to be rekindled, Mao thought. There should be some demonstration, some potent reminder that the making of the People's Republic had been a brave and physical thing—that it had been born not out of textbooks and theorizing, as in Russia, but out of the physical heroism of the Long March, out of long-fought battles and well-deserved victories over Chiang Kai-shek's corrupt armies. To remind the people of the nobility of origins like these, and to galvanize them— and to galvanize the bureaucracy, the cadres and the party elders as well—Mao decided he needed to make a physical display of his own leadership and fearlessness.

---

* Particularly in Wuhan, where students committed the ultimate heresy by demonstrating with banners praising Chiang Kai-shek.

This in itself was nothing new. Chinese emperors had a long tradition of showing off their prowess to the citizenry—by painting, by calligraphy, or by very publicly performing noble deeds. Precisely why Mao chose to show off his swimming was never made clear— except that it was something that, as a young Hunanese farm boy, he had learned to do very well, and perhaps because of his own belief in the importance of the sport. Probably, considering China's peculiar intimacy with her vast hydraulics—and in Hunan, like Jiangxi and Anhui and faraway Jiangsu, the "land of fish and rice," that intimacy ran even deeper—he thought a demonstration of a series of grand swims, in all the swimmable streams of the Empire, would put him in touch with his people in a way that a more intellectual distinction such as calligraphy (at which he was also very good) would not.

Besides, it would also show he was strong and fit and capable and fearless—all estimable qualities of leadership. And if nothing else it would reinforce both his and China's undeniable *uniqueness.* Which American president or British prime minister or even Soviet secretary-general would ever dare indulge in such a vulgar and pro- letarian display?

He took his first swim in the spring of 1956 in the Pearl River, near Canton—a modest but very dirty river, choked with chemical waste. Thirty guards floated downstream with him, as well as a political entourage—all of whom had to swim in their underwear, so precipitate was Mao's decision to go. The exercise seemed to do him no harm: he floated on his back like a great pink bear, as though he were sitting on a sofa. During his two hours of floating he taught Yang Shankun—who went on to be China's president, the man who accompanied Queen Elizabeth to Shanghai thirty years later—how to swim in his own relaxed and confident way. And when he emerged from waters that his doctor had seen were thick with human waste, he chided those who were aghast, who had re- coiled from the idea of the Chairman swimming amid all the filth. "If you put a fish in distilled water," he asked, "how long do you think it will live?"

Mao was none too sure, however, that it was entirely wise to swim in the Yangtze: "If I'm trapped there, they say, no one will be able to rescue me." He sent two of his guards up to Wuhan to swim in the river themselves, and they returned full of tales of the treacherous whirlpools and nematode-carrying snails. But neither dared tell Mao, and there is a painful story of the two men stammering and shivering their way through an interview with the Chairman, one of them eventually telling him, in as roundabout a way as only a Chinese knows how, that the river was indeed not suitable for swimming. Mao exploded with rage at the news, prompting the guard's colleague to change his own story on the spot, and tell Mao that the river was, in fact, an ideal place for a leisurely crawl.*

And so Mao traveled north—passing through his old homeland of Hunan, where he swam in the Xiang River for practice. One of his guards was bitten by a water snake, which didn't augur well. But finally Mao's special train chugged north again to Wuhan, his small steamer *The East Is Red Number One* was pressed into service for the convenience and privacy of the great swimmer, and with a flotilla of eight security boats and four longer-range speedboats in attendance, the expedition edged into midriver.

At a point where today's groups of swimmers were rehearsing for their annual ritual of homage, Mao and forty guards and an even larger entourage of secretaries, doctors, Party secretaries, courtiers and sycophants got down into the water. The general commanding the Wuhan Military Region was frightened and had to be rescued— but the others drifted downstream with the genial and, after two hours of effortless amusement, thoroughly vindicated Chairman Mao. The party touched the far bank, symbolically.

They reboarded the steamer for lunch and for a celebratory glass or two of *mao-tai*. Mao was brimming with pride in his achievement and looked about him for confirmation. Yang Shangkun began the encomiums: "No one can match the strength of the Chairman," he

---

* The guard who gave Mao the news he did not want to hear was soon removed from the palace staff in disgrace and vanished into obscurity. His colleague, who had both betrayed him and lied to Mao, was eventually promoted.

declared. "No other world leader looks down with such disdain on great mountains and powerful rivers. But our Chairman can. No one in history can match him."

There was more of the same, much more. And Mao had proved his point: he was strong, spirited, irrepressible and uncontainable. He had defied the received wisdom, he had turned his back on caution and deliberate care. His swimming was a symbol, and he had meant it to be: he had now invested himself with renewed authority to run the country as he wished, with bravura. He had shown to those around him, and to the people, that he could dare and win.

The victory over the river—which Party legend suggests, improbably, may well never have been swum before by anyone—had given him both the necessary adulation from within his circle and the necessary self-confidence from within himself to renew his attack on the slow pace of the revolution, and to look for victory there. It led, as adulation and overconfidence do, to hubris, and then to Nemesis. It led to excess and insanity: for within two years China had accelerated her radicalism under Mao's personal ministrations, and had given birth to the lunacies—well-intentioned, but lunacies nonetheless—of the Great Leap Forward. The 1956 swim in the Yangtze presaged disaster for China, though no one then had the faintest clue that it might.

Nor had they ten years later, when Mao did the same thing once again. This time he had a far more serious agenda once the swim was done. The swimmers who were threshing alongside us on this particular morning were actually commemorating that 1966 swim, and not the first attempt in 1956. What was taking place today was a rehearsal for a race to be held on July 16, the date chosen every year to memorialize what is still regarded as "Mao's *legendary* swim" or "Mao's *celebrated* swim" in the Yangtze. The first swim was simply the first; he would do another in 1958. But the one that he accomplished on July 16, 1966—when he was seventy-three years old and, as it happened, even more frustrated with his country's progress than he had been ten years before—that was a truly great event, a swim seen round the world.

On that occasion five thousand children and students were swimming too, taking part in a race that Mao's first venture had helped inspire. The cadres were also in the water, in their hundreds. The balloons were arranged in great archways, scores of giant red flags fluttered from flotillas of boats, film cameras rolled to record the event—and for two hours the Chairman floated serenely down his country's greatest and most powerful river, which was in full flood. I remember seeing the blurred newspaper photographs, the strangely impressive images on the television newsreels. At the time I was living in Africa, where Mao had many friends; people would shake their heads in awe. "What an amazing man," they would say. "So strong, so vigorous."

Mao was at the time returning to center stage in China after months of a self-imposed exile, when all the world believed him to have vanished. He had gone into retreat behind the compound walls in Beijing, and then he had disappeared completely, except that now we know he traveled south to consort with that special breed of die-hard Communists who worked and thought and theorized down in Shanghai. Over the weeks and months of his absence he had read and reread books on the vicissitudes of Chinese history. He had prepared lists of those who were in favor of a true revolution and those who were against. And he then decided on a course of action so radical that it would shake the world.

He set the stage for it by traveling down to Wuhan and, on that July Saturday afternoon, immersing himself yet again, before all of his people, to see if he could swim the Yangtze once more.

And he triumphed, as he had ten years before. He swam slowly and deliberately and cheerfully and powerfully, managing the first ten miles in just over one hour. I remember so vividly the pictures of the tiny domed head amid the almost limitless waters of the river— the Chairman overwhelming an ancient force that seemed so much more likely to overwhelm him. He arose from the waters finally, alive and smiling, savoring another total triumph.

They said at the time it was all public relations, the giving of reassurance to a nation that thought he might be ailing. But it was so much more than this. Mao had given his people and his supporters and his foes evidence of his physical prowess, true, but he had also given a splendid demonstration of his authority and power. He received the adulation of the masses once again, and with it, as he perceived it, he won the people's mandate to begin something quite extraordinary.

He returned to Beijing with his mind cleared and his decision taken. The Sixteen Points for the Cultural Revolution were published; the Red Guards were born; and a period of madness and cruelty began that shook his country and the continent to its very foundations. Why it is that, thirty years later, the masses in Wuhan still mark and celebrate that swim—or any swim by Chairman Mao—remains, for me, a mystery. For swimming the Yangtze seems not to be so much a display of vigor or noble achievement, as a harbinger of terrible turmoil.

I remarked on this to Lily, as we watched the teams flailing steadily past us.

"Wuhan people are different," she said. "I don't like them at all. I don't like the city—a very dirty place, very bad people. But they think they are special. They are very revolutionary. They are very patriotic. They look back on Mao with more reverence than most Chinese do. In Shanghai, and back home in Dalian, we know he made mistakes. We give him his due honor, but we know he was a human. I heard the stories about his girlfriends, things like that.

"But the Wuhan people turn a blind eye to that sort of thing. They know they have a special place in China's history and they think they must revere their Chairman. So that is why they swim, I think. Besides, I think they know it is good for them. Ordinary people never used to swim this river. But now it is the modern thing to be fit and healthy. Swimming is healthy—at least, in pools it is. No one can doubt that. This is another reason they do it, I'm sure."

In any case, as I heard on the radio some weeks later, the Great Anniversary Swim of 1995 had to be canceled, because of the floods. The rehearsals that Sunday, the balloons and the shouting and the watery tumult—all had been in vain.

· · ·

When Mao first went swimming on the Yangtze in 1956 he did so just a few yards downstream from the piles of a new bridge that was being built across the river. That bridge was duly finished the following year, and until the Yangtze First Bridge, six hundred miles downstream at Nanjing, was completed eleven years later, it was the closest of the Yangtze bridges to the sea. Mao himself declared it open: "a rainbow of iron and steel," he called it.

It was the bridge from which I had first seen the nighttime Yangtze on my railway journey from London ten years before. Now I was seeing it from below: the piles were being buffeted and washed by waves of floodwater, and the great chunk of engineering looked solid and unmoving, a memorial to the Russians who designed and donated it, and to the Chinese who had welded and wrenched it all together.

Today a still newer bridge crosses the river at Wuhan. We had sailed beneath it while we were watching the swimmers—a soaring tracery of bright steel, delicate where the old bridge had been massive, athletic where its predecessor had been ponderous. It had been opened the week before, someone said; the design was quite beautiful, like some of the new bridges in Korea and Japan, though a man I asked said happily that on this one the Chinese had done all the work, including the design.

It seemed to me that while the two spans, a couple of miles apart, obviously reflected the changes wrought by forty years of bridge engineering, they also seemed to stand for something more significant. There was the stolid and unimaginative and joylessly Stalinist construction on one side, a gift from fellow ideologues at a time when the Cold War was at its coldest and when all on the Marxist side needed to give one another comfort and friendship. And there was this slender and graceful piece of art on the other, glittering proudly in the morning sun.

The one bridge spoke of conformity and obedience, of rigidity and a lack of imagination. The other was suggestive of freedom, of an engineer being given his head, of an idea taking flight. And anchored between them, still smoky in the sunlight of a Sunday morning, lay the city they call China's Chicago.

The three cities, in fact—Wuchang, on the Yangtze's right bank; Hanyang, away on the left bank, on the far side of a huge tributary stream called the Han Shui; and here, where our steamer was now edging in toward the dock, Hankou. Four million people live here, at the Yangtze's most important midstream junction point. This is the city of the new China's heart, beating between the two symbols of the new China's history—on the one hand an image of the strictness of the old, and on the other, an image suggesting the half-free and only too beguiling open-mindedness of the new. More than appropriate, considering that in simple historical terms, this city is—or should be—the most important and revered in all China.

Wuhan's importance is not at all apparent when you arrive there by boat. It has an anonymous, forgettable aspect. On this morning we could have been coming in to almost any big industrial city set down between Manchuria and the Burmese frontier. It looked ugly, dirty, disheveled, crowded and only the slightest bit colored by romance. I was in no hurry to disembark when, with a clang and bump and the screech of chains and hawsers, we docked.

The lower-deck passengers streamed out into the new and soaring concrete terminal building, and I could see them humping their bindles into waiting lines of cycle-rickshaws. The taxis would wait for the upper decks to clear, a few minutes later. I clambered up to the bridge to say good-bye to the captain. He was a kindly man who had spent much of the morning showing me his charts, even though they were stamped "Top Secret" in vermilion—and he had offered suggestions for where we might stay in town.

For a while I stood looking out from the bridge wing, over to the Hankou Bund, alongside which we were tied up. This was where the old foreign concessions had been. There was a ramshackle collection of grimy buildings from which the foreign *hongs,* the trading houses, had once operated, but they could hardly rival their sister structures back in Shanghai.

It had been a very short bund, and the foreigners had been crammed into it in small parcels. The British had the biggest sector, closest to the government offices, because they had been the first outsiders allowed here, courtesy of their triumph in what has been called the Second Opium War. But even this spoil of battle had been a fairly mean allotment of land: my old map showed the inevitable consulate at one end, the offices of Jardines and Swires and British-American Tobacco dispersed at the other, and a few scrawny lanes between, with small buildings of a very faded elegance.

There had once been seven hulks permanently moored off the British Concession and used as floating docks: the clipper ships that raced to London with their cases of China tea all began their voyages here. A cannon was fired to set them on their way, and they raced down to the Woosung Bar in less than two days if the wind was fair and the current strong. London was twelve weeks away, if every shred of canvas was employed and every breath of wind was caught.

Next to the British, downstream, had been the Russians. They were not much involved in Yangtze shipping, but they did a brisk overland trade in brick tea—the compressed dust from the tea factories up in the hills nearby. But I could not recognize the buildings of Litvinoff & Company, which had then dominated the business—indeed, the site on the map now seemed to be occupied by a new skyscraper hotel, the very one in which the captain had suggested we might stay.

After the Russian Concession had come the French, which once sported the city's best hotel, the Terminus; then came the German Concession, and finally the Japanese, a tiny settlement with little to tempt and containing only a barracks and a match factory. Thus were all Hankou's foreigners accommodated, crammed neatly into a flood-prone couple of miles between the railway and river.

The railway and the river! In Wuhan it seems that everything revolves around the existence and the conjunction of the railway and the river. From where I stood scores of feet above river level, the railways were plainly audible. Whenever the wind changed direction and the car horns quieted for a moment, I could hear the background orchestra—the shunting of faraway railway wagons, the yelp of steam engines, the rattle of trains rushing over the points, the rumble of an express passing over the bridge.

The air, thick with industrial smoke, had a familiar edge to it too, the rotten-egg-like smell of sulphur and coke and steam coal—a railway smell, the good old unhealthy smell of coal-driven steam trains, of the railways before they switched to oil. Wuhan is still very much a railway town, sooty and tarry, a terminus town, a junction city of roundhouses and repair shops and signal works. And all set down beside the wharves and the piers, the cranes and the gantries, the mud and the rising and falling waters of the river to whose vast valley the railways had come.

It was the building of the railways that gave Wuhan her peculiar and unforgettable place in Chinese history. This is a long way, both in time and geography, from the Jardines' attempt to build their little line back between Woosung and Shanghai—this was forty years later, and nearly a thousand miles upstream, and central China was now brimming with permanent ways. There was, however, one underlying problem—a problem that had much in common with the proposed Jardines line, and one that rankled with almost all the Chinese.

The main line between Beijing and the Hankou terminal on the north side of the river here had been built in 1905, financed by the French and British, its building directed by a Belgian. (Its terminus station had been put up conveniently behind the French Concession, between the Bund and the racecourse.) And in this way it was typical: it had been built and paid for by foreigners, and such profits as it made went into the pockets of foreign shareholders. Most of the new great through routes in China, all built at much the same time, were the same. The Mukden Railway was built by a Briton. The railways in Shandong were German. Those in Manchuria, Russian. The Manchu Court—then run by regents for the infant Emperor Pu Yi—had for years been gaily handing out contracts to foreign banks and companies that were slicing across the Empire with thousands of miles of track. Why, a growing number of Chinese began to ask, were the Chinese not building the railways, and why were they not making profits from the railways, themselves?

The first questions concerned, specifically, the Beijing to Hankou line that ended here. Toward the end of the new century's first decade, as the questions swelled ever louder and started to evolve into demonstrations and protests, so still more contracts were being handed out by the Court, and that also involved Hankou—the line from Hankou south to Canton, for example, and another line east from Hankou to Shanghai. Hankou, this dirty, clanking, steam-swirled coke town, had from the beginning been at the epicenter of the entire dispute.

In 1910, by which time China had some 5000 miles of railways built and 2000 more a-building, this single issue erupted into a passionate and violent display of nationalism, one that the Manchus could neither comprehend nor control. In every province, groups were formed to protest at the way the courtiers far away in the Forbidden City were giving away to outsiders what seemed to be China's birthright—her transportation routes. Serious demonstrations broke out all across the Empire—the Railway Protection Movement, as the organizing body was called, staged rallies, strikes and boycotts. Even more significant, elements of the newly reorganized Chinese Army were seen to side with the railway protesters. Within just a few months during 1910 and 1911, railways became a focus for all of the long felt dissatisfactions—ranging over matters as far removed as taxation and foot-binding—that millions of ordinary Chinese felt for the performance of the Court. The protesters demanded a change of government—an end, in other words, to the doddering and non-Chinese theocracy, the heaven-directed Manchu Court, which still clung to power in the distant capital. "We must avenge the national disgrace," was a rallying cry. "We must restore China to the Chinese."

Hankou lay at the center of all this revolutionary, anti-Imperial fervor simply because of her strategic position as a Yangtze railway city. Her population—boatmen working on the Yangtze, railway workers, soldiers in what was called the New Chinese Army—was in any case peculiarly militant, much more so than farmers, say, or scholars and members of the bureaucracy. Poetic justice was surely to be served, then, when it fell to this city before all others in China to become the place where the spark of real revolution was first lit. And yet when that spark was lit, it was, ironically, for rather different reasons.

The city is famous today as the place where the first shots were fired: it is the Lexington, if you will, of the Republic of China, the precise place where five thousand years of Imperial rule came to a sudden, shuddering end. Chinese modern history is replete with engaging ironies: here, though the entire Empire was in ferment because of her railways and though Hankou was a rail center like no other, the actual event that precipitated the Empire's end had nothing to do with railways at all. It was an event that took place on the famous day of the "double ten"—the tenth day of the tenth month— in 1911. More than almost any other date in China's story, this is one that is remembered, and revered. The fuse was lit at a place just a few yards from where our boat had berthed—a house in the Russian Concession, around the back of the Litvinoff Brick Tea Factory. Today there is no memorial, no blue plaque; no tour groups come and pay respects. Perhaps that is in part because it all began with an accident.

One of the many revolutionary groups that existed in the Wuhan three-cities region, and which had as a principal aim the subversion of the local army garrison, had secured rooms in a house in the Russian Concession. It seems that on the eve of the day in question they were making bombs and, as so often happens with amateur bomb-makers, there was an accidental explosion. It was a very large one, and the house was badly damaged, and several members of the insurrectionary group were killed, blown to pieces.

Since this was a foreign concession area the agreements on extra-territoriality would in normal circumstances have protected the surviving group members. The local police would be kept out, the Russians would have to deal with the matter themselves. But on this occasion the bomb and its devastation were so large—and the suspicions of the Hankou police were already so heightened—that the local Manchu viceroy ordered his heavily armed policemen to storm the site. In a panic, survivors in the ruins tried to burn documents, but still the police found papers listing the names and the whereabouts of the other revolutionary cells in the tri-city area. Word reached these remaining rebels, who decided there was now nothing for it but to make their long planned move. They had been working patiently for months to talk the soldiers of the local garrisons around to their cause. Now, with their entire political movement imperiled by the police investigation, was the moment to see if their patient persuasion had worked.

It evidently had. At dawn the next day—the glorious tenth day of the tenth month—the Eighth Battalion of the Wuchang Engineers, one of the key regiments among which the rebels had been fomenting insurrectionary thought, formally and decisively rebelled. They seized an ammunition depot and they were joined by soldiers from a local transport regiment and an artillery battery. Between them the three units managed to storm the headquarters units of the Manchu army in the main fort in Wuchang: by the end of a day of vicious fighting the Manchu viceroy conceded defeat. The following day the Manchu commanders across the Yangtze in the cities of Hanyang and Hankou had also done the same. The entire metropolitan area that we now know as Wuhan was by midweek in the hands of a well-organized and popularly backed anti-Imperialist brigade.

It was now the turn of the Railway Protection Movement to spread the revolution across the nation. It was like watching a fast-burning fuse: the movement's disciples rallied soldiers to their cause by the thousands, and exulted as the rebellion spread with astonishing speed, leaping from city to city—particularly in south China—along the newly built railway lines that linked them. There were massacres of Manchus—one particularly noteworthy for its scale in the ancient Chinese capital of Xian. Governors and viceroys and Manchu generals were assassinated, unexpected alliances formed hurriedly to pledge allegiance to forces fighting against the dying Qing dynasty.

The railways sped government troops down from Beijing, but they found that other railways—rebel-held railways—had sped revolutionary forces to intercept them, to slow the progress of the Imperial counterattack. By November government generals in the north were themselves beginning to question the orders coming from within the Manchu fastness of the Forbidden City. There were attempts at compromise, placatory noises came from the Court, from the very regents and the powerful old eunuchs who surrounded the child-emperor. But it was to no avail.

The North-China Daily News in Shanghai (the city's eventual intimate involvement in the rebellion showing once again the importance of the Yangtze valley as its birthplace) published the rebel manifesto on November 14. It is a long document—one whose principal points should be as well-known, perhaps, as those of the American Declaration of Independence, written a century and a half before. The revolutionaries' anger had been triggered by the sale of their birthright to foreign powers, but the real enemy was still the Manchu who had performed the sale. Foreigners, if they were dealt with as equals, could offer China many benefits—but only if the Manchus would get out of the way:

> The foreign powers individually and collectively have stood hammering at the door of China for centuries, pleading for the diffusion of knowledge, a reformation of the national services, the adoption of Western sciences and industrial processes, a jettisoning of the crude, out-of-date and ignoble concepts which have multiplied to keep the nation without the pale of the great family constituting the civilized world. They have failed.
>
> The Manchu Dynasty has triumphantly carried on its reactionary policy despite the strongest pressure exerted

from within and without, until the oppressed people could endure the disgrace and the contumely of it no longer. They rose, and with what results the history of the past few weeks has shown.

The Manchu Dynasty has been tried by a patient and peaceful people for centuries, and has been found more than wanting. It has sacrificed the reverence, forfeited the regard and lost the confidence freely reposed in it by all Chinese.

Its promises in the past have proved delusions and snares. Its promises for the future can carry no weight, deserve no consideration, and merit no trust.

The popular wish is that the Dynasty must go.

On Christmas Day 1911, the man whose ideas had been at the center of all this ferment, Sun Yat-sen, returned from France, where he had been making sure that Europe remained neutral in the conflict.* He came by sea to Shanghai, and was swiftly elected provisional president of the Chinese Republic. He traveled upstream to Nanjing and assumed office on New Year's Day 1912. The revolution that had begun on the Yangtze saw its creator return from exile to the Yangtze, saw him travel up the Yangtze to stake his capital in a city on the Yangtze. There could be no better signal that the river was at the center of the new national entity.

Forty-two days later, on February 12, 1912, the six-year-old Aisin-Gioro Pu Yi, who was known by his reign name of Xuan-tong, formally abdicated.† He was the last of the Manchus, and he was the last Emperor of China.

---

* At the time of the revolution's beginnings Sun had been fund-raising in America: he read news of the storming of the Wuchang fort in a Denver newspaper while he was en route to Kansas City.

† He reigned again nominally for twelve days in 1917, when a short-lived coup restored him. In 1932 the Japanese installed him as the head of their puppet-government of Manchukuo, but he was swept off to Siberia when the Russians routed the Japanese Army in Manchuria. He was later returned to China, was

· · ·

Our hotel was on the very edge of the old Russian Concession, and from my room I could look out over the mansard roofs and the grimy colonnades of houses in the French Concession next door. It was raining by the time I got to my room, and I watched as an old man in his underwear clambered about on the roof outside, retrieving sooty washing from a rusted cable that sagged between two chimney pots. He had disturbed a flock of pigeons, which flapped and fluttered and swooped like a grubby blanket, back and forth over the tops of the houses. In the distance a small red helicopter chattered up and down the riverbank, a television crew on board filming the swimmers who, in their hundreds, were still crossing the flooded stream.

Wuhan in the rain is no city of joy. It bustled, certainly—in the narrow streets at the back of the concessions there were banks and boutiques and amusement arcades, and thousands of people were jammed everywhere, even on a wet Sunday like this, selling and buying, shouting and arguing.

In one scrofulous alley I stumbled across, of all things, an American yogurt shop, a franchise of the highwayside and airport giant known as TCBY, The Country's Best Yogurt. I rushed in to buy something for Lily. She had never had frozen yogurt, and I thought her social awareness might profit from a tub of vanilla-and-chocolate swirl, topped with fragments of a crushed Heath bar. But she grimaced after the first mouthful. "How do you people eat stuff so sweet?" she said, offering the tub back. I motioned to her to hold on to it, and suddenly felt keenly sorry for the young girls who worked behind the counter, and who were gazing at me intently to see if we were enjoying the results of their labors. I shrugged an excuse to the effect I had to eat the stuff out in the street, and made as dignified an exit as I could.

---

imprisoned and "reeducated" by the Communists, and died peacefully in Beijing in 1967, having spent his remaining years working humbly as a gardener.

The simple existence of a TCBY store in Wuhan rang a bell, however. As Lily and I walked farther into town, I recalled a conversation that my wife had had a year or so before at a dinner party in Hong Kong. She had been cornered by a languid fop from Jardines, a young man whose task was to develop the firm's interests in China.

"This cold yogurt stuff the Americans like," he said with obvious distaste, both for yogurt and Americans, "and these Mexican thingies, 'tacos' I believe they're called—do you think John Chinaman would like them?

"I ask," he continued, "because the franchise is up for grabs. Frightful-sounding places I imagine, names like Taco Bell and TCBY. But we can't be too proud, can we?—we're wondering whether to slap up a few in China." He smiled, in a reptilian way.

I had no way of knowing whether market research like this did any good, even whether the yogurt shop in Wuhan was indeed a Jardines venture. If it was, there was an element of drollery to the story, considering that the firm's first sales in the city were of opium, a more obviously addictive product. Whether John Chinaman likes yogurt or not, time will tell: one Jane Chinaman did not. But opium was evidently liked well enough by all.

The West has been trying things out on the people of Wuhan for decades—test marketing them much as they might do in Nottingham or Chicago. It is said that, among other things, the Gatling gun, the fedora, basketball, steam engines and the notions of unionized labor and representative democracy were all first tested on the people of Wuhan. Opium, however, was not among the items that the West *introduced* to Wuhan, or to China. The trade that grew up between British India and China, which was explained in the previous chapter, was created to satisfy—or to exploit, depending on your point of view—an already existing habit. The Indian opium augmented an already very considerable domestic harvest. Even as late as 1908, a trade report for Hankou showed, for instance, that while 34,000 pounds of opium had been landed in the port from the Indian regions of Patna and Malwa, some 65,000 pounds had come *downstream,* from the Chinese poppy fields of Yunnan and Sichuan. The point is often forgotten: the Chinese were already heavy users of the drug by the time the British traders moved in and, like the Mafia, sought to dominate and control the trade.

There was business in more prosaic products too. At the beginning of the century scores of foreign ships—from Britain in the main, but also from Norway, Russia, Germany, France, the United States and Holland—came regularly up the Yangtze as far as Hankou. Tankers brought in kerosene for the Standard Oil Company's bunkers. British and Dutch steamers brought oil from Borneo and Sumatra. Oregon pinewood was brought in aboard British freighters, and a German bulk carrier brought in monthly shipments of cement from Haiphong (the port in Vietnam to which, according to the legend, the Yangtze might have flowed, had the first Chinese Emperor, Yü the Great, not had the source waters diverted).

The imports were of ordinary, unremarkable goods like this, as well as shirting material, pig iron, tin slabs, cigarettes, firebricks, matches, needles, potash, railway ties, tea chests, umbrellas. Nothing exceptional, nothing with a hint of romance about it.

But Hankou's exports at the time—these were the very stuff of China! The manifest of an outbound steamer could read like a page from *The Good Earth*: cargoes of bean cake, white rice, lotus seeds, fungus, raw white silk, cocoons, goatskins, cotton, vermicelli, sesame oil, tung oil, quicksilver, nutgalls, musk, ramie, cowhides, bran, bristles, rhubarb, straw braid and, of course, tea—tea in bags and boxes and half-chests, tea offered as black, brick, mixed, green, log, tablet, oolong or dust.

The docks of a century ago must have been a remarkable sight. The junks would be crowded a hundred feet deep on the banks of the Han Shui, their sides painted every color imaginable. Scores of the shops were riverborne, with the merchant's business, or the craftsman's craft, advertised by an item flying from the mast—a hank of rope, a barber's brush, a shirt, a queue of plaited hair. And on shore the narrow lanes were overhung with crimson and gold signboards, and crowded with jostling and sweating coolies and fat mandarins in their gilded chairs passing to and fro. There would be the sound of cymbals and the whiff of incense and the strange sweet smell of opium drifting up from the dark divans. And, in the background, the ominous sounds of shunting and whistling from the steam trains that would before long play so instrumental a part in changing it all.

Wuhan was more than merely mercantile, more than a simple Chinese Chicago, however: for a while, between the mid-twenties and the late thirties, the city assumed some of the seedily anarchic qualities of Shanghai, becoming an ideological capital of China, a place through which men and women of all conceivable political persuasions passed, en route to somewhere else.

Christopher Isherwood noted the phenomenon in *Journey to a War,* when he wrote that "history, grown weary of Shanghai, bored with Barcelona, has fixed her capricious interest on Hangkow—but where is she staying?" He and W. H. Auden, fixing their own capricious interest on the city, decided that they liked its self-appointed role as a quasi-capital, a place where "Chiang Kai-shek, Agnes Smedley, Chou En-lai, generals, ambassadors, journalists, foreign naval officers, soldiers of fortune, airmen, missionaries, spies" all congregated, betraying and deceiving one another by turn.

It was a center of revolutionary faith and fervor throughout the years between 1911 and 1949—indeed, it was for many years the city where Mikhail Borodin, the amazing and enormous Russian Comintern agent who, it is often forgotten, fashioned the Kuomintang (KMT) into what was initially a properly Leninist organization, was based and where he performed some of his most impressive labors. Chiang Kai-shek did his eventual best to remove the Communists from the KMT—in 1927 sending a campaign of terror, of "punishment without leniency" up along the Yangtze from Shanghai to Wuhan. But it did little to lessen Wuhan's importance as a center of leftist militancy, and the role the city played in Mao's eventual victory in 1949 matched the role it had played in Sun Yat-sen's success in 1911. It was always as rough and gritty in its politics as industry had made it in its atmosphere. Not a pretty place—but an important one.

• • •

Today the ferment and the jostle is much the same, though cars crowd among the rickshaws and there are sleek and brilliantined men with shiny suits, cellular phones clamped to their ears. Plenty of foreigners are here: men from Budweiser setting up a brewery, men from AT&T tinkering with the telephones, the big European information firms—Siemens, Philips, Alcatel—doing much the same, plugging Wuhan into digital networks. These men live well-fed but lonely lives in a tiny hotel well away from the Bund, and they loathe the place, cordially.

The longer-established business houses of the tri-cities are prospering in a thousand brand-new ways, and they are in most cases jammed into the old structures that the foreigners built in Edwardian times. Wuhan bank clerks, who when awakened will honor letters of credit and perform cable transfers and hand over cash on presentation of a credit card from almost any country on earth, sleep their afternoons away under Victorian iron archways and stained glass windows and under the light of dull brass library lamps. Trading companies are crammed into dusty art deco palaces and crumbling godowns; there are real estate brokers and paging firms and couriers where once there were more classically Chinese functionaries, *likin* officials, octroi collectors and compradors.

Hong Kong businessmen have now begun to infiltrate Wuhan with a sudden eagerness not nearly as evident in other cities. It is true that most major centers in China have one or two establishments whose headquarters are in Hong Kong—there are Hong Kong–run hotels in places as remote as Ürümqi, and Hong Kong–owned office blocks in faraway Shenyang and Kashgar. But in Wuhan there is much, much more. The city has been put on a quick and easy non-stop flight route from Hong Kong's Kai Tak airport, and to the southern businessmen who fly in each day, Wuhan is now their most proximate example of *the real China,* the closest big city of the Chinese heartland. (What they have on their doorstep in cities like Canton and Xiamen are still very obviously *southern* Chinese cities, with the southern tongue spoken, southern food eaten, southern attitudes struck.) Hong Kong developers are now pouring in, busily putting up scores of hotels and department stores and trade centers, with promises of multiplex cinemas, nightclubs, and hostess palaces. Hong Kong businessmen are rebuilding the Wuhan airport. They have put money into the gleaming and delicate new Yangtze bridge. There is talk of yet another southern-built bridge, this time over the Han Shui. A Hong Kong bank is financing a new six-lane expressway into the city's heart.

It is in part because of this that I find myself unaccountably prejudiced, and have come to like Wuhan a great deal less than I like Shanghai. Cities like Shanghai and Nanjing are growing fast—too fast for comfort, it is true—but they appear, on the surface at least, to be performing their growth by a large measure of their own hard work, with their own villainy, much of their own money. The city fathers of Wuhan, however, have embarked on a developmental *pas de deux* with Hong Kong businessmen. There is, perhaps as a direct corollary, a temporary and jerry-built feel to the new Wuhan, as though a new metropolis is being constructed with its primary purpose the swift enrichment of *taipans* and their companies in the not-so-far-away territory to the south. Wuhan may be a city with good reason to be proud of its history. But I wonder whether it has much to be proud of in its present. Lily remarked often on the gimcrack, meretricious appearance of Wuhan, and said she disliked the place as heartily as I did. On our last evening there she made a joke about the truism of the old cliché of the city's best feature being the road out.

It turned out that this too was being built by a firm based in Hong Kong. Toll barriers were being welded into place, ensuring that some distant Southerner could make easy money and a quick profit from a city that more than most seems to have become the Southerners' unwitting new client in the Chinese heartland.

Mao Zedong was a very considerable poet—in output, if not always in quality—and he was prone to memorialize what he regarded as his greater achievements with lines of verse. His poem "Swimming" is one of his best known. He wrote it in 1956, shortly after his first swim in the Yangtze: he had come from swimming both the Pearl River in Canton and Xiang River at Changsha, which is why he began this brief gem as he did—lines that retain most of their value, even allowing that Chinese poetry loses much in the translation:

> *I have just drunk the waters of Changsha*
> *And come to eat the fish of Wuchang—*
> *Now I am swimming across the great Yangtze*
> *Looking after to the open sky of Chu.*
> *Let the wind blow and the waves beat—*
> *Better far than an aimless stroll in a courtyard.*
> *Today I am at ease:*
> *It was by a stream that the Master said—*
> *"Life—like the waters—rushes into the past!"*
> *Sails move with the wind,*
> *Tortoise and Snake Hills are motionless.*
>
> *Great plans are afoot:*
> *A bridge will fly to span the North and South*
> *Turning a barrier into a thoroughfare.*
> *Walls of stone will stand upstream to the west*
> *To hold back Wushan's clouds and rain*
> *Till a smooth lake rises in the narrow gorges.*
> *The mountain Goddess, if she is still there,*
> *Will marvel at a world so changed.*

You do not have to read the runes especially deeply to interpret the various meanings that are embedded in these lines. The first stanza is at once philosophical and phlegmatic, a reflection of Mao's self-image, once his swimming was done—his self-confident view of himself as a man now ready to meet the challenges of the revolution yet to come.

I had been given a copy of the poem by a manager at the hotel, the day before we left. She knew that Lily and I were going farther upstream and she wanted me, she said, to take particular note of the second stanza. The lines mentioned the new bridge, of course; but they also mentioned the "walls of stone" that would cause "a smooth lake" to rise "in the narrow gorges." She made me read it, standing in the hotel lobby; and then when I had done so she produced, with a flourish, the first copy of a new booklet that she had received just that morning by express mail. It was called, none too immodestly, *An Epic Undertaking*. It was bound in dark blue, the calligraphy in silver: it was the story of a project that I had felt looming over me, bearing down on me, almost since I had seen the first hills by the side of the great river, hundreds of miles behind.

Just a few miles ahead of us now, and affecting in a myriad of ways the temper of the people and the cities all around, were the beginnings of the most gargantuan project—one that would change the nature of the Yangtze for all time. It has many names: the New China, the Sandouping, the Sanxia, the Three Gorges. It has one name with which all who know the Yangtze today are intimately familiar: the Dam. Upstream the river's flow was about to be halted and constricted by a wall of concrete and iron that would cause a vast lake, and a score of other changes, to fall on the Yangtze valley like no other changes in the river's history. The dam is the defining entity of the new river and of the new China that the nation's leaders promise can be built around her.

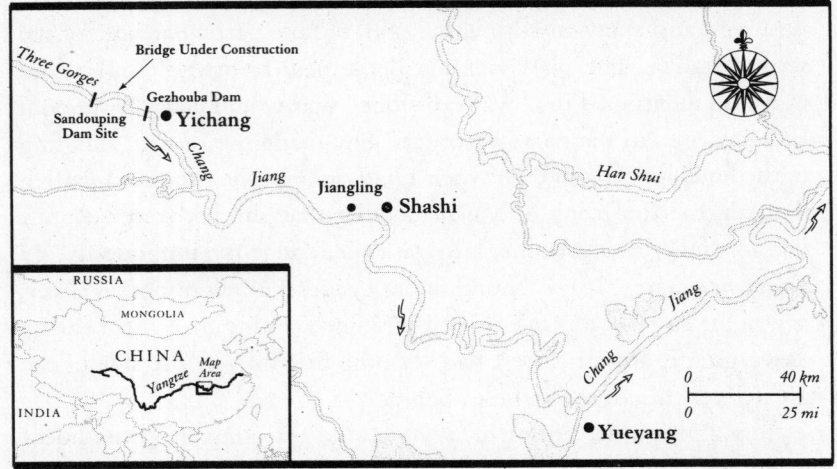

9

A New Great Wall

We decided to travel the next short section upriver by plane—if only to experience the underside of Chinese civil aviation. It so happens that the connection between Wuhan and the much smaller old treaty port of Yichang—a flight of forty minutes, compared with ten hours in a bus or another day and a night in a steamer—is not between what we would conventionally describe as *airports*. This trip would make use of the second tier of Chinese aviation, in which the departures and arrivals are at what might be better classified only as *aerodromes*.

Horror stories of China's conventional air services are legion. I was on a flight once between Qingdao (the city where Tsingtao beer is made) and Shanghai. We were grossly overbooked, as was often the case in those days, and so the staff lugged a number of armchairs from the waiting lounge and set them down in the plane's aisle. The stewardesses, who saw no untoward safety implications in this arrangement, were irritated because they had to clamber over the lumpily stuffed chairs during the flight. But this barely affected the in-flight service: the only item the women were handing out—there was no food or drink—were small empty tins, the kind of thing in which to keep cough drops. There was no discernible reason for the gift: perhaps there had been a surplus in some distant factory.

Then again, about a year later, I was flying to some other Yangtze valley city from Harbin, in Manchuria. I was sitting next to a young man who had never flown before, and he was frightened to death. Despite my being both a stranger and a furry barbarian, he took my hand and squeezed it white as we began the take-off roll. The aircraft accelerated to full speed, after which there was a bang, an engine erupted in smoke and we lurched off onto the grass. We rested there for half an hour while technicians swarmed over the wing, and my new friend sobbed bitterly. Then we started again, trundled back onto the runway, and the pilot said in a nervous voice: "Okay—we try once more." The youngster buried his head in his hands as we took off, this time flawlessly.

On this occasion it took us a good hour even to find the airfield. The normal Wuhan airport is a big affair, with radars, a departure hall, customs officers and touts offering taxis. But the field reserved for flights going to Yichang and similarly obscure places is not much more than a meadow, and is more or less in the middle of town. We had to find our way down a maze of back alleys, past broken-down factories and breeze-block tenements, through middens and swamps alive with black pigs. Ten minutes or so of this and then the buildings fell away and there was open land ahead, with soldiers, a couple of canvas-and-dope biplanes painted in camouflage drab and, parked outside a rusting tin shack, an ancient Russian prop-driven aircraft sporting strange wings that drooped down almost to the ground.

Half a dozen soldiers were playing football with a beer bottle, and the plane's pilot was arguing with a taxi driver. Was this the plane for Yichang? we asked. He grunted and turned away, a response that Lily interpreted as a sign of assent and welcome. No one checked our tickets, and no one minded where, or indeed if, we sat. Eventually the pilot and a rather pretty girl in a sort of half uniform climbed aboard, looked at us and said, Yichang? A couple of elderly men and a schoolboy climbed into the plane along with us; we rolled into position, bumped over a few potholes, and took off.

We flew very low, over a land filled with canals and dikes and lock gates. This was flood country—or, more properly, this was country where, year after year, floods downstream were meant to be taken care of. According to the maps, this was indeed the celebrated Jinjiang Flood Diversion Region, the main bastion of protection against downstream floods. According to ancient design, each time the river crested, so the locks would be opened, the diversion canals below us would be filled, the pressure on the main Yangtze dikes would be eased. Generally speaking the Jinjiang system had worked well since it was improved in the aftermath of the 1931 floods. Very occasionally these arrangements have proved less than adequate, and a few dikes were breached; then there were inundations, wreckage and death. But not this year, or at least not at this place.

From ten thousand feet—our rattling old plane was not pressurized, and so we flew low—all looked quite benign. This was one of the season's infrequent rain-free days, so the visibility was good. Beneath us was far less a scene of disaster and mayhem than the newspapers and television reports of the previous weeks would have us believe. In one large diversion canal, perhaps three hundred yards wide, there was just a trickle of water coursing down the center channel; and when we flew over the cement spillways of its diversion dam, they were quite dry, the iron gates between them and the Yangtze firmly shut.

On the strength of the evidence below it was still difficult to imagine that the floods in the Yangtze valley this year were peculiarly bad. Farther south, in the rivers near Changsha, they could well be worse—I had no way of knowing. But here I still suspected that a useful fiction was being created, and whipped to a froth by the ever cunning government. All the time we'd been in Wuhan the drumbeat had been going on, night after night on television and in morning paper after morning paper: floods, floods, floods. And in truth there were some signs that this was a fairly bad year: the waters off the Bund wharves had been rushing by at frightening speed, and a blue truck that some careless driver had left on a pier was, on the day we left, up to its roof in water.

But at the same time no dike had been breached, no levee overcome, no city street flooded. The river may have been in a fairly robust mood, but what was being put about by the government-run press was, I felt sure, considerably more dramatic than reality. And, uncharitable though it might be, I couldn't shake the feeling that it was very largely propaganda, and if so, all in the cause of winning justification from a highly skeptical world—and a fairly skeptical China—for the building of the Three Gorges Dam.

China, which came spectacularly early to so many technologies—printing, gunpowder, iron casting, the anchor, the compass, the rudder, the wheelbarrow—came surprisingly late to the idea of building dams. The Egyptians had blocked part of the Nile with a masonry dam near Memphis as long ago as 2900 B.C.: and there are Arabian dams dating from the seventh century before Christ. But the Chinese left dam building until nearly three thousand years after the Egyptians—the first, a modest structure on a Yangtze tributary, did not go up until around 200 B.C. One might have thought that the Chinese would have arranged matters otherwise, since the single most important purpose of a dam—the elimination of floods—has long been more necessary in flood-ridden China than it ever has in most other countries.

But there was good reason for the Celestials' apparent tardiness. Hydraulics had long been a Chinese fascination: the country's rivers were so great and so wayward, and the livelihood of so many millions depended on their proper management, that it could hardly be otherwise. But exactly how to manage them? About 2500 years ago a pair of distinct and entrenched schools of thought arose, reflecting the different views of the ruling theocracies: one was advanced by the Taoists, the other by the Confucianists. It may seem odd to westerners that religion had any impact at all on hydraulics: but it is a measure of the peculiar importance of the country's waterways—as well as a reminder of the delicious strangeness of China—that its priests and philosophers did take so seriously the question of exerting control over them.

The views were diametrically opposed. Taoists, followers of what we might call a bohemian way of life, supported the building of only very low levees beside rivers and, generally speaking, letting them devise their own courses to the sea. Confucianists, who took a more rigid approach to governance and life in general, were also much more rigid in their approach to rivers: they believed that massive dikes should be built to corral the waterways along man-made courses and that the extra land thus freed should be intensively used for agriculture. They had a fatalist attitude to the disadvantages of their ideas: they accepted that their approach might well contribute to infrequent but massive flooding disasters—that their dikes would probably prevent moderate floods, but would likely break during serious flooding, causing occasional catastrophes. This, Confucian hydraulicists agreed, was an acceptable trade-off for the intervening periods of fertility and prosperity.

The technologies of the modern world, and the end of dynastic China, brought to a sudden end such dreamy philosophical disputations. The republican governments that ran the country in the years following the 1911 Revolution were undistinguished and inexperienced, and their policies often collapsed in a shambles—but they had grandiose ideas for practical reform. They built courts and prisons, a nationwide school system and a network of new railways; they constructed a central mint, planted forests, organized sweeping reforms in animal husbandry and promoted new breeds of cattle.

Most ambitiously of all, Sun Yat-sen wrote a paper in 1919 entitled "A Plan to Develop Industry"; and there, in a long section on "Improvements of Navigable Rivers and Canals," he set out his ideas for a massive scheme for improving the country's flood control and irrigation system, and for generating electricity, by building scores of big dams.

The one structure that all—and most especially Dr. Sun—felt should be the linchpin of this network, and a symbol of the way in which modern Man could tame and harness ancient and unruly Nature, was to be the mother of all dams—a dam that should, could and would be built across the Yangtze. Sun championed this cause for the remaining six years of his life: one of his last speeches, on the subject "The People's Livelihood," announced his belief that such a mighty dam could create thirty million horsepower, which would produce untold and unimaginable wealth for the peoples of central China.

A spot somewhere along the 140-mile defile known as the Three Gorges would, he declared, be the obvious site for a dam across the Yangtze. It looked just perfect: the kind of place where, if the river was scaled down enough, any playful child would want to raise a toy barrage of mud and sticks. Very big beavers would be in hydraulic heaven at a place like this.

Upstream of the Gorges the river meanders across the former inland sea that is now known as China's Red Basin (called by geologists the Sichuan Basin). This fertile plain, warm, well watered and sheltered and layered with thick brick-red soils, is home to 100 million people. It would be a hugely populous and wealthy country if it were a self-standing nation—which in many ways it seems to be. It is hemmed in on all sides by high mountains, the Chinese spoken there has an unusual and guttural tone and its cuisine, based around a pepper that tastes uncannily like Tabasco mixed with detergent, has a memorable singularity.

The Yangtze gathers and quietens here in the Red Basin, pausing for breath after its headlong dash down from the Tibetan Plateau. It gains its riverine maturity here: it collects huge new tributaries (the four biggest of them giving Sichuan its name, which means "Four Rivers"), as well as a vast new volume of water and a barely imaginable quantity of sediment. At Chongqing the river—here still known as Chang Jiang, the Long River—is 610 feet above the level of the sea at the Woosung Bar. It is also 476 feet above the level of Yichang, the city to which our rattling aircraft was heading.

Between Chongqing and Yichang is a range of mountains— jagged three-thousand-footers all, outliers of the limestones and sandstones of the Tibetan hills that have here uncoiled their tentacles toward the eastern flats. A passerby will notice that once in a while the unfolded hills reveal a granite or a gneiss or a schist; mostly, though, the ridges are of ancient limestones, with softer shales and marls, or harder sills of volcanic rock, sandwiched between. The Yangtze escapes to the coast through them—she descends the 476 feet in just 140 miles of always fast, often turbulent and frequently raging river.* In places the defile through which she runs is squeezed to a width of no more than 350 feet—and the great volume of water, which might have occupied half a mile of width before, and which will spread languidly across a mile or more below, surges through it, slicing away the sides (and causing formidable landslips) and scouring away the riverbed, so that the Yangtze here is one of the deepest rivers in the world.

To a builder of concrete dams, a river squeezing its way through a narrow valley presents a heaven-sent opportunity for spectacular results at relatively low cost. The engineer needs merely to find a good and geologically stable place between the cliffs at the lower end of the rift, and then build his wall of concrete there: the waters will rise and

---

* Through the Gorges the river drops at an average rate of 16 inches for every mile of distance traveled. Once out into the coastal plains, the Yangtze takes 940 miles to drop the remaining 134 feet, at an average of 1.6 inches drifting downward in each mile. When Chairman Mao was warned about the fierce currents and turbulences at Wuhan, it was the sheer volume of water, not the very modest gradient of the river, that concerned his aides.

fill the valley behind, and they will spread only minimally to the
sides. Few people live on such steep valley sides and only where
flooding affects tributary valleys will many lives be disrupted.

All the great structures that were built around the world during
the dam builders' salad days—the Hoover and the Grand Coulee in
western America, the Vaiont in Italy, the Grand Dixence in Switzerland, the Daniel Johnson in Quebec—were constructed in situations
like this. A steep-sided valley and a fast-flowing stream were there
first; the dam went up, and a few years later, in the place of valley and
stream there was a consequently deep lake and a consequently tamed
river—and fewer downstream floods. As an additional incentive,
which the builders could weigh against the likely vast capital cost of
the project, there would be electrical power aplenty to sell, from all
the potential energy stored in the dam-impounded lake.

Dam builders, fired by an almost religious enthusiasm for their
work and its long-term profitability, have been on a construction
spree since the 1930s. This was when men like John L. Savage and his
U.S. Bureau of Reclamation colleagues were persuaded that mighty
barrages across great rivers could have incalculable benefits—both in
power generation and in flood prevention—for countries with expanding industrial economies. So they and their disciples around the
world have put up thousands of dams—of which more than a hundred are the so-called super dams, truly immense constructions of
concrete or earth whose walls soar more than 500 feet.

Almost all of the world's big rivers have been stopped up by
monsters like these—the Ganges, the Zambezi, the Parana, the Nile,
the Indus, the Danube, the Niger, the great Amazonian tributary
known as the Tocantins. Only the Zaire (formerly the Congo), the
Amazon proper—and the Yangtze—remain unblocked by a true
giant dam. And from the thirties on an endless slew of good reasons
have been put forward for adding the Yangtze to the list.

But if flood control had been principally behind Sun Yat-sen's
original idea, his successors turned their thoughts more keenly to
what was initially the almost incidental matter of generated electricity. The Three Gorges, it turned out, is ideally placed as a nexus of

power generation. Most of China's factories—electricity-hungry factories, that is—have been built in the east of the country. Most of her mountains—ravine-rich, river-filled mountains, that is—lie at the other end of the nation, in the west. The Three Gorges site is almost in the dead center of the country; it is, in fact, the closest river-filled ravine to the Chinese east—meaning that, in terms of economy, it has to be the most efficient site for delivering power to the centers of Chinese industry. The power transmission lines—not a trivial factor in the calculation of generating economics—could be much shorter with a Three Gorges site than with one in, say, far western Yunnan.

Developing a hydropower system has perceived environmental benefits, too; not least, it could lessen China's reliance on fossil fuels. The smoke and other emissions from China's vast coal reserves have to be seen to be believed: it sometimes seems a pall of yellow-brown smog hangs over all of the flat country outside the Gorges—a combination of coal-fired power stations and roadside brick kilns, all belching fumes into the air, full blast. A hydropower station somewhere in the Three Gorges, generating thousands of megawatts, would be bound to lessen the nation's reliance on dirty fuels: more and more, the planners who followed up Dr. Sun's bold plan agreed that a Three Gorges dam was an ideal creation for the country's future.

But however ideal the Three Gorges project might seem to an enthusiast, it took engineers and politicians and military experts *forty-nine years* to choose the exact site for it. It took *seventy-five years,* moreover, from the day Dr. Sun made his first visionary statement until the day the first sod was moved. Few construction projects anywhere in the world have taken quite so long to realize. Here was the time scale of a cathedral.

The matter of the right site was the most vexing. Most of those directly involved in the decades of discussions agreed on one thing: that any dam should be built a few miles upstream from Yichang, at the very end of the Xiling, the lowest of the Three Gorges. But then civil war, insurrection, terrorism, shortages of cash, antiforeign sentiment, changes in ideology, power struggles and sudden caprices of the power elite all conspired to slow a more precise choice than this down to subglacial speed. The engineers and the scientists reported and recommended until they were blue in the face: but for half a century, nothing was done.

J. S. Lee—a British-educated Chinese geologist who went on, under the name of Li Siguang, to work for the People's Republic and to become dignified by the title of the Father of Modern Chinese Geology—performed the original surveys in the 1930s and suggested that the best site could be at a turn in the river near the village of Sandouping. George Barbour, the American who worked with Lee, thought much the same.

Then in the 1940s along came John Savage, the American dam builder from Denver who professed himself to have "fallen in love with the Yangtze's water resources"—not with the Yangtze, but with its water resources—"at first sight." Savage was with the Reclamation Bureau; he was a legendary figure in American dam building and his involvement in those early discussions was a harbinger of the intimate involvement of Americans in the scheme.

He suggested six sites, the highest just a few hundred yards down from the lower end of the Xiling Gorge, the lowest at a point some nine miles above Yichang. The bureau drew detailed designs for a long concrete barrage with a series of ship locks that would allow navigation beyond the dam—a critical aspect of a project that, of course, was designed specifically to block what was a very busy ship-ping route. In 1947 a team of fifty Americans worked for a while at one of the sites, only too aware that the Nationalist government that had hired them was, in all likelihood, not long for this world: Mao's Communists were gathering strength day by day. The cancellation of the project later in that same year came as no surprise to the outsid-ers: the torch would have to be passed to a new government, all suspected—and it was by no means sure that Mao, once he had gained power, would be as committed to the Three Gorges dam as his fervent ideological opponents had been.

It was a little later that John Hersey, the China-born journalist and writer who produced what remains the most lyrical of all books about the Yangtze, *A Single Pebble,* offered his vision of the project to the outside world. The hero of his novella is a young American engineer who is taken on one of the great trading junks, a *ma-yang zi,* to survey the Three Gorges and "to see whether it would make sense for my company to sell the Chinese government a vast power project in the river's famous Gorges."

The story's theme is the life of the trackers, the stoic and tenacious men who, with bare feet, broad shoulders and bamboo hawsers, pull his junk up through the Gorges' rapids. But more than once the narrator imagines his beloved dam, with the kind of wild rhetorical flourishings of which Mao Zedong would have eagerly approved:

> The second evening in Witches' Mountain Gorge, just after we had spar-moored for the night against a big boulder in a quiet cove, and while most of the trackers rested on their haunches on the rocks ashore, sipping tea, I sat alone on the conning deck watching blossoms of sunset unfold on the edges of the small delicate misty shrub-like clouds that stood naturalized in the visible sky over the gorge upstream—when all at once I imagined a dam.
>
> There it was! Between those two sheer cliffs that tightened the gorge a half-mile upstream, there leaped up in my imagination a beautiful concrete straight-gravity dam which raised the upstream water five hundred feet; much of its curving span was capped by an overflow spillway controlled by drum gates and tube valve outlets; and a huge hydraulic jump apron designed to pass unprecedented volumes of water stood ready to protect both the dam and the lower countryside against the freshets of springtime. Ingenious lift-locks at either side carried junks up and down on truly hydraulic elevators. The power plant was entirely embedded in the cliffs on both sides of the river. The strength of the Great River, rushing through the diversion tunnels that had been used for the construction of the dam, and through other great tubes and shafts bored through solid rock, and finally into the

whirling gills of nearly a hundred power units, created a vast hum of ten million kilowatts of light and warmth and progress.

The Communists loved the idea as keenly as did John Hersey's narrator, and as keenly as had their Nationalist predecessors. Once they had their house in some kind of order they set up committees to consider the various sites. Drilling rigs went up, core samples were taken—and in 1959 the committee said it would choose one of three sites, all near Sandouping. A year later the uppermost of those three, a narrowing of the river close to a low island called Zhongbao, was finally chosen.

Except it turned out not to be final at all. The military promptly weighed in, and a committee of generals decided that at Sandouping the river was still far too wide to allow for adequate air defense. Since a gigantic dam like this would be a prime site for terrorist or foreign attack, good defense was of prime concern. So the Chinese government went back to look for more sites—and then, in another corner, the Cultural Revolution began. The plans for the dam were, on the one hand, disrupted; and on the other hand, they became embroiled in politics—the dam was seen by Mao and his allies as perfect propaganda for the promotion of his authority and power.

Mao's poem "Swimming" envisaged the structure in two lines of verse, lines that helped invest the project with an almost mythic importance. Building a dam across the Yangtze was in many ways like swimming across the Yangtze—it was a means of demonstrating man's supremacy, and Mao's supremacy, and the Party's supremacy, over the Chinese landscape, as well as being the realization of the worthiest of ambitions. Come the late 1950s, every cadre in the land had started to see in Three Gorges Dam a perpetual memorial to the greatness of the Great Helmsman. If there were any doubts, any concerns about the harsh realities of the dam's construction, of its likely costs, its long-term impact, its risks, its practical disadvantages—all were swept away under the relentless imperium of dogma and fanatic belief.

In the midst of the political chaos of the time there came news of yet more potential sites, and site selection took on as frantic a tempo as that of the Great Leap Forward. The project began to lose contact with reality. Someone piped up to claim he liked a hitherto unmentioned place called Shipai; a committee thought that this was indeed a good place, and for a while all effort was devoted to looking at Shipai. But three years later another committee rejected it: *unstable geology.* Other new names joined the list: Huanglingmiao, Meirentuo, the Nanjin Pass. Two years later still came the recommendation that the dam be built at yet another place, this one called Taipingxi: on this site the builders would need less concrete, but there would have to be more costly excavation. Taipingxi the generals also liked: they could set up lots of antiaircraft guns here, they reported. But the excavation costs scuppered this choice a year or so later.

Back and forth matters went, committee after committee doing and then undoing the work of one another. But finally, once Mao was dead and the Cultural Revolution safely buried and half-forgotten and the Gang of Four in prison, a more serious-minded set of committees—a set that was apolitical, to the extent that in Communist China any government body can be apolitical—made its once-and-for-all-decision. It came via a terse report from the Ministry of Water Conservancy to the State Council in November 1979: whatever the shortcomings of the site for air defense, the original place that had been suggested fifty years before, Sandouping, was where the Three Gorges Dam should and would in fact be built. Now there was merely the question of how big the dam should be, and whether all those who mattered in China and beyond would agree to build it.

The international community was at first excited. The Americans—firms and organizations like Bechtel, the U.S. Army Corps of Engineers, Merrill Lynch, and Coopers and Lybrand, all of whom have expertise in huge capital projects—formed a technical liaison group. The Canadians gave money and said they would be involved. The World Bank began to research the scheme. Sweden and Japan talked openly of pumping in funds. A technical debate began, raging throughout the world's dam-building community.

The question of how high—how tall the dam, and how high the level of the reservoir behind it—has been bitterly debated for years. A high reservoir level—anything more than 500 feet—would mean that more electricity could be generated and deep-draft ships could be accommodated upstream of the dam: but it also would mean that the dam wall itself would have to be taller, and that more people living beside the river would have to be moved as their towns, villages and houses flooded. There would also be little slack available to be taken up in the event of a flood. A lower reservoir level, on the other hand, would cost less—fewer people would need to be moved, and the dam could be lower; but with a proposed low level of around 450 feet, rapids would begin to appear in the upper part of the Gorges, big ships would have difficulty navigating there, and there would be less power potential for the electricity distributors to sell.

A decision was finally announced by Li Peng, the Chinese prime minister, in 1992: the "normal pool level," as it is known, of the proposed Three Gorges Dam would be a stunning 573 feet.* The dam would be 610 feet high, and it would be 6864 feet from one side to the other—more than five times as wide as the huge Hoover Dam. The Aswan Dam in Egypt is twice as long and half as high—but it is a rock-fill dam, and not, like this, fashioned from concrete and iron. The huge wall proposed for the Yangtze would swallow up 26 million tons of concrete and 250,000 tons of steel and it would create a 600-square-mile lake stretching back from the dam for some 372 miles—backing water up in the Gorges and across nearly half of the Red Basin to a point considerably past the city of Chongqing.

The flooding of the valley that would result would be far worse than previously envisaged: it would mean that 1,250,000 people

---

* In what most of the world's dam engineers consider a moment of supreme folly, the Chinese had in 1981 considered building a dam with a pool level of no less than 660 feet. American engineers, horrified by the likely dangers inherent in so gargantuan a structure, told their Chinese counterparts that if there was going to be any American help forthcoming, a significantly smaller dam with a lower-level reservoir would have to be designed. Eventually, realizing the effect of the pressure, the Chinese side complied.

would have to be moved, whether they liked it or not. Thirteen cities like Wanxian (150,000 people) and Fuling (80,000) would be inundated; 140 normal-sized towns would go under, another 1352 villages would be either wholly or partly submerged. Some 8000 recognized archaeological sites would disappear, and scores of temples and pagodas would vanish beneath the waters. The Gorges themselves would cease to be places of rapids and whirlpools, becoming instead a mere section of a deep and placid lake, with only the barest downstream movement of its waters; and even the steep embankments of Chongqing, so much a part of the city's character for so many thousands of years, would be flooded to the point where Yangtze water would be lapping against the city's lower slum streets.

But at the same time—and this is why shipping firms rallied instantly behind Li's announcement—ten-thousand-ton cargo vessels and passenger liners would be able to journey the entire way from the ocean to Chongqing. Nearly 80 percent of China's waterborne trade goes along the Yangtze: the dam and its effects on navigation would increase the tonnage of Yangtze river cargoes fivefold and reduce costs by 35 percent. Chongqing, 1300 miles from the sea and currently limited by the rapids of the Three Gorges to receiving low-water summertime ships of no more than 1500 tons, would become a major Chinese port, able to take truly big oceangoing ships all year round. A hinterland that is truly the heartland of the nation would have its products shipped to world markets with a speed and economy it has never known before.

The power generation establishment rallied behind the government too, and with similar enthusiasm. The plans called for generators to crank out more than 18 gigawatts—18,200 megawatts—of electrical power. This is four times more than any power station in Europe; compared with other dams, it is eight times the power capacity of the Nile's Aswan Dam, and half as much again as the world's current largest river dam, the Itaipu Dam in Paraguay. Truly the Three Gorges Dam was an almighty project: in the propaganda I had received in the mail before I left, a writer writhed in ecstasy as he posed to his readers a rhetorical question:

"This is an opportunity that knocks but once . . . an opportunity to display our talent to the fullest. . . . If a foreign friend asks: *What will you, the Chinese all over the world, leave for this era?* we must reply firmly: *The Yangtze River Three Gorges Project! We'll present this epic undertaking which will benefit the nation and the people not only for the present but for centuries to come.*"

Li Peng needed a project of this magnitude and stature to revivify his image and his fellow leaders' morale, still shaken by the aftermath of the Tiananmen Square tragedies. He joined the chorus of hyperbole: "The Three Gorges Dam," he declared in 1992, "will show the rest of the world that the Chinese people have high aspirations and the capabilities to successfully build the world's largest water conservancy and hydroelectric power project."

Moreover, there was a portent. It did not pass unnoticed that the projected date for the highly symbolic closing of the Yangtze's flow—a central part of a dam-building project, when the waters are passed around the dam site in diversion tunnels—was due to take place in 1997. That was also the year when Hong Kong would revert from British rule back to China's, after 155 years in the barbarian wilderness. The idea that Li Peng's China—or Deng Xiaoping's China, for the former is little more than a puppet of the latter—could in the same year also fly in the face of the barbarian opposition, which was already mounting, and stop up her greatest river: the symbolism of such coincidence augured exceedingly well, in the minds of the masters of the moment.

For by now not everyone, particularly outside China, was quite so enthusiastic. The foreign firms and government organizations that had been so eager to support the Chinese from the start of the project began to have their doubts only a few years later, as the avarice of one decade began to transmute into the more considered caution of the next. In part the doubts arose because of the new zeitgeist: a general feeling had arisen that large dams were ill-conceived projects, that few of them had realized the expectations offered for them, that all were too costly, most had caused grave environmental impacts on their surroundings, and that each was little more than pomposity writ in concrete, with totalitarian regimes favoring them most notably, as a way of impressing the peasantry with the rulers' energy, acumen and skill. The head of the U.S. Bureau of Reclamation made a speech in 1994: from the organization that had built the Grand Coulee and the Hoover and the Glen Canyon Dams came word that, so far as America was concerned, the days of big-dam building were well and truly over. "Large dams are tremendously expensive," said the hitherto uncontroversial American hydrologist Daniel Beard. "They always cost more than you thought and tie up huge sums of capital for many years. . . . There is no more visible symbol in the world of what we are trying to move away from than the Three Gorges Dam."

The Three Gorges Dam—which the big-dam building *industry* still very much wanted to construct, of course, no matter what was being said by official America—soon began to fall into popular disfavor for more specific reasons. A number of key reports on the dam each appeared to have buried within its text at least one major misgiving about the wisdom of so vast an undertaking—misgivings that, when added each to the other, slowly began to assume critical mass.

The U.S. Army Corps of Engineers, for example, concluded that the dam would not, as intended, necessarily prevent flooding downstream. For a start, its engineers noted, a very large proportion of the Yangtze's water comes from tributaries—like the Han Shui, which roars in at the tri-city junction of Wuhan—that join the Yangtze below the dam. Then again, said the Corps technicians, there were very real risks that the dam could be breached—landslides, earthquakes (not uncommon in the hills to the east of the Sichuan Basin) and even war or terrorism could all place the structure at risk—with unimaginably terrible consequences for the huge cities sited downstream. Yichang, for example—this day's destination—would be drowned in a matter of hours: hundreds of thousands of people could die.

The Canadian government's international aid agency wrote a multivolume study of the dam in 1989, recommending that it go ahead. But even this study—which was the basis for Li Peng's announcement of the reservoir height, and which had given him the necessary fillip to inaugurate the project formally—cautioned that in the still waters of the reservoir, huge quantities of silt would accumulate behind the dam wall. These would in time clog the turbine entranceways—and, more significantly, they would produce a lack of sediment in the river downstream of the dam, causing the river to flow more quickly, to scour the banks and the riverbed more severely, and to change the character—and the predictability—of an already wayward and capricious waterway even more. The walls of the Jinjiang flood diversion dikes—over which Lily and I were flying, and in which I saw suspiciously little water—would be seriously scoured by the new fast-flowing sediment-poor waters: they would have to be strengthened and maybe even rebuilt, or else those living beside them would be at dire risk of even more dangerous flooding than they know already. Was this the kind of risk worth taking?

Other reports warned that this same lack of sediment would have damaging effects far, far downstream. Shanghai, more than a thousand miles away at the Yangtze's end, is a city built on top of a plain of sediment that is pushing itself outward into the East China Sea by more than two inches every day. But the arriving silt—so long as it arrives—also strengthens the bed on which Shanghai is built, a bed which is currently being undermined by tunnels and subways and all manner of the kind of human intervention expected in a rapidly expanding metropolis. Because of this, the city is already in danger of subsiding, slowly and perilously: the more the digging and the less the tonnage of arriving sediment, the more vulnerable is this biggest of Chinese cities to inundation by the very sea on which she is built. And beyond this danger, the lessening in the overall flow of the river will allow the tidal effects of the sea to seep farther back in the estuary, changing fishing patterns and altering the salinity of the soils and the groundwater. The effects of the dam, in this one very specialist area of interest, are legion.

Other effects are just as startling. Much was uncovered by the courageous work of a young Beijing journalist named Dai Qing, an engineer-turned-environmental-writer who is also, as it happened, the adopted daughter of one of China's most distinguished army marshals and a woman not to be toyed with. Miss Dai, who knew her subject, was appalled at the risky business of building the Yangtze dam, and throughout the late eighties she carefully collected a series of academic papers by well-respected engineers and hydrologists, each of whom had competent, well-argued and sound reasons for opposing the dam.

She gathered these papers—with nicely turned Chinese titles like "The Limited Benefits of Flood Control," "We Are Very Worried, We Are Very Concerned: An Interview with Zhou Peiyuan and Lin Huainto" and "High Dam: Sword of Damocles"—into a book that she decided to call *Chang Jiang! Chang Jiang!* In a moment of unparalleled chutzpah she then persuaded a publisher, a woman in the southwestern city of Guiyang, to offer the book for sale early in 1989. This was just a few months before the student uprising in Beijing that culminated in the Tiananmen Square tragedy in June: the book was published when the country was in a dangerous ferment, and news of its contributors' opposition to the dam spread wildly across the country. Within months, two things had happened: all of China's elite and intelligentsia knew of the risks that were involved in going ahead with the monster project, and Dai Qing was languishing in prison. She stayed there for ten months, the country's first "green" victim, though in truth a dissident, like so many scores of others.*

The cascade effect of Dai Qing's book was quite remarkable,

---

* Miss Dai dislikes being lumped together with the political dissidents of the time— indeed, she went to Tiananmen Square in a vain effort to persuade the protesting students to go back to their homes, and is as a result somewhat ill regarded by many of the diehards in the opposition camp. But she spent ten months in the Qinchen high-security prison reserved for political prisoners and was threatened with execution. The Chinese government has never explained why she was arrested, though Miss Dai insists it was for her anti-dam writings. Meanwhile the woman who published her book, and who had had a record of printing and distributing controversial and polemical literature and journalism, remains active. Miss Dai, after stints in New York and Canberra, is now back in Beijing, also as tireless a campaigner as ever.

especially since it was to become the central issue in the first attempt at a parliamentary rebellion to take place in the country since the Communist victory in 1949.

First of all, in the late summer, the State Council announced it was postponing the project—not because of the book, of course; it camouflaged its reasons behind a bland and fatuous technical excuse. At the same time, stimulated by the opposition and the project's postponement, more papers began to emerge from the technical theocracies; one of them admitted that sixty small dams and two huge dams, the Banqiao and the Shimantan in Henan province, had all collapsed in August 1975, with tens of thousands—perhaps even hundreds of thousands—drowned. China's ability to engineer dams to withstand the extremes of rain and river was thrown into question—not the purely theoretical question of whether a dam the size of the Three Gorges project could be constructed safely, but whether, since a dam one fortieth as big had burst during a bad rainstorm, the country had the practical skills to be building big dams at all.

But it was the democratic rebellion that then followed that may be Dai Qing's most memorable legacy. The "technical problems" cited as the reason for the 1989 postponement were announced mysteriously "solved" in 1992, following which Li Peng finally went ahead and made the long-awaited construction announcement. But first, the Chinese constitution being what it is, he was obliged to put the matter to, and secure the rubber-stamp approval of, the National People's Congress. The Congress met in Beijing in April 1992, with the delegates being canvassed like rarely before: opposition to the dam, based on Dai Qing's book, on the news of her imprisonment, and on the cascade of new academic papers her troubles had unleashed, was voiced outside the hall. A motion was introduced to present a speech criticizing the project. The meeting's chairman, however—acting on orders from the regime—said there would be no discussion: the vote would be taken there and then, on whether to include the project formally in the final Ten Year Plan of the twentieth century.

Cries of protest were heard. "The Congress has violated its own laws," yelled one opponent, aghast that no discussion would be permitted. She pressed her No button for the electronic tally. So, it turned out, did scores of others. Of the 2613 delegates who had gathered on that cool Friday afternoon, 813—almost one third— either voted against it or abstained. It was, in Chinese terms, a stunning rebellion against Party authority. By the end of the day it had become apparent that although Li Peng had won, it was a Pyrrhic victory, one that the whole world regarded in fact as a sweeping vote of no confidence.

One by one the international community's money sources, appalled by what had happened and by the growing perceived financial risks of the project, dropped away. The World Bank, the Asian Development Bank, Britain's Overseas Development Agency, America's Import-Export Bank, even Canada's International Aid Agency, which had once been so keen—they all said no, they would no longer participate in funding the dam.

The U.S. Bureau of Reclamation, which had earlier signed a technical services agreement with the dam managers, now found itself threatened with lawsuits by seven American environmental organizations, who claimed that by taking part in the dam construction the bureau violated the terms of the Endangered Species Act. The bureau changed its mind hastily. In a terse note to the Chinese it said its technical cooperation would be suspended "effective this day." Risk managers in the big private companies—the merchant banks, the insurance brokers, the construction firms—said in increasing numbers that they now saw the Three Gorges Dam as an insupportable project, one that was vastly expensive, by no means a prudent investment.

The Chinese then had no choice but to do what the Chinese in such circumstances are the best at doing: they began to organize the entire project by themselves. China, in the matter of the Yangtze dam, was by the beginning of 1994 essentially on her own. Or she seemed to be, at first.

Li Peng is a Russian-trained electrical engineer. His determination to have the dam built, come what may, stems both from that fact—his interest in capital projects, the bigger the better—and from his hope that his regime will leave a memorial to Mao and Maoism (and to himself, of course) that will last a thousand years. "The pet project of the red emperor," is how Dai Qing has styled the dam, and both Li and Deng Xiaoping have made it clear they expect their engineers to erect a structure of enduring nobility. But almost all of the criticism of the dam is based on the assumption that it will not last for a fraction of the anticipated time, and that its effects will be by turn minimally beneficial and a wholesale environmental disaster—indeed, that it may turn out to be a catastrophe waiting to happen. The debate can be a highly technical one; but in essence the critics—Chinese and Western both—have homed in since the start of construction on a small number of what they regard as dangerous weaknesses in the project.

The sedimentation problem, the first of these perceived weaknesses, is what critics insist will eventually kill the dam, and it will do so by throttling it to death. Five hundred and thirty million tons of sand and pebbles wash down through the Gorges every year, and the chances are that a large proportion of this material will settle at the base of the dam's retaining wall. Most of this can probably be flushed out—dams have devices that regularly do this, and a most spectacular sight it is when it happens.

But the Yangtze, hydrologists say, throws down far more than mere sand and pebbles. Huge cobbles and boulders are rolled down in this peculiarly violent current, and these, it is believed, will settle unflushably at the base of the dam, binding the sand together and clogging an ever rising mass of detritus as securely as if it were setting cement. The only way of keeping the silt moving is to keep the reservoir level low and the water flow through the dam's gateways as rapid as possible. The power lobby and the shipping lobby won't hear of this: they want a high water level and a low flow-through rate so that they have maximum power potential and maximum ship draft. Li Peng is sympathetic to their views, and believes the sedimentation problems, if they exist, are manageable.

The sediment, opponents argue, will cause other and quite different problems as far away as Chongqing—the city that the dam builders say will become a major inland port. The reservoir waters will be flowing very slowly where they lap against the hills of Chongqing, and because of this they will dump silt precisely where the river presently sweeps it away.* The harbor at Chongqing, initially made deeper by the flooding, will swiftly become shallow again because of the new siltation. The big ships that are expected to use the port will be unable to, unless there is constant and expensive dredging. The dam will thus have contributed, as its critics say it will in many areas, to creating the very problems it seeks to alleviate. In this specific case, it will turn Chongqing, planned as a major center of shipping trade, into a nonport of even less significance than it is today.

Then there is the matter of safety. Dams break—and although not much has been said about dam bursts in China itself, it is now known that at least the two mentioned have broken, with disastrous results, because of either substandard construction or poor design. The Banqiao, an earthen dam on a tributary of the Lower Yangtze in Henan province, was long regarded as "an iron dam—one that can never fail." Torrential rainstorms associated with a typhoon in August 1975 forced the reservoir behind the dam to rise nearly seven feet overnight, and the unexpectedly heavy siltation at the base of the structure prevented the water from flowing away, even when the sluice gates were wide open. Early on the third evening of the storm—a "two-thousand-year storm," the weather bureau said—the water finally overtopped the dam, and the vast structure promptly burst: the resulting lake stretched for thirty miles downstream, and whole villages were inundated in seconds. Various human rights organizations have suggested that almost a quarter of a million people died. The Chinese said nothing about the catastrophe: news seeped out only in 1994, nearly twenty years after the event.

Is the Three Gorges area geologically stable enough? And might not the 370-mile lake that would be formed upstream of the dam—

---

* All of the sewage produced in Chongqing and the scores of other cities above the dam will also end up in the new lake, stagnating and making the waters additionally foul.

with thousands of millions of tons of water pressing down on the fault-splintered country-rock—change the geostatic balance of the area to such an extent that earthquakes might be generated? Might there not be landslips—might not the infamous Huangla Stone, 140 million cubic feet of limestone a few miles upstream of the dam, detach itself from the towering cliffs and crash down into the lake, causing waves 250 feet high, which would surge over the dam, wreck its concrete lip and prompt the structure to crack, leak, buckle and perhaps burst? Earthquakes and landslips damage and destroy dams every bit as often as do flood-induced failures. The Chinese, it is thought, have been dangerously complacent about the seismic risks of this particular project.

Then again, whether or not the Chinese are capable of building or siting big dams at all, there is the question of whether the Three Gorges Dam, so incredibly large a structure, might not become a target for foreign or domestic bombing or sabotage. Dams are inviting targets: Germany's Mohne and Eder Dams were bombed and breached by the British in the Second World War, causing massive flooding of the Ruhr valley. The Perucia Dam in Croatia was badly damaged by terrorist bombs in 1993. In the kind of bizarre twist that only the North Koreans could come up with, the Pyongyang government at one stage threatened to build a dam across their own Han River and then blow it up, so that the resulting surge would flood Seoul, the southern capital. The Damoclean vulnerability of dams can be made to work in all kinds of ways.*

The Chinese are said to be taking extraordinary measures to prevent the Three Gorges Dam from ever being attacked. They are only too well aware of the demonic effect that as much as 400,000 cubic yards of water cascading unstoppably downward *each second* would have on nearby riverside cities like Yichang and Shashi, and perhaps

---

* In 1938 Chiang Kai-shek ordered his troops to blow up the dikes protecting the Yellow River, in an effort to frustrate the Japanese southerly advance toward Wuhan. The resulting floods killed tens of thousands of Chinese peasants—but held up the Japanese vehicles for little more than three months.

even on more distant population centers like Wuhan and Jiujiang. The Chinese Air Force report on the poor defensibility of the Sandouping site was written twenty years ago; today there are plans to deploy some two divisions of soldiers in the immediate area of the dam site, to place guns and missile batteries at every vantage point and to organize a security net around the structure such that the most determined terrorist could not penetrate it. And if the dam were to be destroyed? Not to worry, say the propaganda leaflets sent out by the Yangtze Valley Planning Office, documents of startling complacency, "the dam would be capable of standing up to fairly powerful conventional weapons . . . but if it was attacked by nuclear weapons and totally destroyed, appropriate engineering and managerial measures would limit the damage caused by flooding." It is difficult to draw much comfort from these bland and hardly specific assurances.

The human costs of the dam construction are enormous: the difficulties of moving 1,250,000 people who will have lived all their lives in riverside towns and villages of great antiquity—although also, it has to be said, of an almost universal great ugliness—are legion. Already there have been reports of unrest: in 1992, nearly 180 men and women from what was called the Democratic Youth Party in Kaixian county were reportedly taken away by police and charged with sabotage and counterrevolutionary activity, relating, it is said, to their opposition to the dam. They have not been heard of since.

President Jiang's visit to the city of Jiujiang, hundreds of miles downstream, to plead for room for 200,000 people forced to become refugees was mirrored more recently by suggestions that displaced people might be sent—not asked to go, but sent; this is Communist China—to the miserable uplands of Xinjiang province, a thousand miles to the northwest. Xinjiang and Qinghai, where the Yangtze rises, are gulag country (the Chinese word for the reform-through-labor prisoner, "laogai," is oddly similar to the Russian acronym). The Chinese government is planning a major cotton industry in the area, and advertises its benefits by saying, among other things, that a willing and able labor force of people moved from the flooded Yangtze valley *will shortly be available.*

And then there are the flooded archaeological treasures; and then there is the soon-to-be-ruined environment; and there will be the destruction of the fishes and reptiles and riverine mammals whose normal lifestyle includes using the whole of the lower and middle Yangtze for their spawning and breeding—the near extinct *baiji* and the similarly almost gone Yangtze alligator, the finless porpoise, the Chinese sturgeon, and the Siberian cranes that nest on Poyang Lake. All are now under threat, and the Chinese, except for setting up a couple of underfunded "research establishments" to assuage the most vocally expressed fears from outside, appear to do little, and seem utterly careless of their fate.

A dam that will cost perhaps as much as $36 billion, generating electricity that will have cost $2000 for every kilowatt of capacity—how can the Chinese afford it? And how can an international community bring itself to support or take part in the construction of an outdated monster of such low efficiency, of such great potential danger, of so short a potential life, with such highly questionable economics, and so fraught with severely negative human and environmental implications? Only by getting to Yichang itself, and by seeing the site, could answers to such questions begin to emerge.

We landed forty minutes later at an airport of an insignificance quite equal to the one in Wuhan. It too had biplanes lined up, and here, in a bucolic addition to the scene, a herd of cattle were grazing on the apron.* But I was charmed, now that we had survived the flight: there were dandelions and cosmos flowers in the grass, and the aerodrome had a look of wartime Oxfordshire—except that there was a terminal of worn brick, and inside it a man was asleep at a counter festooned with unsaleable wall hangings of tired-out tigers and smugly obese buddhas. A sign advertised the delights of the Sanxia Bingwan, the Three Gorges Hotel, and so there we went—not so

---

* A brand-new airport was being built outside town: it would have an international terminal, the better to serve would-be investors in the dam.

much to savor its delights as to look for the droves of foreign firms who, I rather cynically suspected, would in spite of all the stated opposition now be flocking to Yichang to try to beg for work on the dam.

The hotel, where we arrived late in the evening, was half-built or half-demolished, it was difficult to say which. It was huge, echoing, empty and awful. It had the advantage of being right on the river-bank, and my room looked out onto the passing ships, of which there were scores, all sounding their sirens as they passed. The hotel's one restaurant closed at eight, and there was no possibility of room ser-vice. There was a bar, but everything in its refrigerator turned out to be frozen solid, which made the child-waitress giggle. I was sorely in need of a drink, and found the idea of a solid one a little less than amusing.

There were also said to be no foreigners in the hotel, except for a young woman from South Africa who was traveling through China on her own. She had the kind of small problem that wanderers find uniquely and, in retrospect only, delightfully Chinese.

She had wanted to check out of the hotel after her night's stay, so that she might catch the night train to Xian. Her bill was three hundred *yuan*. She offered in payment a Visa traveler's check for $100, a type and denomination that the hotel's advertising claimed it would accept and that would in normal circumstances be exchanged for eight hundred *yuan*. The guest could pay her bill, and receive five hundred in change.

But the cashier claimed not to have any money in his till at all: he would readily take the check in full settlement of the bill—but the girl would not receive any change. This would render her quite unable to pay for her train ticket, or anything else for that matter, until the next morning when—and if—she found a bank that would take a traveler's check. By the time I came across her she was on the point of wearily agreeing to do this—to give the hotel, in effect, an extra five hundred *yuan* for nothing.

I weighed in, not minding my own business at all. I told her that she was being presented with a scam as old as the Chinese hills, and that providing she had a totally unsigned traveler's check—which she did—I would change it for her at the going rate. The hotel cashier, a rat-faced little man, looked on with fury as I did this. The South African woman walked off into the night offering undying gratitude. The rat man stared daggers at me, promising by his expression that the service in his hotel would now become for us, if such were possible, significantly worse.

The doorman was a friendlier type. He said that all foreigners who came to Yichang these days—and there were a lot—stayed in the Taohualing Bingwan, the Peach Blossom Hotel. What is more, he said, "there are many beautiful girls there. Girls who like foreigners very much." We flagged down a cycle-ricksha and were at the front drive of the Peach Blossom ten minutes later.

It was a hormonal assault course. Lily walked a dutiful fifty feet behind me for the purpose of the experiment, and as I marched through the gloom toward the brilliantly lit hotel entrance—flashing neon Welcomes and promises of Untold Charms Within—my sleeve was plucked and my shoulders were rubbed by ten, twelve young women, who dashed out from behind parked cars.

The patter was straight from a bad Berlitz course. *You are so handsome. You working for the dam? Your room number, please. I be your good friend. I very reasonable. My massage is excellent. You have much fun. Stop, kind mister, come here and let us have fuck.* Getting rid of these girls was like swatting flies—as one brushed insect broke away, so another zoomed around to get at me on the other side. By the time I reached the hotel building I felt as though I had already had the massage I had been promised. Lily joined me moments later, breathless and not at all amused. The girls, she said, had hissed and sworn at her.

The receptionist, a solid woman in her forties, proved more than amenable when we asked if any foreigners were staying. In the past few months there had been dozens of groups, she said. This week she had, let's see—Japanese, she offered, and Canadians. She turned the computer screen toward us, and let us read down the list of likely surnames. There was a Brown in room 1204, an Ingrams in 1218, a

MacFarlane in 806. All good Scots-Canadian names, it seemed. I called Mr. Brown on the house phone, hoping that he had not succumbed to an Untold Charm Without. But he answered, and I asked him if he had by any chance anything to do with the Three Gorges Dam.

"Too right," he said. "I'm exhausted. But the boss is in the bar. Deep negotiations, you know. Better approach him carefully."

The bar was dark and ice cold. A karaoke machine was showing pictures but, mercifully, it had been turned down so that it was almost inaudible. In the darkest corner sat a group of three foreigners and four Chinese, huddled around a table. The foreigners were nursing beers; the Chinese had peanuts. This was what I had expected to find: for these were the Canadians, chasing work.

The bartender said there had been groups of similarly eager and anxious *lao wai* coming to his bar almost every day this year. They had been meeting the same Chinese, all of whom came from the Three Gorges Project Corporation, which he knew was housed in a modern office building nearby. "They want to be part of our dam," he said. Last month, the bartender said, he had taken his wife and children to see a dam exhibition on the ground floor of the corporation's office. "It is very great, what we are doing. We have good reason to be proud. My children thought it was wonderful. So powerful. So grand."

The Canadians did not take quite so lyrical an approach. Nor, it seemed, had they taken much heed of the world's criticism of the project. They were there quite simply because they wanted a piece of the action.

They turned out to be fairly small players—an Ontario-based firm that had put in for a $35 million contract to design project-management system software, something that would enable the Chinese to organize their work more efficiently. When they met me they were at first dismayed at having been found out, and then became exceptionally discreet. They were well aware that back home the majority of the Canadian public had been appalled by what it knew of the dam, and would not look kindly upon firms from Canada who came to China looking for dam-building business.* But they were far from being alone: it turned out that dozens of other firms from America and Europe and Japan had been scurrying to Yichang in the weeks before, specifically to court business. Still others were expected.

I was shown a list marked "confidential": among the names of those arriving in China and touting for work, or celebrating their having been given some, were General Electric, Hitachi, Mitsubishi, Krupp, Mannesmann, Siemens (who had opened an office in Wuhan), Caterpillar, Nomura, Alcatel, Framatome (the French atomic-power experts, already endeared to the Chinese because of the help they had given to build an equally controversial *can-the-Chinese-really-be-trusted-to-run-it* nuclear generating station at Daya Bay, thirty miles to the windward of Hong Kong), Atlas Copco, Terex Trucks, Brown Boveri and the Finnish Foreign Trade Association. With assistance from companies like these, the Chinese builders will probably not want—at least in the early stages of building—for earthmovers, dump trucks, compressors, drilling rigs, communications gear, heavy steel construction equipment, turbines, electrical transmission towers, ship lock gates or high-powered diesel engines. The only item in short supply in the early stages of building was likely, it seemed, to be money. Given what is known of the state of the Chinese treasury, the want of $36 billion seemed to put the country at least two sandwiches short of a picnic.

The world's financial community had been extremely leery of the project ever since—and indeed because of—the rebellion in the National People's Congress in April 1992 and since the World Bank had pulled out. But the Chinese met this resistance squarely: they decided to go ahead with construction on their own and by doing so

---

* Canada, having been among the first countries to show official interest in the project, felt it deserved prominent participation in the dam. Its highly experienced hydro-engineers were disappointed when Ottawa backed away from the scheme, and a number of big firms promptly formed "Team Canada" to exploit what they could in the Chinese market. But there was still a good deal of opposition at home: the British Columbian government, for example, forbade any formal provincial involvement whatsoever in the Three Gorges project.

demonstrate that the project would eventually become attractive as an investment, even if it wasn't at the outset. It was an adroit bit of gamesmanship; and when combined with adroitly applied doses of blackmail—suggestions to foreign banks that *if you don't help us finance the dam, you won't get any more business in China at all*—it began to work.

The risks of lending money to China are manifold. The country has a total foreign debt of some $90 billion, and a dismal record of welshing that has not endeared her to more prudent minds in the investment community. This particular project, which will take at least seventeen years to complete and will not begin to generate electricity (and thus revenue) until 2003 at the very earliest—and which is plagued by technical opposition, by environmental implications and by massive sociological upheavals—is even less attractive than most. And yet, big American investment firms like Merrill Lynch and banks like Morgan Stanley were early in expressing an interest; while maintaining a discreet distance and the silence of the conclave, they have stuck with the project, offering advice, strategy and, it is assumed, at least promises of eventual funds. Others in America and Japan—Goldman Sachs, Salomon Brothers, Daiwa Securities and Nomura—have taken an interest, too, committing nothing, but keeping their options open and their powder dry. For their part the Chinese offer huge rewards: vast stretches of the Yangtze valley are being opened up to foreign investment, with those who agree to help with the dam being given preference over those who don't.

Politically correct investment strategists have taken a toll on the bankers' enthusiasms, however. A number of investment funds in America now take the view that banks should not invest in environmentally or sociologically unacceptable projects—the Three Gorges Dam being, in their view, a classic of unacceptability. And so they—organizations like New York City Comptroller's Investment Responsibility Office and the Boston-based Franklin Research and Development Corporation—target banks in which they have shares and who are thinking of doing the kind of business of which the shareholders disapprove.

New York's pension funds currently hold $18 million worth of Morgan Stanley shares and $47 million worth of Merrill Lynch: they have clout, in other words. If, following advice from the Investment Responsibility office, the city says it will not touch the Three Gorges project with a barge pole, as it has intimated, then it can bring considerable pressure to bear on the bankers who wish to. Thus is the world becoming more global; in other contexts and from other points of view, thus it is becoming less democratic, thus do international corporations affect the lives of millions, and thus can men in one corner of the world make decisions that have unimagined repercussions on the far side of the planet.

Whether the American and Japanese banks do or do not invest in the project is, for the time being, a moot point. China is raising the first tranches of funding herself, on the domestic market. It has levied a 2 percent sales tax on all electricity consumed in the country. The Bank of China, the People's Construction Bank, the State Development Bank, all have plenty of foreign exchange and have begun lending it to the dam builders. In Hong Kong, there are countless banks and investment houses who are careless of such niceties as environmental ruin and human suffering—a firm called Peregrine, for example, already doing business in North Korea, professed that it would be "fun" to raise money for the Three Gorges Dam. And doubtless firms like Peregrine will end up making money, and will crow lustily at Merrill Lynch and Morgan Stanley, if indeed these firms bow to what the brokers at Peregrine would see as the wishy-washiness of the greens and the human rights advocates, and decide not to help raise money.

The project, in other words, is going ahead, and now looks unstoppable. Li Peng came down from Beijing to pour the first concrete in December 1994—at a ceremony to which foreign journalists were pointedly not invited. Some 20,000 workers toil on the site; by the end of 1996 there will be 35,000. Many of the workers are soldiers. Some are said to be prisoners, laboring on the project at no cost. Coffer dams are going up, lock gates are being cast, canals are being dug, diversion tunnels are being blasted. Yichang will soon have its new, international standard airport. There will be new roads and rail links, and a $3 billion network of power lines. The first of the twenty-six generating sets will be ordered soon: most will come from abroad, and every generator maker on the planet is looking eagerly to get the business.

One of the reasons that is put forward, once in a while, to bolster the case against damming the river, is that by doing so the very dignity of the great stream is being violated. Interrupting the river's flow is seen as an insult, these critics say—and one day the river gods, to the detriment of all, will seek to avenge it.

Toward the end of his masterly novella *A Single Pebble,* John Hersey's narrator, after spending so long among the dangers of the river rapids and after reaching the very upstream end of the Three Gorges, falls prey to the belief in the great river's ancient sanctity. Gazing up at a trackers' path cut into the hard stone of the cliff above him, he starts to reflect:

> To begin with, the path was more than a thousand years old, so Su-ling said: Tang dynasty, she said, and perhaps earlier. Chinese rivermen had been satisfied for a millennium—for more than five times the age of my native country—to use this awful way of getting through the Wind Box Gorge. How could I, in the momentary years of my youth, have a part in persuading these people to tolerate the building of a great modern dam that would take the waters of Tibet and Inner China, with their age-old furies, on its back, there to grow lax and benign? How could I span the gap of a thousand years—a millennium in a day? . . . The sight of the path made me wonder whether a dam was the right thing with which to start closing the gap.

But for all his musings, and for all the opposition to the construction of the Three Gorges Dam, this charming argument is now in fact too late. A dam already has been built, and has stood across the

Yangtze now since 1980. It is a low dam—just 150 feet high, a quarter the height of the barrage upstream. It was constructed by a provincial government, with one Beijing ministry working as an ally, and it was done as a dry run, a dress rehearsal, a test bed for the great dam yet to come, and a source of revenue to help pay for it. And in almost all ways it has been a miserable, ugly source of lamentation.

It is called the Gezhouba Dam, and I could just about see it if I leaned out of my hotel window and peered to the right, upstream. The channel along which the cargo ships beat noisily past our hotel was in fact artificial, part of the Gezhouba's downstream architecture; and at night the klieg lights illuminating the dam's three massive ship locks lit up the sky for miles around. There was also a constant sizzling sound in the background, like white noise: it came from high-tension cables that snaked and looped their way out from the dam's powerhouse, and the pylons that radiated in all directions carried tens of thousands of volts and some of them fizzed and sparked with disturbing displays of energy. Not all of them, however: one, a main transmission line to Shanghai, carries no electricity at all—thus presenting a measure of the technical failure that the dam has been.

Up close the dam was a sensationally horrible thing—a 1½-mile-long wall of gray-brown concrete, patched and rust-speckled, caparisoned with gaunt control towers, festooned with sizzling cables. Behind it the river lay placid, captured and seemingly tamed, hemmed in between the rising hills, a strange embarrassment. To build the dam the engineers had had to stop the river's flow for a day and a half in the midwinter of 1981: the immeasurable indignity that John Hersey had suggested, and for a river that had rushed vigorously along for tens of thousands of years. But such things as halting rivers are meat and drink to dam builders worldwide: an aspect of their pathology that makes them want to tame nature, to stop the unstoppable, to demonstrate the power of cold engineering logic when ranged against the brutish and unfocused forces of raw nature. Communist dam builders take this kind of thing even more personally—actually to stop the Yangtze in her tracks was a feat that Mao Zedong felt proud to have overseen, as though he had somehow drawn strength from it, had derived an even greater measure of popular heroism, and still further sanction for the might of his chosen ideology. And Mao had been personally very committed to the Gezhouba project: after all, it had been started in his honor, and in the midst of the Cultural Revolution, on his birthday—December 26, 1970.

Downstream of the dam, where the sluice gates had been opened, the water gushed and frothed onto the spillways, liberated again, free to feed the great stream below. From the two powerhouses came the hum of the twenty-one great generators that, it is said, were designed to produce 2700 megawatts, enough power to light the houses of 30 million Chinese—or to fulfill the power needs of just 1 million Europeans, for whom electrical power is much more universal a requirement. By any standards the dam is a big one: by the standard of the Three Gorges Dam it is not, however: for every megawatt that Gezhouba is designed to whip from the waters, the big dam is set to produce eight.

The two biggest ship locks were impressive, though, especially from aboard an upriver steamer. I had done the transit several times, and it never failed to awe me, whatever my feelings for the aesthetics of the dam itself. Our ship would nose its way between a cone of flashing buoys to be confronted by the solid concrete wall, looming huge and high. Directly in front was a gateway of two enormous steel doors, so tall it hurt to stare up at their tops.

We would slide gingerly between the gateways, and then into the lock chamber itself, hugging the sides so closely that I could reach out and touch the slimy concrete. Then we were in, along with ten thousand tons of other shipping—empty barges coming up to haul coal downstream, passenger boats, a luxury cruise liner or two, a collection of old motorized *ma-yang zi*—and the huge doors behind would close silently and swiftly. As soon as they had done so, unseen sluices opened in the base of the two upstream doors and the water in the chamber would rise steadily.

Figures of workers and sightseers who were gazing down at us from high above came closer and closer as the ship rose to meet them, until after only four swift minutes we were up alongside them and exchanging greetings and cigarettes. The waters were still, had stopped rising. Bells rang, lights flashed green. Then the lock chamber's farther doors opened and the telegraph on the bridge rang for "Dead slow ahead all," and we moved slowly out once again—seventy feet higher up in what was now a Yangtze lake, heading into the mountains and the Gorges.

If you were to read the papers and believe the handouts, and if you were to accept the dubious veracity of books like the locally published *Large Dams in China* (which has, somewhat unsubtly, a picture of the Great Wall covering its front endpapers, and a so far unsullied Three Gorges at the back), you might think that the Gezhouba Dam had been a splendid success, bringing power and promise to the middle Yangtze valley. In fact its building was a shambles, it was much delayed, was hugely over budget, and since being hastily finished has not delivered either the quantity of power or the myriad of other benefits it was supposed to.

Any big building project begun during the Cultural Revolution should have been suspect: and this one was, in spades. The concrete was rotten. The workers were halfhearted. The management was sloppy. The drawings were inaccurate. Mercifully Zhou Enlai, who at times seems to have been the only sane official in the China of those days, managed to halt this project two years after it had been begun, once he became aware how ill designed and dangerous it was. He had it closed for two years: when work began again, the Cultural Revolution was over and more levelheaded engineers and managers were in charge.

Even so, it was a full twenty years before the dam was fully ready and generating as much electricity as it could. No power ever reached Shanghai, as had been promised—and the costly transmission lines that went up stand idle. Had Gezhouba been a true dress rehearsal for the Three Gorges Dam, the latter might never have been started. As it is, the big dam assumed a life of its own, with its own political pressures driving it ever forward, and the low dam became a small irrelevance, ugly and damaging and almost useless in its own way—an insult to the river, and a harbinger of the troubles to come upstream.

We went in a truck to have a proper look at the great new dam's site. Seeing it from the river is unsatisfactory: from the navigation channel, a quarter mile from each bank, the bulldozers look almost vanishingly small and their work insignificant. The ever present fogs obscure all but the boldest symbols of the dam's approach—gigantic signs proclaiming the glory of the project, extolling the virtues of the workers.* Even so, I made two brief passes by boat this time, just to check on the progress.

I had been there the previous winter and had seen the site through a cold and driving drizzle just before the formal inauguration. Huge rubber hoses extended out into midriver, belching sand onto the river bottom, making shallows where hitherto had been deeps. Excavators crawled along the banks, shoving boulders over the edge and into the water. The fizz and sparkle of welding torches flickered through the gloom, like fireflies.

I was going downstream on one of the Regal China Company's cruising boats, a grand-luxe vessel filled with holidaymakers from far away. I found myself standing on the bridge wing with Norris Mc-Whirter, the editor of the *Guinness Book of Records,* who was on holiday with a group organized by the British Museum. He gestured at the torn hillsides and the mud-stained riverway and, pathologically unable to resist the superlatives involved, said with an endearingly boyish enthusiasm:

"Biggest hydroelectric dam in the world, you know."

---

* These will be as nothing compared to 180-foot-tall *illuminated* billboards with which the authorities say they are planning to decorate the spectacularly lovely cliffs of the Xiling Gorge, advertising local wines and spirits. Their illumination, of course, comes courtesy of the hydroelectric power made by the dams, so at one fell swoop they will be advertising two aspects of the country's modernization.

He looked a little more, asked me to show him the level to where the water would rise, and then, in tones slightly more serious, said:

"Probably the biggest bloody disaster, too."

Six months later, when I went again by ship, the site was more organized, more recognizable as the workings of a dam. There were the twin towers of a new bridge, for example, rising a few hundred yards below the dam wall site. And along the left bank, where the bulldozers had been dumping the rocks, a wall of concrete half a mile long: the approach canal for the ship locks, according to the map.

The greatest activity was on the right bank, however. The previous November there had been the island a few score yards off that bank—Zhongbao, the charts had named it, a quarter-mile-long lozenge of an island, rising perhaps twenty feet above the level of the river at high water. Now the island had quite vanished behind a huge coffer dam of rock and gravel and hardcore: it was surrounded by dry riverbed, and crane and drilling rigs were festooned all over it, pouring and pumping cement onto and into it so that before long it would rise as a giant anchor point for the main dam itself. Zhongbao Island was the linchpin of the entire construction: in a year or so it would be revealed once more, the coffer dams torn down, and construction of the dam proper would begin from its newly reconstituted crown.

Getting permission to visit the dam site was not easy. Lily and I went to the project office and were ushered by a soldier to a quiet and friendly man named Liu Rong Bo, who after the initial cup of tea and thin smile of welcome, wanted to know only one thing: Was I a writer?

I said nothing specific in reply, but reacted with a dramatic expression of distaste. I was a teacher, a historian and researcher, and I had long been interested in the history of the Yangtze River. I had so far traveled all of its length from the Woosung Bar: I planned to travel the rest of its length to the headwaters at Gelandandong on the Tibetan frontier. A visit to this most celebrated dam construction site would be both a privilege and a natural progression for me: I had seen the buoy at the river's mouth, I had seen where the Treaty of

Nanking had been signed and where the pagoda at Anqing stood and where Mao had swum between Wuchang and Hankou—could not a visit be arranged? *Please.*

There was much harrumphing and sucking of teeth, and whispered conversations with an ever impressive, ever persuasive Lily before, at last, a flimsy scrap of paper was written with lines of calligraphy and impressed with a huge scarlet seal of the Three Gorges Project Corporation. A secretary whispered some instructions to Mr. Liu and he began to screw the paper into a ball, before Lily, screeching at the secretary for evidently offering some wrongheaded information, snatched the still unscathed sheet away from him and demanded that he sign it. This he did: a slow and painful Liu, a Rong and a Bo—and then, as a gift, another copy of the newly published booklet which Mr. Liu had edited, and which was called *An Epic Undertaking.* (The hotel manager in Wuhan had given me the first copy a few days before.) Thus armed—book, paper and signed seal of approval—we set out for the site, twelve miles away by road.

The journey took four hours. The road vanished after five miles, to be replaced by a track clogged with every kind of construction vehicle, van, bus, taxi, tractor, crane, backhoe, bulldozer, motorcycle and ricksha imaginable. A giant expressway was being built halfway up the mountainside, and a dozen new bridges soared, half-made, across the deep ravines. But meanwhile this single track of mud and crumbling cliff had to do, regulated at its most congested sections by bored policemen who tried to impose a one-way traffic scheme, but broke it all the time for bribes offered by their friends.

More than once we sat in traffic jams caused by broken-down cars. I went up to one: the driver was sitting beside the vehicle, fast asleep. I asked him what was wrong with the car—he had no idea. I opened the hood to find that the distributor cap had been knocked off by the bumping and the potholes. I clipped it back on, the car started, the driver got in without a thank-you, and all those waiting around laughed, before climbing back into their own cars.

"Bloody cadres!" exclaimed Lily. "No one here cares if they work or not. They just sit around waiting for help, and don't move until they get it. I'm sure it's not like this in New York, is it?" By way of an answer I repeated the old line about the shortest measurable period of time in Manhattan being that between the moment of getting a green light and the blare of a horn from the taxi driver behind. She got the picture.

The flimsy paper, with its impressive scarlet chop, did us little good. Police and soldiers stopped us for an hour at the entrance gate, and then we were escorted to a headquarters building about a mile beyond. Finally—and once again, due largely to Lily's ability to combine a display of well-directed anger, her formidable height and bearing and her highly seductive feminine charm—we were allowed in, unrestricted. No one escorted us, no one followed us. For three hours we were able to walk among the giant bulldozers and excavators, to talk to workers and try to discern something of the plan.

There were 15,500 men at work that day. Half were from the army, and they were all engaged in digging the ship canal, which was being gouged from the left bank, around the northern edge of the dam wall itself. Drilling rigs would buck and screech as they scored countless holes in the rock for the dynamite charges. Every few minutes there would be a soft crump of an explosive charge, and the air would fill with dust, and those fortunate enough to have hard hats would hear the ping of gravel from above. The rest of us knew when to put hands over heads, or when to duck.

The speed with which things were changing was quite literally a subject of awe. I had never been much of an admirer of the Chinese worker: he seemed always to work at half-speed, sleeping whenever he seemed not to be needed. And yet look away—and where he once was, a bridge has risen! a trench has been dug! a building has advanced a floor! The Chinese worker is in this respect just like a snail: you rarely see him in the actual act of moving—but look away for a second, and then look back, and he is somewhere else from where you last remember him, a small trail shows where it was that he went.

From a small knoll of unexcavated rock I could see the entire project, and here, unlike my preconceived idea, there were workers scurrying, antlike and excited, on every part of it. Here I felt that if I stood still for half an hour I would see construction happen before my eyes, like watching the results of time-lapse photography or a slow-motion film. On the far bank they were building the Zhongbao Island coffer dams. On this side there was the ship canal, and down below, close to the river, the footwalls for the main dam itself. Upstream and down were the foundations for the main dam coffers, and in the distance upstream and down, lights pierced the gloom where concrete-laying machines were lining the entrances and exits of the huge river diversion tunnels.

In a little more than two years the flow of this river—90,000 cubic yards of water each second—would be halted, for the second time in her long history. China would be told that this was a moment of which to be proud—a precursor to the building of a second great wall, a monument to man's ingenuity. But there are those who remember that the real Great Wall of China was held together by a mortar made of the crushed skeletons of those thousands who died making it. That the Great Wall was built by slaves; there was no choice: it had to be built, or the Empire would lose face.

This new great wall had to be built too. Thousands might die in its building, thousands might die in its aftermath. Animals and plants and peoples would be affected in a myriad of strange and appalling ways. An immense section of China would be affected, and for the worse, by what was going up here. And yet there was no choice here today either. It had to be built, or the new red empire would lose face too. Two thousand two hundred years separated the building of the two walls—two millennia during which the essential nature of China, by this single standard, seemed not to have changed at all.

Lily and I turned back to Yichang, and sought out a small boat master who would take us past the dam site—and this time, into the Gorges themselves. Here I would see at close quarters what was about to be ruined or drowned deep under the soon-to-be-stilled and soon-to-be-fouled waters of China's greatest river.

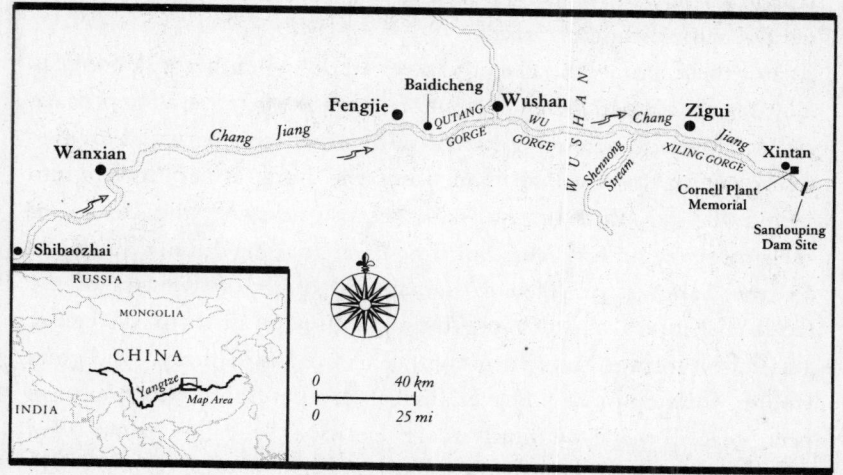

IO

The Shipmasters' Guide

On the banks of the Yangtze there has been only one public memorial raised to a foreigner—or at least, only one that still survives. There is not even a single one for any Chinese, Mongol or Manchu—if one can discount, though not quite forget, the dreadful barbarisms of the dams.

The Yangtze is a river strangely short of heroes. There is no single explorer known for performing heroic deeds in the process of conquering or discovering the river, nor does any merchant or grandee spring to mind who can be said to have tamed or dominated it. The Yangtze, it seems, has ever been a river so great and important that it was always known, was never conquered and was invariably treated with diffident respect.

For the Chinese, the Hsia dynasty's founding emperor, Yü (or Da Yü, Yü the Great), who lived more than 4000 years ago, perhaps comes closest to achieving heroic status. But then he was a mythic figure, heroic because he made sure the Long River flowed into China and not Vietnam, and also because he swept the Gorges of their more trying rockfalls. But if he lived at all he did not do so just for the Yangtze: he lived to manage all of the waterways of the Celestial Empire, and not just the single greatest of them. No statue was raised to him, though temples celebrate his memory. The great Cloud Mountain near the river's Great Bend at Shigu is said to have been placed there by him: it can perhaps be called some kind of memorial, writ large in Carboniferous geology and Miocene tectonics.

For outsiders there are a scattering of men and women who are remembered for what might be called their *association* with the river, and who have left thick volumes of their adventures to molder on the shelves of well-stocked libraries. There was Thomas Blakiston, for instance, who was one of the first to go through the Gorges, in the 1850s, and who wrote scrupulously and elegantly of the birds and the plants of Sichuan. Then there was William Gill, who traveled along the headwater streams of the Yangtze fifteen years later and chronicled the puzzling doings of the minority peoples of Sichuan and Yunnan. There was Archibald Little, who pioneered steam navigation on the river. There was Augustus Margery, who was murdered horribly after entering China from Upper Burma. And as always, and inevitably, there was Isabella Bird, the redoubtable, imperturbable, amazing, thick-tweed-skirted and courageous matron venturer, the chronicles of whose voyages through the Yangtze Gorges return to print perennially today, and whose exploits on the Yangtze and elsewhere unfailingly manage to hoodwink us Britons into believing in our still special singularity.

All these we think of as heroes—yet they are really small-beer heroes when ranged against the likes of Speke and Livingstone and

Burton and Alexander von Humboldt (and even Marco Polo) and those others whose names are linked more closely with the great rivers in the world beyond China.

But there was, for me, one man who truly did rank as a Yangtze hero. I do not mean the Royal Navy captain who took HMS *Amethyst* downstream under the withering fire of Communist guns back in the summer of 1949. That was heroism, to be sure, and it was heroics of a kind that kept young Britons like me riveted to our cinema seats. But it was also a heroism of the moment, a brief few hours of glory; the captain's achievement differs in kind from that of the man whom I think of as a true Yangtze hero, and that was at least in part because my man devoted the greater part of his life to the river, which he came to love.

He was named Cornell Plant. He was an Englishman, born in a North Sea–side village halfway through the last century. His principal fascination, born perhaps from his upbringing near the wide river estuaries—of the Humber, the Thames, the Tyne, the Forth— that saw small merchant ships come and go to and from the North European ports, had always been with river travel and river navigation. He began his overseas career in Mesopotamia, a captain of ships that navigated the slow majesties of the rivers Tigris and Euphrates. He would have stayed in these comfortable parts for years, perhaps, had it not been for a chance encounter in London, while he was home on leave.

It came late in the nineteenth century, when Cornell Plant was dining in the Oriental Club in London. Here, also dining at a table of shipbuilders and marine architects, was the vastly more celebrated figure of Archibald Little. He was telling his companions stories of his own frustrated attempt to steam up the Three Gorges on the faraway river in China. Plant, perhaps wearying of the sunshine and sands of Iraq and Syria, was captivated by the tales, and by the thought of—China! When Little spotted his keen interest and ventured that he might actually come east and command a ship for him for the first major boat assault on the Gorges' rapids, the thirty-three-year-old Plant readily agreed.

He went out east at a time when the Chinese were laughing behind their silken sleeves at the ill-guided madness of the British river sailors. The court authorities had long since assumed it would be impossible for any powered vessel to ascend through the whirlpools and rapids of the Gorges, and yet the British—in the person of men like Little—were busily, insanely in the Chinese view, trying to do so.

The conventional wisdom was that only junks might pass between Yichang and Chongqing, and then only with great effort, with the boats having to be hauled up by hundreds of human trackers. Steam vessels, with their deep draft and their thrashing propellers, had to navigate out in the more perilous center section of the stream, where the Cassandras said they would be simply and swiftly overwhelmed. Even Yangtze explorers like Thomas Blakiston were then advising merchants not to be so foolhardy as to try to match pistons and propellers against the terrific waters of the Yangtze in the Gorges.

The Manchu government had been clever and cynical when it had signed the Convention of Chefoo in 1876. Its mandarins had seemed to be in a generous mood. They had appeared to give in to the foreigners' demand that they be allowed to appoint trade representatives in Chongqing, in the heart of the grain-rich, mineral-rich, coal-rich Red Basin. But closer scrutiny showed that their official stipulation was subtly phrased: trade could get fully under way only when steam navigation was in full swing. Since the Court believed this to be impossible, and since the mandarinate had put forward all kinds of objections,* it turned out that they had managed to offer the foreigners an apparent concession—and yet withhold it at one and the same time. It was a classic piece of Chinese trickery, whereby the Orientals seemed to outfox the barbarians, and not for the last time, either.

---

* Including the notion that the Gorges' cliffs were alive with angry monkeys that, enraged by the noise of passing steam engines, would pelt each ship with stones until the vessel was disabled and the crew dead.

The traders who accepted the early arrangement floundered financially: while it was easy and cheap to send goods downstream, it cost a small fortune to send them up against the raging water. Indeed, someone commented in 1880 that it cost quite as much to send a cargo the five hundred miles from Wuhan to Chongqing as it did to send it the twelve thousand miles from Wuhan to London!

Archibald Little, however, was determined to change all that. He was an unforgettable figure, though not the nicest of men. His travels in China were always done in as much comfort as possible. Little was ill named: he was large and imperious, he liked to eat and drink well ("dinner washed down with a Lafitte from the Café Voisin in Paris, hospitably broached in my honour," he noted after one feast) and he took pride in feeding his dog, Nigger, at the local hotels (where one night's stay for himself "and coolie" cost 132 copper cash, or sixpence in the English money of the day).

By the time he met Cornell Plant in London, he had already built himself a small teak steam launch named the *Leechuan* and, with his wife, as well as a Ningbo engineer and two stokers, he had managed, comically and slowly, to puff and snort and clank aboard it all the way through the Gorges. A Chinese gunboat—a sailing junk, heavily armed—a gang of extra trackers, and a bright red lifeboat went along too, in case of catastrophe. One of his pilots managed to collide with another vessel, a second jumped ship, terrified. But Little was a sticker, and brooked no excuses for failure; and made it, slowly and frighteningly, to his destination.

The eventual arrival of this launch at Chongqing on April 8, 1898, turned out to be one of the greatest events in the city's history, or so the local newspaper said at the time. The entire foreign community of about sixty turned out, and the Chinese, far from being hostile, set off firecrackers by the thousand. But reality soon cooled the enthusiasm. It had taken the craft three weeks to get just 360 miles upstream, and at one time no fewer than three hundred trackers had to haul the fragile craft across one of the scarier rapids. It was clear that, with the marine technology of the time, regular steam-based commerce was not quite ready.

But it was a start. The following year the Royal Navy ordered two of its gunboats, HMS *Woodlark* and HMS *Woodcock,* all the way up to Chongqing. These boats, of shallow draft and with strengthened hulls, had been specially made in sections in Britain, and bolted together in Shanghai. When they received their signal they were on patrol on the central Yangtze station, protecting British trade downriver from Wuhan. Their captain turned them about and sped them past Yichang and into the tortured waters of the Xiling Gorge.

Some four hundred trackers were then involved in getting the vessels over the *tans,* the rapids, and many hours were spent warping the boats with steel hawsers through the whirlpools and boils. The *Woodlark* very nearly foundered: she trembled on the lip of one of the worst rapids with her stern tipped halfway down it—but the ratings were all ordered to run to the bow *at the double,* the ship tilted under their weight, shook herself free of the sucking waters, and moved on.

It had taken thirty-one days for the little warships to dock at Chongqing. But the Admiralty orders had been obeyed, the navy's imperial ambitions realized. By the time Cornell Plant arrived in China at the beginning of the new century, regular steam travel through the Gorges was becoming a distant reality, and the Chinese authors of the Chefoo Convention were becoming less and less confident. Their bluff, after all, was being called.

It was called to final effect in June 1900. Cornell Plant had come out to China to study the rapids of the Gorges; and Archibald Little had come out with the pieces of a brand-new ship, an iron paddle wheeler called the *Pioneer.** Built by Denny's of Dumbarton on the River Clyde, she had been assembled from the kit in Shanghai. She was a big vessel, twice as heavy as the gunboats, and she carried 150 tons of cargo and a full complement of, given the circumstances, very plucky passengers.

And she turned in a bravura performance. She made the journey up to Chongqing in seventy-three steaming hours—over seven days total,

---

* This hardly original name had also been given to the first railway engine that worked the narrow gauge between Woosung and Shanghai.

because one rapid had held her up for three nerve-racking days before a hawser could be secured and allow her to be warped through. When she arrived at the congested dockside in Chongqing, her master— Captain Plant—was able to announce with pride that she had come the entire distance without once having to resort to the use of trackers. The age of steam, so far as the Gorges were concerned, had finally and formally begun.

(History turned inglorious for the *Pioneer* herself. The Boxer Uprising was just then beginning, and the Royal Navy promptly commandeered the vessel, not least because it had such obvious Yangtze aptitude. The Admiralty changed her name to HMS *Kinsha*—the Golden Sand—and used her for twenty years to evacuate civilians caught up in the seemingly endless troubles that blew up along the river, then sold her to a firm that traded chickens between Ningbo and Shanghai.)

Captain Plant then turned his full attention to the river and the rapids. He confessed a tireless affection for the river: it had some ineffable quality that captivated him, he said. "Truly," he once wrote, "the farther one travels along this mighty water highway of China, the more strangely fascinating it becomes." He built a houseboat so that he could live on or beside the rapids of the Gorges for the rest of his life. He designed a nippy little steamer called the *Shutung,* had it built in England and sent over, and saw it perform so well that he eventually ran a fortnightly Three Gorges services that drew a standing-room-only crowd of passengers, carrying freight aboard lighters lashed to its sides—an arrangement still in common use today.

But his heroic stature became properly apparent only when he ventured away from running a shipping business himself and started official duties with one of the most unforgettable bureaucracies that was ever to be created by a colonial power: the Chinese Imperial Maritime Customs Service. This was a body that was every bit as grand and distinguished as its name, and its officers—Cornell Plant had the august title of Senior River Inspector, Upper Yangtze—were giants among men.

The Imperial Maritime Customs had been established under the terms of the Treaty of Nanking—signed on the Yangtze in 1842—which allowed foreigners, the British particularly, to collect customs duties on behalf of the Chinese government. It enabled the British swiftly to exert huge economic and political influence on the Chinese government, and for that, given today's attitudes toward colonialism, it should probably be condemned. But its staff turned out, by and large, to be men of great integrity and scholarship, and their reports, which thundered from the presses, year after year, from every obscure corner of the Chinese Empire, paint—in pointillist style, admittedly—an amazingly accurate picture of how China was, "in the years that were fat."

The great George Worcester, who was until his death in 1969 undeniably the world's leading expert on Chinese junks, and who served for thirty years as a Yangtze River inspector, wrote of his service with affection and respect, many years after it had vanished from existence:

> No serious student of China, her history, people or industries should neglect these publications. Written in faultless prose by men of a bygone generation who where scholars as well as administrators, their work is bound to be of the greatest historical value. Nothing was too unimportant, nothing too trivial for these earnest, lucid compilers of the Trade Reports. Statistics on the movement of umbrellas in Canton, vermicelli from Chinchew, animal tallow from Chinghai and coal dust from Putien were all treated with the same care and attention to detail as was vast "Treasure, Imported and Exported." . . . It must have been a wonderful period in which to have lived.

Cornell Plant's contribution to this vast canon of lucid and elegant scholarship was an eighty-page book entitled *A Handbook for the Guidance of Shipmasters on the Ichang-Chungking Section of the Yangtze River*. It is a far from romantic title, yet it is a deeply romantic book. It represented Plant's life's work, and his life's love: for the first twenty-one years of the century, he would examine with painstaking affection every twist and turn of a river he came to know like no other man before or since. Every rock and cliff, every rapid and whirlpool—this calm, self-effacing, brave and well-loved man noted, plotted, mapped, sketched, and named each one, for his own curiosity, out of duty to Empire, to navigators, and for the safety and well-being of shipmasters ever since.

The rock's names came either from the local Chinese junkmen, or from Plant's steadily fertile imagination: Pearl Rock, one of his charts says, then Second Pearl, Monk's Rock, and Chicken Wings. In one rapid there is a rock that was infamous for the entire upper river, a pinnacle whose whirlpools had pulled a hundred ships fatally toward her: Plant marks it laconically as the Come-to-Me Rock.

In his crib sheets he handed down all the better legends from the old navigators—like that of the Yen-yu Stone at the mouth of the Qutang Gorge, which would block the river at a certain volume of low water, or else be washed over by impassably rapid streams at certain other times when the river was high. The boatmen warned thus:

When Yen-yu resembles an elephant, upstream is totally impossible,
And when Yen-yu is as small as a horse, downstream is highly inadvisable.

Nowadays the rock is shaped like neither beast: a team of Chinese government dynamiters took seven days to drill charges into it and blow it up.

Cornell Plant was a one-man river survey: his maps—beautifully executed pieces of art in and of themselves—still form the basis of all the *Pilot* guides to the river. Today, many of the rocks Plant described and named have been dynamited, and shoals have been dredged and rapids tamed. But his descriptions are still haunting, and for a newcomer, they make good and frightening reading as one's steamer rounds a corner into a stretch of water the old man once knew as especially dangerous:

An immense mass of black rock, some fifty feet high at low level, sticks up right in mid-stream, which, surrounded by a number of smaller ones, during low level, renders the passage on the one hand impassable, leaving only the other which is studded with submerged rocks, the channel between them being very narrow, crooked and dangerous. There are local Chinese who pilot boats up and down these Narrows during low level season. . . . Their services should always be engaged, especially when on the downward passage; an error of judgment in making the narrow fairway between the Pearl Rocks means destruction.

He noted phlegmatically that the native junks—which carried as many as one hundred crewmen and a junkman's family of maybe thirteen members—were all too often lost: one junk in ten was badly damaged by the rocks, one in twenty was totally wrecked. The fifty days it might take a big junk to warp and track and creak her way upstream from Yichang were dangerous, deadly and tense, every one.

His *Shipmasters' Guide* was invaluable, particularly to those who read English—and for big vessels, the fact that the river inspectors and the customs men were invariably Englishmen came as both a comfort and a distinct commercial advantage. But Plant's system of signal stations was available to all, and it remains just the same to this day. Small white houses stand perched on precipitous cliffsides, each with a flagpole and halyards from which the lookout raises and lowers huge illuminated arrows to advise approaching vessels if the way ahead is clear or if the channel is being used by a vessel coming the other way.

To pass beneath one of these stations, a steamer captain once told me as we did so, deep in the Xiling Gorge, is to experience a small but exquisite moment of comfort. "I may be tired from turning round the whirlpools and dodging the quicksands, but I round a bend and there, ahead, is the little station, and the arrow tells me I may go ahead and all is clear upstream—that's something precious.

"Your Englishman—we call him Pu Lan Tian, you know—he did great things. These signal stations, for example. They are a reminder of how man has done his best to make this terrible river safe, or as safe as it can be." This captain was a romantic of sorts: every time he passed below this station and all the others he would blip his siren, and if he was lucky enough, a short fellow in a cloth cap—a river inspector, no less—would peer out over the parapet, and wave him on.

Cornell Plant retired shortly after the sounds of the Great War had faded back in Europe. Out of gratitude the Imperial Maritime Customs and the Chinese government built him and his wife a small bungalow at the village of Xintan, overlooking a deliciously spectacular and murderous rapid—the so-called New Rapid—at the mouth of the Xiling Gorge.

Ships had the most trying time battering their way up through this triple-barreled maelstrom. Junks often had to unload their entire cargo and employ scores more trackers to haul them through the boiling stream. Even today it is fun to watch from on high as a ship lurches and pitches helplessly, like a drunk on a bucking bronco—and then to breathe again as her bow breaks free and she swings into calm water and readies herself for the next ordeal, a mile or so upstream.

The Plants would watch from their terrace for years—the old man's smooth pink face beaming benignly down at the men undergoing their brief misery. A tradition arose that once safely through the rapid the captain of each ship would sound his siren in salute—for it had been Cornell Plant's charts, spread out on the bridge table, that had guided the captain safely ahead, and a small token of thanks was the least to be offered in the circumstances. Plant would always reply by waving a white handkerchief down at the passing vessel, and then would look back downstream again to see if yet another shipmaster was going to be so bold today.

In 1921 the Plants decided to go home to England for a while:

China, warlord struck, was in the throes of strange eruptions of violence and irrational wantonness, and they were tired of it. They took a ferryboat down to Shanghai, and then an oceangoing ship for Hong Kong. But Cornell Plant caught pneumonia on board, and died at sea; his wife died a month later, heartbroken. The pair still lie today in Hong Kong's Happy Valley cemetery, overlooking the racecourse and, if a point can be a little stretched to make their resting place seem an even more suitable one, the bustling maritime madness of that city's western harbor.

There is, it was said, a memorial to him in Xintan village, and Lily and I went looking for it.

Xintan is an otherwise insignificant place, and rightly so. It has a tiny coal mine up in the hills and a tung-oil plantation. Small country boats call there once in a while, and barges stop every week to haul away some of the brownish lumps that pass for coal in these parts. In Yichang I managed to persuade the skipper of a Russian-built hydrofoil to drop us off at Xintan on his way up to Wanxian and collect us on his way back. He was happy to do it—he had heard of Pu Lan Tian and remembered stories of his waving to passing ships.

"The place has changed a lot since his time—landslides, you know," he said. "A big one in 1984, many people died. Half of the mountain came down." He pointed through the windshield to a scar, five hundred feet long, where new pale green vegetation was growing again. "Many houses were swept into the river. I think this will be a big problem if the dam is built. These landslips make huge waves. Maybe they will damage the dam. This is a very frightening piece of river, I have always thought." He shuddered, and watched us nervously as we climbed out onto the sponsons and jumped onto dry land. He roared away quickly in a swirl of foam and fumes to the comparative safety, as he saw it, of the center of the stream.

Xintan was dirty beyond belief, smoky and sulphurous. We scrambled up a bank that was sticky with wet coal dust and as we did so an utterly mad woman suddenly confronted us and started screeching and clucking like a chicken, and spitting at us. A group of small boys were tormenting her, hurling lumps of mud. Suddenly a machine in a small factory thumped into life and its chimney began to emit a thick coil of black and tarry smoke. Dozens of pigs ran through puddles of sewage that stank in the rutted roadway. It was a little difficult to imagine this as a bucolic retirement home for an old English sea captain.

But everyone knew the memorial. It stood at the far end of the village, on a knoll where a tiny tributary, the Dragon Horse Stream, trickled into the left side of the Yangtze. It was quite vast, an obelisk thirty feet high made of blocks of pink granite on a brown sandstone base. It dominated the village and could be seen downstream for miles—I had seen it from the boat, but assumed it must be a memorial to some later revolutionary heroism, and not to a long dead Englishman. It seemed far too grand for that.

Others had thought so too. When I had clambered up closer I could see that every single word incised into the stone had been painstakingly chipped out. The words "Plant Memorial" were still just legible; but the panel below, which presumably had listed his accomplishments in English, had been taken away, and around the side every one of the 130 Chinese characters had been chiseled away—I could still count the holes where they had been—and made illegible. Some terrible vandalism had been executed here.

"Red Guards," said a young woman who had come up beside me quietly and had been standing by while I tried to read what was left. "I am so very sorry. I truly am."

She was pregnant, rather pretty, but tired looking, with wispy hair that blew about her face in the breeze.

"They came here one day in 1968. They tried to blow it up. They said it was evil to have a stone put up in honor of a barbarian. But you know what?—they couldn't destroy it. It was built too well. So they did the next best thing—they had a group of boys with iron tools break out every letter, every character.

"I feel so ashamed. My husband is a shipmaster, and so was his father. All our families have lived in Xintan for many years. They worship Pu Lan Tian. He was a great man. We were proud that he lived here. But his house has gone, and now his memorial has been wrecked as well."

Her name was Mrs. Du and she invited us home for lunch. She had another child at home: she wasn't certain how she was going to deal with the impending arrival—already the nurse at the local hospital had told her she must abort it. She was holding out, for the moment.

After rooting about in a drawer beside her bed she found a piece of paper. She smoothed it out, then stood before us and recited from it:

"The British Consulate in Yichang wrote the inscription on the memorial, which was erected by public subscription among the foreign community, in 1922. It said that Plant was an Englishman born in a place called Fram-ling-gam and that he worked for the Chinese Customs Service during the Qing Dynasty. The first steamboat going up the Yangtze Gorges, the driver of it is Plant. He was born in the Qing dynasty, in the fifth year of the reign of the Emperor Dong Zhi [which would have been 1867]. During the Nationalist government time, in the springtime, he went back home, and on January 19 he died on his way home. His old friends thanked him for all his hard work, and they proudly call him the Father of the Upper River."

Mrs. Du put down the paper. She was blinking back tears, I thought.

"Madness," I said, pointing back at the horribly defaced memorial. She nodded in angry agreement.

"But worse," she said. "In a few years it will be drowned. This whole village will be under water. They have told us to move. What can we do? We will be living far away. And poor Mr. Plant—he will not be remembered at all. And his rapids—they will be at the bottom of a lake. All smooth and quiet. All character taken away."

Later that day another woman, who lived beside the memorial, gave us tea and told us something of the plans for moving—a third of the village would go in 1996, some more in 1998, the rest a year later. There would be an allowance of ten thousand *yuan* for every family member forced to move—thirty thousand for her husband and herself and their small boy, and another ten thousand for her grandfather, she said.

"It will be expensive—we have to get the new house for ourselves. It is already selected where we will go, a village called Qian Shan Po, up in the hills behind." She jerked her hand back, contemptuously. "It is much cooler up there. We will not be able to farm the peaches and the oranges and the limes. Sweet potatoes and lettuce will be okay, and the corn too. But life will not be the same. And we won't be able to see the river any more. It'll be difficult—not so much for my child, nor for my husband and me.

"But what of my grandfather?" She nodded toward a figure sitting at the end of her garden. "He is too old to change."

Her grandfather was seated under a persimmon tree at the edge of the cliff, smoking a pipe and gazing down at the boiling river below. He was quite deaf and made no move when I walked up to him and then stood beside him. He was dressed in an old gown of dark blue silk adorned with dragons. He looked perfectly at peace with his world, warming himself in the late spring sunshine, puffing on a tiny nut of tobacco, watching the ships churn by.

In a couple more years government officials would come and order him to move elsewhere. "There is no point in arguing with our leaders," sighed his granddaughter. "Besides, this dam is a national project—an international project, I've heard them say. We have no rights. We cannot complain. That is the way it is in China today."

She sighed deeply—she was more unhappy for her ancient relative, I thought, than she was for herself. He had seen so much change in his lifetime, and so little of it had been for the better.

When he was a young man all the upstream boats would have been hauled by trackers, teams of naked men harnessed by bamboo hawsers and struggling along the broken shores or in the crouch-high galleries that ran along the cliff walls.

When he was a child the Manchus' power was still a bright memory, and some young men of the day wore silk robes and had their hair in queues and some of the women still bound their feet. Since then steam power had come to the river, the trackers—with their songs and their poetry and their guilds and their rude good fellowship—had been replaced and vanished into riverside villages like this, and some had said it was good that man was a beast of burden no longer.

Some kind of social justice, affecting the trackers and the coolies and concubines and the *mapus* and all the other drones of Imperial days, had come to modern China—but had rested only briefly, and a rude and greedy kind of commercial world that had overtaken those brief promises of fairness and equality now seemed to dominate everything. It was no good: the Confucian calm and order that this old man once knew had long since been swept away, and the changes were coming faster and faster, so that if to his granddaughter it seemed as if the Chinese world might suddenly spin off its axis and explode in a million pieces, consider how it all must appear to him.

And now, because of a cascade of decisions made without a care for whom they might one day affect, this old man would have to spend his final years far away from the river beside which he had lived, so his granddaughter said, for the last ninety-four years. "He loved the river," she explained. "It will break his heart."

I decided not to disturb him, and instead walked away, between the corn rows and the orange bushes and down the hill toward the river. Lily and I waited for an hour, talking to some women loading rice flour onto a waiting barge. Then I spotted a group of four Tibetans, dressed in their burgundy robes, walking quickly upstream along an old trackers' path: they were selling herbs, someone said.

They were the first Tibetans I had seen, a reminder of how close China's frontiers were now, and I wanted very much to talk to them, to show them a picture of the Dalai Lama I had tucked into the bottom of my rucksack, back in New York. But just at that moment our Russian speedboat appeared around the bend, and the captain waved to us to come aboard, and swiftly. He was late, and didn't like stopping under these unstable cliffs for longer than he had to.

I craned my neck as we passed below the Plant Memorial. The old man was still sitting, motionless, under his tree, his hawklike eyes watching our ship pulling away from the bank and into the whirling foam of the New Rapid. I stood up and waved to him and, for just a moment, he took one hand away from the stem of his pipe and gestured down back at me. Whether it was a wave of resignation or farewell I could not be sure; but I thought in that moment that he did know that his peace was about to be interrupted, but that he had chosen not to think about it, and would savor such rest as he still could, up there in the afternoon sun.

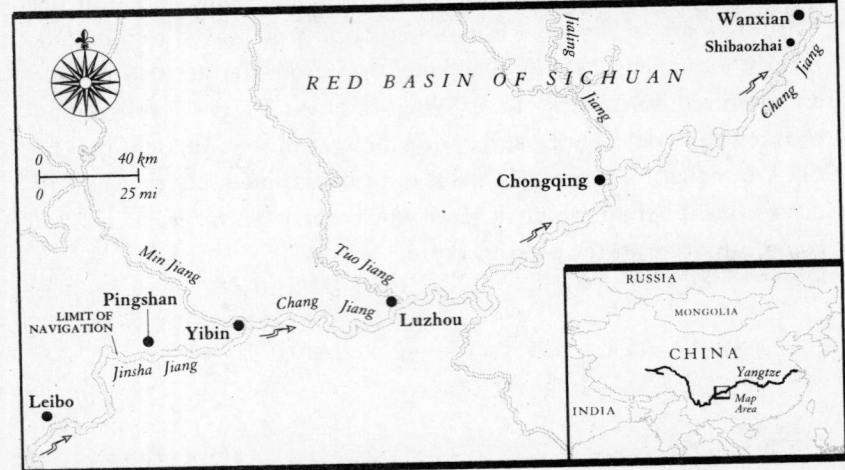

II

The Foothills

The moon was high and the sky was clear when our ship lumbered up to the dockside under the hills of Chongqing. It was the kind of night that, during the war, the local citizenry would have dreaded— for it was on moonlit nights like this that the Japanese bombers came and wrought terror on the streets below.

Back then it did no good to black out the lights and stop the traffic: the squadrons of Zeros would come in from Wuhan, or from the field at Yichang—the same aerodrome where we had landed some days before—and follow the river sparkling silver under the moon. Then, when another silver stream joined it from the north—the Jialing— they would know where to strike. There, the darkened pubic triangle at the confluence of these two huge rivers, was where to drop the bombs: it was as easy as shooting fish in a barrel, an aerial rape.

Down below, the people of Chongqing—China's capital, since Chiang Kai-shek and his government and all the foreign embassies had fled there from Nanjing in 1937—suffered almost undefended. They huddled inside caves that had been hollowed from the rock: some suffocated, others died of thirst. Until the Americans came, and the Flying Tigers took to the skies and gave them some kind of shelter, the citizens and the newly arrived refugees had to put up with six, seven or eight raids each day and night, throughout the terrible hot summers of 1938, 1939 and 1940.

Not for nothing is Chongqing called one of the four *Yangtze furnaces:* from May to October the humidity is terrific, the heat sweltering, everyone is bathed in sweat for all the hours of light and dark. And when to the murder of the heat is added the exploding of the bombs, the hiding in tunnels, the constant burials and a pile of unburied dead, the lack of running water, a total want of sanitation—back then Chongqing must have been one of the hardest cities in the world in which to try to live. And amid all the anarchy and the squalid mess, this was one of the Great Power capitals: in theory it ranked alongside London, Washington and Moscow, and generals and ambassadors and heads of state came in and out, via the most tortuous of air routes, to deal with the Generalissimo and his men, and to work out how to defend China from enemies both foreign (the Japanese) and domestic (the Communists).

Chongqing is still a grim and unlovely city, though now with 16 million people crammed into its hilly streets, compared with the 600,000 who lived there back when it was China's capital.* It may have been clear and moonlit when we arrived—but the most memo-

* The city housed the Nationalist government twice—once during the commonly remembered eight years from the fall of Nanjing in 1937 to the end of World War II and the Japanese defeat in 1945; and then again for three strange months at the end of 1949. When the Nationalists fled to Taiwan, they did so from Chongqing, after which the new capital was set up by the Communists in the city where it exists today—Beijing.

rable feature of the city's climate is quite the reverse: a thick, pallid, warm, wet, yellow-gray fog that lies on it like a mildewed blanket. For most of the winter the combination of smoke from cheap coal fires and the soot from briquette ovens, the teeming factories and the daily atmospheric temperature inversions makes for an atmosphere like gray soup, and Los Angeles in August seems by comparison sparkling clear.

"Coketown," someone called it. The air is usually like that of Leeds or Dundee in Victorian times, with a sharp smell of half-burned coal gas, rust, scorched tin, and dirt. And yet what a mercy all the fog has been: in the winters of wartime the gloom made it impossible for the Japanese to bomb, and what the city lost in the clear summer days and nights, it rebuilt and recovered on almost every dreary day of the winter.

We had been caught in an unexpected fog the day before, near the city of Wanxian. "The radar is no good—I have to be able to see," said the captain, as he shut down the engines and dropped two anchors, paying out three hundred feet of chain before they reached bottom. "We will have to stay till the weather clears. All ships will stop."

It was oddly quiet—the river sucked and gurgled softly, and once in a while we could hear a truck passing on the right bank. We could hear the crewmen talking on another ship moored nearby, but we couldn't see it. Then a fierce searchlight suddenly pierced the fog from astern, there was a deafening roar of a siren, and a pair of barges that were being pushed by an enormous black tug throbbed past, kicking up a wake that shook our ship like a small earthquake. "Bloody fool!" said our captain, and he raced to the bridge wing to shake his fist at the tug skipper, who simply grinned.

We waited all night, calling in vain on the radio for the Chongqing inspection station, trying for a weather forecast. "It would have been better in the old days," the captain grumbled. He fingered a pencil nervously and paced back and forth across the length of the bridge: like all mariners he was only content when in deep water and clear air, far from land and other ships. Here there were obstacles all around, and matters were worse, for he could see none of them.

But in the morning came a brassy early summer sun, and the fog began to lift. A dozen yards offshore there was an elderly man in a *sampan,* sheltering from the chill beneath his craft's arched matting roof. He had an otter with him, tied to a length of rope. Once in a while it would leap smoothly into the water and swim ahead of the little boat, before returning to its master and neatly leaping back aboard.

Otters are the upriver equivalents of the famous Guilin cormorants, experts at catching fish—but much more trustworthy. While each bird has to have a grass or iron ring around its neck to forestall any swallowing of the catch, the otter is more obedient and releases its fish on command, like a retriever with a pheasant. Most good otters come from Tibet, and take months to train; when fully operational one will catch as many as 30 catties of fish a day—33 pounds. I shouted to the man, asking how he had done. "Ten catties only!" he said. "Fog—the otter doesn't like it."

We were moving again by lunchtime, steaming fast to make up for lost time as we passed under the factories and housing blocks of Wanxian city. A hundred years ago there were stands of cypress trees on the hills and bamboo plantations, and Wanxian was the foremost junk-building city on the Upper Yangtze. Today, silk spinning is the major industry. There is still a bamboo market, and the locals talk of a Wanxian man who can supposedly balance himself in midriver standing on a single pole of floating bamboo, using another pole as an oar. Wanxian is an inauspicious-looking place, and few passersby give it more than a glance. But it played its own part in recent history: the infamous Wahnsien Incident of 1926.

Back then, the Yangtze was a perilous place for the foreign shipping lines that operated between Chongqing and Shanghai. A few large companies dominated the business: the Americans had the Yangtze Rapid Steamship Company, Russell & Co., the Dollar Line, Standard Oil Company of New York, and a few smaller operations with impressive names, like the American West China Navigation Co., American-Chinese Steam, and Yangtze Transport Co., as well as tiny wood-oil shippers like Gillespie & Co. On the British side the rival firms of Jardines on the one hand and Butterfield & Swire on the other slugged it out (as they do to this day in Hong Kong)—the former with Indo-China Steam Navigation, and Swires with what all knew as C.N.Co., the China Navigation Company. The Chinese government had its own China Merchants Steam Navigation Company (whose vernacular name was translated in more submissive language as The Bureau of Merchants Invited to Operate Steamships), and there were Japanese, Italian and French companies operating too.

And all had their naval gunboats steaming upriver and down, patrolling, keeping the trade lanes open, protecting citizens and compradors alike from the strange irrationalities of Chinese warlords. It was the collision, in August 1926, of these two aspects of Chinese life—warlords and gunboat diplomacy—that came to be called the Wahnsien Incident.

Sichuan in those days was controlled by a particularly vicious, clever, cunning, and iron-hard local warlord named Yang Sen.* He was almost uncontrollably powerful in the Upper Yangtze valley, and he had thousands of troops loyal to him. But he needed to move them, sometimes at short notice, along the river—and the problem arose that although the French and Japanese, typically, would allow warlord soldiers to travel on their cargo vessels, the Americans and the British would not. They were neutrals, they pleaded: they were not to become involved in the internecine rivalries of the Chinese themselves.

Warlords—and not just the local General Yang—were incensed by this ruling, and their strength in numbers allowed them to disregard it. Customarily they would board a party of their men dressed as civilians; once the ship had cast off, the men would draw their hidden sidearms, storm the bridge and hijack the ship for their own

---

* These days it is reckoned as politically incorrect to call Yang a warlord as it would be use the word to describe Nelson Mandela or, indeed, George Washington. He could perhaps be more properly termed "a local political leader in command of a small and highly mobile army," and there were many like him. But in China few were motivated by ideology or much more than territorial greed. Mr. Yang was not; he was no Mandela. He was, rather, a menace.

purposes. The shipping companies responded by welding iron gates all around the bridges and the sensitive doorways of their vessels— iron bars and locked wire cages kept the local passengers and the foreign crew members rigidly apart.

On August 30 two of C.N.Co.'s ships were seized by Yang's men off the port of Wanxian. Two Royal Naval gunboats, HMS *Widgeon* and HMS *Cockchafer,* were sent to sort matters out. (A French gunboat sat idly by, with characteristically Gallic sangfroid.) Negotiations came to nothing, and within a short while murderous gunfire broke out. The British ships, which had been sent first on an innocent rescue mission, became swiftly engaged in what was obviously a punitive expedition. They opened fire with their big guns, and subjected the port to an intense barrage. Scores of Chinese died as six-inch shells went whistling through the city streets, demolishing some of the more fragile buildings simply by the velocity of their passage. "Shell no hit—Chinese man die anyway," a local exclaimed, incredulous.

At the end of the affair seven British sailors were dead and an uncountable number of Chinese—by some accounts, three thousand. The two Swires ships were badly damaged and on fire, and one of the officers was drowned. The warlord General Yang had scuttled off into the cypress woods, to fight again. And the whole sorry issue of gunboat diplomacy was out in the open.

The western press fulminated. "The new China will not tolerate such intrusions of Western power into the heart of the country," wrote the *Nation.* The *New York World* agreed: gunboats were an anomaly, probably more dangerous as an irritant to the Chinese than a force for good policing. (Forty years later the mood was to be summed up perfectly by Richard McKenna's classic novel, later a Hollywood film, *The Sand Pebbles.)*

And as the press and public complained, so the gunboat-happy policies of the Western governments slowly changed. The Wahnsien Incident, the bombing of the *Panay* convoy eleven years later,* and a

---

* In December 1937 Japanese dive bombers attacked the American gunboat *Panay* on Yangtze convoy duty in the mistaken belief she and her charges were Chinese.

growing general distaste for the idea that western ships should have a prescriptive right to trade and shoot in eastern rivers—in the face of such events and such sentiment, the river was slowly and steadily abandoned. The Italians slipped away, and the French, then the Americans and finally the British. Come the Pacific War, and the untidy four years between the Japanese surrender and the Communist revolution, and eventually all the foreign warships had weighed their anchors and steamed off into the sunset. By 1949, after the *Amethyst* Incident had sounded one final tocsin to those foreigners who dared steam the river, the Yangtze was cleared of barbarians, left to her own devices. The time of the foreign gunboats, which during the twenties and thirties had provided so much material for novels and films and not a few newspaper headlines, had come to an end. And the town of Wanxian, which was now slipping into the oily haze astern, and which was a place that had played a considerably more important role in modern Chinese history than her grubby innocence seems to declare today, was where that end had its beginning.

At the Chongqing docks, the river today is more than a hundred feet below the city, and it has to be reached by way of long flights of well-worn stairs, or via flotillas of rickety funicular devices that haul small passenger railcars sideways up and down the slopes. Invariably the steps, slippery with mud and dripping sewage, are jammed with porters hauling bales of cargo suspended from bending and bouncing bamboo poles. Files of expensively, incongruously and unwisely dressed foreign tourists can often be seen as well, picking their way gingerly down toward their boats.

Their presence invariably strikes me as rather odd. Chongqing has little enough to interest foreigners. Yü the Great, the emperor whose influence on the course of the Yangtze is legendary, was born here,

---

The incident, in which several vessels were damaged and several American sailors died, enraged public opinion at home and caused an immediate wave of anti-Japanese hysteria—but also, more seriously, pointed up the dangers inherent in allowing foreign warships to operate deep inside China, on a Chinese river.

and there is a mountain—Yu Shan, not surprisingly—south of town, where the foreign ambassadors and Chiang Kai-shek once had their mansions. There is a museum to "Vinegar Joe" Stilwell (the Chinese like him because he loathed Chiang Kai-shek and privately called him "Peanut"), an array of prison cells in which Communists once languished, a museum with a couple of mangy dinosaurs and a few restaurants serving the local hot pot, and other Sichuan food. The city is almost alone in China in having no bicycles—the hills make even the modern Chinese-made mountain bikes all but useless. There are on-again off-again plans to build the world's tallest skyscraper in the city center, and a New York firm of architects has spent a lot of time and money on various local villains, trying to win the contract. That is essentially all that can be said for the city—that, and the interminable, greasy, lung-fouling all-weather fogs.

But, despite the dearth of real amusement, a lot of foreigners do pass through Chongqing, and the sight of expensive furs swishing and inappropriately high heels teetering down the slippery stairways is not uncommon. This is because the city is the chosen starting point for almost all of the Three Gorges tours, and ships grind out of here, as many as a dozen a day, bound the 727 miles downstream for Wuhan via the 120 miles of the Gorges themselves.

I have rarely met anyone who, under close questioning, admits actually to having been wholly pleased with taking a voyage through the Gorges. The natural scenery is stunning—all agree on that. And the retrospective pleasure is clear: the haunting beauty of the narrower of the gorges (and there are many more than three; this number is a purely subjective construct, which has somehow stuck) is something quite impossible to forget. It becomes, like so much in the Chinese landscape, the stuff of dreams. But it has also to be said that, during the process of any voyage up or down the gorges, it becomes painfully and unremittingly evident that humans—and by that I mean twentieth-century humans, and almost certainly twentieth-century Communist humans—have made the most terrible mess of the place.

The ruination—by pollution, squalor, filth, ugly architecture, wanton tree felling, factory building and artificially induced land erosion, and by that characteristically modern Chinese combination of greed and carelessness—is something that every visitor is bound, eventually, to notice. Those who come and see—especially if they have paid a lot of money to do so, or are on a once-in-a-lifetime-journey and so gamely and understandably try to ignore this reality and choose to view the grandeur through the grime—all invariably confess to a keen sense of disappointment, and wonder at the nature of a people who can so comprehensively befoul one of the wonders of the natural world. How can it be, they ask, that a place that was for so long thought so special by so many—writers, painters, poets, classicists, aesthetes—is now in reality so grubbily unspectacular, so wholly unmemorable, and, most tragic of all, so poorly husbanded?

It doesn't help that many of the boats also fall far short of the standards that are expected by the kind of travelers who can afford to make such a journey. But there is worse: the sights—if the boat trip is well enough organized to allow one to see them (I once went on a trip where one entire Gorge transit was performed in the dark)—are often so ineptly explained, the towns in which tourists stop are so vile and so jammed with tawdry goods and populated by the unashamedly crooked, the coal-smelling pollution is everywhere so appalling, the factories and the workers' houses are so ugly and such a blot on a once pleasant landscape, that it is not surprising that so many who disembark in Wuhan three days later are eager to put the trip behind them. They all seem to categorize the Three Gorges trip as an *experience,* something all are glad to have *done,* but unlikely to ever want to do again.

"The Taj Mahal—definitely yes," said one elderly American from Cleveland with whom I once traveled on a Gorges trip. "The Grand Canyon—yes. Paris—yes. China—most certainly yes.

"But the Three Gorges—quite frankly, I hate to say it, but it's pretty much a waste of time. Better to read about it. And yet, my god—did those writers have imaginations! They described things that simply aren't here."

His wife chipped in, agreeing with what her husband had said, but wanting to record her own grace note of disappointment.

"Where," she wanted to know, "are the naked trackers? Why aren't boats being hauled over the rapids by naked Chinese men?" She showed me a brochure: there were pictures of nude men with well-muscled buttocks and backs, lashed together with braided ropes, bending in their scores to haul a ship up and over a raging whirlpool. Some were in the water, their skin glistening like silver. Others, with the bamboo-fiber ropes bent over their backs, hauled from on land, their feet clamped onto the rocks, their arms loose and their fingertips touching the earth, their heads low, their eyes staring fixedly at the ground. On board the ship, a trackers' master beat a drum, and one could almost hear the singing and the grunts as, foot by painful foot, the army of men drew the huge wooden vessel onward against the rushing might of the stream.

I was sorry to disappoint her and to snatch away what had clearly been, back in her Ohio bedroom, a delicious erotic expectation. I explained to her that like the whiffletree, the Yangtze trackers were now all gone, victims of reciprocating engines, the power of steam, and the liberal use of dynamite in blowing up the rapids that remained.

The only trackers who could be seen on the river now work for the benefit of tourists. They are only half-naked, as it happens, with fetchingly small loincloths and bare and callused feet, and they work on a tiny Yangtze tributary called the Shennong Stream. Foreigners who visit are driven for two hours up from the main river by dusty bus and are then taken, by staircase or palanquins, down to its crystal-clear waters, to be set in ten-person wooden boats that are paddled slowly back downstream. Half-naked steersmen armed with iron-tipped poles guide these boats through the more treacherous little rapids they encounter—there is no need for tracking on a boat going downriver, of course. But upstream is a different matter, and other half-naked men with bamboo hawsers looped around their shoulders track the empty tourist boats back upriver. In due time these tracked craft pass the fully laden downriver boats: each encounter is greeted with squeals of delight and the click and whirr of cameras. Some of the trackers stop, retrieve postcards from plastic bags they have secreted in the folds of their loincloths, and try to sell the cards while standing up to their waists in the icy water. Others peddle marble eggs and necklaces made of translucent quartzite. It is all decidedly vulgar: fake Rolexes cannot be far behind.

And their tracking skills are clearly vanishing, too. What were once, after all, the practices of a highly sophisticated craft started to be lost upon the introduction of the steamboats. The decline of this cruel art has been much written about—by Isabella Bird and John Hersey, most notably, and also by legions of anthropologists, who recorded the trackers' songs and listened to their laments, and of sociologists who studied the trackers' clan systems, their economics and their health. Tourism then kept the skills alive, if barely, and those men who were still physically able to track continued to be studied, if no longer by academics, then at least by enthusiastic amateurs and by makers of films.

But then, in 1995, there was a terrible accident on the Shennong Stream. A rapid proved to be far stronger than expected, the iron-tipped poles failed to grip on the passing cliff faces, and a team of trackers did the unthinkable—one by one they lost their staves, and the team lost control of the boat. The entire vessel went under and stayed under for ten minutes, trapped between the rocks and the tons of foaming water. Eleven Taiwanese tourists drowned. Since the modern Chinese authorities are greedily eager to promote tourism in this region for as long as the soon-to-be-flooded Yangtze Gorges will allow, the tragedy was a commercial catastrophe for which the authorities had to find a scapegoat. The trackers, unschooled, illiterate and unchampioned, were the obvious victims: the drownings have probably put paid to the future of their displays, even as a Yangtze sideshow, and what skills they had will probably now fade away completely.

Not far from where the foreigners died is an accidental necropolis—a resting place of far, far greater antiquity that tourists are rarely able to find, but that anthropologists have recently declared to be of the most profound importance. It is called the Longgupo or Dragon Hill Cave; it is on the south side of the Yangtze, hidden deep in a jumble of limestone hills that lie about fifty miles west of the valley of the Shennong Stream. The sandy clays and gravels that fill the cave were, when first found, solid with bones of animals that had died there many thousands of years ago.

There are countless caves in these parts of China—the action of water on limestone has seen to that—and the many bones that turn up in them have long been mined by the local farmers, and sold. They are colloquially known as "dragon bones"—particularly the bigger specimens—and farmers have traditionally made fair sums of money on the side by selling the bones to pharmacies, who grind them up and sell them as tonics and cures to the ever gullible local peasantry. But the entrance to Longgupo Cave had collapsed several thousand years ago, preserving its contents and keeping the inquisitive out. When a farmer chanced upon a bush-covered hole in 1984 and squeezed his way inside, and then for some happy reason decided to report the existence of the cave to the government rather than plunder it for profit, he was able to show off, to the team of paleontologists promptly sent down from Beijing, a vast space that was still filled with a pristine and quite undisturbed range of bone fossils. Cursory digging showed there were no fewer than twenty layers of bones—with the oldest bones at the bottom and the youngest, the most recently deposited, at the top. Government scientists began their official excavations in 1985, and for the next four years they carefully pulled tens of thousands of bones from the sands and wrote long reports on the wonders they had so serendipitously uncovered.

They made what was by any standards an excellent haul, a collection that would provide museums-full of spectacular new fossils. There were, for example, the bones of a huge herbivorous ape that looked rather like an orangutan. There were specimens of *Ailuropoda,* an ancestral pygmy form of today's nearly extinct giant panda. There were large skulls of mastodon elephants, as well as recognizable pieces of a rare horse species called *Equus yunnanensis.* There was the occasional hyena, plenty of ancient types of deer, and many tons of coprolites, the fossilized droppings that are much sought after by collectors. Evidently the cave had been used as a lair by beasts like the saber-toothed tiger and the large porcupine: many of the bones showed gouge-marks, indicating where the prey had been seized by its long-toothed predator and then dragged in out of the rain for lunch.

But the most extraordinary find at Longgupo was at first blush what seemed the most prosaic: two very small fossils of animal teeth. One was of an upper incisor; the other was part of a lower jaw with two still attached molars. The paleontologists who examined them quickly recognized that these teeth were very unusual indeed, in that they had belonged to hominids—the three-foot-tall hairy animals of the genus *Homo* that, around 800,000 years ago, walked erect on their hind legs and are generally regarded as antecedents of man. The scientists tentatively identified the teeth from Longgupo as belonging to a new subspecies of *Homo erectus;* and when, shortly afterward, they discovered two stones in the cave that appeared, from the marks on them, to have been used by some primitive beings for hammering and cutting, they became as excited as only paleontologists can. They promptly declared they had discovered a brand-new site for pre-human settlement of almost a million years ago, a place on the Yangtze that would at least rival the great 1927 discovery of the *H. erectus* known as Peking Man in the valley of the Yellow River; and one which would easily rival the finding of Java Man over near the Indonesian village of Trinil in 1891.

But then in November 1995 came a stunning announcement, made from an unlikely source: the Department of Anthropology and Pediatric Dentistry at the University of Iowa. An American paleo-anthropologist there named Russell Ciochon reported—on behalf of a large international team, including three Chinese—that two highly accurate series of tests had been performed on the Longgupo fossils, which demonstrated beyond all reasonable doubt that the teeth were not a mere 800,000 years old, as had been thought; nor were they a million years old, as some others had speculated. Instead, tests on the residual magnetism in the various levels of deposits in the cave showed that the age of the level where the teeth had been found was more than *1.8 million years*. Moreover, electron spin resonance testing, an even more precise tool for age determination, showed them to be *1.9 million years* old. The teeth, in other words, were from hominids of a far, far greater age than either Peking Man or Java Man.

More was to come. Dental examination showed that the cusps on the three teeth shared features with early small hominids whose fossils had been found far away in East Africa. Specifically they were similar to the teeth of *Homo habilis* and *Homo ergaster,* two of the very earliest examples of the genus *Homo*. And the existence of the two stone tools underscored this point: for they were very similar to the tools that had been used by *H. habilis* in Africa.

There was an inescapable conclusion to be drawn from what, to the world of anthropology, was a spectacular set of discoveries. The hominid found in the Yangtze valley was of a far more primitive kind than had been found either at Peking or in Java, and in the absence of any other discovery it was reasonable to suspect that it was the original Asian hominid, the ancestor of all Asian mankind. The little stone-bearing beasts had evidently limped out of Africa, traveled across the southern part of what is now the Arabian peninsula and spread, slowly and steadily, all the way to Asia. The first evidence of their having arrived in the East was thus to be found here at Longgupo, in a half-collapsed and newly discovered cave a few miles south of the Yangtze—a river that now, if still not able to claim a role as the cradle of any specifically Chinese civilization, can at least now in all certainty lay claim to being the cradle of all the world's Asians. It is far from unreasonable to say that, with this discovery, it is now abundantly evident that the Yangtze and its valley have played a crucial and pivotal role in the development of all civilization, and of all mankind.

Above Chongqing the river starts to narrow significantly, to speed up, and to become more richly colored with silt and soil. It takes a long southwesterly swing across the Red Basin, through scores of miles of farmland. This is *Good Earth* country—peppers drying on bamboo poles, banana palms, thatched cottages, acres of rapeseed, fields of wheat and paddy. The basin is the Kansas of China, a granary protected by hills, warmed by the sun, steamy and fertile and rich. There are cedar trees, pines, ash and bamboo—the bamboo of the basin, being peculiarly strong and inflexible, is used all across China for boat hooks, sounding rods and quanting poles. There are also curious tree-living insects that produce copious quantities of wax: cakes of it are collected to make candles, or to add gloss to paper, or a sheen to types of cloth.

The river performs a sizable U-turn between Chongqing and the Yangtze's next main town, Yibin. For want of a change we decided to take a short cut on the bus, and to make a straighter line to Yibin across just a hundred miles of this splendid and colorful fecundity. The town is an ancient trading station, set down at the junction of the Min River and close to the head of navigation, and to where the real mountains, the Himalayan outliers, begin in earnest. Driving across the Red Basin toward Yibin is rather like driving across Colorado to Denver: you begin in the morning, and the land is flat on all sides. In the late afternoon the sun, now directly ahead, inches down to reveal a long line of jagged hills: in America, the Rockies; here, the great ragged ranges of Sichuan and Yunnan, the granite and limestone temple guardians of Tibet.

The town used to be called Suifu, and there is an old eight-story pagoda at the point where the Min River pours its relatively clean, relatively translucent waters into the reddish gold waters of the mother-river. Until quite recently the Chinese believed the Min to be the mother-river, and many still do. The Min, for a start, is navigable for 130 miles—or even, when the water is high, the 180 miles up to Chengdu. It is vastly more important for trade than the Yangtze is above Yibin. It rises suitably far away, up in the Tibetan Plateau. By contrast, the Yangtze's rapids close it down for upstream traffic only 60 miles above Yibin, and there is no significant boat-borne trade and there are no big cities at all for the remainder of the river's length.

But length, pure length, is what counts to students of rivers. And while the Min winds a perfectly respectable 500 miles to its source—

and would on its own rank high among Asia's bigger rivers—it is dwarfed by the Yangtze itself, which continues upward from Yibin for no less than 2200 and some further miles (the precise distance depending on which of the three headwater streams is chosen as the origin).

However, the nomenclature changes at this point. Above Yibin, the Yangtze ceases to be the Yangtze, or, more accurately, the Chang Jiang ceases to be the Chang Jiang. From here on the river is known as the Jinsha Jiang, the River of Golden Sand—a name that will seem particularly apt to anyone watching it ripple its voluptuous way beneath the Yibin pagoda. The Jinsha glints with sand; the Min sparkles with nothing worse than a foam of industrial effluent, and the two streams flow for a couple of miles quite separately, before mingling and becoming the sludge-brown, *eau de nil* water of all the downstream reaches.

Like the Wedding of the Amazon Waters below Manaus, this is a spectacle of raw hydraulics: a reminder, too, of the erosion and abrasion of all that vast expanse of rough geology that, for the Jinsha Jiang, marks every further mile of its course.

On shore, sophistication seemed to be dropping away more rapidly as we got farther and farther away from the sea, closer to the frontiers, nearer to the *ur*-China. The constants of the Yangtze valley cities—taxis, cell-phones, neon signs, working lavatories—were thinning out now. A small indication that we were getting into backcountry was to be seen on the bedside table of the little hotel in which we stayed in Yibin: a list of the Punishments, so-called, that management warned would be handed down in the event of any guest damaging or stealing any of the Equipments, as also so called, in the rooms.

The notice was stern and uncompromising. For taking or ruining the Mattress, a fine of 450 *yuan* would be meted out as Punishment. For ditto to what was called the Singular Sofa, 140 *yuan*. For the Thermose, 37 *yuan*. Anyone strong enough to haul away the entire Contents of the Bathroom could do so on payment of 1800 *yuan*. The Mosquito Driver, whatever that might be, went for 15, the Lock on the door for 70, the Gorbage Buckets for 3 *yuan* each. All Hangers would be checked at the moment of departure, and thieves of same would be marked down 2 *yuan* for each offense. In all, the list had thirty-two separate categories of sixty-one items that were there for destruction or theft: if you removed everything and left the room quite naked, your bill would be swollen by no less than 8323 *yuan*— about $1000.

Moreover, added the rubric below, "If your cigarette end burns the carpet, furniture, wall-paper, curtain or anything else in the room, you will be punished 50 *yuan* for each hole.

"If the end burns anything on the bed, you will be punished as wholly as it costs.

"Welcome," the notice ends with a flourish, "to our hotel."

Sichuan is the birthplace of Li Peng, China's premier; it was where Deng Xiaoping was born, too, and the guttural accents of both men remain. In Yibin the locals claim Mr. Li as their own, though official biographies published in more disinterested cities say he was born in Chengdu. His picture is everywhere, however, and most notably in the one institution for which the town is known across all China— the great Wuliangye distillery, where China's best-known liquor has been fashioned for the last six hundred years.

It is called the Five Cereals Liquid, and I was shown around the piles of fermenting rice, sorghum, buckwheat, winter wheat and sticky rice that are used to make it. I thought it tasted quite foul, but the emperors have liked it for generations, and a lovingly misspelled brochure—"every sip of Wuliangye awakens the sweatest reminiscence of affection or experience"—lists the hundreds of gold medals it has won during decades of food fairs in such culinary epicenters as Plovdiv, Leipzig and Panama. A man the Chinese know as Jin Richen was also shown taking a glass of the stuff: the rest of the world knew him as Kim Il Sung, the founder of North Korea, and at the time I was given the brochure he had been dead for more than a year.

White-coated and anxious company officials tried hard to kindle my enthusiasm, plying me with sips of ever rarer types of the liquor as my tour went on, but to little avail. Only when I found a room dedicated to a joint venture with a Scottish distillery did my senses waken: then another booklet was instantly produced, with a chronicle of the distillery's flirtation with the manufacture of scotch.

The first step was the unveiling of a liquor called the Orient, "a fine Chinese whisky made by traditional Scottish methods, offering the typical flavour of whisky, as well as some oriental features.

"On opening a bottle a fascinating scent will emanate. You may enjoy yourself by having it on a chafing dish [come again?] taking it to the beach in the summer. You will feel enchanted. It is delicately packaged, yet the prices are very reasonable. It carries the tender sentiment of the Home of Wine."

Someone pressed a glass into my hand. I took a hesitant sip. It was not at all bad. I gave a thumbs-up. A roomful of white-coated men nodded with delight. "It has been very triumph," said one.

Emboldened by the success of this fascinatingly scented beach drink, the bosses of Wuliangye took the further step of arranging a joint venture with Burn Stewart, a small distillery in Fifeshire. The result was a blend of scotch and local distillates that the Chinese then aged, bottled, and sold under one of two names—Ampress for their own people, and Empress for foreigners. And foreign, said one of the white-coated men, included Scotland.

I paused in my note taking. "Coals to Newcastle?" I asked. He simply beamed.

His confidence has a certain unchallengeable charm. And if a six-hundred-year-old company that had made its name distilling grains mixed with "the intoxicating waters of the River Yangtze" felt confident that Chinese whisky would sell well in the snug bar of the Station Hotel in Inverness, then who was I, a simple Sassenach, to disabuse them of the notion? Besides, I remarked as I had a final sip, Ampress Whisky was sweetish, peaty and really not at all bad. Empress would probably be better still.

Next morning we embarked on our final boat, the last it would be possible to take up the river Yangtze—or, more properly, the first and last we would be able to take up the newborn Jinsha Jiang. It is only 60 miles to where the rapids become too strong for any forward progress. The captains of such boats as make the trip are nervous men, wary of being in places that common sense tells them they should avoid.

It was a fussy little craft, with a close-knit family of a crew—six men and a motherly young woman who bustled about, bringing rice and tea onto the bridge whenever anyone looked too fraught. The steersman was a roguish-looking fellow with alarmingly long hair, unusual for a Chinese. His captain, Mr. Lu, was fifty-seven years old and had been working on the Upper Yangtze since he was twelve. All of his crew had been apprenticed under him; he had been apprenticed to his father.

The first few miles of the River of Golden Sand looked manageable, though it was rarely more than a hundred feet across, and the banks were steep and all the rapids merged into one, so the whole river frothed and boiled as it sped by. From time to time we stopped, nosing in to the black mud on the bank and here allowing a woman passenger to jump off, there letting a couple clamber on with their goats or their bindles, or with small children strapped to the mother's back. Soon, though, the muddy banks became tiny rocky coves, and then there were no stopping places at all and the cliffs began to close in beside us and, more ominously, ahead. The mountains reared ten and twelve thousand feet into the sky, according to my American charts, and their peaks were sharp, and glinted wetly in the midday sun.

"Ayeeah!" Captain Lu complained at one point, but smilingly. "She is a difficult bitch, this river here. Too narrow. Too twisty. Too much boiling and swirling. Too many things get in the way. The fellows back in the Gorges have it easy. Here we have to be tracked by engine—they pull us up near the top. Better than when it was done by the *qiaofu*—those men were always getting themselves drowned and killed."

A signal station was displaying a large down arrow on its flagpole, meaning that we would have to wait until traffic passed. We idled enough to keep steady in the stream and waited, though for no more than ten minutes. The downstream shipping turned out to be a trio of great sailing junks that swept swiftly into view, and then went flying past us in the current. Their sails were patched and old, and on one a couple of the bamboo battens were broken—but otherwise the men who sat perched on the stern cabin looked to have good reason for their expressions of jauntiness and pride, as their ships rode smoothly and elegantly past through the roiling waters.

The signal station's arrow was then taken down and replaced by another, this one pointing up. Captain Lu gunned his engine and we inched slowly forward again, pushing hard against the rushing, noisy water. It became steadily harder to move: everyone on the bridge seemed to be willing the little craft on, like a driver with a slipping clutch urging his car to get to the top of the hill.

Then we spotted our target—an iron buoy in midstream, topped with a big flag. This was where the warp would begin. Everyone sighed with relief once the buoy came into sight. We headed steadily for it and eventually, taking fifteen minutes to do a hundred yards, we came alongside. As we did so, a *sampan* came whistling down toward us on the flood, and a tough little man handed one of the workers on our fo'c'sle a black steel hawser, which was promptly doubled around a capstan and then tightened. A cable rose dripping out of the water ahead. It led, I could see with my field glasses, to a steam donkey engine that was cemented onto a rock a hundred yards ahead.

There was an exchange of hoots from sirens on land and on our bridge, and then our engines began to roar and at the same time smoke poured from the donkey's chimney and the cable went as taut as a piano wire. We began to move forward again, painfully, slowly, the noise of straining metal and tightened bolts and roaring water filling the air. The captain began to perspire with nervousness, and the long-haired youngster at the wheel concentrated hard, his brow creased deeply with unaccustomed urgency. The sound of the stream crashing against us heightened, and huge eruptions of spray drenched the bridge as wave after wave crashed against our slow-moving bows.

And then, quite suddenly, it was all over. The waters smoothed out, the current lessened. The donkey engine—now near enough so we could see its drivers and wave to them—fell quiet. The *sampan,* which had been pulled upstream in tandem with us, came alongside and took the cable away, and we were moving under our own steam once again, beneath the dark cliffs, and to the delighted yells of a gang of watching children.

A mile farther and there was a small dock at a place called variously Xinshizhen or Pingshan. The captain clapped his hands and lit a cigarettes and said simply "No more go," in English. The signs spelled out the name in Chinese and in another, unrecognizable script that looked like the daubs of a hyperactive child. That was Yi writing, the captain explained: the people of the town of Leibo nearby, and for a hundred miles farther west, all belonged to the Yi.

He shuddered. "I don't like them. They frighten me."

He gave us a farewell dinner, which he extended by offering copious draughts of Wuliangye liquor, until the bus for Leibo arrived. Then he went back and began shouting excitably to his boys, readying them to take the little boat back to Yibin. He was quite alarmingly unsteady on his feet. But there was little point in his staying at Pingshan. As the great scholar of Chinese boats, George Worcester, had written sixty years before, "It is a small town with nothing remarkable about it except for the fact that it marks the limit of continuous junk navigation for a distance of 1,700 miles from the sea on the fifth largest river in the world."

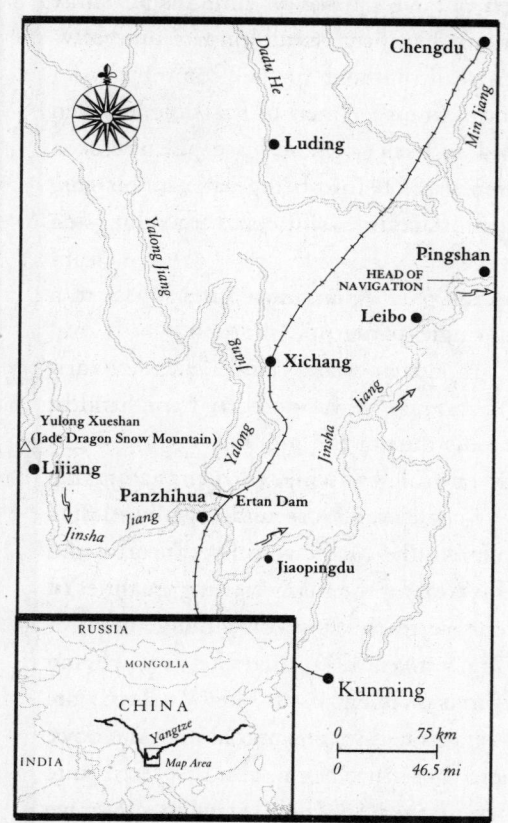

Map labels:
Chengdu
Dadu He
Luding
Min Jiang
Yalong Jiang
Pingshan
HEAD OF
NAVIGATION
Leibo
Xichang
Jinsha Jiang
Yalong Jiang
Yulong Xueshan
(Jade Dragon Snow Mountain)
Lijiang
Panzhihua
Jiang
Ertan Dam
Jinsha
Jiaopingdu
Kunming
RUSSIA
MONGOLIA
CHINA
Yangtze
INDIA
Map Area
0   75 km
0   46.5 mi

12

The
Garden
Country of
Joseph
Rock

Not long before arriving in China for this journey I came across the oddest of picture captions, its wording quite hauntingly bizarre. It appeared in a volume of photographs taken by an eccentric Austro-American botanist-explorer named Joseph Rock; it was beneath a black-and-white picture, dated 1924, of a scene he had captured in the mountains of the Upper Yangtze valley, which showed two teen-agers supporting between them a curious-looking object, like an un-formed sculpture of soft clay, as tall as each of them. Whatever the object was—plasticine torpedo, melted petrol pump, alien being, squashed motorcar—it seemed to have a nose; on close inspection it looked as if, once upon a time, it had been some kind of animal.

Indeed it had. The caption read, without further comment:

"Two Moso boys displaying a fine specimen of the Boneless Pig. After being slaughtered, boned and salted, these huge pigs are used as mattresses for up to a dozen years before being eaten. This custom, originally a protection against famine, still exists today in Muli and Yongning."

Beg pardon? I read the caption once again, more carefully. Somehow the corralling within a single paragraph of such words and phrases as "pig," "mattress," "a dozen years," and "eaten" had a surreal quality to it, and for a moment I wondered if I might have taken a surfeit of unfamiliar pills during the night.

But apparently not. A day or so later, while further reading up about this corner of the world, I came across a second, equally strange reference, this time to a people like the Moso, who lived nearby and who were known as the Nakhi. Among the many sterling qualities of these folk was the habit, exclusive to the lovelorn among them, of committing suicide by drinking a mixture "so that the vocal chords become paralyzed and the victim is unable to cry for help." Clearly the people who lived in these mountains had some rum habits—and since the mountains in question were those that begin, almost precisely, at Pingshan, where the boat traffic up the Yangtze is forced to a halt, we were now fast moving into their territory.

"This is the demarcation line," writes a guide, "between the Han people and the Yi minority ethnic groups, and the other many ethnic minority groups of the Tibetan foothills." Downriver, where Lily and I had been traveling for the past weeks, had been what passes for the normality of mainstream China, or what geographers call China Proper. Ahead of us now lay the very much more wayward world of the non-Chinese, the world of those who have been incorporated into the Chinese Empire, but who live irredeemably and steadfastly beyond it. In one sense, the Pingshan city boundary is the far western expression of what might be called the Chinese Pale.

It was in Leibo, the seat of a semiautonomous Yi county, that matters began becoming a little strange. Lily and I had managed to get rooms in a small inn, and after noodles at a restaurant run by a memorably handsome Yi woman, we retired to our respective beds, exhausted. At one in the morning there was a thunderous hammering on our doors, and a squad of Chinese goons demanded that we present ourselves for questioning before the local office of the Public Security Bureau.

We came down in our pajamas, befuddled from sleep. There were three men, all Chinese, greasy-haired, smoking, wearing black leather jackets. Why were we in town? they wanted to know. Did we not know that foreigners were prohibited here? Was I not aware that the hotel was forbidden to accept guests from outside? Lily, who was blamed for having led an innocent abroad, was given especially harsh treatment—to which she responded by standing up to her full and daunting height, and with a stentorian voice demanding respect and courtesy from men who were, she insisted, no more than mere officials whose duties were to serve the citizenry.

It was a stunning, high-stakes outburst, the kind of response to a police inquiry that would hardly be dared in London or New York, let alone the rugged hinterlands of western China. But perhaps I didn't yet know Lily to the full: her outburst was the first of many, and it worked a charm. The three policemen became promptly craven, they offered to settle their argument with us—fully justified, since Leibo (which means "thunder and wave") was very definitely a closed city—by levying a fine of about one dollar apiece, and they asked only that we leave town by sunrise.

Once the mood had become calmer and more friendly, and cigarettes were being offered around, and cups of tea, I asked one of the men why they had been so suspicious, so eager to throw us out.

"Because of the Yi," he said. "They are a very troublesome minority.* They hate us. This is their town, in their eyes. Relations be-

---

* There are about six million Yi, a people who have high-bridged noses, speak a Tibeto-Burman language with a crude phonetic script and are generally farmers and hunters. They dress colorfully, make much use of felt—unwoven cloth, in

tween us and them can be very poor. Foreigners often stir things up, and we don't like that at all."

So we left next morning, after having had breakfast on a grassy knoll overlooking the river, which uncoiled soundlessly a thousand feet below. There were small wild strawberries here, intensely sweet. In the distance ducks squabbled and chuckled, and large brown buzzards swung lazily in the thermals. All was perfect peace. Up here the arguments between Han and Yi had no relevance at all: only the river mattered, and made all the difference. It was a ferocious-looking beast, a rich syrup, lined with white streaks, squeezed between cliffs every bit as steep and forbidding as those back in the Gorges—an unforgiving place for any shipmaster.

Downriver the Yangtze may have been impressive for its power and width and might: here it was speed and sharpness and caprice that made it all so daunting. From high up on this perch the river looked just as everyone had said it would: the most difficult and dangerous big river in the world. There were rapids every few hundred yards. I watched idly the progress through the rapids of some of the endless procession of logs that had floated downstream from the faraway forests of northern Sichuan. As each one breasted a rapid so an end rose, arching high out of the river before then tumbling back deep below the foam, and then the whole log skittered from bank to bank in a way that no ship could ever have survived. In one or two places small *sampans* dashed from bank to bank, taking farmers to the water meadows opposite: but I noticed they never ventured up- or downstream, for fear no doubt of being caught in the currents and ripped to pieces on the rocks below.

Navigation was out of the question. But crossing the river—that, as the *sampans* below were demonstrating, was not by any means an impossibility. In fact the boats were providing a timely illustration,

_____

which the fibers are pressed together—in their dress and shelter, and hunt with poisoned arrows. Unlike some other minorities, they never had their feet bound. They are also known as the Lolo, and are divided into two castes, the White Bones and the Black Bones—the latter, less numerous, once making up a Yi ruling aristocracy.

since my next destination, a couple of hundred river-miles upstream, was the most famous crossing point of all—the place where Mao Zedong and his Red Army managed to make it from the river's south side to the north, in the early summer of 1935. In fact it was sixty years before, almost to the day, when Mao managed the most decisive act of what has since come to be known as the Long March.

To reach such a place so hallowed on the Chinese political landscape is still not easy—though hardly as trying as it had been for Mao's weary and underfed young soldiers. First we found the bus to Xichang, a town well to the north of the Yangtze on a huge tributary known as the Yalong Jiang. The ride in normal circumstances might have been merely terrifying—for its first few miles the bus roared and smoked along narrow dirt roads on top of cliffs hundreds of feet above the river, and more than once a tire smashed the retaining mound of dirt and became instantly suspended in space, those riding above that wheel looking down a dizzying void into the river foaming below. At such moments all the passengers were asked to get out, slowly and carefully, while the driver and his men pulled the unladen vehicle back onto the roadway.

My confidence in our survival was hardly helped by the braking arrangements. The driver had a contraption of small rubber hoses that ran around the back of his seat: it providing cooling water for the brake shoes, and was supplied from a bladder on the roof.* Whenever the bus began to run downhill, usually on a road with a sharp turn and a cliff at the bottom of the slope, the driver would reach behind him and turn a small brass spigot on the tube, allowing the water to flow; but more often than not the tube would become loose, water would flood the floor of the bus, and the driver, aware that his brakes were starting to smoke and were not arresting our downward progress one bit, would call for a passenger—me, usually, since I was sitting directly behind him—to find the tube and reconnect it, quickly! It always worked—we had the system down pat

---

* Other buses had enormous black rubber bladders covering the entire roof: these were filled with natural gas, the cheapest fuel available locally.

after fifty miles or so—but it made the ride more interesting than perhaps it needed to be.

Had ours been an ordinary bus service the degree of onboard terror would probably have been limited to this. But in fact ours was a bus that crossed—once the red-and-white striped barrier of the Pale was passed—into territory controlled by the Yi; and that simple anthropological reality transformed a journey that was merely frightening into an experience more akin to nightmare. For the Yi—the men huge, handsome, large nosed, chocolate brown, reputedly fierce, turbaned (with their hair protruding through a hole in the turban top), and the women equally attractive with blue-and-white striped costumes that in other circumstances could be thought of as charming—demanded that they had a prescriptive right to ride in this weekly bus, no matter how many were already in it and with utter disregard for any trivia like the paying of fares, or for any Han Chinese who tried to lay down the rules for running this particular service.

The bus was built for perhaps 50 passengers. By the time we were halfway to Xichang I had counted 140 people on board, as well as several dozen chickens and a pig that kept getting caught in the automatic door and might well have been rendered boneless and fit for mattress duty by the time the trip was done. Men would squeeze into the smallest of spaces that remained and still, around the next bend, another group of Yi would be waiting, would flag the bus down and insist on jamming themselves inside: woe betide any driver who might refuse. "I knew a man who didn't stop," said the driver to me in a private moment, "and he was never allowed to drive that route again. They threatened him and his family. They terrorized him."

By the time the 140 were tucked inside, the vehicle was as full of humanity and assorted zoology as physics would permit—whereupon fresh members of the minority clambered up the outside and parked themselves on the roof rack. The driver had taken about as much as he could and pleaded with them to get down—in the ending hurling stones at them to try to dislodge them. The men simply caught the stones and hurled them back, sending the driver scampering into the shelter of his cab and trying to drive on.

We ground slowly up a range of hills to a plateau where a weather station recorded the winter snowdrifts—and although we made it down the far side and into a tiny village with a dusty main street lined with hovels, there was a shriek of metal and a gasp of mechanical exasperation; the engine had finally given up its attempt to transport the gross overload, and the bus sagged to a halt. The huge crowd of people and animals promptly spilled out and gathered around, laughing and staring down at the driver who was trying gamely to work out what was wrong and then make repairs.

But by the time the seriousness of his situation had begun to sink in, Lily and I had already found ourselves a substitute—a friendly policewoman, a Yi herself, tall and handsome and with what Lily later enviously remarked were "spectacularly large breasts." For a small sum in folding money, she agreed to drive us the remaining distance across the final range of hills to Xichang. We made it by dark: I imagined by then, and probably until late the next day, that all the Yi from the bus were still waiting, since so far as I could tell it had blown its main gasket and shattered a half-shaft at the same time—the kind of repair that even a normally ingenious Chinese driver would be hard-pressed to effect.

Xichang, blessed with so clear an atmosphere that locals call it "Moon City," is China's Cape Canaveral—the principal site of the country's (currently unmanned) space effort. Satellites are lobbed up into orbit from here with impressive regularity, using the commercial work-horse rocket that is known, appropriately, as the Long March.

Once, when I was being shown around the gigantic Hughes Aircraft headquarters in southern California, I came across one of the satellites that was about to be sent up from Xichang. It was a huge drumlike communications satellite that had gone wrong sometime after its first launch; it had been plucked from orbit by the American space shuttle and brought back down to earth for repairs. At the time I saw it, it had just been bought by a consortium of businessmen in Hong Kong; a few months later it was shipped off to Xichang and eventually launched back into space by a Chinese rocket in April 1990—inaugurating, as it happened, one of the most profound cultural revolutions the modern East has ever seen.

For the satellite soon began beaming down the various programs of the Hong Kong–based organization that the owners set up—Star TV, it was called, Satellite Television for the Asian Region. The effect of the programs was to erase, with consummate ease, a whole slew of cultural boundaries that extended from Kuwait to Japan. Within the huge broadcast footprint of the satellite, an unending diet of popular music, sports, news and old films became instantly available to anyone below who had a satellite dish—meaning that Chinese in Shanghai could watch Taiwanese films, and Indians in Bombay could dance to Seoul music, and Iranians and Koreans could watch football from Hokkaido and Singapore.

The implications—a cross-pollination of ideas among the region's young, a steady homogenization of cultural icons, the creation of a new, Pan-Asian identity among the millions of viewers—have already proved fascinating, despite being little anticipated by the satellite's owners.* They have been hardly recognized in Xichang itself, however: it is one of the few towns where satellite dishes are hard to find, and when I asked a taxi driver what was the main business of the town, she replied simply, "Wood."

Lily and I had a fight on the day we were due to leave Xichang. We had been together for several weeks, the journeying had been trying and we were both tired. But what happened was almost entirely my fault; the way it developed offers an illustration, perhaps, of that most

---

* They were recognized very swiftly, however, by the media mogul Rupert Murdoch, who bought a controlling interest in Star TV soon after its creation and now has ambitious plans for increasing the reach of his various news and entertainment organizations into this immense potential market. One of his early decisions, which sparked some anger, was to drop BBC World Service News: the Chinese, whose favors he sought, found it unpalatable, preferring their viewers to exist on a diet of music and old films, which Murdoch's managers were more than happy to supply.

misunderstood sensitivity common to almost all Asian peoples, which we have come to know as "face."

The circumstances were simple enough. Earlier in the day I had discovered that there was a young Scotswoman living on the campus of a small college in the Xichang suburbs; she wasn't in when I called, but I arranged to stop by on my way to the railway station. Lily and I were due to catch a 9 P.M. express to a Yangtze-side steel town called Panzhihua; I supposed that if we left the hotel at eight we could pass by the college, I could deliver my message and the miniature of Johnnie Walker I had as a gift, and then drive on to catch the train. We duly left the hotel in a taxi, and I sat back to enjoy the drive.

But ten minutes later I realized we were going the wrong way—we were heading directly to the station, and not making the expected detour. I asked Lily why and she fell suddenly silent, embarrassed. Then—and here was my big mistake—I yelled at Lily, demanding that she have the taxi turn around and go back to the college. The driver did so, but said there was now not enough time—if we went to see the teacher we would surely miss the train. So I exploded, screeched at Lily and, with a cry of exasperation, ordered the man to turn back around again and head for the station. I would write to the woman and explain later. She, I knew, would be waiting, and would be disappointed. I certainly was: this all could have been so easily avoided.

Lily refused to speak to me. She boarded the train, sobbing. She asked the conductor if she could continue to Kunming, and on being informed that she could, she told a fellow passenger to tell me that I could get off at Panzhihua on my own. She would not come any farther with me, but would fly back to Shanghai. I could continue the rest of the way alone. She had never been treated so badly; all westerners, she said, were crude and ill-tempered bullies; I was the worst she had ever met, and I had no idea about the sensitivity of the situation in which I had placed her.

But mercifully the journey to Panzhihua takes a good five hours, even in an express. That gave me time to explain and cajole and apologize with sufficient fervor that, when the express lurched at last to a halt, she had agreed at least to get down and come into town with me and to consider the situation afresh. We talked late into the night, and, under the influence of several bottles of Tsingtao beer, she explained the problem.

It wasn't that I had been angry, she said—that she could well understand. She had misunderstood, and it was her fault that we hadn't asked the taxi driver to make his detour. She felt bad for the Scottish student, and she realized that both the student and I had been disappointed. But that didn't forgive the crime that I had committed—and that, so far as she saw it, was that I had been angry with her *in front of the taxi driver*. It meant she had lost her dignity, her standing, *her face,* in front of a stranger. I had made her lose face, and that was an unpardonable error.

But, I spluttered—who cares about the driver? She had no idea who he was, nor did he know or care who she was. He was a stranger, and his opinion of her, of us, was of neither value nor interest.

"That's not the point," she retorted. "It makes no difference how little I knew him. The fact is, as far as I am concerned I *did* know him. He and I had been talking. He and I had been friendly. He and I had been party to a relationship, and it makes no difference how tenuous it was and how brief it had been.

"And then you, great clumsy western ass that you are, you shamed me in front of him. You made me look an idiot before him, and it changed his relationship with me. You western people do this kind of thing all the time. You are so damned unsubtle, so totally unaware of how we feel."

There were tears in her eyes at the end of this speech, but I could see that her rage was spent. I offered more apologies, I agreed I had been an insensitive brute of a *lao wai,* I promised that in future I would try and be more aware of her feelings and those of all the Chinese with whom I dealt. She sniffed, dabbed at her face and then smiled and ordered another beer.

"Okay—all over," she grinned. "Problem over. Now let's see where the Long Marchers did their stuff."

. . .

A driver named Wang, and his girlfriend, Pu Ping, agreed to drive us to the place where Mao had crossed the Yangtze. They expected it would take us two hours to get there: it took fifteen. The main roads out of the city were straight and lined with the eucalyptus trees the British had imported from Australia; but within ten miles or so we had to turn off toward the river valley, and there were few roads better than cart tracks; we inched our way along the precipices and across huge ranges of hills, slowly and painfully. "Ayaaah!" Wang kept crying, "I had thought Mao's memorial would be easy to get to."

Mao had already commanded his forty-five thousand marchers for five months by the time it became clear he had to cross the Yangtze and move northward from the hills of Yunnan into the vitally important province of Sichuan. He and his senior planners had chosen three places where they might do so—all of them were in these upper reaches, above Yibin. The central place, where Mao and Zhou Enlai would place their headquarters and where most would cross, was to be at the well-known caravan crossing point of Jiao-pingdu—the place where the merchants from Yunnan would traditionally bring opium and placer gold and exotic cloths north from Burma and Annam; and where traders from Sichuan would wait in their caravanserai on the left bank, with salt and silver and hides and Tibetan medicines and herbs for their colleagues traveling up from the south.

Jiaopingdu might be difficult to get to today, by car; but the mule trains of old plodded their way there with regularity, and the site where the traders boated their wares across the stream has an antiquity to it as venerable as the great passes and stopping points on the Silk Road, five hundred miles to the north. Quite possibly this is where the ancient Burma Road crossed the river, where the merchants from Prome and Pagan and Mandalay, on their way to the old Chinese capital then known as Changan—now Xian—dealt with this most formidable frontier of rushing water.

The caravanserai was full of waiting traders on the day in late April 1935 when Mao's scouts, coming from the south, first reached the river. Their reconnaissance was to ensure a safe river crossing for the so-called Cadres Regiment, the unit in which the Communists' top leaders were marching, along with their infantry guardians from the famous First and Third Army Groups.

The scouts demanded boats—any boats, in whatever state of repair they could acquire. "We are Red Army men," they reassured the traders. "We are here to kill the landlords and the evil gentry. In ten years we will come back and give land to you." Faith or naïveté—or coercion, more probably—impelled the traders to find five rickety boats for them, two on the northern (the Sichuan) side, three on the Yunnan bank. A Nationalist sentry detachment was surprised while playing mah-jongg—its stacked weapons were captured, its members were shot. Another couple of days and the scouts had acquired two more boats, and by early May most of the scouting party was safely installed on the Sichuan bank. The Nationalist troops had been frightened away: they hid, presumably, in the hills across which Lily and I, Mr. Wang and Pu Ping were now bumping our uncomfortable way.

Mao and his senior colleagues crossed the river before dawn on Wednesday, May 1. They found a collection of eleven caves hollowed out of the sand cliffs on the Sichuan shore and made these their headquarters for overseeing the river crossing: Mao had his own cave, Zhou Enlai another, and there were separate caves for radio operators, other senior members of the Party and the security guards.

From here they watched as the seven boats shuttled back and forth over the stream. Each crossing, each boat full of soldiers, took three minutes. The horses were frightened and had to be forced to swim alongside. By day the operation was quite easy, so long as there were no KMT air raids—and the river's formidable cliffs acted as a kind of protection, for few bombers dared make it down beside them. By night, huge bonfires were lit on each bank, to guide the boatmen in.

The thirty-six local men who ferried the thirty thousand soldiers from south to north were paid either a Mexican silver dollar or five ounces of opium—it was an axiom of the highest public relations value that the Long March organizers should bend over backward to be fair to all potentially sympathetic workers they met along the way. No food was stolen; no house was ransacked (other than those belonging to landlords, which were adjudged fair game); no women was molested; no peasant was insulted. And the ferrymen were paid fair wages.

By all accounts the operation took nine days, and not a single soldier, man or woman,* was lost. When the boats were finished with, they were released into the furious stream and were swept away and seen to break up on the rocks a hundred yards below, as expected. The soldiers of the KMT bombarded the marchers from the cliffs and hills, as expected; but Mao's men had breached the most important barrier on their long progress north and their morale was hugely boosted as a result. The existence of mere Nationalist gunfire was as nothing compared to the rigors of crossing the greatest river in all of China's vast geography.

Today there is a suspension bridge where the crossing took place. There is no need for a caravanserai, for such traders as make the trip hurry across the river on a steel roadway in about half a minute. The caves are still there on the northern side—dark and dank. In the largest is a hand-scrawled piece of agitprop graffito, the epitaph "Long Live Chairman Mao." The official memorials are on the southern side—a statue of a marcher with a huge paddle raised like a banner, a poem in Mao's memorably wild calligraphy, a museum, which an obliging old man opened for me. I was the first foreigner he had ever seen, he said; and though I doubted him, I could not actually find, on perfunctory inspection, another barbarian name in the visitors' book.

The museum had more on its walls than in its display cases—maps, charts with arrows, blurry photographs in sepia, drawings of the passing heroes and brightly colored posters were everywhere. Under the glass were just a few broken paddles and lanterns, some straw

* Of thirty-five—one of whom had bound feet.

sandals and a leather sailmaker's device known as a bosun's palm, and which some marcher had evidently used to repair a tent. But most of what the marchers had, they took on with them—filing cabinets, guns, food, paper, swords, chairs, ammunition, books—and little is left but the footprints, the memories and the legends.

A thunderous explosion suddenly shook the building and Lily and I rushed outside. A cloud of gray dust was rising from the bank of the river—iron ore, explained the museum keeper. In fact only the ore trucks on their way to the smelters at Panzhihua use the new bridge—those, and the occasional school buses that come here from Kunming and Chongqing, bringing youngsters to have the heroics of the Long March firmly instilled into their half-formed minds.

On the way back to Panzhihua that evening, Driver Wang made a chance remark that, as it happened, triggered another long and happy cascade of coincidences. "A lot of foreigners live near the city," he said. "They are building a dam. The biggest in China. And I don't mean the Yangtze dam. They are working on something else. You should go see them."

I did, next morning. The dam site turned out to be on the Yalong—a huge, double-curved concrete dam being erected across a narrow gorge in a river that, in its own way, is quite as impressive as the Upper Yangtze. The Yalong Jiang was the source of all the logs we had seen down near Leibo—the woodsmen of the forests of upper Qinghai province use the river to transport hundreds of thousands of logs each year, a trade so important that the dam's designers have had to build a special spillway for the logs alone, and a tunnel to take them around the dam wall and keep them well away from the turbine blades.

The foreigners who worked on the project—Italians and Germans, Wang had said—lived in a compound of bungalows a mile or so from the site. I hailed the first obvious outsider I spotted going in through the security gates—a smallish man with a bushy chestnut beard—and I asked him if by any chance he spoke English.

"I'd be a bluidy fool if I didna'," he replied. "Name's Walker, Frank Walker. From Lochcarron. That's Scotland, if you hadnae guessed. Why not come up and have a wee bite to eat?"

And within a lightning flash of a moment I was plucked from the hot, dusty, alien center of China, where I had been thinking only of Long Marchers and straw sandals and Sichuan peppercorns and whether or not the Public Security Bureau would interfere with that night's sleeping arrangements, and transplanted instead to ice-cold air-conditioning in a room hung with pictures of landscapes of Wester Ross and soccer heroes, at a table covered with red gingham, drinking from a glass of Newcastle Brown Ale, talking to people with names like Irene and Jonathan and Gemma, watching them watch a Ken Dodd comedy special on their television, listening to them making plans for tennis that afternoon and bridge that evening and the fancy-dress party on Saturday night, and in an instant forgetting as readily as if I had been molecularly transported that there was quite another world outside the iron fences through which we had passed just minutes before.

Frank Walker's life was that of the professional expatriate. China today had been Iraq three years before,* and next it would be some godforsaken site in Africa or deeper Asia or who knows where. He and his family took their two- and three-year postings in their stride; they existed in a world of foreign schools and pen pals and video rentals and The Club and advertisements for tax havens and discussions about exchange rates and vaccinations and trying to learn brand-new languages and dealing with security guards and looking forward to the weekly mail calls from home and having to pay for long-distance telephony and going months without butter or fresh milk and having to eat dinners of baked beans and Danish biscuits from cans and dealing with the afflictions of strange insect bites and crowds who stare at you and of living with unfamiliar and half-worthless coins and listening to odd radio stations playing weird

---

* He was held hostage for several months, a victim of the turbulent politics of the region.

music and driving odd-looking cars and waiting for the six-monthly long-haul flights home.

His job was to look after the fleet of huge trucks that haul dirt and rocks away from the excavations: their brand name is Terex, the company belongs to General Motors, and the factory is in Glasgow. There were thirty of them, reinforced giants of steel and tungsten thirty feet tall with tires bigger than a man: they had come by land all the way up from Canton—no train was big enough to carry them—and Frank in his Peugeot had led the convoy twelve hundred miles, going no faster than twelve miles an hour over rutted roads where no foreigner had been for years. The looks on the village children's faces, as they spotted this vast armada of western iron rumbling through—"never to be forgotten." It had taken three weeks to go from Canton to the Ertan dam site—a memorable journey, said Frank with a grin.

Frank invited me to ride a Terex on a working expedition into the heart of the mountain—a terrifying half hour, as it turned out, of heat and dust and insufferable noise. The Chinese driver was an irrepressibly cheerful little man, five feet nothing and seemingly quite unsuited for driving the forty tons of mixed metals that constitutes a Terex earthmoving truck. He told me he had been a farmer until the dam builders had hired him the year before—and now he was having great fun, the power steering and computerized brakes allowing him to throw his gigantic toy around as though it were made of straw and tissue paper.

We roared through the portals of a huge tunnel and, belching thick smoke from our exhaust, we gunned downward into the center of the mountain, under a glistening roof of wet granite. A chain of dim lights marked the way: every so often there would be an open cavern with a gaggle of men and strange machines that were digging, burrowing, tunneling. Sirens would sound, red lights would flash, there would be the crump of distant explosions, and the walls would throb and pulse. The driver would merely pause and grin, then gun his engine, and roar forward again into the abyss.

Ten minutes later and we were at the site where we had been ordered to collect and haul away the fifty tons of newly broken rock. The driver spun the vehicle around like a London taxi and then backed gingerly downward into a brand-new raw-rock tunnel, the wheels slipping and scratching for a hold on the newly fractured gravel on the floor. The mighty vehicle at first slid this way and that, the cab scraping angrily against the dripping walls, the headlights uselessly illuminating the rock ceiling. There was no other lighting in the tunnel—and there was still smoke pouring from the blast site and ghoulish screams and yells from an excavator crew, who were eagerly talking us backward to where they could dump rock onto us.

Then there came a sudden cry to stop! The driver locked the brakes and we held our breath as, with a deafening roar and a terrible bouncing and rocking and the wails and shrieks of tortured coil springs, we reeled under the assault of tons upon tons of rock that were now pouring onto us from on high. Then a hiss of final gravel and dust and there was a blessed silence; the driver lit a cigarette, but as he did so there was a shout from outside, the crew urging us to be on our way and make room for another truck, another load. The driver snapped his gearshift into forward and slammed his foot down on the metal pedal, and we creaked slowly, but then faster and faster, back up the slope, out into the lit tunnel, and after ten more minutes and to my eternal relief, back into the sunshine again.

A foreman ticked off the driver's load—another forty *renminbi* added to his pay slip. I jumped down, thanking him profusely, declining his kind suggestion I might enjoy another go.

"They kill themselves all the time," Frank announced cheerily. "They've no idea how to handle these monsters. Last week three lads stole one from the parking lot and drove it straight off the cliff into the river.

"They've not been found. Nor has the Terex for that matter—the river's powerful deep. And you know what? One of the boys had just been married, and his widow came up to where the Terex had gone over, and she jumped in the river too, killing herself. Pretty girl. Stupid, too, so far as I can see.

"I'll never understand these people. If they're not working they're asleep. If they're not sleeping they're eating. And if they're not doing either of those then they're killing themselves. Odd folk the Chinese, if you ask me."*

Some of the single men took a more tolerant attitude. I spent one afternoon in a bar with two Britons, one a crane driver from Middlesbrough and the other an electrician from Cleveland, and with the six young Chinese tarts they had managed to find who, when we met, were entwined around them like convolvulus, vowing not to leave, and getting stickily drunk on enormous glasses of Bailey's.

"Our interest in these girls?" said the crane driver, when I asked him. He pinched one, whom he had introduced as Hourglass, and she giggled warmly. "It's purely sexual. Oh sure, they say they want to marry us and come back to the West—but quite frankly, and I can say this out loud because they haven't the faintest idea what I'm saying, we're only interested in screwing them. And very good at it they are, too.

"And you know what the nice thing is—they're so fucking backward in these parts they'll do it without asking for money. They think they're in love with us! They think the sun shines out of our arseholes. Have you ever heard anything so stupid?" And he thwacked Hourglass on her backside again, making her coo with delight.

Lily, who was appalled, was about to say something—but the expression on the man's face changed suddenly.

"You keep quiet, young lady," he said, wagging a finger at her. "This is my business—hers and mine. No poking your nose in where it don't concern you."

---

* Suicide turned out not to be a Chinese monopoly, by any means. A combination of alienation, loneliness and stress had already driven a significant number of the bachelor expatriates mad: only the week before, one engineer had taken a room at the Nan Shan Hotel in Panzhihua, attacked staff with a carving knife and then thrown himself to his death out of a tenth-floor window.

· · ·

I found a dead man on the street that evening. I saw him from the corner of my eye, lying beside the road as we drove back to the hotel. I told the driver to turn around and go back for a look.

The man was lying on his back, his eyes wide open. He was quite naked. He seemed to have a head injury—perhaps, I thought, he had been knocked down by a car.

On the other side of the road a group of men were sitting around a small fire, tucking into blue-and-white bowls of rice. They were no more than thirty feet from the corpse. I asked them if they knew what happened.

"Oh, that fellow!" said one of them, laughing and pushing great balls of rice into his mouth. "He was just a crazy man. Always around here, shouting at the cars. Never wore any clothes. Some minority, I guess. I could never understand what he was saying. Hit by a car a couple of hours ago."

The men seemed not in the slightest bit concerned that they were having their dinner beside a cadaver, and none of them had bothered to see—after the car hit him—if he had been killed outright. I suggested that we might cover him up.

"Suit yourself," said the same man, pausing briefly from his feeding and gesturing with a chopstick to where a roll of matting stood by a wall. "Use that."

And so I unrolled the matting and carried it across to the man and knelt and closed his eyes, before placing the mat over him so that his head and most of his body was covered. His feet stuck out of the end; they were dirty and calloused from years of walking, barefoot. He may have been mad; but he had had a knotty stick, which I found and placed beneath the mat, beside him. When he was alive, a few hours before, he probably looked like a harmless mendicant, or a Chinese palmer. We were near Tibet; there were lots of pilgrims in these parts.

On the way home I called in at a police station, and they thanked me. Later that night I drove past and the man had been removed.

The group were still sitting around the fire, and they waved at me as I passed, doubtless thinking that I was quite as crazy as the man who had met his end beside their evening dinner table.

Our taxi driver's first remark about a dam being built and the foreigners working on it had triggered a cascade of coincidence. Frank Walker was the first link in this trail: his translator, a rather sulky young lady named Ena, was the second.

Ena was a pretty and willing girl who, her pouting aside, enjoyed something of a following among the young male inhabitants of Panzhihua. One of her friends, an insurance salesman who dreamed of greater things, turned out to have as his hobby a passionate interest in the headwaters of the Yangtze. Ena knew that Lily and I were going there; and one day she introduced us to her young man, who was named Wu Wei. He fell on us with glee: as an insurance salesman his life was rather dull. But nine years before, he said with evident pride, he had been a member of one of the all-Chinese expeditions of river rafters who had managed to paddle their way down the entire length of the Yangtze. He himself had only been on the upper reaches, specifically along the tributaries known as the Dam Qu and the Tuotuo: any help he could give to us, he would. And perhaps we would like to see some videotapes?

And so for the next two days, dawn to dusk, amid the blaring car horns and the grinding din from the city's steel mills, we watched tape after tape of the expedition's progress along the upper reaches of the river. Wu's interest was in Tibet—and even though he was a Han Chinese, born and brought up in Yunnan, he kept a photograph of the Dalai Lama taped to the inside of one of his living room cupboards and was constantly critical of China's repressive policies toward what the government officially called Xizang Autonomous Province, but which he insisted on calling Tibet.

"We have been brutes—no doubt about it," he said. "I love the Tibetan people. I have always said we should cherish them, regard them as brothers, as equals. We should not seek to dominate them.

They are different. Their way of life, their religion—all different. Who are we Chinese to tell them how to live their lives?"

Lily blanched on hearing this. We had not discussed Tibet in much detail; but whenever we had, and whenever I had said how terrible a shame it was that China's policies toward the Tibetans had been so cruel, she had reacted defensively. I knew that she was secretly proud of—or at least a supporter of—her country's foreign policies, and that she saw the Tibetans as primitive innocents who had been consistently misled by religious zealots and egged on by western romantics; but now Wu—a Chinese like herself—was taking the same position as I. She fell quiet, but I knew we would have to face the problem in a day or so. I knew also, if I was to avoid a scene like that on the Panzhihua train, that I would have to deal with this disagreement with the utmost caution and tact.

Wu then came up with an idea. He would make contact with a friend who had also been on the expedition, a man who lived in Chengdu and worked for an organization that had access to four-wheel-drive cars, which would surely be needed if we hoped to get high up on the river. He had a feeling the organization would be eager to help. But that was for the following weeks. For now, he said—can I lend you my own car and let you explore the reaches close to Panzhihua? If you like, he added hopefully, I can come along as well, and be your guide.

Never before in my dozen years of traveling in China had a private individual ever offered—or been able—to supply me with both transport and his own time to show me around a corner of his country. There were always official guides available—Local Guides or National Guides, a corps d'elite of half-English-speaking and too often woefully ignorant young men and women, screened and cleared as faithful adherents to the Party line, who would, for a sizable fee, escort you along a predetermined route to show off the nation at its best. There were also enthusiastic amateurs like Lily, who would jump at the chance of touring companionship, of helping a stranger in exchange for learning more about the cultural fingerprints of foreigners. But never before had I come across a sedate, employed, and politically independent-minded man or woman who would be willing or able to stop everything, drop everything and come away for no better reason than to demonstrate a part of his country of which he felt proud. Why would he do such a thing? I could only think of one kind of person who might do it.

"I suppose you think I'm actually a policeman," Wu replied, reading my mind, chortling. "And I suppose you think that I think you're a spy. So that's the only logical reason we can travel together—me to show you what the Party wants and to keep an eye on you while you're traveling. That must be the logical view.

"In fact it's more simple. I really am just fascinated by the Yangtze. Meeting someone else who likes the river—well, I just want to do anything I can to help. Believe it or not as you like. I think your people might do the same for me, if I ever come to your country."

(I was ashamed to say this latter seemed rather improbable. The notion that a lone Chinese traveler might fetch up in Arkansas, profess a fascination with the Mississippi River, and promptly find a local insurance salesman who would take a week off to drive him from Osceola to Eudora was frankly laughable. The Chinese often have a stern and forbidding visage; but behind it, equally often, is a kindness and a hospitality few other people can imagine.)

Wu had two cars—a sporty-looking Toyota LandCruiser and a ratty-looking red Beijing Jeep, which showed that the spoils of the insurance business were every bit as handsome as in America or Europe. To our slight chagrin he elected to take the Jeep, and at five o'clock one sunny summer morning we set off westward, away from the blighted industrial landscape of Panzhihua. The last we saw of the steel city—a town that had been deliberately created by Mao's planners, and to which, during the fifties and sixties, the Great Helmsman had exhorted workers to move—was a long line of steam trains dumping torrents of molten slag down a slope that led directly into the Yangtze. It seemed a suitable memorial to the insanity of the Great Leap Forward—the making of a cliff of iron, the creation of industrial pollution on a titanic scale and with a callous disregard for the greatest of China's waterways. Wang Hui, Li Bai, Da Fu and

Meng Jiao and all those other painters and poets who once loved the river—thou shouldst most decidedly not be living at this hour!

If there was to be some recompense for the dismal aspect from the rearview mirror, it was the beauty of our destination. I had a hint of it that morning when we climbed over some low hills and passed through the octroi post into Yunnan and came, via the steep valley of a tributary, to the Yangtze once again. Here we were on the Golden Road, so-called—the main route by which heroin (as well as rubies, and other more mundane trade goods) comes into China from the Golden Triangle of Burma, three days' hard driving away. The Chinese keep close watch on the trucks coming eastward: a group of policemen wearing machine guns were tanning beside the road, and they stopped us briefly, asking jokingly if we happened to be returning drug couriers, then waved us on. We stopped at a gas station and drank tea with a pair of Tibetan truck drivers: when I showed them a picture of the Dalai Lama, they clapped their hands to their foreheads in prayer and insisted on paying for the tea.

It was a warm and sunny early afternoon when we reached the main stream. The skies were a perfect blue, the air was alive with birdsong. In the short stretch of still water, the hesitant end of the tributary stream before the bar where it entered the ferocious whirlings of the Yangtze proper, two teenage girls—they were probably Yi, but perhaps Bai, a people whose homeland was a little south of here—were swimming. It looked like something out of an H. E. Bates story, filled with rustic bliss, sunshine and rude good health. The girls were astonishingly pretty; they were swimming in just their bras and panties, their bodies were strong and tanned, their hair close-cropped. They were blithely unconcerned when Lily, Wu, and I drove up: they stood in the shallows and waved at us to come down and go swimming too, and they seemed genuinely disappointed when we shouted down that we had to be in Lijiang by nightfall.

We stopped at a small café beside the old stone river bridge and lunched on black chicken soup (made of a local bird with unusually dark and strongly flavored flesh) and bowls of noodles. On the wall was a reproduction Madonna, fifteenth-century Italian, probably torn from an Alitalia calendar. A large red hen had made her nest against this wall, and the combination of old wood, Renaissance brushwork, a sleeping chicken and hanging baskets of Chinese spices made for an intriguing conversation piece. Wu smoked a couple of cigarettes and then tossed me the keys to the car. He was tired, he said, and it was as well if I became used to driving, however illegal such a thing might be. Besides, he would bribe any policemen we might meet.

And so, slowly and steadily—Beijing Jeeps having a tendency to boil on long uphill stretches, as well as a host of other problems—we inched our way up the western side of the valley. We passed small groves of banana palms and newly tilled fields where young boys were planting soybeans or rapeseed. Small fields of lavender, red stands of poppies, yellow mists of buttercups—it was all energetically colorful. Behind stood the jagged blue ranges of the Yunnan mountains, and down below the brown river was coiling and uncoiling thickly and quietly around their bases.

After climbing for half an hour the road suddenly flattened, and we came out onto a plateau of pine woods. It became greener and cooler and more moist, and there were flashes of falling water, with kingfishers darting in and out of rainbows. And then without warning, in the northern distance, there rose a huge, rugged and totally snow-covered mountain. The sight of it made Lily gasp with astonishment, and Wu snapped awake.

"My God!" he said, and rubbed his eyes. "It is Yuelong Xueshan—the Jade Dragon Snow Mountain! It's so rare that you see it as free of cloud! Good fortune, so they say. We will be very lucky!" My American map showed the peak as standing 18,400 feet high, the tallest point for scores of miles around. It rose over the plain of Lijiang, where there were cornfields and rice paddies glinting in the sunshine. Below it, to the southern sunlit side, which I could see from my vantage point, the land was flat. The Americans had built an airstrip there in the late thirties, and from it they sent bombers up to protect Free China from the Japanese and flew sorties over General Stilwell's Burma Road.

Behind Jade Dragon Mountain, on the north side that I couldn't see, the Yangtze passes through what is said to be the deepest and most ferocious gorge of the entire river. The Tiger Leaping Gorge is a defile all too little known to the outside world—in the mid-1980s one expedition reported that only three westerners had ever glimpsed it—and it far outranks the Three Gorges in depth and spectacle. Nowadays it is quite easy to reach, and I had plans to be there in another day or two. What a changeable stream, I thought: down where the two young girls had been swimming, beside the bridge just half an hour behind, the Yangtze was just a decorously swirling stream—powerful, but not obviously murderous. A short way ahead, behind the hills, it apparently turned into a monster.

The town of Lijiang is one of western China's true gems—one of the very few way stations in the Middle Kingdom on what, archaically perhaps, is still known as the Hippie Trail. Youngsters from around the world come to Lijiang, en route between the equally delightful towns of Dali and Xishuangbanna in Yunnan and Yangshuo in Guangxi province. They are on a circuit—the same people who visit the back streets of Chiang Mai, Kathmandu and Lhasa, or Panajachel, Goa and Trivandrum, end up with equal enthusiasm and curiosity and camaraderie in towns like Lijiang. No matter what regime is in power, nor what rules are in force, there is a universality in the appeal of such places—laid-back, easygoing, with colorful people and cheap and wholesome food. In the normal and depressing order of business, the youngsters come to such a place first as rucksack-carrying pioneers and discoverers; the tour buses come next; and then the airports and the big hotels.

Lijiang is currently poised delicately between the first two phases of this evolution—the youngsters are still making it here, but on buses as well as by hitchhiking (I picked up two young Israelis, taking six months off from their kibbutz, and they were typical of the breed); and the hotel lobbies have notices offering the day's program to the tour groups of Dutch and Belgians who have found out about the local delights. No groups of Americans or Japanese, nor of Chinese "compatriots" from Taiwan and Hong Kong, not yet; no airport yet, either, though one was due to open, imminently); and no Holiday Inns or other chains, although I met an unpleasant Frenchwoman who had plans for a Sofitel, once the airfield opened. The developers are eyeing Lijiang, greedily and warily at the same time.

What tempts them all is a combination of the scenery, the weather and, most notably, the fact that the inhabitants are not Chinese. The dominant population of Lijiang are members of the Nakhi tribe, a people who have created for themselves a small and most unusual paradise. True, there is a Mao Square in Lijiang; and there are dusty and ugly streets lined with the boxy modern buildings that look like anywhere else in postrevolutionary China. Lijiang is run by the Chinese—there are Chinese policemen in their running shoes, and Chinese officials in the various government offices. But theirs is a colonial administration, as it is over most of cis-Himalayan China.

There is a low hill in the center of town, with a television tower at its summit: this marks the dividing line between the dismal and the delightful. To its west, all is ugly, drab, modern and Chinese; to its east, however, is fussy antiquity—an exquisite collection of old wooden houses, with cobbled streets and tiny canals, high-walled secret courts like Oxford quadrangles, and everywhere the smell of warm pine and wood smoke. Tall men walk by with hunting falcons on their sleeves. Imposing-looking women, who wear blue bodices and trousers and stiff white aprons, and who have T-shaped, star-embroidered padded cotton capes across their backs, stand outside their little homes, minding their children and their most common household pets, parrots. These are the Nakhi, and they have been the object of Chinese disapprobation for hundreds of years, and western fascination for scores.

There are some quarter of a million Nakhi, most of whom live on the Lijiang plain: they are said to be descendants of Tibetans and they were long regarded by the Chinese as utter barbarians. They listen to their wizards, they cling to shamanism and to a Tibetan heterodoxy known as Bon (which is claimed to be far older than the Lamaist Buddhism normally associated with the Tibetans), they have a pictographic script that is unrelated to any other in the world and which is made up of entirely recognizable creatures and objects. And though technically they run their society along conventionally patriarchal lines, there is an odd matriarchal aspect to their lives, which penetrates deeply into even the spoken language. The addition of the feminine suffix to any noun, for example, makes it bigger, more powerful and dominant, while the addition of the masculine denotes weakness, delicacy and submissiveness. A female stone is a cobble or a boulder; a male stone is a pebble, or even gravel or a grain of sand.

To underscore the more conventional aspect of Nakhi life there is one well-known patriarch in town—a bespectacled eccentric ethnomusicologist named Xuan Ke. He is not a man who is overfond of the Han Chinese: during the Cultural Revolution he spent years in prison and forced-labor camps, often tied up with wire,* for the dual crimes of playing Schubert's *Marche Militaire* as an ironic welcome to a group of revolutionary troops, and for suggesting that Mao's greatness might not outlive that of Jesus Christ, with whom the Great Helmsman shared a birthday. Xuan Ke says he has been officially forgiven now, and he brandishes his passport to show he is allowed to leave the country whenever he wants. But Public Security Bureau men keep tabs on him, he says, and they were there, ostentatiously noting our arrival, when we came to call on him at his house.

He runs a small Nakhi museum in the upper floors of his old family house. It holds clothes, paintings, old musical instruments. For the last decade he has also led a small orchestra of elderly men, who play Tang dynasty Tao temple music. On our first evening, we went to listen: the concert seemed to be for the benefit of an obnoxiously Brylcreemed lounge lizard from Kuala Lumpur who claimed to be a Taoist master and was filming everything with one of those video

---

* Once for singing "Twinkle, Twinkle, Little Star" in his sleep.

cameras that have a large screen instead of a viewfinder: he held it in front of him and all of us behind could see the orchestra twice, once full-sized and real, and again on the four-inch screen.

There was also a group of geologists from Kunming—they were drilling test holes, they said, close to the Tiger Leaping Gorge. There was a possibility that a dam might be built below the Gorge in due course. "We have a duty to exploit the water resources of our rivers," said the group's leader, as the musicians were tuning up. I asked him if perhaps the Gorge was sacred, too beautiful to change. "There is too much beauty in these parts. A little less will not be a major loss."

But now the musicians were ready, and this promising conversation had to come to an end. All the men in the orchestra, Xuan Ke explained, were Nakhi. Most were very old—five were more than eighty, three more than seventy. The five who were in their mid-sixties Xuan Ke called "my boy musicians."

The oldest man of all, Sun Ziming, was eighty-three, and he had a long white beard that smelled of mint and tobacco. He had a gentle expression that belied the fierceness of his musical task, which involved thumping a large brass gong at the kind of irregular intervals that are said to be peculiar to Tang temple music. Old Mr. Sun told me proudly that during the war he had been a caravan driver on the Burma Road, and that he would walk to Calcutta, taking four months. He would occasionally also walk to Lhasa, but all the other roads out of China in those days had been cut by the Japanese.

Another old-timer used a Persian lute, said to date from the fourteenth century and to be a relic from the Nakhi royal court, back when there was one. There was a frame of ten cloud gongs, a bamboo flute as small as a chopstick, a fish-shaped temple block that sounded if beaten with a mallet. Jew's harps are part of the local musical scene, too, and a man at the front played one, though with less of a role than the *er-hu* and *pi-pa* players, for the orchestra was geared this evening to playing Chinese music and did not bother itself with the decidedly odd sounds of the Nakhi themselves. They were taking the Nakhi music to London later in the year, they said. It was their first foreign journey, and probably also the first time that Londoners had been able to hear the sounds of what was billed as "The Land Beyond the Clouds."

"I think we are the only orchestra in China that plays good classical seventh-century music," said the director after a concert of two hours of ethereal, strangely blissful sounds. He grinned. "The Chinese must think it rather ironic that it is a minority people who have preserved it, and not the Chinese themselves."

After the concert, and after we had shaken off the importunate Malay, Xuan Ke and I went down the road to the Din-Din Café, one of the myriad of small restaurants that are favored by the young backpackers. We had banana pancakes and homemade granola, fresh orange juice and Italian coffee, so-called. The one supposedly local dish was Nakhi cheese, fried with sugar, which was none too exciting. A hand-chalked sign read, Please accept our apologies if your preference is not available due to previous passenger selection. "Yes," said the owner, when I asked her if she had ever traveled by plane. "How did you guess? Bangkok. My only time." She had spent 20,000 *renminbi* decorating her restaurant, and she now made 4000 a month, clear profit. "Soon I will have chain," she said. "Like your Kentucky Fried, yes?"

I asked Xuan Ke to explain the rumor that Lijiang was the suicide capital of China. He became immediately animated and cheerful.

"Yes, yes!" he said. "This is a distinction we do claim. It is all to do with love. I like to think of Lijiang as the love capital, really. The boys and girls here, they fall in love in a most unfortunate way—the morals of the Nakhi people have never been very good. Much promiscuity, I think you would say. And so there is much disappointment, and many couples kill themselves to end their affair. It is a long, long tradition.

"They have their special places to do the deed—a lake here, a mountain pass there, a riverbank there, a meadow up along the road below the Jade Dragon Mountain, near the American airfield. There is a ritual to it. The youngsters write notes, they call in the wizards to bless the event, and then they drink a mixture of black aconite boiled up with oil. It sounds very disagreeable to me. But it has the advantage of paralyzing the larynx. Once they have drunk it they cannot cry out. They die quite quickly and quite peacefully—but totally in silence. No one can come to help them. If they are far away, and no one sees them, then it is all over. They drink the mixture, and they are found dead the next day. The wizards perform another ritual, and it is all over. Joseph Rock was the great expert on it. He knew how they killed themselves, and where, and why. He knew the wizards. He wrote all about it. I have the books."

Xuan Ke and his father had known Joseph Rock well, and the little museum housed some of the great man's relics—his desk, his bookcases and some of his books, and the enormously wide chair that suggested, wrongly, that Rock had been an unusually portly man. His gold dinner plates and his folding canvas bath from Abercrombie & Fitch were no longer there; but the garden he planted, and his country house a few miles north, also near the American airfield, remained, memorials to a strangely memorable man.

Joseph Rock had been born in Vienna; his father, a melancholy man, was majordomo to a Polish count. He wanted his young son to enter the priesthood. But Joseph, who lost himself in bizarre nighttime fantasies that included the learning of thousands of Chinese ideographs by the time he was a teenager, had other plans: he vaulted out of Vienna, signed on as a steward on a transatlantic steamer, arrived in New York in 1905, pawned his clothes, worked as a dishwasher and a waiter and at a score of other menial tasks before arriving, hungry and penniless—but already speaking ten languages, including Arabic and Chinese—in Hawaii.

He had the magical combination of formidable chutzpah and an unquenchable wanderlust. For a while he taught; but soon, surrounded by the delicious greenery of those overfertile islands, he turned to botany as by turns a diversion, a fascination, a hobby and then an obsession. Without either a degree or any formal knowledge of plants, he marched into the Honolulu office of the U.S. Department of Agriculture one day in 1910, insisted that they needed a herbarium and won his way. Within a year, he was teaching botany at the College of Hawaii, and he published papers that are still regarded as classics.

But a craving for travel could not be ignored. He went to Washington and persuaded the Agriculture Department there that he should become an official plant hunter—a paid agricultural explorer, with his nominated territory that part of western China where the rhododendrons, the camellias and the tea varieties were being found in such abundance. He came out first in 1922; and for the next twenty-seven years, until the Chinese Communists dismissed him along with most other foreigners, he lived and explored with memorable energy and acumen, in that vast and tumultuous series of mountain ranges between Dali in the south and the cold deserts of what was then Amdo, and is now called Qinghai, in the north.

He worked first for the government, searching for sources for a substance called chaulmoogra oil, which was then thought to be a treatment for leprosy, and which was used in huge quantities in the great sad lazarettos of Hawaii and Louisiana. Before long, however, he began to chafe under the restriction of government work, even so far from home, and he transferred his professional allegiance to the more liberal board of the National Geographic Society.

He wrote papers and popular articles by the dozen, steadily transferring his affections, as he did so, from the region's plants to the region's people. He sent thousands of specimens home, but he never wrote a single serious paper about the botany of China. Within a few years of his arrival he had taught himself to be the world's greatest expert on the Nakhi people, and a translator of their terrifyingly complex pictographic language. He befriended a colorful figure known as King of Muli, and made similar comradely alliances in principalities called Choni and Yungning. He wrote vast tomes about the Moso—a people, related to the Nakhi, who lived on the northern side of the Yangtze and whose practices are more rigorously matriarchal than their country cousins. (For instance, their family names pass down from mother to daughter.) It was these people who slept and fed on the Boneless Pig, the animal of the mattress and of the slices that are eaten a dozen years later with locally whipped and straw-filled yak-butter and chunks of homemade cheese.

The Moso are a people who also have a highly libidinous reputation across China—whose reported eagerness for sex rivals that of the Trobriand Islanders, far away in the western Pacific. Moso women lead the charge here: they can take as many lovers as they like, and those drawn into these brief relationships are known as *azhu,* good friends. A survey carried out in 1983 found that of 1878 mature Moso women, no fewer than 393 carried on *azhu* relationships. The men invariably returned to their own homes when the night was over: if any children resulted from the mingling, the woman—who might begin her sexual activity as a young teenager—was allowed to keep them.

Not surprisingly the rate of sexually transmitted illness among the Moso has been staggering. Peter Goullart, a Russian-born Frenchman who came to know the area well and who wrote a biography of Joseph Rock, recalled a conversation with a Tibetan trader he met coming down from Moso country. Goullart, who was called on to treat occasional sickness, examined the man and discovered that he had indeed contracted a case of what one might call Moso Rose.

"No! No!" the man protested. "It is only a cold."

"How did you get it?" Goullart asked.

"I caught it when riding a horse," the trader replied.

"Well," said Goullart, "it was the wrong kind of horse."

Joseph Rock, who was not drawn to this kind of activity, instead drew maps, keenly but not very well. He surveyed mountains (managing on one occasion to make an absolute ass of himself by claiming in a telegram to Washington that a peak called Minya Konka was the world's highest, at 30,250 feet—his amateur use of the theodolite having misled him, it later transpired, by almost a mile). But wherever he went, he traveled in the grandest style, like a Victorian in Africa. Porters carried him everywhere in a palanquin, often trembling under the lash of his formidable temper. When it came time to halt, there was always a cook, an assistant cook, a folding table, starched napery, table silver, a leopard skin to sit upon and from which he would contemplate the view he always had his bearers select for him. There were bottles of well-traveled wine, no matter how far into the wilderness he had penetrated; there were Viennese dishes he had taught his staff to prepare; and after dining there was tea and a selection of liqueurs.

Then he would set off once again for more discovery and amusement—and glancing around happily, he would note in his diaries how his column of hired men stretched half a mile into the distance and how any village chief would regard him as a potentate from some fabulous kingdom and treat him accordingly. As well as his folding bath and his gold dishes, which impressed all who saw him, he invariably took a wind-up gramophone, and he would regale the villagers he met with scratchy Caruso arias played full-blast.

He remained in Lijiang throughout most of the anti-Japanese war, to the irritation of the authorities in Chongqing: he raised vegetables and listened to advice from his sorcerer friends, and to the news on his short-wave radio. When, on one occasion close to the war's end, he traveled back to America, he fell almost insane with grief on learning that his collections, which had followed him home on a ship, had been torpedoed in the Arabian Sea.

"Followed him home" is perhaps an inappropriate phrase. Joseph Rock never had a real home, nor did he ever settle with any particular person, male or female; only in Lijiang was he content, and he said he wanted to be interred there, under the towering range of the Jade Dragon Mountain. We visited the house and the garden where he had wanted to be buried, in a village an hour north of town: it is cool, among the foothill pines, and there are meadows and crystal springs. A family of Nakhi live there now, and there was a cow in Rock's study, which is now used as a byre. A beautiful young Nakhi woman, her hair covered in a white bandeau, was nursing her baby in the room that Rock had used as his library: perhaps he would have been content to see that at least his house was being used by his beloved Nakhi, and not by the Chinese.

The latter threw him out in the end. The Communists distrusted those they regarded as barbarian priests and wizards and sorcerers, and they killed scores of them, and sent others off to be reeducated. Rock left finally in August 1949, two months before Mao Zedong declared the formation of the People's Republic. By then it was all over, so far as fun was concerned, up in the wilds of the west. He wrote to a friend: "if all is OK I will go back—I want to die among those beautiful mountains rather than in a bleak hospital bed all alone."

But China never did let him return. He stayed in America, working in solitary misery, and he died in a Honolulu hospital in 1962. His books remain, and an Italian publisher brought out his definitive study of the Nakhi pictographs, completing the work in 1972. They remain as Joseph Rock's memorial—his books, his remarkable photographs—and three species of flowers: *Rhododendron rockii, Primula rockii* and *Omphalogramma rockii.* Considering that this son of a dreary Viennese manservant never took a degree in botany, or in anything else, and that he achieved all he did by an unquenchable combination of courage and bare-faced cheek, the flower memorials seem touchingly appropriate.

Although he was memorialized by the names of plants, there were others who tramped these same hills and who made a great deal more of the region's extraordinary botany than Rock ever did. There was, for instance, Augustine Henry, a medical officer with the Imperial Maritime Customs and a colleague of the very unbotanical but properly named Cornell Plant. Henry, who found expatriate life tedious, explored in great detail the mess of vegetation zones that Yunnan's precipitous mountains piled on top of one another. He, like other plant hunters, would travel uncomfortably in a *huagan,* a chair, slung from the shoulders of local bearers. The work was dangerous and difficult, but well seasoned with rewards: Henry had numerous flowers named after him—a rhododendron, a viburnum—and he was one of the first westerners to sight the famously beautiful dove tree, which grows wild in western China, and nowhere else.

More famous still were the French missionaries Père David and

Jean André Soulié, whose decades spent in the isolation of the western Chinese hills were amply rewarded by the discoveries of scores of splendid specimens. It fell to Père David actually to find the first dove tree—a delight that offers the illusion, created by paired white bracts that sprout beneath each flower, that scores of doves with outstretched wings have alighted on the branches and are waiting to fly away. The Linnean Society gave it the name *Davidia involucrata,* and seeds from it were brought back to London by another hunter, the Royal Horticultural Society's great Ernest Wilson, a few years later.

Seeds from countless plants that were first found by these brave and inquiring men came pouring into Britain and America during Victorian and Edwardian times. Today, the fact that gardens and hillsides in the West are colored by tea roses and peonies, by azaleas, camellias, chrysanthemums and rhododendrons is owed almost exclusively to the efforts of these men. Christian converts in western China remain something of a rarity: botanical converts in western gardens, however, suggest that the missionaries and their friends performed memorable tasks—even if, like Joseph Rock, they were not quite the tasks to which they were first assigned.

I had one more task before leaving Lijiang, and I was prompted to undertake it by a newspaper article that Bruce Chatwin had written of a trip in 1986—three years before his early death of what those who cared for him said was an illness that he had contracted in China, and perhaps even on this trip. Ironically the man about whom he had written then, and who I was now coming to see a decade later, was a healer, a herbalist. He was a man whom Bruce Chatwin has made almost famous.

He is named Ho Shi-xiu, and he lives still as he did then, in a small Nakhi village called Baisha, halfway between Lijiang and the hamlet where Joseph Rock kept his country villa. Lily and I drove the six miles there, parked the Jeep in the grounds of a school, walked to the main street and turned south. Farmers and housewives and children were busying themselves on all sides—threshing grain, washing clothes, noisily spilling in and out of classes. Where would we find Dr. Ho? Lily asked. I told her not to worry: Dr. Ho was such an avid self-publicist that it would only be a matter of moments before he found us.

Turning south was in fact a mistake. We walked for more than a mile, pleasurably but pointlessly, drinking in the mountain air, peering up cross streets, asking questions. The street was lined with willows, and a bright stream tumbled between the flagstones. A teacher asked me to spend a few minutes telling her class of ten-year-olds exactly where I was from; an old Nakhi woman asked me to help her untie the bridle of her donkey, which had become snarled on a tree; another woman, her daughter, showed me how to shave garlic to the thinness of gold leaf.

The guidebook I had with me struck a rather irritable tone about Dr. Ho and Bruce Chatwin's somewhat overripe profile of him as "the Taoist physician in the Jade Dragon Mountains." The publicity had gone to his head, said the book: now everyone wrote about him, everyone visited him, he was formidably wealthy compared to his fellow villagers, and he never let visitors pass without impressing his fame upon them. But where exactly was he? No one here seemed to know who he was; if he existed at all he had evidently gone to ground.

We retraced our steps, frustrated. After twenty minutes we found ourselves back in the stone-paved central piazza and struck off to the north. Two hundred yards along the way there was an almond tree in the middle of the road, and from behind it, as if responding to a stage manager's cue, stepped a slight man dressed in a blue wool cap and a long white doctor's coat.

"My friends, welcome!" he said, in the familiar and oily way of a man who is about to sell you something you know you don't want. "How very good of you to take time to visit my humble village. You have time to come to my little home?"

Dr. Ho had found us. His having done so there was now no getting away from him. He looked quickly around to make sure there were no other potential clients coming up the street, then bundled us into the front room of his cottage, beneath a small sign that said Jade Dragon Snow Mountain Chinese Herbal Medicine Clinic. It was by no means an extraordinary house: the walls were of wood and a dark reddish mud from which poked tiny bristles of chaff. Inside there were shelves of papers and a desk covered with vials and bags of seeds, and there was a pleasant smell, like an old Irish Medical Hall.

Dr. Ho spoke English quietly, just comprehensibly, telling us his life story in the compressed manner of a telephone pitchman who knows that at any moment his listener may put down the receiver. If ever I showed a sign of wearying he would put his hand gently on my knee. "Wait for just a moment, kind sir—you have come a very long way to hear my story." He said he had learned his English at the nearby American air base: but it sounded quite Dickensian, not at all as though he had been schooled by the men of the Flying Tigers.

The Cultural Revolution that swept through Lijiang came as something of a mixed blessing for Dr. Ho, who had returned to the town from Nanjing after falling ill some time in the early 1960s. The Red Guard detachment assigned to this part of Yunnan selected the doctor promptly for *reform through struggle,* or some such madness: he was immediately suspect for no better reasons than his ability to speak, not only fair Dickensian English, but an alarming number of other foreign languages as well, a skill that in the eyes of the Guards rendered his commitment to Han supremacy and Maoist ideals very far from certain. So his house was ransacked, suspect goods and books were confiscated and he was forced outside to work, set to tilling the mountainside and making orderly fertility out of wild Yunnanese fecundity.

But what the Guards did not realize was that the work they had set Dr. Ho as punishment brought him into contact with the makings of a new and very profitable career. Working in the fields halfway up the Jade Dragon Mountain, he came across samples of some of the rare and unusual plants that forty years before been studied assiduously by Joseph Rock. Dr. Ho knew Rock's work and he recognized the possible importance of the flowers and shrubs that were growing in such abundance on these slopes.

He started to collect them, keeping them well away from the scrutiny of his minders, bringing them back each night to the small plot of land behind the house. There he began to grow them in pots and under glass. Thus was born the tiniest and most exotic of physic gardens, with strange and exotic samples of botany that exist to this day. As part of his discourse Dr. Ho takes visitors to see them: there is a lichen guaranteed to cure shrunken ovaries,* the root of an orchid that is said to be good for migraine, a delicate green grass known as heaven's hemp—said to be peculiarly efficacious in seeing off bladder problems—and something called *Meconopsis horridula,* which, as its name half implies, works wonders for the temporarily dysenteric.

Dr. Ho ground his plants to powder and soaked them in hot spring waters—trying them out on the villagers, varying the amounts and the mixes depending on the ailments presented and the age and sex of those he treated. Before long he had a following: the Chinese have always been eager for natural cures, for their own version of the ayurvedic arts practiced farther west, and Dr. Ho's discoveries on the mountainsides seemed to work wonders, either from their chemistry or from their placebo effect.

He next combined his newfound pharmaceutical skills with his professed lifelong commitment to the way of Taoism—a philosophy that in any case sets great store by internal hygiene, the quest for immortality, internal alchemy and healing. And in 1985, formally and with some ceremony attended by Taoist priests, he established himself as a full-blown Taoist herbal healer. He sat back and anticipated a late middle age of well-meaning obscurity. What actually happened, however, was that a few months after setting up shop, and by pure chance, he was visited by the Adonis-like figure of Bruce Chatwin, his hand-tooled leather rucksack on his back, who swung into town with his pencil, notebook and an assignment from an American newspaper. Chatwin plucked Dr. Ho from nowhere and cast him into the blinding spotlight of thoroughly respectable fame.

Whether or not there is any therapeutic value to any of Ho Shi-

---

* Or bronchitis, if it is taken with grease from a boiled-up mountain bear.

xiu's seemingly limitless range of teas, decoctions, infusions and tisanes, there is no saying—there have been no laboratory tests, so far. But such was Bruce Chatwin's following that, on his say-so alone, a string of the distinguished and the gullible promptly started to stream into Baisha to seek solace and comfort and the botanical assistance of Dr. Ho's tiny clinic.

The doctor, a man not at all backward at coming forward, presents to anyone who is interested—and to most who are not—a thick stack of files and visitors' books that demonstrate the vast number of the great and the good, as well as the ordinary German tourists and Japanese bus-tour groups, who have come a-calling. There were the signatures of British ambassadors by the score, of television personalities like Michael Palin and John Cleese ("interesting bloke—crap tea" he had written), of writers like Patrick Booz, of society ladies from the Upper East Side, and of regiments of Californians and health nuts from Oregon, Montana and the hills of Bavaria. There were newspaper articles in all known languages, preserved in folders of cellophane: he took them reverently from the stacks, offered them for viewing as though they were fragments of the True Cross.

Finally he peered at me, placing his wispy little white beard close up against my face and examining my skin and eyes. He leaned back: "Blood pressure, anxiety, loose bowels," he declared. And though I protested that I had none of these afflictions—although my daily inspection of the leavings below dozens of Yunnanese hole-in-plank lavatories had convinced me that the latter problem was endemic in rural Chinese life—he pressed a bag of powder into my hand, then a leaf or two and a twig, which he pressed between the pages of the book I was carrying, and cocked his head on one side.

"These will clear up all your problems, I have no doubt," he said, and cocked his head again, an expectant expression on his impish face. I twigged: he wanted cash, and Lily counted out some ten-*renminbi* bills into his hand, one bill, then two, then five—until finally he smiled, closed his fist on the money and stood up.

"You have been so kind to give me of your valuable time," he said, in as non–Flying Tigers a patois as it is possible to imagine. "I hope you will tell your friends to come and visit me too." Not *I hope you will come back;* just *I hope your friends will come,* listen to my spiel, hear about my fame, listen to my diagnosis of a life of diarrhea and dyspeptic discomfort, buy samples of my potions and make me richer, and pass it on in due course.

He was a rogue, I thought—a lovable old rogue of a snake-oil salesman, an amiable bit player in a circus of a grand tradition. He and his Taoist wizardry had taken me for fifty quite affordable *yuan*. But he had taken the late and much missed Bruce Chatwin, I thought, for really rather more.

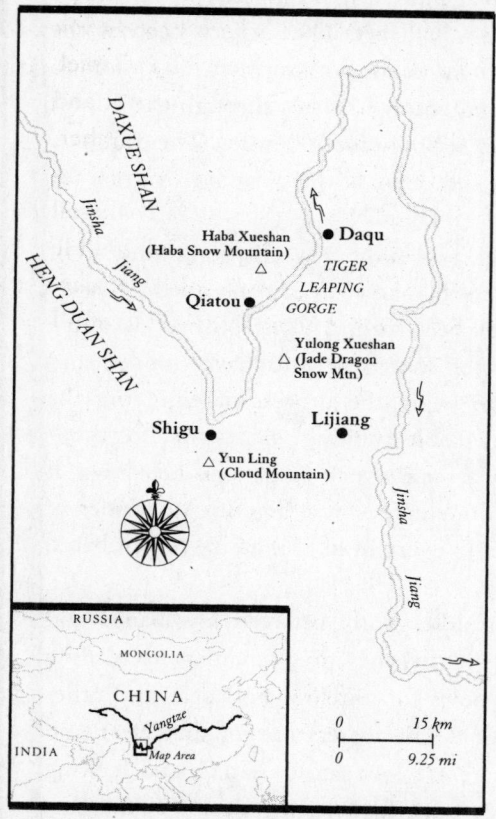

DAXUE SHAN

HENG DUAN SHAN

Jinsha

Jiang

Haba Xueshan
(Haba Snow Mountain)
△

Qiatou ●

● Daqu

*TIGER
LEAPING
GORGE*

Yulong Xueshan
△ (Jade Dragon
Snow Mtn)

Shigu ●

Lijiang
●

△ Yun Ling
(Cloud Mountain)

Jinsha

Jiang

RUSSIA

MONGOLIA

CHINA

Yangtze

INDIA   Map Area

0   15 km

0   9.25 mi

I3

The River
Wild

During its 3964-mile passage from the fringe of glaciers at the foot of
Mount Gelandandong in Qinghai province, to the navigation buoy
on the East China Sea, the Yangtze drops 17,660 feet—three and a
third miles. Most of that drop occurs, as is the case with almost all
rivers, in its first half. Between the glaciers and the distillery city of
Yibin—a distance of 1973 miles, which happens to be almost precisely half the distance between the source and the sea—the river
drops very nearly 17,000 feet—almost all of its total drop, in other
words. Below Yibin the river is wide and generally placid: it is
flatwater, as mountain boatmen like to say.

But above it, on that first half of the river, the water is anything but flat. Above Yibin, every river mile of the Yangtze sees its waters falling an average of eight and a half feet. That is very steep by the standards of any major river. It is worth nothing that the Colorado slides down along a similar gradient as it passes through the Grand Canyon—but manages to do so for only for 200 miles. The Yangtze, by contrast, keeps going down and down at the same average rate for fully 1900 miles.

The upper half of the Yangtze is, in other words, for almost all of its length, a very turbulent, very fast and very steeply inclined body of water indeed. Once it has been properly established as a big river—once the dozens of lesser source streams have braided and knitted themselves together to begin the process of emptying the high Tibetan Plateau of all available running water—tens of thousands of cubic feet of water course every single second down it toward the sea. And though on average these gigantic quantities of water fall more than eight feet in every mile, it must be remembered this is *on average*.

In some places the waters sidle gently between low banks and sandy beaches. They pass by silently, they give sanctuary to wading birds, they provide watering holes for antelope and bear and other animals of the high cold plains. The waters are icy and clear and shallow; the river is wide; there are low sandy islands; and looking down from a boat one can see huge fish waving slowly in the current. Places like these are rare and beautiful; and their beauty has an ominous quality, since invariably beyond the lip of the downstream horizon everything changes, and what is placid up here becomes down there a place of speed and foam and spray and, for any humans caught there, a place of matchless danger.

At these much more numerous other places—both on the River of Golden Sand and on its upstream extension that the local Tibetans call the Tongtian He, the River to Heaven—and once the Tibetan Plateau's encircling hills have been breached and the waters begin to roll inexorably down toward the ocean, the vast volumes of water steadily transmute into terrifying, awesome stretches of river where the power and fury of the rushing Yangtze become barely imaginable. All these millions of tons of roaring water are suddenly squeezed between gigantic cliffs, are contorted by massive fallen stones and by jagged chunks of masonry, and they sluice and slice and slide and thunder down slopes so steep that the waters hurtle down ten, twenty, fifty feet in no more than a few hundred furious yards.

In places like these the water is not so much water as a horrifying white foam—a cauldron of tortured spray and air and broken rock that is filled with the wreckage of battered whirlpools and distorted rapids and with huge voids of green and black, the whole maelstrom roaring, shrieking, bellowing with a cannonade of unstoppable anger and terror. The noise is almost more frightening than the sight: the sound roars up from the cliffs, echoing and resounding from the wet rocks so that it can be heard from dozens of miles away, a sound of distress like a dragon in pain.

These stretches of wild water are nothing at all like the troublesome boils and shoals and whirlpools of the Three Gorges, across which trackers were able to haul the great trading junks, and where Cornell Plant and Archibald Little eventually triumphed with their iron boats: these are upriver rapids where any survival is impossible, where any craft sucked in would emerge only as matchwood, and where any passengers or cargo swept down would be pulverized by the ceaseless might of the roaring waters. These are the Upper Yangtze's rapids, and they are worse than any others in the world.

There are many of them, all unutterably dreadful, all formidably dangerous. But none is more dangerous and dreadful—nor more spectacular and unforgettable—than those in the gorge near Lijiang, where the river squeezes itself through a twelve-mile-long cleft that in places is no more than fifty feet across: narrow enough, some say, for a tiger fleeing from a hunter to have once jumped clear across. This notion is almost certainly quite fanciful, but the name has stuck—Hutiao Xia, Tiger Leaping Gorge, unarguably the most dramatic sight on the entire route of the river.

During these twelve miles the river falls at least six hundred feet—by some estimates, a thousand. That means it falls at the rate of between fifty and eighty feet each mile, a drop with more of the characteristics of a waterfall than of a river rapid. According to the Chinese there are three main groups of white water in the Gorge and twenty-one separate rapids. All of them are dangerous: two in particular, one close to the beginning of the Gorge itself, one halfway down, are truly terrifying.

The river courses along a natural fault line, tearing through rock that has already been crushed and weakened by the tectonic forces that have shaped this geologically chaotic corner of the world. Near-vertical cliffs of limestones and granites, porphyries and slates, soar directly up on either side of the stream for fully seven thousand feet; the mountains of which they are faces rise behind them to twelve thousand feet, and from the dark gorge shadows below one can peer up into the narrow strip of blue sky and glimpse snow and ice sparkling on the upper slopes.

There is a pathway clinging to the left bank of the river, and Lily and I planned to walk down it. We started on the Gorge's upstream end, at the bridge at a hamlet called Qiatou, where the river flows silently and placidly under groves of weeping willows and looks for all the world like the Thames at Bablockhythe. There was little indication here that things were about to change, except that the river's progress seemed to be blocked a few hundred yards ahead by the huge wall of mountains rising sheer to the north of the grubby little village.

But soon there turned out to be another clue: while not so long ago Tiger Leaping Gorge was rarely seen by westerners,* today the local authorities have become only too well aware of the profit they can make from those outsiders who have a fondness for strenuous journeying, and so they have built a sort of turnstile on the path and employ an old man to sell plastic tickets to walkers. Ours read, Hutiaoxia Tourist Scenic Spot Management Office of Zhongdian County and it had a sketch of an improbably long tiger jumping

---

* At the downstream end of the Gorge there still is a sign saying No Foreigners Allowed.

across an improbably narrow defile between cliffs. Permission to undertake the walk costs about a dollar, and the man told me he sells about twenty tickets a day in the summer.

"Be very careful," he said morosely. "Two killed already this week."

The path, an old miners' mule track, is hewn out of an almost vertical cliff face. The mountain rose mossy and dripping to our left, the cliff wall dropped off sheer to our right, directly into the river. And while the path more or less followed the contour line, the river itself began to whip down the dizzying slope, starting the fall of nearly a thousand feet down the twenty-one gigantic sets of rapids. This meant that the cliff on our left-hand side became ever higher as the river fell away. We hugged close to the mountainside, imaging what might happen if we strayed too close to the other side, a slippery piece of rock, a gust of wind . . .

About a mile in, as the walls of the Gorge began to close and the sun was blotted out by the walls of rock, we crossed a pile of blinding white debris, the spoil heaps of a marble quarry. Where was the quarrying? I wondered—and as I did so a van-sized piece of rock whistled down from above, crashed onto the spoil heap, bounced off it and then hurtled down over the edge. I heard a vast splash from below. The quarry, I realized, was five hundred feet above our heads, on the side of the mountain.

This was where the walkers—both North Americans, it turned out—had been killed three days before. They had been doing just what we were doing—walking slowly and carefully along the tiny track, daring not to venture too close to the river side. Suddenly and without any warning a huge piece of marble, dislodged by a careless worker up above—most of the quarry workers were prisoners, it was said, and could be expected to take an understandably cavalier attitude to the safety of those around their enforced workplace—slammed down on top of them, and dashed them away and off the path and down into the river below. They may have been killed by the rock; they may have died in the fall into the river; they may have been drowned. Whatever: their bodies, mangled beyond recognition and with every bone broken, were found at the lower end of the Gorge later that evening.

We walked even more nervously, keeping a hundred yards apart so that if one of us was hurt, the other might survive. From time to time the path petered out and we were clambering over soft talus that would slide over the edge as we shuffled through it, and would threaten to drag us with it. Once in a while we met walkers coming the other way: they looked white faced and nervous, and greeted us with queries that we echoed to them: *What's it like ahead?*

Then the path widened, and there was a small stall built of rock where a young Moso man was selling soft drinks. A steep path led down from here, and someone had suspended a rope alongside it to give walkers added purchase: it went down to the bellowing and spray-drenched side of the worst rapid of all, a place where the river is cinched into its tiniest cleft and where a mansion-sized pyramid of black limestone stood in the middle of the stream, splitting the roaring white waters into two, like a half-horizontal Niagara ceaselessly churning and bellowing through the defile.

We went down and stood alongside it, struck dumb by the thunderous might of it all. This, of the twenty-one measured rapids of the Tiger Leaping Gorge, was probably the worst, the meanest dog of all. Great torrents of white and green water hurtled toward us, taking boulders and spars and trees along with the flood as though they were feathers and balsa-wood sticks. This was the quintessence of the Tiger Leaping—the rapid we had come to see, where the river showed itself as a thing of raw and unimaginable might. This was a place where no human being could ever pass. Or so I once had thought.

Someone had managed to get onto the rock in midstream, for a start: he or she had written the characters for *hu* and *tiao*—tiger and leap—in vermilion paint on the rock's most prominent surface. How this unknown painter—or this graffiti artist, or this vandal, depending on the viewpoint—had managed to get across, to daub his paint and get back without being swept away is an achievement that beggars belief.

• • •

But man has an unquenchable eagerness for the conquest, as he likes to put it, of such challenging places. Mao Zedong had swum across the Yangtze down at Wuhan, and so had conquered it, in a manner of speaking. Other men, and at later dates, had tried to voyage their way down the entire length of the river, paddling it in specially strengthened boats. This was their version of conquest; those who tried were among the best and the worst of humankind; their efforts, in which the puniness of man was matched against the strength and caprices of the river, led to some success and also to a great deal of painful failure. Tiger Leaping Gorge—and in particular this huge rapid near its beginning, officially known as the Upper Hutiao Shoal, with a sixty-foot drop through two suicidal pitches—was where that failure had been most vividly demonstrated.

The "conquest" of an *entire* river demands of course that one knows where the river begins and ends—knowledge that, for the world's big rivers, can be notoriously difficult to acquire. Close to their beginnings big rivers have a habit of splitting themselves into countless fine tendrils or capillaries, and several of these may compete legitimately for being the true *fons et origo*. Is it the stream that is farthest from the sea? Is it the stream that is at the highest altitude? Is it the stream with the greatest flow of water? There is little agreement on this point among either hydrologists or cartographers; and so explorers can make names for themselves even today by finding, or claiming to find, supposed new sources for well-known rivers.

The beginning of the Mekong, for example, was reportedly found by a Frenchman in 1995. But it may well be that another source, with an equally legitimate claim and yet equally difficult to verify, may be found by some other wanderer ten or fifty years hence. That, after all, is what happened with the Yangtze.

Until the closing years of the Ming dynasty, in the 1640s, the source waters of the Yangtze were thought to lie at the head of the Min Jiang, the big and (in those prepollution days) unexpectedly clear stream that joins the muddy Jinsha Jiang, the River of Golden Sand, at Yibin. The reason was simple: the wide and rushing Min was navigable for as much as 180 miles above Yibin, while the Jinsha, narrow, rocky and furrowed by turbulence, was closed off to boatmen by a line of mountains no more than 60 miles above town. The Min was by far the more important river for trade; logic suggested, therefore, that it had to be the origin-river.

Exploration soon put paid to that theory. A Ming dynasty geographer named Xu Xiake looked closely at the Min, and found that it splits into its various capillaries and minor tendrils only about 500 miles above Yibin. Even the most ambitious source-searcher could not discover a spring or a glacier that was more than 500 farther miles upriver from that. But Xu went on to discover that the Jinsha Jiang, by contrast, burrows into the hills for nearly 2000 miles— changing its name above the town and the bridge at Yushu to the Tongtian He, the River to Heaven. This, Xu reasoned, must be the origin-stream of the Yangtze.

Later travels confirmed that this must be so—if only because the Jinsha and its tributaries were so very long. The Tongtian He, it was found out two centuries later, went on to attract three substantial tributaries—the Qumar, which brings waters down from the north; the Dam Qu, which swirls in from the south; and seemingly most powerfully of all, the Tuotuo, which comes directly from the high snow peaks of the west. Which of these three rivers is actually the origin-stream has been a matter of debate and wonder for much of the last half of this century.

The Qumar was discounted early on: it had neither the water volume, the length nor the altitude to be a serious candidate. Its attraction lay simply in the fact that it vanished, and that it did so into some of the wildest and least hospitable plateauland on earth. The Tibetan Plateau has fewer than three people inhabiting each hundred square miles—it is a place of many black yaks, a few black tents, huge expanses of grass, sudden outcrops of rock and ice and an endless, endless sky.

The Tuotuo and the Dam Qu, however, were real candidates, and in 1976 the China Geographic Research Institute dispatched a serious expedition from Beijing, armed with systematic methods, to determine which was the true source. After a summer in the field these explorers decided it was the Tuotuo, and specifically that the Yangtze began its 3964-mile journey to the sea in a tiny lake called Qemo Ho, which lay at the foot of the Jianggudiru Glacier, at the base of the 21,723-foot-high mountain called Gelandandong. For nine years this spot remained the official source—and to many it remains so today.

But in 1985 the American National Geographic Society sponsored an expedition of its own. A group of explorers led by a Hong Kong Chinese named Wong How Man first went back to the Qemo Ho source; then doubled back to the point where the Dam Qu river splits from the Tuotuo and headed to the source of that—their argument being that more water appeared to stream into the Tongtian He from the Dam Qu than from the Tuotuo. If it was the more powerful stream *and* if it was longer, then its beginning should be officially considered to be the source.

And longer the Dam Qu turned out to be—though by a little more than a mile. The explorers headed east, following the Dam Qu's great recurving path to a point where it split into two tiny streams, the Shaja, which headed south, and the Guangzhuguo, which meandered to the north. The Shaja was short, the Guangzhuguo half as long again—and it petered out into (or rather, started from) a small and clear pool lying at the base of a hill that the local Tibetans call Jari.*

This, according to Wong's claim—which was backed up by an official Chinese report in 1986—was almost certainly the true, technical source of the Yangtze. It was nearly a full mile lower than the Tuotuo's source in the glacial lake, but it was one and a half river miles further away from the sea, and it provided much more water. It lies at 32° 7′ North, 94°6′ East, is at a height of 18,750 feet above sea level, and is 3965 miles from the ocean.

* On the far side of Jari Hill rises another tiny stream—the declared headwater of the Mekong.

So the choice for anyone wanting to journey down the entire length is this: whether to accept this tiny and unnamed meadowland lake as the source, and so journey from Jari Hill, down along the Guangzhuguo, the Dam Qu and the Tongtian He to the Jinsha Jiang and finally onto the Chang Jiang proper; or to begin at the icebound Qemo Ho (Qemo Lake), then pass down the entire length of the Tuotuo, and only then join the Dam Qu.

Drama tended to force the choice. All would-be explorers of the river seemed to want the very same thing: to begin their journeys at the foot of a mountain range, in a lake that was surrounded by a frieze of blue-white glaciers. This setting was by far the more dramatic. It had the look of a great river's source: it was not merely a place of muddy oozings from a dismal and half-frozen Tibetan pasture. Mount Gelandandong was part of the poetry of the great river: it was how Wang Hui's painting had captured it, in the seventeenth-century imagination: it began among the clouds, spilling from ice and snow, emerging with grace from the heavens. Gelandandong was just right—it was *spiritually appropriate*.

And so when, in 1985, a thirty-two-year-old freelance photographer named Yao Mao-shu decided that he would try to become the first person ever to float the entire length of his country's greatest river, he arranged to begin his epic at the base of the mountains, and set his raft on the crystal cold waters of Qemo Ho.

He was powerfully motivated. The year before he had heard that an American team was planning to raft the river, and he had applied to go with them, but had been turned down. His dander was up. Why should the honors for such a conquest go to barbarians? The river was part of the soul and fabric of China. Only a Chinese should have the right of such triumph. He, Chinese to his very core, would go off alone, and would conquer the great river himself.

He was a tough and resourceful young man, and alone in his twelve-foot craft he went through the hell of the upper reaches with dignity and courage. After six hundred miles he arrived at Yushu, and blurted out his adventures—of catching and trying to tame a lynx for company, of being threatened by wolves, of coming across an island filled with thousands of swan eggs, of going hungry for days, of being ice-cold, of being so terribly lonely in the Tibetan plains that he felt he would go quite mad. They liked him in Yushu and gave him fresh supplies, and when he drifted off downstream again the whole town wished him well.

But he never made it. Somewhere in the canyons where the River to Heaven becomes the River of Golden Sand, Yao's boat, the *Dragon's Descendant,* capsized. His body was found by herdsmen, drifting in an eddy in a downstream calm. He left a widow back in Chengdu. And he left a China that—once the tragic tale had been told around the nation—became suddenly determined to avenge his death, by conquering the river once and for all, by concerted Chinese effort, the following year.

The expedition that the luckless young Yao Mao-shu had wanted to join was led by a man who had wanted to run the Yangtze ever since 1976, when he had paddled down the white waters of one of the origin-streams of the Ganges, on the other side of the Himalayas. He was named Ken Warren; and the fact that he patted his mane of white hair into shape with mousse, and that in 1986 he took a case of said mousse along as part of the ten tons of supplies with which he intended to beat the Yangtze, should have been warning enough that he was never the man to do it.

This onetime vitamin salesman—who began his attempt on the river by praying before the cameras at the source, affecting tears and pleading with choking voice, "Oh beautiful Yangtze . . . we ask you to take care of us and we promise you no harm"—led an expedition that turned out to be both a failure and a disaster.

One man—a young photographer from Idaho named David Shippee—died of altitude sickness along the way; four other members of the expedition deserted because of Warren's questionable leadership; and when the going became too rough for comfort—when the rapids in the Tongtian He became too dangerous, too unrunnable—then Warren himself walked out on the remainder of the party. The Americans' permit to raft on the river expired when they were still 3000 miles short* of their intended goal—a fact that did not prevent Warren from declaring to the television cameras that what he had done really had been a success, that he would be back for more, and would return to the river with a "secret weapon" that would defeat the rapids that had thus far defeated him.

Ken Warren was an essentially disagreeable figure—but he was handsome, and exceptionally telegenic. The film which ABC-TV commissioned of his expedition, and which was paid for by the sponsoring insurance company, Mutual of Omaha, suggests that the expedition was honorably conducted and even heroic. But once it was over, and sober questioning replaced the hyperbole and the flattery to which television and its subjects can fall prey, so the truths about the expedition's lamentable organization and leadership began to emerge, and the bitterness began.

Margit Shippee, the widow of the dead photographer, sued for her husband's wrongful death; Warren in turn sued the four men who had abandoned him; and the whole fiasco vanished within a miasma of costly lawsuits and acrimony. Warren himself died in the early nineties, and today on the Yangtze his name is ill regarded indeed. One Chinese boatman to whom I mentioned the name simply shuddered, and remarked caustically that "this American above all should not have been allowed to come onto the river."

Inevitably, and perhaps properly, it eventually fell to the Chinese to become the winners of the dangerous and often fatal competition to be the first to "conquer" the Yangtze. The contest was already well under way in the summer of 1986. By the time the Warren team had stage-whispered its prayers and set off, no fewer than six Chinese expeditions (one of them with our friend from Panzhihua, Wu Wei) had already set out from the Gelandandong glacier-lake source. They remained well ahead. By the time the Americans had pushed their boats off in early summer the leaders of these Chinese parties

---

* And 300 miles short of Tiger Leaping Gorge, which all had said was the most dangerous stretch of the river.

had reached more than a thousand miles downriver—and yet, tragically, already three of their number were dead. (It was first thought that eight had died: but in fact five from two of the competing parties were found safe and sound. After their boat had shattered on a rock they had clambered up the walls of a canyon and survived for days on a diet of leaves, roots and snails.)

Once matters had thus begun to become more dramatically dangerous on the river, official China unexpectedly began to take an interest. Up until now the political leadership in Beijing had looked on these home-grown efforts merely as a way of avenging the previous year's tragic death of Yao Mao-shu, who, with his good looks and his clear-eyed idealism, had become something of a minor national hero. Now, with three of the youngsters who were trying to shoot the rapids again already dead, the effort began to assume, as had Mao's swim thirty years before, the familiarly powerful man-versus-river symbolism. What was being attempted out on the Yangtze, the political leadership in Beijing decided, was now nothing less than a trial of national honor, a test of the modernization that had been brought about by the glories of socialism and the command economy. All efforts should be poured into the attempt, it was said: the youth of China should be helped and supported and egged on in the nobility of their cause.

And so by midsummer all China's eyes were on their great river, and on the teams of men who were daring to try to conquer it. The rafters, it was clear, now feared the worst from a river that was proving far more dangerous than they had anticipated. Most of the members of four teams swiftly dropped out, and those remaining were by midsummer grouped into just two competing crews, battling on gamely. These teams managed to raft all the way down from the Tibetan Plateau town of Yushu downstream to Dêgê and Batang, towns that are way stations on the great southward sweep of the river where it marks the frontier between Tibet and China Proper. They stopped, for rest and reconnaissance—reconnaissance mostly—at Qiatou, by the willow trees, and at the point where Lily and I had strolled and where the stream looked innocently placid like the

Thames at Bablockhythe. They then walked, just as we had, along the perilously narrow path of the Gorge, and they dodged beneath the marble quarries, where the prisoners even back then were prying loose the tumbling slabs. They came to see and study and examine, with ever mounting apprehension, that first rapid—the sixty-foot half-horizontal Niagara of a monster known variously as the Upper Tiger Leaping or the Upper Hutiao Shoal. It was, they thought at first from where they stood, quite unrunnable.

But then one of the teams had an idea. They built an enclosed capsule-raft out of rubber inner tubes, added a tightly fitting pneumatic doorway to one side, and lashed everything together so that it looked like a squat Michelin Man. They carried this down to the waters just above the Upper Tiger Leaping Rapid, found an unsuspecting dog, placed an oxygen mask onto its face, thrust it inside the raft, sealed up the door and kicked the capsule out into the stream. The vessel, highly buoyant and cushion-soft, careened out into the cauldron of foam and, after turning over and over a dozen times, vanishing deep into the yards-deep foam, flying up into the air, hurtling off sharp rocks and slamming itself against the canyon banks, bobbed out into the calmer waters below the rapid, still afloat. But the door had been ripped off, and the dog was missing, never to be found again.

With a logic that can only be fully understood by a Chinese, this first test run was considered to have been a success—as in *the operation went very well, but the patient died.* So they built a second of these seemingly unsinkable rubber capsules, this one slightly larger—for humans, not dogs. On the morning of September 10, 1986, two of the party's more experienced members—one, a thirty-four-year-old history teacher named Lei Jiansheng; the other, a boiler worker at a railway station, a thirty-two-year-old named Li Qingjian—climbed inside the capsule, and Lei read a brief statement to the watching crowd:

> I think China is one of the greatest nations, but its development is hindered by some backward ideas. We

should encourage the opening up of minds, and the spirit of adventure. Rafting the Yangtze is a very small wave in the long river of history, but it is worthwhile if it can help move forward the development of our country.

And then the rubber door was shut tight, and the capsule was pushed out into the center of the stream.

For a tantalizing while it hung there, as if the rubber itself was frightened and did not dare move. But then, after some prodding with sticks and a push from a man who swam out while tied to the bank with a rope, it was swept out into the maelstrom. The film of the event, one that I have now watched with horrified fascination scores upon scores of times, shows the flimsy craft being sucked whirling down into the white foam, vanishing, reappearing, going down for a second time and then, only moments later, bobbing up in the still waters downstream. Then the door is opened and two wet, smiling faces peer out blinking in the sunlight. Their friends lift them out, check their arms and legs, find all still there in good working order. The run was over, and the pair were badly shaken—but they were all right.

There are many more rapids within Tiger Leaping Gorge—some, like the Meteor-Studded Rapid five miles below, even worse than the first. But in essence, with the running of the Upper Hutiao Shoal, the great deed was done. The second Chinese team completed its own run through the Gorges without incident, at about the same time as it was announced that Ken Warren's venture had failed, and that the Americans were all going home. The two Chinese teams, now without competition, savored the remainder of their journey—down through the lower reaches of the Jinsha Jiang to Yibin and the confluence with the Min Jiang, and then along the much more placid hundreds of miles of the Yangtze proper. It was not all plain rafting: another rafter died on the way; and a reporter was killed when he was hit by a falling stone—a total of five people had died by the time the teams reached the flatwaters, and before the remainder of the journey became no more than a tedious tide-lapped routine.

The two parties reached the buoy in the ocean in November. The first to do so, on November 12, was the team that had titled itself the Luoyang Expedition for Sailing and Exploring the Yangtze; two weeks later came the China Yangtze River Scientific Observation Drifting Expedition. All told, when the deaths of the American David Shippee and Yao Mao-shu were added to those who died on these two Chinese expeditions, and when a group of others were later discovered to have died as well while making other and lesser attempts on other parts of this terrible river, it was realized that much had been sacrificed during that extraordinary Yangtze year. And for what, other than the sustenance of China's national pride? There seems in retrospect to have been—at least once the government became involved—a gladiatorial aspect to the entire affair, in which young men were sacrificed to the terrors of the great river, in part to keep the people entertained, and to maintain them in harmony with the political temper of the time.

Above the Gorge that water is clear and calm and wide again. There is a paper factory on the left bank, which discharges a horrid gray stain into the stream a few miles farther on; and then, at Shigu, named after a stone drum that still stands there as a memorial to an ancient battle, the river executes its most obvious and extraordinary physical feature. It spins around, in the space of a few hundred yards, from heading due south, to due north. Because of this sudden redirection of the river it can fairly be said that at this very place, where there is now the town, all China's destiny was once held hostage by the whim of ancient tectonics—and specifically by a hill, lying to the south of town, called Yun Ling, Cloud Mountain. I knew it well from studying the maps: now, at long last, I had the opportunity to see it, to walk up its slopes and see for myself why it was so crucially important—if unwittingly so—to the story of China.

Late in the afternoon Lily and I reached the little town. The heat was like a furnace, and was made even hotter by the unmistakable and oddly soapy scent of Sichuan fire-pepper. From time to time there was a relieving waft of northern air, a breeze that was liquid with the thick smell of new-mown hay. But generally it was quite still, the valley shimmering and hazy. The cattle drowsed in the slowly lengthening shadows of the jagged mountains to the west, the Heng Duan Shan, the Horizon Splitting Range. All the town of Shigu seemed asleep, tier upon tier of adobe houses rising up the hillside, hushed for the siesta under their sinuous blankets of tile.

Down below the memorial that held the old stone drum—a millstone-shaped slab with scores of lines of incised verses giving details of the long-ago battle—a group of children were diving noisily into a rock pool from the town's old wooden bridge. It was a lovely bridge, three hundred years old at least and suspended, like so many in these parts, from a pair of heavy iron chains. There are still early Qing dynasty gates at each end, with patches of peeling vermilion and gold paintwork and elaborate bronze locks that the village elders shut each day at sunset.

A woman was creeping slowly along a cobbled path, her old bones creaking under the weight of her wooden back-frame with its afternoon crop of corn. She was evidently mother to one of the boys below.

"Come on home and help me thresh this lot!" she called down.

"Just a little while. It's far too hot to work!" the boy shouted in reply. The woman nodded and walked on, trailing stalks of corn and a furrow of yellow dust.

To get up to the side of Cloud Mountain one must climb the long staircase of slabs that snake through the old part of town, a normally busy lane with open-fronted shops lining each side. In one of these a man with a screw-topped Nescafé jar half full of green tea lay snoring under a billiard table. No one was stirring, no one noticed my passing. Shelves in the little stores were stacked high with supplies for the evening: cylinders of powder-dry noodles wrapped in old copies of the *People's Daily,* plastic bags of peppers, whole pigs' heads cut raggedly from their shoulders, cans of Coke, piles of white cabbages, tall bottles of Pabst Blue Ribbon beer with the labels stuck all askew, bricks of dust tea, watermelons, thermos flasks, primrose yellow sachets of Pantene hair conditioner (made under license in Shanghai). On each storefront table was an abacus and a steelyard. Under almost every table was a dog, asleep.

Before long I came to a tall cement monument with a red star on top and a plaque. Three children, all wearing the red scarves of the Young Pioneers, were sprawled asleep on the podium. I trod as quietly as I could. The plaque above the children was dominated by a long revolutionary message and then a short poem in the familiar sprawling, looping calligraphy of Chairman Mao. I managed to read a few characters: it was yet another of his hymns to the Long River—a river which, now that I was a few hundred feet up, was just coming into sight.

From the angle of the sun it was clear that Cloud Mountain's lower slopes, directly ahead, lay to the south. They were meadowlike Chinese alps with short grass and a dusting of white camellias. The upper few hundred feet of the mountain were different, lightly forested with camphor laurels and rhododendrons. Above that the hill seemed to have a rounded, stony summit. The top was elongated into a lozenge shape that ran very noticeably east and west: up there it had a shape rather like a Brecon Beacon, or the Red Hills of Skye, or a very small edition of Kilimanjaro.

It is a hill that looks to be a thing of no consequence at all. It is something of a dwarf: it rises sedately, almost sheepishly, from the turmoil of this eastern extension of the Himalayas where much grander mountains—like the Horizon Splitting Range, in whose shadows the cows were settling down—are thrusting themselves into the skies on all sides. It is not exactly a holy mountain, like the more famous Chinese and Tibetan summits of Emeishan or Taishan or Kailash: it has never attracted pilgrims or mendicants. It is far too far away from anywhere to be of much interest to tourists. A hundred years ago the plant hunters from Harvard and Kew came here to look for primulas and gentians and perhaps (though without success) for samples of that marvelous piece of botany known as the dove tree, which some, because of its huge white flowers, called the hand-kerchief tree.

But the hill does have a certain importance, and it has given the otherwise rather ordinary—pretty, but ordinary—town of Shigu a kind of fame that no nine-story pagoda or ruined lamasery or Maoist resting place could ever bring. Cloud Mountain, it is fair to say, is regarded by Chinese myth to have guided and directed China's very *being*.

To grasp its standing in legend, one must remember that the Chinese believe that their origins as a people mimic and parallel those of the origins of the planet itself. The history of the World and the history of the East are to their thinking inseparable, party to the same divine plan—one of the reasons that they are the Celestials, and the rest, barbarians. The Chinese, to their own belief, never came from anywhere else: they were always, in their minds, *there*. The world was created, China was created, the Chinese were created: all was one, seamless and of high purpose. The details of this story tell of a vast expanse of years during which myth and proven history were hopelessly and inextricably entwined.

Most of these protohistorians believe that the world—and hence China—started after the Egg of Chaos had spawned a deity named P'an-ku. This remarkable proto-God grew ten feet a day and lived for 10,000 years; he is perhaps best known in the Chinese context for having chopped into two parts the mighty universe stone and by doing so separating for all time the Heaven from the Earth. Immediately after this, China was created and was promptly blessed by the successive presence of twelve Emperors of Heaven and eleven Emperors of the Earth (who each ruled the new land for 18,000 years), followed by nine Emperors of Mankind (who ruled for a total of 45,600 years).

Next came sixteen nondescript kings about whom almost nothing is known, and then three sovereigns who had (or, at least, two of them had) the heads of men but the bodies of snakes. One of these (or maybe not; maybe he belonged to a group of five, slightly later on) was Huang Ti, the so-called Yellow Emperor, father figure to the nation, the revered founder of the Chinese civilization.

Huang Ti's life marks the notional end of primitivism and savagery: it is from the time of his reign—perhaps around the year 2697 B.C.—that China becomes heir to an organized and sophisticated system of society and government. It was during his time that people began to live in wooden houses, to wear silk clothing, to ride in carts, to sail in junks, to fire-harden ceramics, to hunt with longbows, and, most important of all, to write. The much vaunted "five thousand years of history" begins with the reign of the Yellow Emperor. All Chinese think of themselves as this great man's sons.

It is said that the towering figures who then lived immediately after the founding Emperor went on to invent all the pillars of China's early civilized life. Fu-hsi, the Ox-tamer, domesticated animals. Shen-nung, the Divine Farmer, invented the plow and the hoe and set up the organizing of produce markets. Yao, the Fourth Emperor, created the calendar and organized some kind of central government. But it was Shun, the Fifth Emperor, whose decisions were to devolve eventually, onto Cloud Mountain. It was in 2200 B.C., or thereabouts, that the work was performed which makes Cloud Mountain so vital a site in the creation and development of modern China.

It came about because, during the Imperial reigns of both these men, Yao and Shun, China was plagued by the most terrible floods. One or the other of these two emperors called upon a young and apparently technically competent bureaucrat named Yü to try and control the waters—to dredge new channels, to stop up dangerous rivers, to create lakes and, in a decision of potent symbolism, to try and keep all of these tamed waters within the orbit of China. China's waters were a great national treasure, the two emperors declared during each of their reigns: they must be made to behave themselves, but *they must remain in China.*

Yü, working under the orders of either one or both of the emperors, rose manfully to the task. With the assistance of a small brigade of dragons he ranged across China for the next fifty years, reshaping the hills and the valleys in such a way that—in theory at least—the country would be protected from the seasonal ravages of her great waterways. He did his work so well he came to be an emperor himself, Da Yü—Yü the Great; and even today he is referred to by Chinese who know about Christianity as "China's Noah."

He was said to have been utterly obsessive, and an instance of his dedication is still taught in schools: he is said to have passed by his family house on three occasions as he tracked across the kingdom, and each time heard his family weeping for him to come home. Never once, the Chinese say proudly, did he soften. He went right on to stop up another river and dredge another canal, and to save China, and China's waters, for all time. His family, he declared, would have to wait.

The achievements of his flood control era are legion, and there are said to be moss-covered memorials to his works dotted beside rivers all around China. But his greatest success, the most spectacular triumph of his half century of earthmoving and shaping, is said still to have been the siting of Cloud Mountain. From halfway up its slopes—and from any large-scale map of China, or indeed, of the world—it is abundantly clear why. For by placing the mountain where it now stands, Yü changed the course of the Yangtze, keeping the huge river inside a China that would otherwise have watched impotently while its potentially most important waters streamed away.

Any good map will amply demonstrate the strategic positioning of Cloud Mountain. In this part of western China all of the hills around are clearly ranged to the north and the south, spearing down from the jumbled ranges of Sichuan. I could see this, more or less, from where I stood: the ranges tumbled into the blue haze of the northern sky in serried ranks, regular, like soldiers. And the rivers that run in the valleys between—the Yangtze, which I could see, as well as others, like the Mekong and the Salween, which I could not because they lay a few dozen miles off to the west—all run north and south as well. The trend continues to the south of where I stood as well: seventy miles or so away to the south is a long lake called Erhai Hu and it, too, is aligned from north to south. Every geographical feature, in fact, seemed to be aligned like the folds of a concertina—

sharp valleys, narrow ranges of hills, up and down, up and down in rank upon rank, and all beginning in the north, all ending in the south.

All, that is, except Cloud Mountain, where Lily and I were standing. Though it is smaller, less spectacular, more modest than its rivals, it lies right across the lay of the land. In a land of such unyielding north-south predilection it is an eccentric, an erratic. And most of its bulk lies—and in this lay Da Yü's triumph—*right across the path of the oncoming Yangtze.*

Regarded from its source, the Yangtze had up until this point been roaring due southward for the last one thousand miles. But here in Shigu, and, according to Chinese legend, on the specific orders of the Imperially charged Yü the Great, it slammed suddenly and unexpectedly right up against this newly placed and massive wall of Carboniferous limestone. It collided against the wall and rebounded dramatically in a huge, tight hairpin bend that has it thundering northward with as much vigor and determined might as, a few hundred feet before, it had been thundering and roaring south.

I could see it below me in the afternoon shadows. Just on the left of my field of view the river came heading toward me like a train, fast, unblinking, unstoppable. But then in an instant it halted, it hesitated in a boil of small pools and oily undercurrents and then it promptly turned and began to speed away from me. If ever a river could be said to have turned on a dime it was the Long River, here in deepest Yunnan, among the rapeseed fields and the yak meadows of the Nakhi.

The implications of this screeching, rubber-burning turn are profound. They are most obvious from a glance at the map, when one can see what the region's geography would have been like if Da Yü had *not* placed the mountain exactly where he did.

Without the barrier the southerly streaming Yangtze would have carried on in precisely the same direction—and six hundred miles later, in an undistinguished mess of mud and mangrove swamps, it would have left China for good.

The valley along which it might do so exists today. The declivity that currently brings the river down to Shigu continues through the lake bed at Erhai and on down to become the bed for a weak but also southward-flowing river called the Lishe Jiang. This stream is soon nudged a little southeastward by a range of low hills called Ailao Shan—the Misty Foothills Mountains—and, as the gradient declines, it begins to slow and widen. Before long it leaves the hill country altogether, mumbling past miles of rice paddies and bamboo groves and stands of jungle before it reaches a frontier town called Lao Cai. There it sails in stately fashion onto the steamy plains of what was once northern Annam, where it suddenly and silently escapes from China. It has entered Vietnam. It goes past towns like Yen Bai and Phu Tho and Vinh Yen and then finally it passes the great capital city of Hanoi and its port of Haiphong and reaches the Gulf of Tonkin and the sea.

What began as the River to Heaven and the River of Golden Sand thus might have gone on to become the Red River. The waters that drip from China's high glaciers might have fanned out eventually in a delta that belonged not to the People's Republic of China, but to one of her lesser neighbors.

Instead, and thanks to Da Yü, not a single drop of Yangtze water is actually permitted to escape from China. From my vantage point on the boulder—it was getting darker now, and my maps were flapping in a hot evening wind picking up from the west—I could see the diverted direction in which it was heading: it was going north and east, deep into the center of the Middle Kingdom. It would twist and swivel for a while until it plowed through Tiger Leaping Gorge. There it would turn briefly back south, as though still trying to nudge its way out—but the hills would now be too tall for it to slip away, and besides, the old north-south grain of the land has vanished here and there is no pattern at all in which to ease and find a convenient exit. The river is now resolutely pinioned inside China. Its way out, its path of least resistance, is no longer south, but east. And thus does it find its way to Panzhihua and Chongqing, through the Three Gorges to Wuhan, and thence to Nanjing and Shanghai and the sea.

Had it not been for Cloud Mountain, it would not have passed that way at all—and the third-longest river in the world would not exist, a valley in which a twelfth of the world's people now live and work would not exist, and all China would present a very different geography, a very different anthropology, and a very different history from that with which she is blessed or cursed today. Cloud Mountain, in short, is the axial point of China's very being.

Geology and tectonics present a more mundane explanation, of course. When India broke free of the Africa to which it once was joined, drifted north to Asia and then collided with it between Eocene and Miocene times, the Himalayas were thrown up, coughed up into the air by the explosive force of the collision. At the eastern end of this collision zone there was terrible tearing and distortion, and gigantic blocks of crust were spun slowly clockwise as they tried to get away from the slow but never-ending impact to their west.*

The Yangtze, in ancestral times, flowed to the south, into the valley of what is now the Red River. The tremendous tilting that took place after the India-Asia collision wreaked havoc with this tidy plan, and a side stream began to take Yangtze water away from the tilted uplands, heading east. Soon the strength of the tilt and the depth of the new valley won out, and all of the Yangtze water began to course east, not south. The Red River lost its biggest tributary, and China gained her greatest river.

Da Yü's involvement in this grand plan can never be known. To the Chinese his role is implicit—or at least it is to those Chinese who believe him to have been a real person. To more disinterested schol-

---

* Since Eocene times India has plowed nearly a thousand miles northward, and it is still heading that way at two inches a year—enough of a velocity (nine times the rate of fingernail growth) to impose enormous stresses, and to trigger the devastating earthquakes—like that of October 1995—that plague the chaotic countryside of Yunnan and the Burmese border.

ars in distant laboratories, poring over their polarizing microscopes and fault-zone maps, a more impersonal explanation seems appropriate. The Chinese claim geologists have no poetry in their souls—and from halfway up Cloud Mountain, with the western sky turning to indigo and the great first bend of the Yangtze shining below like gunmetal, a poetic explanation seems, as up at Gelandandong, more spiritually appropriate to the story of this vast river.

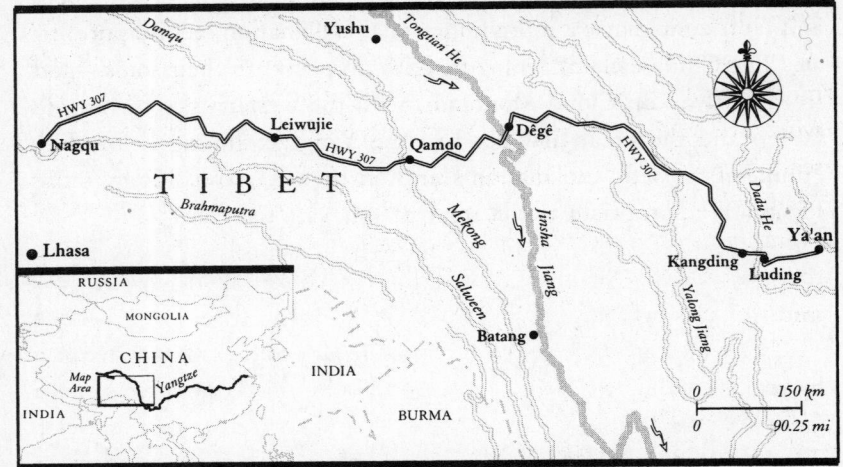

14

Harder Than the Road to Heaven

We had pitched our tent on the slopes of a Tibetan mountainside, above a bright green meadow that was crowded with very large yaks. Camping had not been in our plan; but our car had broken down, and now lay seemingly beyond repair. The diagnosis was plain: the two mild-steel bolts that were supposed to hold the radiator secure had both sheared simultaneously, buffetted by scores of miles of vicious bumping along what is laughably called National Highway 307. Once the bolts had snapped, the radiator had fallen backward, directly onto the cooling fan. The whirling metal blades had promptly cut a series of concentric arcs into the copper tubing, causing all of the car's cooling water to pour out onto the dry and stony ground.

In London or New York such a mishap would be serious, but not mortally so. Even if there was no service station nearby, some man would be within hailing distance who could jury-rig the radiator, sealing its leaking tubes for long enough for us to limp onward for a permanent fix. But in Tibet, hundreds of miles from anywhere, an event like this turns into a disaster on an epic scale. So we broke out the tent and readied ourselves for a long and hungry stay in the midst of this broken wilderness.

The tent was Chinese-made, overly well weathered and decayed by years of use. The zippers intended to hold together the flaps of the front entrance and its fly sheet had been ruined and refused to work. This in itself would be no major problem—provided the weather held. But Tibetan weather is notoriously fickle, and within seconds of my putting up the tent and clambering into it and showing Lily— who had never camped before in her life—where to stash her gear, the wind suddenly picked up and marble-sized spheres of hail began to tumble from the sky.

They sounded just like bullets—a fusillade that began slowly at first and then became as intense as a wild celebration of battle, with the chunks of ice, larger and larger and rougher and with ever sharper spurs and spikes, hurtling viciously down from the clouds.

I was keeping the unzippable doors closed with my hands, and the ice was beating against the exposed skin, bruising it and then cutting it until blood flowed freely and dripped onto the tent floor and onto the ice-carpeted grass outside. Lily was terror-struck, and she fled into a corner of the tent like a wounded animal—until a torrent of hail thundered down through the fly sheet and began to bruise and batter her, upon which she sensibly moved to the center of the space, away from the wall. She sat whimpering, her crying drowned completely by the thunder of the hail, which went on and on, becoming ever louder, half burying the tent in a thick rime of frozen water. What with her wailing, and the thunder of the ice, and my bleeding hands, and the thought of the ruined car buried in white outside, the day was turning out to be rather trying.

We were on the road to the Yangtze's headwaters, and getting there—involving a lot of backtracking—was proving anything but easy. It had seemed very much otherwise some weeks before, when the cascade of coincidences that had begun with the taxi driver miles away eventually took us to two men who had access to cars—Mr. Wu back in Panzhihua, and more recently Mr. Xu Xiaoyang, who lived and worked in the Sichuan capital city of Chengdu. Xu was a devoted fan of the Upper Yangtze River, and he had stated flatly that if he could help anyone wanting to get there, he would: as he told his story in his office above a local department store, reaching the headwaters would be almost child's play.

We had been given his name and a letter of introduction by Wu of Panzhihua, and he—Xu—was waiting for us at the Chengdu railway station when we pulled in after our daylong ride from the south. It had been an astonishingly beautiful journey—a combination of scenic beauty and awesome engineering as, via tunnel after tunnel after tunnel, the line pierced the eastern flanks of the Daxue Mountains and raced high above the Anning River.

The railway had been built in the seventies by gangs of convicts and soldiers, and it must have been one of the most technically difficult pieces of permanent way construction anywhere in the world. The reward for a traveler is one of perpetual astonishment, of being hurled from the bat blackness of a tunnel into the glare of a section high up on a cliff above the river, then dashing back into darkness again before once more—two hundred times, all told—being thrust into vivid sunshine higher up the mountain still, with the rice farmers working their paddies and the fishermen poling their *sampans* hundreds of feet below. We reached the plains of Chengdu quite tired out, exhausted by the huge emotional overload of seeing so much unforgettable scenery, and being so overawed for so many hours, without respite.

Xu Xiaoyang was in his early thirties, an owlish man in pebble-thick glasses; he was with a friend whom he introduced as Mr. Tang, who had long hair draped over the top of his shoulders, and a vaguely Tibetan cast to his features. Tang had been to the head-waters ten years before, and would guide us; Xu would organize everything: it would be his pleasure, he said, and his privilege.

His organization, which was based in two large and spartanly furnished rooms above the department store, was called the Sichuan Corporation for International Cultural Development. How it raised funds, how it paid Xu and his pretty secretary and the rent and the office machines, remained a mystery during the initial days that we waited in Chengdu, getting my Alien's Travel Permit and our car—another Beijing Jeep, as it happened. But money it seemed to have in abundance: there were cellular telephones, air conditioners, expensive dinners offered to us each evening, visits from moguls from Shanghai and Hong Kong, and a good deal of talk about future cooperation, of "putting Sichuan on the map," of making films about the Three Gorges Dam, and about the headwaters themselves.

Then came a clue as to whence came the corporation's riches. A glossy brochure was delivered to our hotel one day showing the worldwide extent of its business. Most of the links appeared to be with countries in Africa—Tanzania, Kenya, Niger. There were photographs of banks and office blocks, grand houses that might have been presidential palaces, factories and hydroelectric schemes—all in gleaming white concrete, all being happily run by smiling Africans. They had all been built, it turned out, by Sichuanese—by men who had been sent out by Xu and his predecessors, to live and work in camps all over Africa, as part of what is generally known as bilateral cooperation.

I had seen such camps before—they were usually well-guarded barracks, with the inmates permitted neither to leave nor to welcome visitors. The workers' costs were met by the Sichuan provincial government, which in turn received a subvention from Beijing's foreign assistance ministry. The organization that made all the arrangements—Xu's in this case, though each province invariably had a similar foreign-assistance program—took the provincial and national grant money, and maybe some subsidy from the foreign power to whom aid was on offer. It seemed to do very well—allowing in this case Xu, who was the manager, to drive a large Japanese car, to live alone in a comfortable house near the American Consulate (he was divorced, and his current girlfriend lived in Tokyo) and to dine famously every day.

It allowed him also to be unusually generous to friends and friends-of-friends who stopped by with what in other circumstances might seem outrageous requests. I had mentioned to Wu that Lily and I wanted to be able to see the far Upper Yangtze in a place where it was narrow enough to jump across—something that would ordinarily require months of planning and the granting of permissions. He had duly passed on this intelligence to Xu.

"There will be no problem," Xu said excitedly, "I have the most excellent *guanxi* here. We will get all we need. You will get your wishes."

By *guanxi,* he meant "connections"—the complex system of favor exchanging, of mutual back-scratching, of the calling-in of old debts which, overlying a byzantine network of family and business and school and military ties that acts as China's new-style class system, forms the essential lubricant that allows China to function, unfairly but quite efficiently. An impoverished peasant without any *guanxi* at all might not always get all of the rice he deserved or to which he was entitled; nor would a vexed citizen who lacked connections find true justice at the hands of the system. But I knew I would get a car and a driver to take me to the Yangtze headwaters because—*and only because*—I would be perceived as someone who might, one day, be able to repay a favor that would most assuredly one day be called in. This was *guanxi* in its most perfect essence: I would get all I needed because I could get them what they needed.

But what I nearly did not get was my Alien's Travel Permit. "I have serious suspicions about this man," complained the head of the Chengdu Public Security Bureau, when he was asked to give me permission to travel down Route 307, the old Lhasa brick tea road.

He refused to say why he was suspicious: I had offered myself to him innocently as a teacher, bent on traveling to western Sichuan for reasons of scholarship and curiosity. But my passport was perhaps a little overfilled with stamps from previous visits to China, and he may have wondered why. Anyway, he turned me down.

So we went instead to another office, one that Xu knew had equal powers to issue permits, and eventually—and to a triumphal war whoop from Xu, who had been in danger of losing face because of the bureaucrat's obduracy—I was handed the gray folded insert for my passport, which allowed me to visit the towns of Kangding, Luding and Dêgê.

I would not be permitted to cross the Yangtze, however. The river here marks a firm frontier: on the far side, the western side, the right bank, was the province the Chinese now call Xizang, and which the rest of the world calls Tibet. The officials were adamant that I should not go that far, especially during what was said to be "troublesome times." I was equally determined that I should: Lhasa may have been far from the Yangtze, but in the plan that Xu and I had conceived, it seemed an essential way station.

Back in Shigu, where the Yangtze makes its first big turn toward the north and east, I had taken a close look at the large-scale map. The road that headed north, up toward the old local capital town called Batang, was indifferent at best. It was a narrow dirt track used only by logging trucks and it led through hundreds of miles of difficult and frankly uninteresting wilderness. It would be far more interesting, I thought, to make a large zigzag of a journey, crossing the river and in doing so sampling a richer cross section of life and topography.

According to this plan, I would travel west from Chengdu along the southern branch of the tea road to the point where it crossed the Yangtze; then I would pass deep (and illicitly) into Tibet, I would cross the valleys of the rivers Salween and Mekong until I reached the only properly metalled road in the entire province, the great north-south highway that ran between Lhasa and Golmud, a dreary northern potash-mining town that lay in the gulag-land of central

Qinghai province. If I took this road north from Lhasa I would then cross the Yangtze once again—and I would at this point be just a very few miles from one of the great river's supposed sources, the Tuotuo stream and its rising at the pool below the Gelandandong glacier. A brief trek into the moors near there, and I should perhaps find a Yangtze that was as narrow and as pristine as I wanted.

In this plan, journeying into Tibet and all the way to Lhasa was essential. Yet now I was told—not that I had truly expected otherwise; everyone was saying that Tibet in 1995 was a tricky place to visit—that the greater part of the road I needed to travel was off-limits. The permit that allowed me to travel along it as far as Dêgê was firm in forbidding me to proceed any farther. Besides, cautioned my Australian guidebook, the roads leading to Lhasa from here (and there are actually two) "are some of the wildest, highest and most dangerous routes in the world. They are not open to foreigners. If you do travel along them do not forget the physical dangers—take food and warm clothing. Travel on these routes usually takes several weeks, hitch-hiking on trucks . . ." The auguries were not so good.

Tang arrived on the morning of our departure in a bright red Beijing Jeep—our second. They were common enough cars in China—made under license in what was said to be a disastrously run joint-venture factory Chrysler had set up in the mid-eighties in the Chinese capital. He was sitting in the front passenger seat: the driver was a small and nervous-looking man named Mr. Miao. Normally Miao was employed by the organization that owned the car—the Propaganda Department of the Chengdu City Government, with which the owlish Xu had such excellent *guanxi*. He knew perfectly well where we were wanting to go, and he thought there was a good chance we would get there. "You may have some trouble with the police," he said with a twitching grin, "but you probably also have many dollars, yes? Out there they are more interested in dollars than permits."

Xu was up early to see us leave and he made a brief speech offering prayers, in guttural Sichuanese, for our good fortune. We then crunched into first gear, with a grinding noise that said little good about the mechanical quality of our conveyance. Miao patted his gearshift lever with an affectionate gesture that was to become his most obvious nervous habit (the more nerves, the more rapid the patting rate) and sputtered smokily out into the traffic and toward the distant mountains.

For several hours we motored southwestward, the hills looming rigidly on our right. This was still China, the far corner of the Red Basin of Sichuan, and the roads were good and fast; there were factories and airfields and a dismayingly large number of army bases, with heavily armed soldiers pacing back and forth on sentry duty outside the gates. Chengdu is a major staging post for troops bound for duty in the Tibetan highlands: whenever a rebellion is to be put down, or monks arrested, or borders closed, the soldiers who do the work are flown in from Chengdu, or sent by convoy down the met-alled highway from Golmud. Of the two ways to get troops to Lhasa fast, the bases and the aerodromes around Chengdu are by far the more important.

Then we crossed a bridge and turned smartly right, to the west. The land began to rise. This was the beginning of the hills about which Li Bai had written his most famous couplet: "Oh how danger-ous, how high! How hard is the road to Shu! It is as hard as the road to Heaven." We were leaving China Proper and we were entering what once had been Tibet Proper, but which had for the last three centuries been a half-world, a place where the two so very different cultures came together and either merged or collided according to the mood of the moment. Between the edge of the mountains and the banks of the Yangtze—250 miles as the crow flies, but five times that once the mountain passes were negotiated—lay a chaotic wilder-ness of craggy ranges and deep gorges that the Qing dynasty admin-istrators had briefly called Sikang province, or in the words of today's Chinese historians, Xikang. The very existence of a state here had much to do with an engagingly eccentric Briton, Sir Francis Younghusband, who invaded Tibet on Britain's behalf in 1904.

This area between the river and the eastern edge of the mountains was always a wild and lawless place, peopled by volatile rapscallions who owed their allegiances to various local chieftains. The Moso, those who favored lying upon and then wolfing down the Boneless Pig, were one such: there were others, petty states—more than thirty—with names like Chala (into which we had come when we made our sudden right turn over the bridge) and Lithang and Gye-morong. All were lumped together under the name of Kham, and the people were collectively known as Khampas. They were widely thought of as warlike, unruly and deeply holy, and were feared by Tibetans and Han Chinese alike—said with admiration by today's Tibetans to have been the region's best killers and the greatest saints.

Sir Francis Younghusband had come to Tibet—from India, and via Sikkim—in 1904 on what has often been described loosely as Britain's Last Imperial Adventure. The excuse provided by the Indian viceroy at the time for his doing so was laughably flimsy: Tibetans were said to be stealing Nepalese yaks, he said, and must be dealt with. The underlying purpose was very real: it was to keep Tibet out of the sphere of influence of the increasingly voracious Russians.

This action was the Great Game between innings, and when Younghusband's soldiers were firmly settled in place under the Potala in Lhasa—having been put there by superior force of arms and, as Hilaire Belloc summarized, because "Whatever happens, we have got/The Maxim Gun, and they have not"—Britain forced the Tibetans to sign a convention that would keep the Russians firmly at bay. The side effect, unanticipated at the time, was that China would begin a long process that would culminate in her becoming the dominant influence on Tibet. "She climbed back into Lhasa," wrote one of Britain's critics, "on Francis Younghusband's shoulders."

The first act of the Qing dynasts, the Manchus, was to annex the region of Kham, to create a buffer state between the Chinese Empire and what was then seen, supposedly, as an outpost of British imperial interest. So they sent west a ruthless killer named General Zhao Erfang, charging him with a mission to take Kham for the Chinese and wipe out any resistance in the towns through which we were due to pass in the coming days. The general became known as the Butcher of the Monks as he sacked lamaseries by the score, and executed Buddhist leaders from Yushu and Dêgê down to Batang and the Yunnan border. He crossed the Yangtze and made for Lhasa, looking for the Dalai Lama of the day: but the Lama had fled to India, just as his successor was to do when other Chinese came to get him, fifty years later on.

The Chinese turned the Kham they had thus conquered into the entire new province to which they gave the name Xikang—a process of Imperial administration that came to a screeching halt less than half a decade later, in 1911, when the Manchus were themselves driven from power by the republicans. But the idea of having a buffer state between China and Tibet (and at the same time of making a springboard by which the Chinese could ultimately make their leap to Lhasa itself) still carried weight. In 1928 it was revived, and there was more stern battling in the mountains as the Chinese fought to carve Xikang into an administrative reality.

It never truly happened. Governors came and went. Bureaucracies were set up and dismantled. The capital was shifted from Batang, beside the Yangtze, to a town that was then called Dardo and which is now known as Kangding. But even that capital never became much more than an exercise in wishful thinking; and in 1955, after years of halting starts, Xikang was formally abolished: the land was swallowed up by Sichuan, though its people were made semi-autonomous, and they were recognized as racially different from both the regions that marched beside it. (But in Taiwan today the province is regarded as still being in existence, and there is a representative, notionally from Xikang, who sits in the National Assembly in Taipei.)

The thought that Sir Francis Younghusband might have some responsibility for the unique existence of the country through which we were passing did not seem to press with undue weight on the local inhabitants. There were other diversions for them. In Ya'an, the frontier town where we spent the night, there was a very noisy market, and across from the inn some wily entrepreneur had set up a small zoo behind hastily hung mats, and he charged people one *yuan* to come and see his tired collection of exotica.

I was hoping to find one of the big blue-horned pheasants that are native to these parts, and which go by the magnificent name of Temminck's Tragopan; but instead there was just one flyblown porcupine and a ratty old snake or two. There were a number of pages torn from ancient copies of the *National Geographic* that showed teenage African girls with bare breasts: Lily was convinced that this was the true attraction on offer by the hustler who owned the zoo—it was not to show animals at all, but to offer sex-starved Chinese men a chance to feast their eyes on tits.

Next morning we started to climb hills in earnest, razor-sharp ridges so newly elevated that they were still crumbling and hurling down torrential landslips. I could well believe that the Indian tectonic plate was in continuing collision with its Asian cousin: the land seemed half alive here, and with the mist swirling through the rhododendron groves and the rivers coursing down every ravine, it was a place quite lacking in stillness, or in any sense of serenity or bucolic peace. It was one of these rare places—New Zealand is another, I suppose—where the land seems far more charged with energy than do the people.

The roads were narrow and dangerous and clung to the side of huge black cliffs. Long diversions—one of them at least a hundred miles long—kept us away from the more serious landslips. One road across a high pass was only open westbound—the direction we needed—before two in the afternoon, and we arrived to find barrier poles up and police telling us to try the following day or take another long detour, which we did.

The route took us, fortuitously, along the frighteningly fast-flowing Dadu River and to the small town of Luding on its left bank. There, a black iron chain bridge that had been slung across the river in early Qing times, almost three centuries ago, was still standing: it had attained heroic status in late May 1935, when Mao's Long Marchers fought their way across it, under a withering fusillade of

Nationalist machine-gun fire. Their action had been just as heroic as—but much more widely publicized than—their crossing of the Yangtze back at Jiaopingdu: brightly colored pictures of the grim-faced soldiers battling through the fires, clinging to the great iron support chains, can be seen at most patriotically inclined shrines in today's China, as important an image for the collective mind as that of Mao standing before the microphones in Tiananmen Square, declaring the People's Republic born, or of him standing erect, his right arm pointing to some just attainable promise, a worthy goal for the distant Chinese future.

There was no artist to record the crossing of the Yangtze, though, and as a result today most Chinese seem to believe that the Luding Bridge actually spans the Yangtze, and not its lesser—but scarcely less impressive—tributary.

I strolled across the swaying planks, having paid one *yuan* for the privilege: Lily paid less (being Chinese) and came too, but she was frightened by the sight of the torrent swirling by below and demanded that I hold her hand as we, crossed. On the other side she tried (in vain) to find a boat to take her back.

When finally we arrived at Kangding, which as well as being the capital of Xikang had been the seat of the King of Chala—we were all exhausted. As was the car: it was already showing acute signs of distress, not least because the hood had broken free of its cast-iron hasps after an encounter with a particularly deep pothole, and had fallen off, bouncing down onto the highway and into a ditch.

This town had at last the *feel* of Tibet about it. It was huddled in a fold among the mountains, and a small stream coursed under a string of bridges in its middle, sending up a constant roar that went echoing into the hills. I climbed up for a view: scores of red roofs glowing in the evening sun, the green of the forest-covered hills, the white of the little river rushing between the houses—this was a pretty place, and I felt a sense of relief that I realized, perhaps unkindly, came from winning some slight relief from China, and the Chinese.

Our hotel was beside a small lamasery, the Anjue Si, which was in the midst of being restored. Old women spun prayer wheels silently, young monks in burgundy robes strung flags from the scaffolding. This has long been a religious center: up on the hill to the south of town is a small white stupa, known as a chorten in Tibet, the first of many such shrines. Until the first half of this century the French had kept a cleric here, the head of their Mission Étrangères, of which the plant-hunting Père David had been one of the best known. Kangding's bishop was once the redoubtable Abbé Huc, who made friends with the Tibetans and was thrown out by the Chinese for so doing: he wrote one of the best-ever travel accounts of the little-known China of the mid-nineteenth century, which became something of a worldwide best-seller.

Kangding is a crossroads town, once a terminus for the brick tea trade, now an important rest stop for anyone bound into or out of Tibet—it is the true beginning of ethnic Tibet or, for someone coming from the far side, the true beginning of the real China. The little cafés here serve Tibetan tea—a powerful decoction brewed from tea dust and twigs, with copious amounts of salt added to impart extra flavor and with large globules of rancid, hairy yak-butter floating on top. It is an acquired taste that I was not to acquire—finding it even less attractive a comestible than *tsampa,* the principal food of the Tibetan peasantry, which consists merely of flour worked with water and yak-butter, and which is eaten raw and has a taste like rotten dough.

The brick tea from which the brew is made was once the main reason for Kangding's existence as an entrepôt. Mule or yak trains took it from here deep into Tibet—the bricks wrapped in colored paper, put into tubes of bamboo matting and then sealed in waterproof bags made of yakhide. The shapeless bundles that resulted, hard as iron and heavy as lead and containing perhaps scores of pounds of precious Chinese tea, were carried by pack animals or by human bearers over the worst and most dangerously exposed roads in the world—roads that took their traffic more than three miles high, across snowfields and beside seracs at the top of windy mountain passes. The road is little better today, even though trucks have replaced the mule trains, and even though the only people who travel on foot are the pilgrims, who go on their hands and knees and take many years to get to Lhasa.

The fact that Kangding is a crossroads came home vividly to me as I was sitting down to dinner at a small Chinese restaurant beside one of the river bridges. I was well into my steamed fish and spicy tofu when there was a commotion at the door and a young woman walked in—someone I knew very well. She was an archaeologist from California, a woman named Pam Logan who had borrowed my New York flat some six months before when she had been on her way to Paris. Neither of us could believe it—meeting at all was fairly improbable, but meeting in a small foothills town in eastern Tibet even more so. She knew the area well, and regained her composure rapidly.

"Perhaps it's not so odd," she said finally. "This is Kangding, after all. When you come to think of it, it's probably more likely that we meet here than anywhere else. People have been meeting here for centuries. That's why the place exists."

She was on her way back from Dêgê, where she had been working on a plan to restore a number of lamaseries that had been sacked during the Cultural Revolution. She was going to Chengdu, thence to Irkutsk and the once independent statelet of Tannu-Tuva, which lay in a series of valleys west of Mongolia. I knew Tuva fairly well, having been there to see a monument to the supposed geographical center of Asia, which an Englishman had raised there, inaccurately, a century before. I gave her the number of some people to make contact with in Kyzyl, the capital; she in turn gave me a letter for the Dêgê police chief, a Mr. Ma. She owed him fifty *yuan,* and tucked that into the envelope as well. Then we hugged and said our goodbyes—she would be in Tuva in a week, and I should be on the banks of the Yangtze, and at Dêgê, in another couple of days—if the car performed properly.

· · ·

Next morning the road climbed high onto the basement of the Tibetan Plateau. There would be many more great ridges and plains before we reached the plateau itself, but these hills now had an organization about them, as though we had left the chaos of the collision zone behind us and were on the way to the high upthrusts of the Asian plate itself. There were villages of the strangely boxy stone houses of the settled Tibetans, and down in the meadows the large black tents of the nomads. It was all staggeringly beautiful—clean and glittering in the early sunlight, with dew-fresh grass, towering peaks, piercing blue skies and, dotting the scenery with ragged char, hundreds upon hundreds of grazing yaks. Like sheep in Scotland, yaks always acted skittishly when we swept past: they would rear up and race away, their hooves sending sprays of earth behind them, and the ground rumbling under their speeding mass.

There were other animals, too—small creatures like groundhogs, and big waddling rodents, like stunted capybaras, that were said to be Tibetan marmots. Birds, too: eagles and owls by night, and small blue and red and orange perching birds by day. The dreariness of China was well behind us now: we had come up into a new altitude, and the world was new and excitingly different.

But the road was still terrible, and the car performed less and less well. Poor Miao, whose gearshift patting rate was becoming almost manic, kept having to stop and cleanse this nozzle or rebraze that point or demand that local welders—who were becoming rare animals indeed in these parts—reattach pieces that had fallen off. The Jeep was looking very sick indeed; and inside we were choked with dust, and all we owned was filthy and, in many cases, broken by the constant battering. Lily had rarely before been in a car for more than two hours: so far we were four days into a journey that might take at least two weeks. Her morale was not the best.

Gas stations were rare as well, and those who found them tended to stay in them for long periods, unwilling to plunge on into the wilderness once having discovered an oasis of relative civilization. At one, deep in the middle of nowhere, I came across a beautiful young woman who spoke flawless English. She was from Sikkim and had been working in the hills a hundred miles from here, helping to build a new lamasery, to replace one torn down by Red Guards in 1968.

She was called Changchup Dolma, and we arranged to have dinner together that night. Lily refused to come: Tibetans, and those who sympathized with Tibetans, were far from being her favorites.

The young woman was indeed young—only twenty-seven, and though her family was from Sikkim, she had been educated in the town of Vizakapatnam in southeast India, taking a B.A. in art history. Her uncle, under whose auspices the new lamasery was being built, was an exceptionally holy man—the incarnation, she said, of the great Dêgê Lama. He had been recognized as such when he was nine years old, he had come to Lhasa in the 1950s to study, as was decreed, and then gone on to Kangding, to a lamasery under the control of the Lama of Chala. During the Cultural Revolution he had been arrested, and spent twenty years in prison, for no greater crime than claiming himself to be (as did his followers) a reincarnate deity, a *trulku*.

The girl was almost weeping as she told me this. But she was not sad, she said—rather she was just tremendously happy to meet me, a foreigner who listened. She loathed the Chinese, and had made no efforts to learn their language. She spoke Sikkimese, Hindi, Tibetan, and this excellent English. "But Chinese is the tongue of our oppressors," she declared. "I would think of it as a betrayal to learn it." Since nearly 90 percent of the local population—most of whom were nomads anyway—were Tibetan, she had little practical reason for learning the language.

She was tall and graceful, and when she begged me to stay for some months and try to learn something of the plight, as she put it, of the Tibetan people, I was more than a little tempted. During dinner she tried to teach me to write Tibetan, which I told her I had long thought one of the prettiest-looking of languages. But I could manage only *om mane padme hum,* which I already knew from

having seen it so often carved on the thousands of roadside stones, set
there by patient masons who wanted no more than for the mantra to
be carried away by passing breezes. She was a patient teacher,
though, and smiled beatifically through all my clumsy errors.

Later I had a letter from her, posted in a town called Luhou, the
nearest to her lamasery: she said she had had to ride two days in a
truck to post it.

> I hope you remember me [she wrote, as if I could possibly
> forget],
>
> I am the girl you met in Luhou, Tibet. I am sure when
> you get home you will have many adventures to tell your
> friends. . . . Being a poor talker I couldn't tell you much
> about Tibet. In China there is no freedom of speech, as
> you must know, and you can hardly talk about what you
> really feel. Living in Tibet for nearly three years now I
> really don't know what people feel in their minds and
> hearts. No one seems to believe any other person. They
> may be spies, or maybe they had been tortured badly dur-
> ing the Revolution. It still has an effect on them, this
> past—the older ones tell the younger generation to keep
> quiet and not to believe the third persons. Even the small
> children follow the rules.
>
> I might be late in writing to you some more. I mean I
> might not be able to write to you very often. I hope you
> won't mind. You see, we don't have a post office here and
> going to town is difficult as there is no bus or cars. I have
> to go and look for a truck passing by, and they hardly ever
> give a lift. But I will do my best to write to you as often as
> I could.

That was the only letter that ever came. She enclosed a photograph of Domand Gunpa, the lamasery she was building for her
uncle. It had room for forty student monks, she said, and there was
to be a large chorten built nearby. What had gone up so far was a

grand and colorful two-story structure of wood, and in the photograph there is a milling crowd of monks and abbots, and the local Tibetan girls in the foreground look happy enough.

On the surface, in many ways, it might seem as though the Chinese are allowing, if cautiously, some resurgence in Tibet's religious traditions. The fact that westerners are being invited to help rebuild lamaseries and that Sikkimese devotees like Changchup Dolma are being allowed to cross what was once a rigidly controlled international frontier speaks of a growing liberalization—at least to Lily, who consistently argued that China's policies toward Tibet had been universally beneficial and were now marked by an excess of tolerance. But this letter, which was waiting for me at home, postmarked in Chinese and Tibetan script, spoke of other, less pleasant attitudes—and knowing the Chinese, and their low regard for the barbarians who are their neighbors, I had to doubt that matters were improving in any significant way.

The road got steadily bleaker and more lonely, and the idea grew that we were journeying well beyond all law and beyond all organization—a notion that was in some way exhilarating, in another quite daunting. An example came a hundred or so miles outside Luhou, on a stretch of road near one of the many opencast gold mines that pepper this hazily administered part of Tibet-cum-Sichuan. It was when I watched two truck drivers—in the only trucks I had seen for dozens of miles—having a spirited argument. The one had climbed down from his truck and was standing on the running board of the other, gesticulating wildly at the man inside. As we passed by, this man suddenly pulled an automatic pistol from his jacket and, while the scene diminished steadily in our rearview mirror, had thrust it into the face of his antagonist. What happened next I can't say, but it had rather the look of violence to it. That the locals call this part of the world the Wild West seemed at the moment only too appropriate.

The gold mines are run by gangsters, too—claims are staked,

locals are trucked in to work in near freezing conditions for a few cents a day, and the gold is divided up between a government official and the man who first found the lode. Officially, all gold belongs to the Chinese treasury: unofficially, a lot of local farmers are getting rich, and, more to the point, a lot of corrupt government officials—a phrase that in China has the ring of tautology to it these days—are getting even richer.

We were on the northern branch of the brick tea road, a longer route to Lhasa than for those who go by way of Batang, so there was very little traffic, no more than two or three trucks a day. Occasionally we would find broken-down vehicles, and once a bus that lay at the bottom of a canyon, wrecked almost beyond recognition, and still smoldering. The passengers, if any had survived, were nowhere to be seen.

And every day, every hour, we climbed higher and higher toward the great plateau. On our fifth day, after lunch at a hot, dry junction town that looked like a rest stop in eastern Montana, or Wyoming, we began to inch our way up the sides of a long couloir that the maps said led to the summit of Chola-shan, the final mountain chain before we reached the Yangtze.

The scene was unforgettably dramatic. In the background was the immense massif, scoured by three mighty glaciers that left razor-sharp peaks to slice through the racing clouds. In the foreground, beside a stream of cloudy ice-milk, was a sloping meadow, with pines and junipers where it joined the rocky slopes, untidy piles of tussock grass in the middle and then acres of sweet, lush, and damp grass closer to the road, where the land was flat. A dozen yaks grazed contentedly, and in front of her family's large black tent sat a young Tibetan woman, nursing her baby. In her right hand she held a prayer wheel, which she whirled like a top, sending blessings out on the wind. Her left arm supported her child, pressed tight to her breast.

She had long pigtails, and her hair was decorated with amulets made of yellowed amber; on her arms she wore bracelets of braided silver. I thought then I had never seen anything quite so beautiful. There was distant birdsong. The icy water tinkled merrily between the grasses, and some of the yaks wore bells, which pealed slightly as they changed feet and moved on for another mouthful of meadow. Blue smoke wafted from a dying fire, and a black pot hissed on its embers. The young woman looked up at me and smiled warmly, quite unconcerned at my presence as she continued to turn her prayer wheel in silent, practiced devotion.

Behind and above, the mists spun through the peaks like gossamer trails and tiny puffs of cloud lazed in the summer sunshine, their shadows briefly darkening the grassland. I wanted to stay here, my own Shangri-la among the hills, for always.

But we had to cross the Chola hills, and so I said my good-byes—blithely ignored by the young woman—and we continued, whipping the broken Jeep into some semblance of forward motion. The road was a switchback—"twenty-five bends to the summit!" said Tang, who had been here before. Soon the meadow was just distant patchwork, and the sharp peaks were all around us, and melting snow was leaking onto the gravel. A half-wrecked snowplow lay in wait in a road menders' hut, and a cold wind rattled the corrugated iron of its driver's cabin.

There was a cairn at the summit—4916 meters, 16,100 feet said the sign, not quite accurately—and lines of prayer flags fluttering wildly in the gale. It was bitterly cold, and the thin air was making Lily feel unsteady. In the distance I could see the black cleft where the Yangtze ran, on the far side of which was Tibet proper—and another roadmen's hut. We headed there for shelter, and a cup of tea.

It was entirely run by women, tough old brutes dressed to their chins in wool and padded green coats from the army. They volunteered for the work, they said, and were paid sixty *yuan* a month—nine dollars. The contract called for a five-year stint up at these altitudes—and there was a bonus paid to those who stuck it out and didn't go back to Dêgê or Luhou, pleading for easier duty.

"But you know what bothers me?" said one woman, thinking that I could perhaps improve her lot because, being a foreigner, I should have plenty of good *guanxi.* "The bosses say this pass is at 4916 meters—you saw the sign? Well they put it up—but it's wrong. We're actually at 5500 meters [18,000 feet]—but they changed the sign just so they don't have to pay us the extra money that's supposed to be given to anyone who works over five thousand meters. They're cheating us. Cheapskates! Damn bastards!" She kicked her boot furiously against a broken-down truck, and added: "You write about it. Then maybe they'll change it." I assured her I would do just that.

The fields on the weather side of the hills were covered near the summit with yellow tuliplike flowers and mats of blue heather, and lower down there were poppies and rapeseed fields—the hillside was a riot of primary colors. But as I was admiring the prettiness of it all, a huge black cloud roared in out of nowhere and it began to hail, the ice clanging angrily off the wrecked cars and trucks that had fetched up at the way station. We got back into the Jeep and raced downhill, until the hail turned to rain and then stopped altogether. A scattering of grubby little shacks showed that we were on the outskirts of Dêgê.

Sixty thousand people live in this ugly little settlement, wedged into the valley of a noisily rushing Yangtze tributary. None of the buildings seemed to be complete—they were either being built, or falling down. Our hotel was as grubby a place as I expected, without water of any sort—I had to wash in public under a hose that builders were using to help make cement. I drew quite a crowd of nut-brown watchers, especially at the more intimate ablutionary moments.

Dêgê is an overwhelmingly Tibetan town (it used to have a king, like Muli and Chala) but with a large number of Han Chinese immigrants. "Solidarity between the Han and the Zang* people will make China strong!" said a poster above the police station. Inside, the

---

* The character *Zang,* used now to denote the Tibetan people, also denotes "a depository for precious things," or "the Buddhist scriptures." Since Xi means

police chief, Ma Lu—who was Tibetan, but not a believer in the primacy of the Dalai Lama and thus trustworthy, in Chinese eyes— beamed with pleasure at our arrival.

"I have heard from your friend Miss Pam," he said. "She has already told me you might be coming." I then handed over her letter, with the fifty *yuan* enclosed. "Another letter from her?" He opened it, and exclaimed: "How good she is!" He was a kind and helpful man, and he knew where I was hoping to go, and agreed readily to write a note of recommendation to his colleague across the border in Qamdo, the first true Tibetan town of any size on the far side of the river. This is what Pam Logan had hoped he might do. He sealed his letter with a huge red chop and signed his name for further authentication.

"This will ensure you have no trouble," he said, though he looked a little doubtful, and added, "I hope."

Officer Ma took us next morning to the one institution for which Dêgê remains well known—the Bakong Scripture Printing House, where, for the last 250 years, monks and their apprentices have been printing Tibetan bibles and prayers, for dissemination around Tibet, China and the lamaist world.

The building is wooden, constructed around a courtyard, and fes- tooned with flags. On its flat roof are golden-plated sacred birds and a gold chorten, beneath which lie the relics of the founding lama. In- side, on old and sagging wooden floors that are connected by a maze of steep staircases, hidden trapdoors, secret passages and corridors, scores of young men were about the printing of thousands of sheets of biblical texts, their energy astonishing, their hurry overwhelming.

They were screen printing from carved blocks of pepper wood, a peculiarly durable local wood that is stored for decades to be sea- soned, so that it never cracks. The process was perfectly mechanical, except that the mechanisms were young Tibetan lads. Two of them would sit facing each other, the one holding the block between his knees with the lower end resting on the floor. His partner would then

---

"west," then Tibet—Xizang—is, in the Chinese syllabary, the Western Depository, or Western Buddhists.

swiftly roll an ink wheel down over the block—some pairs of boys were working in red ink, others in black—and then the first boy would with equal swiftness take from a pile on his right a sheet of fine mulberry paper, about thirty inches by five, and place it on top of the ink-glistening wood. The other boy would pass an uninked roller firmly over the paper, pressing paper to ink, transferring the Tibetan symbols—or the Hindi symbols, for Sanskrit versions of the bibles were exported to Sikkim and Nepal, as well as to the devout in India proper—from block to sheet.

The first boy then lifted the paper away and placed it, face up, on a pile to his right, as his colleague inked the block again and waited for the fresh sheet of paper to be set before him.

I counted: one pair of boys did a sheet every second. A Tibetan bible has 1800 pages. One hundred boys were working on the day we visited. The numbers seemed staggering.

"It may look frantic," said the ancient lama who seemed to be in charge and who, with a lame left leg, limped gamely past his charges, to make sure they were working well. "But we have to make up for lost time. During the Cultural Revolution, we did nothing. We didn't print a thing. And there's a lot more than just bibles."

He took me upstairs, puffing and wheezing his way up the attic flights. Older men were working under the eaves producing prayer flags, or slips of tissue paper imprinted with mantras that would flutter away in a breeze and produce a scriptural litter that the world would not mind.

One particularly ancient fellow, so thin that it seemed for a moment as if it was only a bagful of burgundy robes hunched over the wood block, was carving flat plates of *hujiao-mu*—pepper wood— which would be used to imprint prayers on water. The idea, he explained, in the croaky voice of an ancient more used to silence, was that a divine would squat beside a flowing stream and, once every couple of seconds, push briefly down with the prayer side of the block, impressing the inscribed prayer onto the surface of the water and letting the river carry the words of the deity to the river's mouth.

I told him that I was going to the Yangtze headwaters, and he became animated, his faced creased with smiles. He looked around his shelves and found a small block, which he pressed into my hand. "Take it with you, my son," he said, "send prayers down the waters. You will become saintly if you do so. You will gain much merit. You will give me much pleasure. And you will please God."

Half a mile above the printing house, at the end of a valley road lined with almond trees, lay a small lamasery. Four elders were sitting in the sun outside, warily watching the group of wild dogs that were pacing on the far side of the street. The men beamed with pleasure at the prospect of having a visitor, and they spent much of the rest of the morning shuffling ahead of me, showing me the altar rooms and the huge prayer drums and the portraits—all treasures of great antiquity, and all of which had mercifully escaped the rigors of the Cultural Revolution. Dozens of temples had been wrecked, thousands of icons smashed; sacred texts had been used as toilet paper by Chinese marauders, so say countless books on the tragedy of Tibet. But here in Dêgê at least, this one lamasery survives, more or less unscathed; and I suspect that there are very many more. The destruction of Tibetan culture may have been savage; but it was most assuredly not complete.

The following morning we crossed the Yangtze. The river was narrow up here—scarcely surprising, since Dêgê is 3100 miles up from the buoy in the East China Sea, and less than 900 miles from the source. It was so far from the river mouth and so different that it might have been in another world.

Down on the banks men were offering ferry rides to the far side in coracles made of yakskin. Some of the men had homemade kayak-style oars, which they used in the familiar style, dipping one end in, then the other on the other side. I had seen a film of them being taught this technique by an American, a visitor who came with the ill-fated Warren expedition of 1986: beforehand they had used single-ended oars, and paddled slowly and erratically. It seemed likely that they were now indeed using the American technique—or perhaps more accurately, the Inuit technique. If so, they were displaying one of the very rare advantages that have come to these corners of the world from contact with the supposedly more advanced outside.

A grumpy-looking Chinese policewoman was on picket duty on the Sichuan side of the narrow stone bridge, but she did not even glance up from her breakfast noodles as our Jeep stuttered across. On the far side—on what was now legally and properly Tibet, Xizang, there was a red-and-white pole barrier blocking the road, and I readied myself for interrogation and a smart return to China. But the ancient who manned the post turned out to be friendly and he raised the pole high. Before he could change his mind, Miao pressed his foot to the floor and the car, trailing more smoke than was healthy even for a Sherman tank, raced up the slope on the far side of the valley. For the time being we were leaving the Yangtze valley and would have to drive several hundred miles through forbidden land before seeing the Long River again.

The topography here reflects more than anywhere else the precise point of collision between this part of the world's two great tectonic plates. It is not an edgewise collision, the kind of collision that produces the chaotic kind of geology we had seen back in northern Yunnan. Here the plates had hit almost exactly head-on—so while the world here was rumpled, and violently for sure, it was rumpled in a somehow *orderly* way, with all the hills arranged in steep and equally tall ranges, and the rivers rushing through deep and equally narrow valleys, and all aligned precisely, as though with a compass.

The hills were arranged in an almost exactly north-south pattern—and the three huge rivers that drain this corner of Asia ran through the mountains parallel to one another, north-south also. Compounding the strangeness of the topography, they were also very, very close—making this one of the best-drained parts of the world, with rivers shearing away like railway lines from a city terminus.

First there was the Yangtze, heading south to Shigu and—but for the intervention of Cloud Mountain—the Gulf of Tonkin; then, a mere fifty miles to the west, was the upper part of the Mekong, which drained through Laos and Cambodia before entering the South China Sea near Saigon; and thirty miles farther west was the Salween, a lesser-known river that watered the Shan States of upper Burma, and flowed into the Andaman Sea by the town of Moulmein, a place made famous only in a poem by Kipling, the one about the Burma girl a-settin' by the old Moulmein pagoda.

We had our first spot of bother with the Chinese police when we arrived at Qamdo, a large town on the upper Mekong. We had found a ramshackle hotel, and were finishing an equally ramshackle dinner, when a young man sidled up beside me.

"You have a permit?" he asked, in halting English.

He was a civilian, or so I thought. In fact, he was a nark, and Qamdo was full of them. I ignored this one, but within minutes another, rather larger and more insistent, came up to me and asked the same question. Would I perhaps like to accompany them to the police station?

Lily spoke fast and well. I was a distinguished geographer, she said, a foreigner with a lifelong fascination with the Yangtze. I was traveling this way only as a means of reaching the river's headwaters in Qinghai. I would not be stopping for any reason other than rest. It was a matter of common courtesy, she insisted, for the authorities to let me pass. The future of Anglo-Chinese geographical cooperation could be thrown in jeopardy if I were sent back. . . .

Sent back. The thought was chilling. To reach this town we had already driven over another vastly high pass across the Ningjing Range, which separates the Yangtze valley from the Mekong: it would be depressing beyond words to have to retrace our steps. Besides, the car was deteriorating rapidly, and there was likely to be a mechanic only in Lhasa, five days ahead—closer than Chengdu, now six days behind.

The official was a small, ratlike man. He had brought his ten-year-old son to the interview, and the boy had taken my passport and was trying his best to read it, stumbling on the extravagant rubric in the front, which spoke about Her Majesty's Principal Secretary of

State for Foreign Affairs Requesting and Requiring Such Persons (as his father) to Let the Bearer of the Document Pass Without Let or Hindrance. He translated it, badly. His father ruminated. Then he took out a piece of paper and began writing furiously.

"I will fine you a large amount—say, five thousand *yuan*—and give you a piece of paper guaranteeing safe passage to Lhasa. Will that do?"

I was about to agree, when Lily shushed me. No, she said, it would not do at all. The sum he had in mind was outrageous. Five hundred *yuan,* maximum. He glared at her. She glared back. The child translated some more, trying to explain the difference between a Let and a Hindrance.

Finally the man backed down.

"Okay—five hundred. And I will write this. It should be good for four hundred kilometers more. The rest of the police zone will present no problem."

But he was wrong. The very next day, at a dreadful high-altitude village called Leiwujie, we were detained once again. Lily was taken away alone this time, and I had to kick my heels in the street outside, listening to her screeching inside, as she raged hysterically against what she called the tyranny of the police. She was, I thought, an exceptionally brave young woman.

She emerged after an hour, white faced and in tears. But, as it turned out, triumphant. Shakily she explained what had happened inside.

"I was on the telephone with the chief of police back in Qamdo. I argued with him. I shouted at him. I can't believe it—I told him to shut up! Many times. He was quite afraid. I argued and I argued. The policeman here said he has occasionally seen foreigners here before, begging, on their knees, trying to get permission to go on. He has always sent them back.

"He had a man last year who fell over and over on the ground, rolling back and forth, weeping, offering money. But he said no. He said he has never once let any foreigner he has caught pass this point.

He is proud of it. 'If I see a foreigner, this is as far as he gets.' He told me that.

"But for some reason, he decided to agree, in this one case. He listened to me, he understood my passion for this river. He was very impressed that we had come all the way here from the sea. He knew that if he said no the whole voyage would be in danger, and that you would write and hold him up to ridicule. So he said yes. We can go. No fine. No nothing. Just go. Immediately. Back to the Jeep!"

Propitious or not, it was the Jeep that was the next to go. The wretched car sputtered to a halt two mornings later, when we were deep in the mountains and miles from the nearest habitation. I had to clamber down five hundred feet to a stream to get water: the wrecked radiator, cut to shreds by the spinning fan, spewed it out before we had gone a mile. Down to the river again, another bucket of water, another mile's progress—and so on for ten miles, by which time we reached a road menders' camp, and Lily and I pitched the tent.

There were only Tibetan women in the camp; their menfolk would be back by dark, they said, and one of them had the equipment necessary for mending the radiator—a welding torch, I assumed. The women took us in out of the storm: they gave us soup and let us sit in the warm while a battery-powered prayer wheel by the door hummed its mantras into the howling gale. And then the storm quietened, and the men returned.

The "equipment" turned out to be a two-inch bar of solder, a jar of flux, and a sharp-edged hammer that could be used as a soldering iron. Miao fell upon these items with glee. As evening darkened and the Tibetan stars came up we watched this remarkable man as he performed, in that classical Chinese way, a miracle of improvisation. We watched him heating the hammer to red heat in the jet flame of a gasoline stove, and then melting silvery globules of solder onto each one of the eighty-three cuts and gouges we had counted in the radiator. It was painstaking work—every break had to be crimped closed, every closure welded shut with solder, every joint then tested under the high pressure that water attains in a car's cooling system.

But by dawn he was done. The final test worked—no appreciable amount of water spilled onto the roadway. The radiator was secured with two new bolts and wired on for good measure and additional safety. We had breakfast of barley-flour *tsampa,* and Miao and Tang gulped down some buttery tea. And then we started off once more— Lily and I dipping down in our seats every time we spotted the police, or truckloads of troops—and we continued climbing onto the plateau.

Nine days out and we had reached it. The hills fell away, and ahead were endless plains, cold and windy. We camped out each night, now that I had managed to repair the zippers on the tent. The camping was quiet and lonely: there were no villages, no permanent habitations, and only very occasionally a gathering of nomad farmers on the horizon. Nor was there much by way of wildlife. This had been antelope countryside as little as a decade ago, with flocks of thousands; but their numbers had been savagely reduced by systematic poaching and the encroachments of the yak herders. Human influence in this part of Tibet is recent—the ever rising population of China and the government-ordered movement of peoples being the two most obvious causes—and so far as the indigenous animals and plants are concerned, it is almost wholly malign.

The few people we saw working on the roads were prisoners, guarded by soldiers. I asked that we speed past, for these were men from the *laogai,* the labor camps, and no foreigner should see them. Were I to be stopped by their guards there is little doubt that the expedition would be over: the Chinese authorities are sensitive about their political prisoners, and merely seeing these gangs of gray-skinned men, masked against the cold, shackled to one another, wielding picks and hammers with dispirited weariness—this was enough for my deportation.

It was cold, and the air was thin. Lily was miserable—she had headaches and found it difficult to breathe, and in the tent at night she tossed and turned, worried by fearful dreams. I had read about the physical deterioration that precedes severe altitude sickness and listened to Lily to see if I could detect those problems: but no, she was in fact as strong as an ox—her symptoms, I felt sure, were brought about by the strange abnormality of her situation, of not knowing, of not being prepared for the bizarre side effects high altitude can bring.

And then finally, eleven days out, in a slight depression in the plains ahead, there were the radio towers and tenements of a dreary junction town that I knew from my maps was called Nagqu. The town is of no interest—it is the administrative center of one of Tibet's five regions, just as Qamdo five days behind had been—but little more. Except that it is the junction of the brick tea road, or the convoy road that goes between Chengdu to Lhasa, and the main highway that links Lhasa with the north. A road that, unlike the one we had suffered along for the last eleven days, was paved with asphalt, was fast, and, in places, had even the luxury of being a divided highway. We drew up at the traffic circle where the one road joined the other.

I was faced with one small problem—which way to go. If we turned right we would be at the Yangtze headwaters in little more than a day. If we turned left we would be in Lhasa in about four hours.

I looked at Lily, pale and exhausted. I looked at the ever stoical Tang, the man who knew the headwaters and who was smiling through it all—he had a stern look about him, and his eyes were nodding shut. I looked at Miao—he was chewing hard on something, his face was screwed up in a frown, and he was slapping the gearshift mightily, with the rhythm of deep anxiety.

I asked him to turn left. Later that evening, and to our general delight and relief, we were at the Lhasa Holiday Inn, sleeping between clean sheets and eating yak burgers. The manager turned out to be a Frenchman I knew, and he gave us three rooms for no charge. We stayed for three memorably pleasant days. I spent hours in the ancient shrine of the Jokhang and at the Potala, the former seat of the Tibetan government and the Dalai Lama's gigantic winter palace. I strolled around his summer house, the Norbulingka. I took a car to the Drepung Monastery, once so huge and proud, but now savagely reduced by the Chinese. And I rested. I was happy to be here, and to be so close to the India where I had lived some years before, and which I loved. I met a man from San Francisco, who gave me pills for Lily's sickness. We found a mechanic who repaired the car.

After the days of rest and restoration, and with the car washed and with its tires pumped up and Lily high on her new medicine and Miao slapping his gearshift lever only once an hour or so, we set off back up the asphalt highway. Five hours later and we were passing Nagqu once again, and the junction with the cordially loathed (but later, fondly remembered) brick tea road. Then the land began to rise. We were coming up onto the southern flanks of the Tanggula Range of mountains, to the hills where the Yangtze has its beginnings.

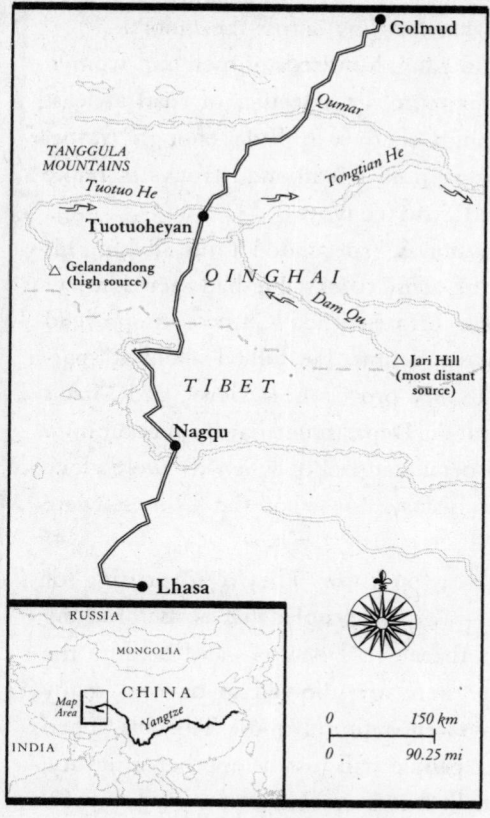

15

Headwaters

The road between Lhasa and the north is good for almost all of its length—except, travelers are always warned, for the hundred miles or so where it heaves itself up and over the Tanggula Range. There, even in midsummer, the weather is dreadful, the terrain wretched and the road usually stripped to its gravel foundations.

It was midsummer in the rest of the northern world, but on the day we broached the slope of the great range, wet snow began to fall, a wind whipped up, and soon we were grinding our way up the endless gradient in the teeth of a July blizzard. The car was misbehaving yet again—bad fuel, explained Miao, without conviction—

and it took us several hours to make the summit, by which time it was pitch-dark and the wind was howling across the moors.

We had passed another chain gang, hundreds of men and women lashed together in small groups to repair a section of road at least twenty miles long. Even though there was little enough traffic, soldiers with flags were holding up all northbound trucks to make way for a string of southbound army convoys.

"Trouble in one of the monasteries," speculated Tang, shaking his fist at the taillights of one of the army trucks. He had seen some of the rioting in Lhasa ten years before, when Chinese troops had beaten monks, and it had incensed him. He talked about it sparingly—he knew that Lily held very pro-Chinese views, and Miao's job with the Chengdu Propaganda Department hardly made him a likely sympathizer with the Tibetan cause. But when we were alone Tang spoke openly about his distaste for what the Chinese were doing.

"It's more insidious these days, you know. They're advertising for people to come and live here—Chinese people, that is. Before long there will be as many Han as there are Tibetans—and because the Han people who come to live here are allowed to have as many children as they like, they may well outnumber the Tibetans. Then this will stop being Tibet. The people will just be another minority, like the Yi or the Nakhi. They'll lose everything.

"I know the arguments—that before the Chinese came, the Tibetans were ruled by despots, by cruel old priests. That may be so. But at least it was their country. It was up to them to decide what to do about it. It's not up to us. It's none of our business. We come in, and give them good roads and water and hospitals, all the things they never had. But we think that gives us a right to tell them how to live their lives.

"And if they don't do it the way we tell them, then"—he jerked his hand in the direction of yet another convoy, the fifth, another hundred trucks steaming southward toward the capital. "Then we send in force and crush them."

The people were reportedly up in arms just then about Beijing's decision not to acknowledge the youngster who had recently been chosen as the reincarnation of, or successor to, the Panchen Lama, the senior legal Tibetan lama. A group of wise men chosen by Beijing had settled on a candidate some weeks before, and the candidate—a boy of nine living in a remote part of western Tibet, near Shigatse—had been accepted by the Communist leadership. But then the wise men had made the error of telling the Dalai Lama, living in exile in Dharmsala in India—and he had agreed with the decision.

His agreement, which legitimized the boy's candidacy for the thousands of followers of the most revered (as opposed to the most legal) of Tibet's lamas, made Beijing promptly change its collective mind. The national leadership condemned the choice, criticized the child for all manner of sins and his parents—blameless people to their very core—for corruption and publicity seeking. A new child was chosen, and was due to be formally installed as the future Panchen Lama later in the year. The Dalai Lama was pointedly not consulted: he had already made his choice, said Beijing, and unhappily it was the wrong one.

This row would dominate the rest of the year, and almost certainly did result in some disturbances across Tibet, particularly in the western monasteries, where support for the Dalai Lama is at its most fervent. Now there seemed little doubt but that these soldiers—officially heading south for "routine resupply"—were going to help put down an incipient rebellion, yet again.

Which made it unlikely, I thought, that we would be given much by way of hospitality when, late that night and in the middle of a howling snowstorm, we hammered on the iron gate of the army base at Tanggula township and asked if we might possibly be allowed to bed down for the night.

On the face of it, the request seemed reasonable. Lily was sick again. The car was faltering again. We were tired and hungry. There was no other accommodation, and the weather was foul and getting worse. This—at 15,100 feet—was said to be the highest permanent human settlement on the face of the earth. We should at least be able to park in the courtyard and sleep in the car in some kind of shelter from the icy gales.

A sentry opened the iron door a fraction, his face wrinkling with distaste at the blowing snow outside. I asked him to get an officer, and a few moments later a young man appeared, his shoulder showing the rank of captain. I explained the problem, and asked if we might stay.

"No," he replied. "Certainly not."

I put on as innocent an expression as I knew how.

"Pray—why not?" I asked.

He thought for a moment.

"Three reasons," he then replied. "First—you are a *lao wai,* and we don't let *lao wei* stay in Chinese army bases. I'm sure your army wouldn't welcome a visiting Chinese traveler, right?

"Second—you are all civilians, and we don't let civilians stay in army bases. And third"—here he seemed to be casting around for a third reason when suddenly he remembered something—"and third, last night, for some so far unexplained reason, *thirty-seven of our men died here* of some mysterious ailment."

He looked at the four of us, gazing at our faces as we registered our shocked surprise. Suddenly his expression was triumphant, as if he had blocked us at all our exits. I thought hard for a second.

Not so fast, I realized. I raised my hand.

"But in that case, surely that means you'll have thirty-seven empty beds. Doesn't it?" The question of available space was a red herring, but it was the only herring I had. And I wasn't too worried about how the men had died*—we would quite probably freeze to death if we stayed out here.

The captain's face cracked into a smile. He swore, using some imprecation that I couldn't catch but was obviously racist in its implications, and then he opened the door. Yes, he said, he supposed we

---

* From what I heard later it sounded like carbon monoxide poisoning from a blocked heater flue.

could have four rooms, and would we perhaps like some dinner? Army rations were not so good up here in Tibet, he said, but they could probably rustle up rice and meat of some kind.

I now had doubts about my theory that the convoys of troops were off to beat up local monks: here the soldiers were totally relaxed, performing the drear routines of garrison duty as though nothing had happened in this part of Tibet for years, and nothing was likely for the rest of their tour. So we spent a warm and peaceful night; and it was only when we awoke at five for the final push that the spell was broken. The dawn broke gray and it was snowing still, and it was bitterly cold once more.

From the base the road sloped downward a little for the next twenty miles, then passed a lonely menders' camp and a small settlement called Yanshiping. Through the driving snow I could occasionally see the outlines of nomads' black tents, their walls plastered thickly with ice. The yaks had gone to ground, presumably huddled down in depressions on the moors, waiting out the blizzard.

We drove on and on, mile after wretched mile, stopping from time to time to scrape the accumulated ice from the windshield. Finally, late in the morning, we came to a wretched little settlement sprawled across both sides of the road that was called Tuotuoheyan. We were at 14,500 feet. There was a meteorological station here, and a hydrometric station that measured the flow of the river, and there were barrack blocks with mud walls, where the long-distance truck drivers took their ease, a break more or less halfway between Lhasa and Golmud along this terrifyingly bleak highway.

Here the Yangtze was really narrow, and so it was where the first of the river's many bridges had been built. In this foul weather it was also quite probably as far as we were going to go. We all got out to investigate.

The bridge was concrete, standing on a dozen buttresses, and it was about three hundred yards long. The river itself, murky and grayish, made an unappealing sucking noise as it passed under our feet. It was divided into a number of channels, each separated from the others by bars of brown gravel—on high-water days they would be submerged, but here, on this midsummer's day, the river was quite low. All told, it was perhaps a hundred yards wide, and it wallowed along quite placidly, compared with the wilder sections just a few score miles downstream.

There was a furious blast of snow, and the others skittered back to the car. But I was determined that this should not be quite the end. Not yet. So I fastened the zipper on my polar jacket and put on my gloves, and I jumped down onto the grass on the left-hand side of the bridge, at its far end.

I began walking. My compass showed that I was going due west. I was on the river's left bank, and if I kept on walking for perhaps another week, and if I climbed up another three thousand feet, then I might reach the source—the spiritually appropriate, wholly photogenic, mountain-ice-fed but nevertheless not-exactly-correct source— at the Gelandandong Glacier. But then again—and here was the rub—I could walk in quite the opposite direction, keep going for about two weeks and climb up a little less far, and I might reach the other correct but unappealingly ugly ooze-of-a-source on the puddle-sized lake at the head of the Dam Qu stream. And whichever source I reached would, in someone's eyes, be quite the wrong one.

So I had made more modest plans. I strode along through the muddy grass for an hour or so, following the lazy twists and turns of the riverbank. The gusts of wind slowed and then suddenly, and just as I had hoped, the snow stopped altogether. The clouds swirled away, and I found myself standing quite alone in the middle of a vast white plain, crisp with frost, under the perfect blue sky and a low late-morning sun.

Behind me I could see the smoky smudge of the gray-brown buildings of Tuotuoheyan. To my right was a small encampment of nomads, and a man was riding slowly toward me on a pony. I waved at him, and he waved back and yelled something unintelligible, but clearly friendly.

I looked ahead of me, to the far west, and then just a little south.

There, rising starkly from the high plateau of the Tanggula Range, stood the ring of high and snowy peaks called Gelandandong. Through my field glasses I could see arêtes and *bergschrunds* and couloirs and all the other features of Alpine geography. In the midst of this magnificent scrum of young mountainhood was the glacier and the small circular pool from which, said most—and from which, said Wang Hui, in the painting at which I had looked so carefully all those thousands of miles away in New Hampshire—this great river started its long journey.

The great river was not great here, not at all. It was beside me now, shallow and quite clear, running fast through a gravel-bottomed channel that was ten feet wide. There must have been a dozen such channels, each glinting blindingly in the sun. This was a braided stream, meandering its way through the boggy flatlands of the plateau, not quite knowing which was the path of least resistance along which gravity should most effectively direct it. I didn't care to know: all I was interested in was this single narrow rivulet beside me, a rill of ice-cold and pure water: the Yangtze heading eastward to the sea.

I reached into my pocket for the tiny prayer block that the monk had given me back in Dêgê—I had hoped, I think, that I might imprint a few good thoughts on the waters and send them scurrying down to sea level. But it was not there: I had left it behind, carelessly. It was back in the army base. In any case, I told myself, for me to do such a thing was more than a little out of character: I was no Buddhist, I had no real idea what sentiments had been inscribed on the wood, and would feel plagued that I had performed some disingenuous act, just for the symbolic sake of it.

So instead I got out a cigar. A friend had given it to me in Hong Kong. The Mandarin Hotel had imported a Cuban maestro from Cohiba in Havana, and had set him to work hand-rolling cigars in a corner of the hotel lobby. My friend had bought two for me, for some exorbitant sum. One, he said, was to be smoked at the start of the Yangtze journey, and the second was to be savored in mood victorious if, and only if, I reached the headwaters. This battered and somewhat stale object that I pulled from my jacket pocket was the very one.

I straightened it as best I could and listened to it: there was a slightest crackle of a few stale leaves, but not too much—it seemed to have kept most of its supple softness, and it might not be too bad. So I tilted my head out of the breeze and lit it slowly and carefully, then blew a cloud of pure blue smoke out into the chilly air.

Once, a few weeks back, this had been a grand cigar; now, old and tired from its journey, it had just a hint of its glory: in any restaurant it would have been sent right back. Out here, though, it was the best smoke I could ever, ever imagine. And so I sat there in a state of utter contentment, listening to the gurgling of the stream, listening to the lone Tibetan behind me marshaling the yaks from a herd that had been scattered in the storm, and listening to the soughing winds. They began to pick up again, and they started to scatter the grass and to riffle the calm surface of the river waters once more.

The furious caprices of the great Tibetan Plateau: four seasons in an hour, they like to say. It had just been high summer for ten minutes, and now wintertime was blowing back. It started to get cold once more—and so I stood up and turned back, and walked to the waiting friends in their car beside the Tuotuoheyan bridge. It struck me that for the first time in nearly four thousand miles, I was traveling in the same direction as the waters of the river. It was heading seaward, and I was too.

All the cars and trains and boats and planes that I had booked for the coming days would take me in the same direction, too, carrying me until I ended up in Shanghai once again. Then, just like the river water here, I would push out across and over the Woosung Bar and its red canister buoy, and I would pass the winking lighthouses and the huge navigation buoy just off what they had once called Cape Nelson, and I would soon be out onto the ocean once more, and back on my way to the rest of the world.

Back on my way to what they call the outside world. Back from having been at its very center, and along the river that runs right through it.

Afterword
The Yangtze

At the end of June 1997, the sovereignty and the administration of that tiny but astonishingly valuable piece of real estate known as Hong Kong—or Heung Gong or Xianggang, depending on your linguistic preference—passed from the hands of the faraway United Kingdom into those of its neighbor and geographically natural parent, China. In those days immediately before and after the change it became something of a sport to wonder at the future of the enclave—would it be a place that would continue to astonish and amaze? Would it remain prosperous? Would it—could it, indeed—remain free?

I took part in such sport, arguing long into many nights with colleagues, friends, and foes—and in the end I came up with what at the time was a much-derided prospect, a notion that, for me at least, seemed a reasonable endgame for Hong Kong's existence. *The China of the mid-*

twenty-first century, I would say, *would have as now Beijing as its Washington; but it would in addition then have Shanghai as its New York— and Hong Kong as its New Orleans.*

The notion was, as I say, widely derided—by supporters of Hong Kong, at least. No less a figure than Chris Patten, the last of Britain's colonial governors and a wise observer of all matters Chinese, thought it nonsensical. Hong Kong was so important, he insisted—and important in global terms, not merely regionally or locally—that to reduce it to the status of a southern American coastal port city was little short of lunacy.

But I remain convinced that something like this will happen. Not that it will come about because of any inherent failings in the nature of Hong Kong—though its cultural and ethnic southern-ness does make it more of an obvious gateway just to southern China than to China as a whole—but because, quite simply, of *competition.* And chief among those cities that compete, and a place that even back in 1997 was jockeying hard to topple Hong Kong from its perch as the preeminent commercial hub of modern China, is of course, the great 18-million-strong waterfront city of Shanghai.

It is now a decade since I researched the book to which this is the afterword. The Shanghai that I described back then was busy flexing its muscles, readying itself for the challenge it had set itself, and which was, now seen with all the certainty that is an advantage of hindsight, to become the leading metropolis of a China from which all foreign empires had at last been purged.

It was obliterating most of the remnants of alien dominion—bulldozing avenues of the French Concession; tearing up the kind of houses that could only ever have been suited to foreign-devil *taipans,* rendering the grand structures of the Bund into gaudy caricatures designed for tourists. And it was beginning, at the time, to create a brand-new city, Pudong, on the east side of the Huangpu River, and to excavate subway lines, to build a new airport—to make itself, in other words, into the kind of city that post-Imperial China (and I use the phrase in three senses—post-Ching dynasty, post-Maoist, and post-foreign) amply deserves.

At the time of writing now it is clear that the city fathers have done most of what they had then set out to do. Shanghai is today, and, without any stretch of the imagination, a truly incredible city—a multicolored fantasy world, a future city plucked straight from the pages of a 1950s *Popular Mechanics,* a vibrating, noisy, polluted, pulsating, sleepless Blade-Runnerish agglomeration of immense high-rise structures tricked out in the most gaudy of architectural styles, all brilliantly lit, all crammed with young professionals and hopefuls all participating, or doing their uneducated best to try to participate, in the wild joyride of a capitalist dream-state that is today's China.

Whether it will work remains to be seen: but for now Shanghai is, quite clearly, a Manhattan-in-waiting; and Hong Kong by contrast—though abundantly clean and more or less honest with its arrangements based on the equity of international law and its streets free from invading hordes of rural bumpkins on the lookout for riches—seems dazed and submissive, reeling from the one-two punch that the oh-so-rapid aggrandizement of Shanghai has just delivered.

And Hong Kong's more dejected and realistic supporters acknowledge some manifest home truths about Shanghai. The cleverest and most cunning and commercially adroit Hong Kong businessmen were, if you looked closely, all from Shanghai. Racially—and China is a nation in which race still counts, hugely—the Shanghailanders were always regarded by the rulers in Beijing as being much like themselves, and not at all like those shorter, swarthier, and darker folks from the coastal cities of which Hong Kong was one. And that in practical terms (and unlike Hong Kong, which was connected to the rest of China only by the most delicate of threads of rail and road) Shanghai was sited, essentially and conveniently, at the very mouth of the Yangtze—and that meant she had a four-thousand-mile slipway running from her backdoor right into the heart of China and Tibet, and enjoyed in consequence access to the middle of the middle kingdom to a degree unknown by any other city in China.

Many anticipated changes have occurred in China since I made the journeys for this book. The Three Gorges dam is at last all closed up, the waters behind it are rising fast; the majesty of the Gorges themselves is being submerged in an immense lake of stagnant sewage; an unhappy few million people are being shunted off to execrable replacement cities that tower above where their old homes are now beginning to drown.

Farther to the west there is now a highway above the Tiger Leaping Gorge, and greed and development have started to ruin some of the wildest corners of the China that, in those days, I had come to love for their serenity and savage charm. Beyond that, Tibet is being vandalized yet further; Chinese families are being settled there in immense numbers, the better to drown the rebarbative local culture in a opiate ocean of the purest Han ethnicity.

All of these drownings—whether they are of their own people in middle China, or of Tibetans at the edges of the nation—are being conducted at the direction of the Zhongnanhai politburo, and are being done with the basest and most chauvinist of aims. Though to millions they are a matter of infinite regret, they are not developments that were entirely unexpected.

The extraordinary growth and development of Shanghai—which has been conducted, after all, on the city's own initiative, and permitted only with some reluctance by the graybeards of Beijing—is, however, another matter. True, the Yangtze rolls on through its boundaries, as it always has and always will, and with the kind of mighty imperturbability for which all the world's great rivers are revered. But in the river valley and now on its estuary banks a vast new China with vast new cities is emerging with an almost frightening speed and energy—fast turning itself into a global power the like of which it is almost impossible to imagine.

I had some last-minute hesitation when I decided on the title of this book ten years ago. Today I have no doubt at all—this river is most decidedly at the center of China and China, whether the world likes it or not, is the nation that is at the center, in the focus, in the crosshairs, of everything that this planet does or has yet to do, and where it will remain for many years—perhaps many centuries—to come.

—SBAW

Sandisfield, December 2003

Suggestions for Further Reading

The River in General

In recent years the Yangtze, despite its immense size and obvious importance, has been more often the subject of journalistic adventuring than of longer inquiry. Of the large number of essays only one, written by Paul Theroux for the London *Observer*, has lasted. Sensibly he had it published as a small book, illustrated with charming woodcuts. It was called *Sailing Through China* (London and Boston, 1984) and anyone wanting the briefest of introductions to the general mysteries of the river would do well to look at it.

Also short, but still majestic in its sweep and tone, is John Hersey's *A Single Pebble* (New York, 1956), the novella which he wrote exactly a decade after his better-known work from the ruined city of Hiroshima. The protagonist is a young American engineer bent on building a dam across the Yangtze: the hero of the tale is one of the

Chinese trackers who hauls the American's boat up against the stream—two images that remain as haunting and topical at the end of this century as they were when the book came out to wide acclaim in the middle of it. Those contemplating seeing the river in what the dramatic might call its death throes—before the dam is finished— should slip this into the coat pocket: it remains a classic.

Lyman van Slyke's excellent *Yangtze—Nature, History and the River,* which was published as a Stanford paperback in 1988, offers a rag-bag of fascinations about the river, and is eccentric, scholarly and amusing. It has countless maps and diagrams and photographs, and a good list of suggestions for further inquiry.

And finally there is Judy Bonavia's splendid guidebook, *The Yangzi River,* in a new edition (Hong Kong, 1995) with additional comments by the knowledgeable Madeleine Lynn. The book has precious little information about the river anywhere upstream of Yibin, but for coverage of Chongqing and the Gorges, and of the more placid and more historically notable sites below Yichang and downriver to Shanghai, it is unrivaled. To fill in the gaps in those parts of Sichuan, Yunnan and Tibet that are overlooked by this guide, one might with profit consult either a recent edition of Lonely Planet's *Travel Survival Guide to China* (Melbourne, 1994), or the *Odyssey Guide to Sichuan* (Hong Kong, 1993).

There are two good Admiralty charts of the river: number 2916, covering Shanghai to Datong, and 2947 for ships and their passengers wishing to go up to Yichang and the Gezhouba Dam.

The best easily available topographical maps of the area are the American 1:500,000 Tactical Pilotage Charts: the numbers of the ten sheets needed to cover the entire river are as follows (they begin as I did, at the sea): H-12B, G-10D, H-12A, H-11B, H-11A, H-11D, H-10C, H-10B, G-8C and G-8D. The less easily obtained JOG charts, which are at the very useful scale of 1:250,000 (four miles to the inch), have a very different notation system: for instance, the JOG chart of the Great Bend at Shigu is sheet number NG 47-7, and that covering Tiger Leaping Gorge is NC 47-3.

Ships and Shipping

There can be few books more indicative of a lifetime's passion than G. R. G. Worcester's *The Junks and Sampans of the Yangtze*, which the Naval Institute Press of Annapolis sensibly put out as a revised single volume (there had been four) in 1971. It reads easily, and is copiously illustrated with Worcester's own line drawings: every imaginable detail about the river, its boats and boatsmen, and its boatsmen's lore, is tucked away in this sea chest of history.

But even Worcester's great effort must pale in comparison with Joseph Needham's *Science and Civilisation in China*, which a team working for Cambridge University Press is still laboring to produce, even though Needham himself, the originator, has now died. The volume that covers matters of interest to river travelers is *Volume 4, Part III—Civil Engineering and Nautics*, published in 1971. It is well worth hunting down in a used-book store. I found mine, a treasure true, at Lion's Head Books of Salisbury, Connecticut, on payment of what I still think of as a bargain $75.

The Royal Navy's *Yangtze Pilot*—later the *Ch'ang Chiang Pilot*—is a typically unsmiling and bloodless sailor's account of the river from Cape Nelson to the Head of Navigation, prepared for use on ships' bridges, and in the bathtubs of those who, on cold winter nights, derive great pleasure (as I do, and as did Mr. Mitty) from sailing on imagined journeys to exotic and faraway ports. Sadly the *Pilot* went out of print after its 1954 London edition, largely because the Communists sharply limited foreign access to their rivers; but a shortened version of the material is to be found still in chapter 9 of the Admiralty's *China Sea Pilot*, Volume 3, printed in London in 1982 and still available in chart shops.

I would also strongly recommend reading Richard McKenna's *The Sand Pebbles*, a deservedly classic novel set among the Yangtze Patrol sailors and the missionaries they helped protect during the turbulent warlord years. (There is no connection between McKenna's *Pebble* and Hersey's—the gunboat in McKenna's story is called the USS *San Pablo*, and *Sand Pebble* is her nickname.) See the film too: a very winsome Candice Bergen and the late Steve McQueen appear in it, and the mood that it captures—even though it was largely made on location in Hong Kong—has an uncanny truth that all travelers in China will recognize.

David Grover's *American Merchant Ships on the Yangtze 1920–1941* (Westport, 1992) and Admiral Kemp Tolley's *Yangtze Patrol* (Annapolis, 1971) present useful and competent accounts of foreign shipping on the great river. Captain Graham Torrible, who worked on a number of C.N.Co. boats from 1925 until the outbreak of the Second World War, wrote his amusing and informative *Yangtze Reminiscences,* which was privately published by Swires in London in 1975.

The Three Gorges and the New Dam

Dai Qing's *Yangtze, Yangtze* (Earthscan, Toronto, 1994), the publication of which in China won her plaudits for her courage, is available in English now, and presents a formidable collection of engineering papers and polemics that may be too technical for many readers' tastes. I rather prefer the lighter but none the less passionate tone of Caroline Walker's *On Leaving Bai Di Cheng* (the title is that of one of Li Bai's best-known poems about the river), which was published by NC Press, Toronto, in 1993. It is a somewhat ill-organized book, but the four writers share a deep concern for the loss of so much of China's archaeological relics, once the waters from the dam begin rising.

Since Cornell Plant is such a hero of mine, I can find little to criticize in his slim volume *Glimpses of the Yangtze Gorges* (Shanghai, 1936), which some enterprising publisher may one day see fit to republish, given the new topicality of the Gorges story. The somewhat matter-of-fact writings of Mr. Plant are enhanced hugely by Ivon Donnelly's charming pen-and-ink drawings, and the book is a collector's joy.

Archibald Little's *Through the Yangtze Gorges or, Trade and Travel in Western China* (London, 1888) has the cumbersome literary style common to most Victorian travel writings; but his achievements were such, and his journeyings so extensive, that it is still a book to be read, more than a century on. Similarly Isabella Bird's *The Yangtze Valley and Beyond,* which first came out in London in 1899, but which was republished in London and Boston in 1985, should be consulted as a record of amazing personal achievement—as well as being an advertisement for the continuing benefits of Mrs. Bird's thick tweed skirt—but it is a somewhat trying read today.

In Addition

There are countless books about the city of Shanghai: I have long liked Noel Barber's *The Fall of Shanghai* (New York, 1979) which more than most has managed to capture the feckless and amoral mood of the place and time that made up this great whorehouse of a city. The 1983 Hong Kong reprint of the 1934 edition of the *Standard Guide Book to Shanghai* does much the same, though in a more mannerly fashion.

Henry Hobhouse wrote engagingly about the Chinese tea industry in his astonishing *Seeds of Change* (New York, 1986). Joseph Rock's monumental work, *Ancient Nakhi Kingdom of Southwest China* (Cambridge, 1948), is complemented today by a book of Rock's pictures, *Lamas, Princes and Brigands,* edited by Michael Aris (New York, 1992). This elegant coffee table book tells much of Rock's amazing story and offers a full bibliography including references to all nine of his *National Geographic* magazine articles, which should be read by anyone thinking of venturing to this most fabulous part of the world.

The Thistle and the Jade by Maggie Keswick (London, 1982) is the Jardines account of its operations in the East; and ten years later Swires published its *Pictorial History of China Navigation Company Limited:* both volumes, though vanity books, offer a wealth of detail about the operations in the Yangtze valley during the height of European penetration.

Finally, Richard Bangs and Christian Kallen, both of whom are well skilled in the rigors of the outdoors, have written a splendid account of the bizarre contest during the late 1980s between the teams of Americans and Chinese who were determined to be the first to raft the entire length of the river. *Riding the Dragon's Back* (New York, 1989) turns out to be a simply excellent book—about China, about the river, about the history of both, and almost incidentally about the fatal lunacy that propelled men and women from around China and the world to try to descend through terrible stretches of white water like Yunnan's Tiger Leaping Gorge. If I had to read only one book about the river, it would probably be this. The story evidently so captivated the authors that they managed to make this a general and wide-ranging book about the Yangtze, with the race and its attendant disasters a mere metaphor to display the might of the world's most important river.

Index